Bulk Surveillance, Democracy and Human Rights Law in Europe

This book discusses contemporary standards of lega[illegible] in the area of bulk electronic surveillance from the perspective of the European legal model. Bulk, or untargeted, surveillance, although traditionally associated with the interception of electronic communications, is increasingly used as a convenient tool for collecting information on large groups of society. The collection of redundant information, which is intrinsic to bulk surveillance, is no longer a side effect but an important objective of the use of bulk powers. As a result, untargeted surveillance is everywhere increasingly being implemented, and without any clear link to state security or crime-fighting objectives. This work examines the origins of untargeted measures, explores their mechanics and key concepts, and defines what distinguishes them from other forms of surveillance. The various elements of the legal safeguards in place, which are fundamental to protecting individuals from the risks of abuse of power, are analysed in detail. The book discusses not only the different standards of legal safeguards, but also gives examples of their implementation in individual European countries. It also examines the relationship between the development of the global data market and untargeted surveillance powers, in particular in the context of the risks associated with algorithmic surveillance, client-side scanning, the privatisation of surveillance – or surveillance as a service – and the increasingly widespread use of preventive content filtering mechanisms. The book will be a valuable resource for academics and researchers working in the areas of law, international relations, public policy, engineering and sociology. It will also appeal to professionals dealing with various aspects of the use of surveillance measures, such as experts, members of the legislature and law enforcement agencies.

Marcin Rojszczak is Assistant Professor of Cybersecurity and Privacy Law and Head of the Emerging Technology Law Team at the Warsaw University of Technology. His research interests include cybersecurity, electronic surveillance and cross-border aspects of data protection law.

Routledge Research in Human Rights Law

Sports Investigations Law and the ECHR
Collection, Use and Exchange of Intelligence
Björn Hessert

The Right of the Child to Play
From Conception to Implementation
Naomi Lott

Social Media, Fundamental Rights and Courts
A European Perspective
Edited by Federica Casarosa and Evangelia Psychogiopoulou

Housing, Land and Property Rights
Residential Justice, Conflict Zones and Climate Change
Scott Leckie

The European Convention on Human Rights and the COVID-19 Pandemic
Ronagh J.A. McQuigg

International Human Rights and Local Courts
Human Rights Interpretation in Indonesia
Edited by Aksel Tømte and Eko Riyadi

Defamation and the Right to Freedom of Speech
The UK in Comparative Perspective
Mariette Jones

Bulk Surveillance, Democracy and Human Rights Law in Europe
A Comparative Perspective
Marcin Rojszczak

For more information about this series, please visit: www.routledge.com/Routledge-Research-in-Human-Rights-Law/book-series/HUMRIGHTSLAW

Bulk Surveillance, Democracy and Human Rights Law in Europe

A Comparative Perspective

Marcin Rojszczak

Routledge
Taylor & Francis Group
LONDON AND NEW YORK

First published 2025
by Routledge
4 Park Square, Milton Park, Abingdon, Oxon OX14 4RN

and by Routledge
605 Third Avenue, New York, NY 10158

Routledge is an imprint of the Taylor & Francis Group, an informa business

British Library Cataloguing-in-Publication Data
A catalogue record for this book is available from the British Library

ISBN: 978-1-032-58252-8 (hbk)
ISBN: 978-1-032-58253-5 (pbk)
ISBN: 978-1-003-44926-3 (ebk)

DOI: 10.4324/9781003449263

Typeset in Galliard
by Apex CoVantage, LLC

The Open Access version of chapter 1 was funded by Warsaw University of Technology.

Mojej Ani,
która mnie nieustannie wspierała
i przeczytała niezliczone wersje tej pracy.
oraz naszemu Synkowi
Mareczku – dziękuję Ci za każdy dzień
pełny Twoich uśmiechów.

Contents

Key cases

Note: The page number indicates where each case is referred to for the first time.

European Union

Opinion on the EU-Canada PNR Agreement (Opinion 1/15) EU:C:2016:656 [p. 91]
Österreichischer Rundfunk and Others (Joined Cases C-465/00, C-138/01 and C-139/01) EU:C:2003:294 [p. 165]
Poland v. Parliament and Council (C-401/19) EU:C:2022:297 [p. 105]
Privacy International v. Secretary of State for Foreign and Commonwealth Affairs and Others (C-623/17) EU:C:2020:790 [p. 174]
Prokuratuur (C-746/18) EU:C:2021:152 [p. 81]
Promusicae v. Telefónica de España SAU (C-275/06) ECLI:EU:C:2009:68 [p. 160]
Sayn-Wittgenstein v. Landeshauptmann von Wien (C-208/09) EU:C:2010:806 [p. 79]
Scarlet Extended v. SABAM (C-70/10) EU:C:2011:771 [p. 48]
Schrems II (C-311/18) EU:C:2020:559 [p. 190]
Skype Communications Sàrl v. Institut belge des services postaux et des télécommunications (C-142/18) EU:C:2019:460 [p. 38]
SpaceNet (Joined Cases C-793/19 and C-794/19) EU:C:2022:702 [p. 149]
SS SIA v. Valsts ieņēmumu dienests (C-175/20) EU:C:2022:124 [p. 60]
Tele2 Sverige (C-203/15 and C-698/15) EU:C:2016:970 [p. 80]
TK v. Asociația de Proprietari bloc M5A-ScaraA (C-708/18) EU:C:2019:1064 [p. 59]
Van Duyn v. Home Office (41/74) EU:C:1974:133 [p. 78]

European Convention on Human Rights

Ahmet Yıldırım v. Turkey (3111/10) 18 December 2012 [p. 121]
Akgün v. Turkey (19699/18) 20 July 2021 [p. 76]
Al-Skeini and Others v. the United Kingdom (55721/07) 7 July 2011 [p. 116]
Amann v. Switzerland (27798/95) 16 February 2000 [p. 87]
Association "21 December 1989" and Others v. Romania (33810/07) 24 May 2011 [p. 130]
Association for European Integration and Human Rights and Ekimdzhiev v. Bulgaria (62540/00) 28 June 2007 [p. 114]
Azer Ahmadov v. Azerbaijan (3409/10) 22 July 2021 [p. 121]
Banković and Others v. Belgium and Others (52207/99) 10 May 2001 [p. 116]
Bărbulescu v. Romania (61496/08) 5 September 2017 [p. 87]
Ben Faiza v. France (31446/12) 8 February 2018 [p. 139]
Big Brother Watch and Others v. the United Kingdom [GC] (58170/13, 62322/14 and 24960/15) 25 May 2021 [p. 122]
Breyer v. Germany (50001/12) 30 January 2020 [p. 101]
Bucur and Toma v. Romania (40238/02) 8 January 2013 [p. 76]
C.G. and Others v. Bulgaria (1365/07) 24 April 2008 [p. 76]
Centre for Legal Resources on behalf of Valentin Câmpeanu v. Romania (47848/08) 2 August 1984 [p. 114]
Centrum för rättvisa v. Sweden [Chamber] (35252/08) 19 June 2018 [p. 142]
Centrum för rättvisa v. Sweden [GC] (35252/08) 25 May 2021 [p. 123]
Cevat Özel v. Turkey (19602/06) 7 June 2016 [p. 133]

Germany

BVerfG 5 December 2022, 1 BvR 1865/22, ECLI:DE:BVerfG:2022:rk20221205.1bvr186522. [p. 22]
BVerfG 16 February 2023, *hessenData/Palantir Case* (1 BvR 1547/19) DE:BVerfG:2023:rs20230216.1bvr154719 [p. 219]

France

Conseil Constitutionnel 23 July 2015 (2015-713 DC) FR:CC:2015:2015.713.DC [p. 177]
Conseil Constitutionnel 18 June 2020 (2020-801 DC) FR:CC:2020:2020.801.DC [p. 233]
Conseil d'État 21 April 2021 (393099) FR:CEASS:2021:393099.20210421 [p. 201]
Conseil Constitutionnel 17 May 2023 (2023-850 DC) FR:CC:2023:2023.850.DC [p. 229]

United Kingdom

Liberty & Others v. the Security Service, SIS, GCHQ ([2015] UKIPTrib 13_77-H_2) 22 June 2015 [p. 156]
Privacy International v. Secretary of State for Foreign and Commonwealth Affairs ([2018] UKIPTrib IPT_15_110_CH) [p. 201]
Privacy International v. Secretary of State for Foreign and Commonwealth Affairs ([2021] UKIPTrib IPT_15_110_CH) 22 July 2021 [p. 201]

United States

United States v. Curtiss-Wright Export Corp., 299 U.S. 304 (1936) [p. 118]
Katz v. United States, 389 U.S. 347 (1967) [p. 61]
United States v. Verdugo-Urquidez, 494 U.S. 259 (1990) [p. 118]
Kyllo v. United States, 533 U.S. 27 (2001) [p. 61]
United States v. Jones, 565 U.S. 400 (2012) [p. 61]
Jewel v. NSA, 965 F. Supp. 2d 1090 (N.D. Cal. 2013) [p. 119]
Klayman v. Obama, No. 14-5004 (D.C. Cir. 2015) [p. 119]
United States v. Ulbricht, 858 F.3d 71 (2d Cir. 2017) [p. 42]
Wikimedia Foundation v. National Security Agency/Central Security Service, No. 20-1191 (4th Cir. 2021) [p. 95]

Abbreviations

BND	Bundesnachrichtendienst; German Federal Intelligence Office
BVerfG	Bundesverfassungsgericht; German Federal Constitutional Court
CJEU	EU Court of Justice
COMINT	Communications Intelligence
DGSI	Direction générale de la Sécurité intérieure; French domestic intelligence agency
DPD	Data Privacy Directive; EU Directive 2002/58
DPI	Deep Packet Inspection
DRD	Data Retention Directive; EU Directive 2006/24 (repealed)
ECHR	European Convention on Human Rights
ECtHR	European Court of Human Rights
FISA	US Foreign Intelligence Surveillance Act
FISC	US Foreign Intelligence Surveillance Court
FRA	Försvarets radioanstalt; Swedish signals intelligence agency
FRT	Facial Recognition Technology
FVEY	Five Eyes; the signals intelligence agreement between the United States and the United Kingdom, and later also Australia, Canada and New Zealand
GCHQ	Government Communications Headquarters; UK signals intelligence agency
GDPR	General Data Protection Regulation; EU Regulation 2016/679
IPA 2016	UK Investigatory Powers Act of 2016
IPT	UK Investigatory Powers Tribunal
LED	Law Enforcement Directive; EU Directive 2016/680
NSA	National Security Agency; US signals intelligence agency
SIA	Security and Intelligence Agency
SIGINT	Signals Intelligence

1 Electronic surveillance yesterday and today

1.1 Introduction

Surveillance as an instrument of covert observation has been used for hundreds of years to monitor the activities of individuals of interest to those in power.[1] As societies have evolved and new possibilities to communicate and exchange views have emerged, surveillance techniques have also been modernised, and the purpose of their use has changed. Surveillance has not only become a means to gather strategic knowledge of military movements or other governments' plans, but it has been increasingly used as a tool of domestic politics. Therefore surveillance is certainly not an invention of the modern age. As David Lyon aptly observed, "surveillance may be seen as an unfolding process over time, a process that often involves technological mediation."[2]

The purpose of this chapter is to present the genesis of modern electronic surveillance measures and to explain how their emergence has been influenced by technological and social developments in recent decades. These considerations will, on the one hand, form the necessary background for the subsequent analysis of legal regulations and, on the other hand, provide a better understanding of the challenges to be taken into account when discussing the direction of the evolution of surveillance legislation.

Untargeted surveillance was for years closely linked to defence and foreign intelligence. This was primarily due to technological constraints: bulk data collection involved massive data processing, which until the late 1980s was a task that required large technical capabilities and even larger budgets. It was only the development of digital services, which began in the 1990s, that led to the gradual spread of the technologies also needed to implement unrestricted surveillance programmes. The dynamic development of bulk surveillance is also often linked to the geopolitical changes associated with the end of the Cold

1 Andreas Marklund and Laura Skouvig (eds), *Histories of Surveillance from Antiquity to the Digital Era: The Eyes and Ears of Power* (Routledge 2022).

2 David Lyon, 'Situating Surveillance: History, Technology, Culture' in Kees Boersma and others (eds), *Histories of State Surveillance in Europe and Beyond* (Routledge, Taylor & Francis Group 2014) 32.

DOI: 10.4324/9781003449263-1

War. These resulted in a shift in the priorities of electronic intelligence services and their greater focus on domestic operations. In reality, however, while geopolitical issues were the catalyst accelerating the emergence of today's surveillance apparatus, they were not the decisive factor. It was social change and increasing digitalisation that created the environment for indiscriminate surveillance.

Hence, in addition to historical issues, this chapter will present contemporary technical capabilities which both facilitate and limit the implementation of modern surveillance measures. Although the technical aspects of technologies subject to regulation are rarely discussed in legal analysis, it seems that their omission would make it difficult to fully understand the relevant aspects concerning the quality of the applicable laws.

1.2 Origins of bulk surveillance

Contrary to how it is often portrayed, electronic surveillance is not a by-product of the development of the Internet. Rather, its emergence should be linked to the invention of the telegraph and telephone, and above all to the spread of radio communications. It was the advent of these technologies that contributed to the revolutionisation of the way in which communications relevant to intelligence operations were transmitted – in particular, those exchanged by government and military centres.

As early as the beginning of the 20th century, intercepting the enemy's communications became a standard task of reconnaissance units at different levels of armed forces' organisation, providing information useful for planning tactical, operational and strategic actions. Thus, in addition to traditional military intelligence units, dedicated teams were created to carry out the so-called *signals intelligence* (SIGINT) radio reconnaissance tasks.[3] Initially, they were focused on performing radio-targeting, and later also sought to gather any useful information on the enemy's structure, deployment, mode of communication or plans. This knowledge was gained by both intercepting radio emissions and eavesdropping on dedicated communication channels (e.g. telegraph wires). Already during the First World War all parties to the conflict were actively developing their intelligence capabilities in this field, with increasing success.[4]

Evidence of the importance of electronic intelligence to military operations is provided by the Polish-Soviet war fought in 1919–1921, in which the Polish military successfully opposed the much more numerous Red Army and

3 Peter Matthews, *SIGINT: The Secret History of Signals Intelligence 1914–45* (History Press 2013).

4 Ronald Lewin, 'A Signal-Intelligence War' (1981) 16 *Journal of Contemporary History* 501; Jim Beach and James Bruce, 'British Signals Intelligence in the Trenches, 1915–1918: Part 1, Listening Sets' (2020) 19 *Journal of Intelligence History* 1.

eventually defeated General Tukhachevsky's groupings in the Battle of Warsaw in 1920. An important role in the victory was played by the intelligence capabilities of the Polish intelligence service, particularly those related to the interception and decryption of Soviet ciphertexts.[5] As early as 1919, Polish cryptologists carried out an effective cryptanalysis of Soviet ciphers and then – thanks to the construction of a network of listening stations – gained access to vast amounts of intercepted ciphertexts. In this way, SIGINT made a valuable contribution to the military success and victory against a stronger adversary.

The case of the Polish-Soviet War not only confirmed the usefulness of signals intelligence on the battlefield at the time, but also heralded the dawn of a new era of intelligence in which critical information could be obtained remotely without conducting traditional intelligence operations on enemy territory. However, to achieve this goal it was necessary to build up the entire process of intelligence acquisition and processing, starting with capabilities for data collection (listening stations) and their subsequent decoding (decryption), and ending with a substantive analysis of the acquired information and its transmission to decision-makers in a reasonably short time. Even the most skilled cryptologists could not decode messages that had not been intercepted. And the best listening stations could not contribute to defence capabilities if the messages captured are not analysed in a timely manner. In other words, it doesn't matter how many messages can be intercepted if in the end no one reads them in a sufficiently timely manner. Despite the passage of more than 100 years since the Polish-Soviet War, this argument has lost none of its relevance and even today defines one of the main axes of the debate over the legitimacy of untargeted surveillance programmes.

Even during the Second World War, SIGINT capabilities were developed in close correlation with cryptanalysis teams. The Allies' efforts to crack the Enigma cipher were led first by the Polish Cipher Bureau[6] and then, as part of the ULTRA project, by the British Government Code and Cypher School (GC&CS, the predecessor to GCHQ).[7] As Enigma employed a novel way of encrypting data, it also became necessary to develop new cryptanalysis techniques. This is how the first decryption devices were developed, including Rejewski's famous cryptologic bomb.[8] Later, already during the Second

5 Jan Bury, 'Polish Codebreaking during the Russo-Polish War of 1919–1920' (2004) 28 *Cryptologia* 193.

6 Władysław Kozaczuk and Jerzy Straszak, *Enigma: How the Poles Broke the Nazi Code* (Hippocrene Books 2004).

7 For more on the history of the GCHQ and the ULTRA programme, see: Richard J Aldrich, *GCHQ: The Uncensored Story of Britain's Most Secret Intelligence Agency* (Harper Press 2011); John Ferris, *Behind the Enigma: The Authorised History of GCHQ, Britain's Secret Cyber-Intelligence Agency* (Bloomsbury Publishing 2021).

8 David Link, 'Resurrecting *Bomba Kryptologiczna* : Archaeology of Algorithmic Artefacts, I' (2009) 33 *Cryptologia* 166. See also Marian Rejewski, 'Mathematical Solution of the Enigma Cipher' (1982) 6 *Cryptologia* 1.

World War, a decryption centre was established at Bletchley Park, a precursor to modern computing centres. The cryptanalysis of Enigma thus ended the phase when breaking ciphers could be a manual task and began the era of using automated systems for this purpose.[9]

With the end of the Second World War, the Allied SIGINT capabilities were quickly adapted to meet the data collection needs of the Cold War realities. The dynamic development of not only nuclear programmes, but also missile and satellite technology, resulted in new needs in the area of signals intelligence. State-of-the-art systems for the interception of telemetry data were created, allowing for data collection and automatic processing.[10] The global nature of the Cold War also necessitated a different approach to setting up listening stations. As a result, as early as 1946 the United Kingdom and the United States agreed on the terms of SIGINT cooperation and concluded their first agreement,[11] which initiated the intelligence cooperation between the two countries that has continued to this day.[12]

In the 1950s, more countries joined the agreement: Australia, New Zealand and Canada.[13] This agreement, as well as others that were later concluded by the same parties, is commonly referred to as the Five Eyes Agreement (FVEY). The intelligence cooperation thus established allowed for the creation of a global listening system for radio, telephone, and later Internet communications. One of the much-discussed projects under the FVEY partnership was the ECHELON electronic listening system, which was de facto more a set of technical capabilities than a specific intelligence programme.[14]

Each of the parties to the FVEY established a dedicated service specific to electronic intelligence (communication intelligence, COMINT)[15] and declared cooperation in the exchange of foreign electronic intelligence information.[16] Although the Five Eyes agreement was established more than 70 years ago – in

9 RA Ratcliff, *Delusions of Intelligence: Enigma, Ultra and the End of Secure Ciphers* (Cambridge University Press 2006).

10 Matthew M Aid and Cees Wiebes, 'Introduction on The Importance of Signals Intelligence in the Cold War' (2001) 16 *Intelligence and National Security* 1, 4.

11 *British-US Communication Intelligence Agreement*, 5 March 1946 http://cli.re/gnxJ7k.

12 For a detailed analysis of FVEY, see Richard Kerbaj, *The Secret History of the Five Eyes: The Untold Story of the International Spy Network* (Blink 2022).

13 More countries were parties to the FVEY partnership, but only Canada, Australia and New Zealand, by virtue of Art. 7 of Appendix J to the Agreement of 10.05.1955, gained the status of "UKUSA-collaborating Commonwealth countries." See *UKUSA Communications Intelligence Agreement*, 10 May 1955 <http://cli.re/6kZedX>.

14 Lawrence D Sloan, 'Echelon and the Legal Restraints on Signals Intelligence: A Need for Reevaluation' (2000) 50 *Duke Law Journal* 1467; see also Kerbaj (n 12) 149–150.

15 These parties were the NSA (the United States); GCHQ (the United Kingdom); ASD (Australian Signals Directorate [Australia]); the CSE (Communications Security Establishment [Canada]); and the GCSB (Government Communications Security Bureau [New Zealand]).

16 Despite the adoption of a broad definition of the term "foreign communications" in the 1946 Agreement, it is clear that only information relating to foreign governments and entities and persons acting on their behalf was covered (see FVEY Agreement of 1946, 2).

the early days of the Cold War – and undoubtedly served to enhance Western countries' defence capabilities through the rapid exchange of relevant intelligence, the principles of cooperation laid down at that time still operate in almost unchanged form today. However, the surveillance techniques used are being adapted. With the development of the Internet and information society services, they enable the collection of increasingly large data sets and the immediate cross-border transmission of those data to foreign partners.

Although the FVEY is the best-known intelligence agreement on SIGINT, it is not the only one. From the perspective of European countries, an equally important one is Maximator, which has only in recent years become of wider interest to researchers.[17] This partnership involved the cooperation of the electronic intelligence services of Denmark, France, Germany, Sweden and the Netherlands.[18] The programme was set up in the 1970s on the initiative of Denmark and was geared towards cooperation in the area of diplomatic communications. Although the members of the Maximator partnership exchanged information on the methods of obtaining data and their cryptanalysis, the programme did not aim to build a common database of intelligence information. As a result, each country developed cryptanalysis capabilities on its own, without directly providing access to the acquired electronic intelligence to each other.[19]

Particular states also pursued bilateral cooperation programmes in the field of signals intelligence.[20] An example of such an arrangement was the RUBICON programme, run by the US NSA and the German BND for several decades, in which deliberately weakened cryptographic products were created and marketed through a controlled Swiss-based company, Crypto AG.[21] Until the technical breakthrough of the 1980s, cryptographic tools had been offered not in the form of software but as hardware devices. Crypto AG was one of the leading manufacturers of such devices, supplying them to customers in more than 70 countries. The NSA-BND collaboration allowed both countries easy access to the content of the ciphertexts exchanged by the users of Crypto AG products, which provided an invaluable source of information over the years.[22]

17 Bart Jacobs, 'Maximator: European Signals Intelligence Cooperation, from a Dutch Perspective' (2020) 35 *Intelligence and National Security* 659.

18 Although Aldrich points to the existence of another European intelligence programme in which other states were to participate – see Aldrich (n 7) 416.

19 Jacobs (n 17) 661.

20 Interestingly, cooperation regarding SIGINT was not only between intelligence agencies, but also the military – see, for example, information on the Dutch Air Force's cooperation with their German counterpart in: Cees Wiebes, 'Dutch Sigint during the Cold War, 1945–94' (2001) 16 *Intelligence and National Security* 243, 260.

21 The Swiss Parliament, 'Case Crypto AG. Report of the Delegation to the Control Committee of the Federal Assembly' (The Swiss Parliament 2020) BBl 2021 156 <www.parlament.ch/centers/documents/de/bericht_gpdel_fall_crypto_d.pdf> accessed 6 September 2023.

22 Richard J Aldrich and others, 'Operation Rubicon: Sixty Years of German-American Success in Signals Intelligence' (2020) 35 *Intelligence and National Security* 603.

Interestingly, Crypto AG was not the only cryptographic equipment manufacturer whose products were deliberately weakened to facilitate surveillance programmes. Another, less well-known, example is Philips, which at the behest of the Dutch electronic intelligence agency (then *Strategisch Verbindingsinlichtingen Centrum*) created a version of the Aeroflex device in which flaws were deliberately introduced to allow easier cryptanalysis of messages sent through it. A weakened version of Aeroflex was sold to, among others, Turkey – notably a NATO member – which also gave rise to tensions between European intelligence agencies.[23]

Given the triangle of effective electronic surveillance defined earlier – (1) data acquisition; (2) data processing; and (3) analysis and exploitation – the SIGINT programmes conducted in the second half of the 20th century were modernised to provide increasing automation of the activities carried out in steps (1) and (2). As a result, the capabilities associated with the interception and initial decoding of data increased significantly, but the final stage of the process still remained the manual analysis of the information acquired. Although the various services were expanding their capabilities in this area in terms of both personnel and technology, it was clear that the future of electronic intelligence lay in solutions that would also make it possible to process information automatically, and not just decode it into a format readable by the recipient. The aim, therefore, was to automate not only the classification of messages, but also the processing of their content.

Communications that were traditionally of interest to intelligence services, such as diplomatic or military ones, were typically protected from unauthorised access not only by encryption but also by the use of dedicated limited emission devices or separate transmission channels. However, the development of modern telecommunications services meant that an increasing amount of information was being transmitted without specific protection mechanisms. This data stream also contained a great deal of information that could prove useful for the purposes of intelligence operations. Moreover, the accumulation of increasing amounts of data provided a strong impetus for the development of new digital means of storing them.

This led to the creation of the first databases containing the digital equivalents of traditional binders of intelligence files. This data organisation soon proved inefficient, as it did not allow easy information retrieval. Hence, systems containing keywords began to be developed to facilitate the evaluation of the content of the information captured.[24] These systems helped to identify communications that would then be routed for manual analysis. Given the then technological possibilities, carrying out this type of processing required a large (at the time) amount of computing power, which could only be provided

23 BND has not agreed to sell Crypto AG products to Turkey. See more: Jacobs (n 17) 664.

24 Jens Wegener, 'Order and Chaos: The CIA's HYDRA Database and the Dawn of the Information Age' (2020) 19 *Journal of Intelligence History* 77.

by extensive data processing centres. As late as the 1970s, the BND was still using for this purpose the system operated under the CHERRY GLOVE programme made available by the NSA.[25] It was only in the following decade that the German service carried out a major investment programme to develop its own data processing capabilities, tailored to the needs of the growing digital market. At the time, similar programmes were also being carried out by other electronic intelligence agencies. Their common aim was to digitise data processing not only to expedite the processing of the information captured, but also to facilitate its use thanks to the creation of digital information banks, and to enable intercepted data to be decrypted more quickly.

Although in the days before the fall of the Berlin Wall the electronic intelligence services of democratic states were also involved in tasks other than foreign intelligence, these cases were incidental.[26] The main objective of SIGINT invariably remained the strengthening of defence capabilities. It is, therefore, not surprising that most of the specialised services – dealing exclusively with electronic intelligence – originated from military structures. Because electronic intelligence was not associated with domestic operations, the way it was organised, the procedures used, and the oversight mechanisms in place were not subject to detailed statutory regulation.[27] Suffice it to recall that the very existence of some of these services, including the NSA, was kept secret for years.[28]

Progressive digitalisation led to a situation in which electronic intelligence could gather more and more information and acquire it in previously unavailable ways. Traditional listening stations began to be supplemented (and then partly replaced) by modern satellite systems, allowing mass interception of communications from a selected region of the world. The vast amount of information thus available far exceeded military needs. Electronic intelligence has gained access to virtually all communications exchanged by individuals anywhere in the world. It is not surprising, therefore, that it was already in the 1980s that the GCHQ's activities accounted for 80% of the information collected by British intelligence.[29] At the end of the Cold War, electronic

25 Erich Schmidt-Eenboom, 'The Bundesnachrichtendienst, the Bundeswehr and Sigint in the Cold War and After' (2001) 16 *Intelligence and National Security* 129, 138.

26 And they often led to controversy over the legality of the actions taken – see e.g. information regarding the pre-1980 SHAMROCK programme in: James Bamford, *The Puzzle Palace* (Houghton Mifflin 1982) 302.

27 In many cases, this was also due to the location of electronic intelligence within the structures of the military. For example, the German Foreign Intelligence Service, although officially established in 1956, had previously been developed within the Gehlen Organisation in the US occupation zone and worked mainly for the CIA. See Hans-Henning Crome, 'The "Organisation Gehlen" as Pre-History of the *Bundesnachrichtendienst*' (2007) 7 *Journal of Intelligence History* 31.

28 Although the NSA had been established in 1952, its existence was not officially confirmed until 1975.

29 Aldrich (n 7) 441.

intelligence was a key part of the intelligence community, with a budget as large as its surveillance capabilities.

1.3 Electronic surveillance in the digital era

In the years immediately after the fall of the Berlin Wall, a shift in foreign and defence policy priorities necessitated the adaptation of electronic intelligence tasks. An example is the German BND, which became geared more towards fighting terrorism, international drug crime, and arms trafficking.[30] In this way electronic intelligence agencies, historically rooted in military structures, with gigantic data collection and processing capabilities and scarce external control, came to be engaged in tasks traditionally associated with internal security services. However, it is one thing to systematically gather information on another state's extensive military, diplomatic or economic structures, and another thing to seek information on the activities of individuals or (relatively) small and dispersed criminal groups. The limited use made of the intelligence capabilities available at the time is reflected in the data presented in 1998, showing a small number of intelligence reports provided by the BND in connection with its activities concerning the new areas.[31]

A new era in the history of electronic intelligence followed the tragic attacks of 11 September 2001. One of the responses of Western countries to the growing threat of terrorism was to acquiesce to the implementation of a new generation of mass programmes for the surveillance of citizens. These measures were intended to help identify unknown sources of threats. And although in many cases they were still carried out in the context of foreign intelligence, given the then rapidly developing global data market it became increasingly difficult to draw a clear line between foreign and domestic operations.

Even though in the first decade of the 21st century the public was informed of the increasing focus of electronic intelligence services on programmes targeting civilian communications, this issue could not be analysed in detail due to the lack of reliable data and the understandable concern about the ever-present terrorist threats.

It was not until the disclosure of NSA documents by Edward Snowden in 2013 that a more comprehensive understanding of the current potential and scale of the involvement of electronic intelligence agencies in the conduct of mass surveillance programmes was possible. The information disclosed by Snowden mainly concerned the NSA and GCHQ, and to a lesser extent the services of other countries, limited to instances of their cooperation with their US counterparts.

30 Klaus Gärditz, 'Legal Restraints on the Extraterritorial Activities of Germany's Intelligence Services' in Russell A Miller (ed), *Privacy and Power* (Cambridge University Press 2017) 404 <www.cambridge.org/core/product/identifier/9781316658888%23CT-bp-16/type/book_part> accessed 9 October 2020.

31 Schmidt-Eenboom (n 25) 165.

According to the documents published, the NSA runs a set of different programmes, which can be subdivided according to the scope of data collected and the manner in which they are acquired. First of all, one can distinguish programmes that allow the collection of data accompanying electronic communications, i.e. the so-called metadata (including the MAINWAY and MARINA programmes), as well as programmes also related to the interception of the substantive content of communications (e.g. PRISM).[32] According to the method of data collection, it is possible to further distinguish activities related to eavesdropping on telecommunication channels (the UPSTREAM group of programmes) and those related to direct access to the IT systems of leading Internet service providers (including PRISM and MUSCULAR).

Under PRISM, the NSA gained ongoing access to the data centres of the major global digital service providers located within the United States. According to 2012 data, it was possible to access data stored by Microsoft, Yahoo, Google, Facebook, Paltalk, YouTube, Skype, AOL and Apple.[33] What is important here is that the NSA had direct access to the information collected by the service providers, so the data did not come from the interception of electronic communications. Therefore the NSA could access the full content of information collected by hundreds of millions of users, including from email (e.g. from services such as Gmail, Yahoo or Exchange) and file repositories, as well as from electronic communications services (such as Skype) or content published on social networks. Notably, it seems that PRISM enabled any information to be extracted without the service providers being able to control the process or the users' awareness of it.

Thanks to the documents disclosed by Snowden, the PRISM programme is one of the better-known contemporary mass surveillance programmes run by the NSA, but it is not the only one.[34] Of equal importance from the perspective of European users is the UPSTREAM group of programmes, whose common feature was (is?) the interception of electronic communications, usually transmitted over international fibre-optic links. Activities of this type were carried out both in the United States (e.g. the FAIRVIEW, STORMVIEW or OAKSTAR programmes) and in third countries (RAMPART-A) in cooperation with foreign secret services as well as telecommunications operators. Within the framework of the individual programmes, different types of communications – in particular metadata, but also the substantive content of the transmission (e.g. emails) – could be intercepted. According to the

32 A description of the technical capabilities associated with the various surveillance programmes is provided in the NSA documents disclosed by Snowden, including 'Special Source Operation Overview' <https://goo.gl/2uQFBQ> accessed 6 September 2023.

33 Barton Gellman and Laura Poitras, 'U.S., British Intelligence Mining Data from Nine U.S. Internet Companies in Broad Secret Program' *The Washington Post* (7 June 2013) <https://cli.re/XAdAnp>.

34 Glenn Greenwald, *No Place to Hide: Edward Snowden, the NSA, and the U.S. Surveillance State* (First Picador edition, Picador 2015).

information disclosed, communications transmitted via Deutsche Telekom fibre-optic cables in Germany (code name EIKANOL)[35] and also Denmark were to be intercepted under RAMPART-A.

The RAMPART-A programme was geared towards cooperation with the so-called third countries, in this context partners not belonging to the FVEY agreement. In turn, the countries party to the FVEY agreement jointly carried out additional activities related to the interception of electronic communications. Examples of this type of programme include TEMPORA (discussed later in this chapter) and MUSCULAR, conducted jointly by the NSA and GCHQ. Under the MUSCULAR programme, communications exchanged between the data centres of Google and Yahoo were intercepted. And under the OPTIC NERVE programme, also run jointly by the two intelligence agencies, images from webcams of the Yahoo! Webcam application users were recorded on a massive scale. According to the documents disclosed by Snowden, images from more than 1.8 million Yahoo user accounts[36] were obtained in this way over a 6-month period in 2008. According to GCHQ's assessment, about 7% of the photos were intimate, and some were of an explicitly erotic nature.[37] The OPTIC NERVE programme was untargeted, which means that images from all users were intercepted, regardless of whether a particular individual was suspected of any activity of interest to state authorities.

As a result of its activities, the NSA collected vast amounts of data, gathered from many sources, on a daily basis. This enabled it to conduct global surveillance programmes, targeting not specific individuals but whole communities or, in the extreme variant, entire countries. One example of a surveillance programme of this type is MYSTIC, which according to the information disclosed allowed for the interception of all electronic communications (e.g. voice calls, emails, instant messaging) originating from designated countries for further analysis.[38] The mass interception of communications also made it possible to carry out programmes such as GHOSTHUNTER, which aimed to identify in real time wanted persons logging on to the Internet, thus contributing to "a significant number of capture-kill operations."[39]

Data extracted through surveillance programmes were collected in multiple data warehouses and used for further analysis by means of dedicated tools such

35 Kai Biermann, 'Daten Abfischen Mit Lizenz Aus Dem Kanzleramt' *Zeit Online* (4 December 2014) <https://cli.re/KDpWbJ>.

36 Murad Ahmed, 'GCHQ "Watched Millions of Yahoo! Customers on Their Webcams"' *The Times* (27 February 2014) <https://cli.re/rmBK3K> accessed 6 September 2023.

37 '*OPTIC NERVE – Yahoo Webcam Display and Target Discovery*' *GCHQ* (December 2018) 3 <https://cli.re/zEro79>.

38 Barton Gellman and Ashkan Soltani, 'NSA Surveillance Program Reaches "Into the Past" to Retrieve, Replay Phone Calls' *The Washington Post* (18 March 2014) <https://cli.re/MAoXvn> accessed 6 September 2023.

39 Ryan Gallagher, 'Inside Menwith Hill' *The Intercept* (6 September 2016) <https://cli.re/xz3xdJ> accessed 6 September 2023.

as XKeyScore. This system made it possible to quickly access information of interest using any identifier, such as an email address, an IP address, or other Internet identifiers.[40] Unlike a traditional search engine, however, XKeyScore was also intended to allow modification of the selectors used in individual surveillance systems, thus enabling the rules of data collection to be changed. It was, therefore, a system with a dual functionality: it enabled not only the analysis of already collected data (like classic analytical systems), but also the management of the process of capturing new data. According to 2008 data, the XKeyScore platform alone used 700 servers deployed in 150 locations worldwide.[41]

The set of documents revealed by Snowden also provided a better understanding of the GCHQ's intelligence capabilities. The British service has been running its own mass electronic surveillance programmes for years, and one of the most important remains TEMPORA. Its aim is to eavesdrop on transmissions sent over some 200 transatlantic fibre-optic links.[42] Due to its geographical location, much of the international telecommunications traffic (including Internet traffic) between Europe and North America is transmitted through the United Kingdom. This gives the GCHQ the ability to intercept vast amounts of data, including voice calls, user data and files, emails, and instant messaging. However, there is no reason to believe that TEMPORA is the only European fibre-optic communications eavesdropping programme. Similar activities were already carried out by the BND in the 1980s as part of Operation DELIKATESSE, the aim of which was to intercept communications transmitted over fibre-optic cables linking Europe with North Africa.[43]

1.4 Between targeted and untargeted measures

With the development of the technical capabilities associated with surveillance activities, the relevance of the distinction between targeted and untargeted measures, which has been made for decades, is gaining more and more attention. In fact, it should be borne in mind that the term *surveillance* itself is imprecise, and it would be more correct to speak of measures with a surveillance effect. This is due to the simple fact that many of the technical solutions are not developed with the implementation of surveillance activities in mind, and the surveillance area is just one possible application of the technology in question.[44]

40 Edward J Snowden, *Permanent Record* (Metropolitan Books 2019) 276–279.

41 Mark M Jaycox, 'No Oversight, No Limits, No Worries: A Primer on Presidential Spying and Executive Order 12,333' (2021) 12 *Harvard National Security Journal* 58, 94–96.

42 Ewen MacAskill and others, 'GCHQ Taps Fibre-Optic Cables for Secret Access to World's Communications' *The Guardian* (21 June 2013) <https://cli.re/3R3QwW> accessed 6 September 2023.

43 Schmidt-Eenboom (n 25) 156.

44 Neil M Richards, 'The Dangers of Surveillance' (2012) 126 *Harvard Law Review* 1934.

In targeted forms of surveillance, the activities of the authorised authorities focus from the outset on gathering information on specific individuals or groups of individuals. Even if, at the time of initiating proceedings, it is not possible to indicate the identity of the subjects of surveillance, it is possible to use other distinguishing factors to determine the scope of the measures to be applied. Targeted surveillance is traditionally associated with the activities of law enforcement agencies and the implementation of criminal procedures, in which case such measures are applied under external review (most often by a procedural authority or a court), and the correctness of the entire process is subject to subsequent assessment at the stage of criminal proceedings.

In democratic states, untargeted surveillance is not a measure that is primarily used in the area of criminal procedure. Indeed, its primary purpose is not to collect information on persons of interest to law enforcement agencies, but to intercept large amounts of information and subject it to subsequent analysis in search of patterns or correlations that may reveal events previously unknown to the secret services.

While targeted surveillance is generally exercised by law enforcement agencies, untargeted surveillance is the domain of secret and intelligence services (SIA). This is due to the simple fact that untargeted surveillance is, from the outset, geared towards the collection of any available information that may prove useful to the conduct of the services' activities. However, this *usefulness* should in no way be linked to the necessity of gathering this information. Therefore an intrinsic feature of untargeted surveillance is the collection of redundant data, which may or may not prove useful for further analysis.

For this reason, untargeted surveillance is often referred to as "mass" or "bulk" surveillance.[45] These adjectives are intended to emphasise that the technical aspects of this form of surveillance are based on the collection of vast amounts of data. Although they are used interchangeably, in practice, they are not synonymous.

Indiscriminate surveillance is a concept that refers to the extent of the data collected, in particular indicating the lack of use of distinguishing factors to identify specific individuals subject to surveillance. Therefore it can include, for example, the collection of information relating to specific social groups or to individuals with links to specific political, religious or cultural groups. Bulk surveillance, on the other hand, refers to the technical method of data collection and involves the interception of all information that can be obtained in a given manner (e.g. from a particular transmission medium). Bulk surveillance tends to be indiscriminate surveillance, and indiscriminate surveillance is, in turn, usually carried out using bulk collection of information. However, this is not always the case.

45 'Report on the Democratic Oversight of Signals Intelligence Agencies' (Venice Commission 2015) CDL-AD(2015)011 12–13 <https://cli.re/ApE7Ad> accessed 6 September 2023.

For example, some consider that the bulk capture of communications by the GCHQ under the TEMPORA programme should not result in these activities being considered indiscriminate surveillance.[46] Advocates of such a view point to the use of selectors in the processing of data, which allows the scope of the data collected to be significantly reduced. In this way, according to this conception, although the GCHQ does, in fact, have access to the entirety of transmissions sent over telecommunications fibres, it is at the same time targeted surveillance, as only information meeting certain filtering criteria is passed on for further processing.

However, this view has a fundamental flaw which its proponents seem to overlook completely: to search for specific information in a dataset, one must first have access to that dataset. A search is an operation on data, and it is impossible to search a dataset without having access to it. Therefore if it is a secret service that has access to the transmission medium, and it is the same service that controls the flow of data and determines the choice of selectors, the resulting processing is still indiscriminate in nature, and the use of selectors is only a further step in data analysis. In this case, data filtering is usually dictated by technical limitations (related to the analysis of large data sets) rather than the need to reduce the severity of the surveillance measure applied.

Thus, the mere use of selectors is not enough for a measure based on bulk interception to be considered as targeted in all cases. Recognising this problem, some legislators have established mechanisms to separate the power to control the interception of data (and the process of pre-filtering the data) from the power to carry out their subsequent analysis, the latter of which is done by the secret service. An example is the Swedish model, in which the intelligence service (FRA) does not manage the interception process.[47] This task is carried out by a separate office, the National Inspectorate for Defence Intelligence (*Statens inspektion för försvarsunderrättelseverksamheten*), according to a court-approved order.[48] This is, therefore, a qualitatively different solution to that used by the German BND, the British GCHQ, or the US NSA, where the same entity is responsible for data interception and its subsequent analysis.

Importantly, additional safeguards have been introduced in the Swedish model to exclude the possibility of bulk systems being used in a manner similar to targeted systems.[49] Indeed, any untargeted system can be used for targeted surveillance: it is sufficient for this purpose to use identifiers directly pointing to a specific person as keywords. This also leaves considerable room for abuse,

46 David Anderson, 'Report of the Bulk Powers Review' (Independent Reviewer of Terrorism Legislation 2016) 3 <https://cli.re/97RkoJ> accessed 9 June 2023.

47 See Art. 12(2) of the Swedish Act on Signals Intelligence Defence Activities, SFS 2008:717.

48 The powers and duties of SIUN are detailed in the Ordinance with Instructions for the National Inspectorate for Defence Intelligence Operations, SFS 2009:969.

49 For more on this topic, see section 6.2.

as in most cases the application of bulk measures is subject to separate (less restrictive) regulations than the use of targeted surveillance.

As bulk measures have historically been in the domain of intelligence services and the military, their use was not subject to the regulations established in criminal procedure. The primary purpose of using such systems was to gain knowledge and provide information to decision-makers rather than to gather evidence for court use. As a result, when designing this type of solution, no particular attention was paid to the legal constraints arising from, for example, the obligation to respect fundamental rights or the principles of necessity and proportionality.

In practice, in addition to the division into foreign and domestic surveillance, it is possible to distinguish yet another type. An example is the so-called strategic surveillance carried out by the German BND.[50] The purpose of this programme was to collect information on foreign electronic communications transmitted between German territory and selected third countries of interest to the German secret services. Strategic surveillance thus created the appearance of targeted surveillance, while employing untargeted surveillance mechanisms.[51] In fact, this was a "third" type of surveillance, in addition to the surveillance used in criminal cases (targeted surveillance, for which indiscriminate surveillance measures could not be used) and the so-called foreign-foreign surveillance (carried out between persons located abroad, for which German law for years did not provide for any legal restrictions on the surveillance measures used).

The basis for the use of strategic surveillance (and many bulk surveillance programmes) is the increasingly difficult-to-prove assumption of the (at least partly) foreign nature of the intercepted communications. In the case of monitoring voice communications over traditional telecommunications services, establishing the locations of communicating parties seemed straightforward and could be done automatically. However, the dynamic development of digital services means that attempting to infer a user's location solely on the basis of the location information contained in network traffic involves a high risk of error.

This is because determining that emails sent from a cloud email service (e.g. Gmail) come from a user located in a particular country would require

50 For more on strategic monitoring, see: Christian Schaller, 'Strategic Surveillance and Extraterritorial Basic Rights Protection: German Intelligence Law After Snowden' (2018) 19 *German Law Journal* 941. The strategic monitoring programme has also been reviewed several times by German courts, including the Federal Constitutional Court and the Federal Administrative Court. See in particular the following judgments: BVerfG 14 July 1999, 1 BvR 2226/94-1 BvR 2420/95-1 BvR 2437/95; BVerwG 14 December 2016, 6 A 9.14, English translation available at: <www.bverwg.de/en/141216U6A9.14.0>.

51 The basis for its conduct is the so-called G10 Act – i.e. the Gesetz zur Beschränkung des Brief-, Post- und Fernmeldegeheimnisses [English: German Federal Law on the Restriction of Letter, Post and Telecommunications Secrecy], BGBl. I 1254; 2298.

collecting and analysing a larger set of information than just a single email. In practice, with a simple filter it is not possible to separate domestic traffic from foreign traffic. It is necessary to intercept all communications and only at a later stage to filter out a specific traffic type (domestic data). In this case, however, it would be necessary not so much to base the filtering on the geolocation of the communicating parties (which, in the case of many services, cannot be determined based on IP packet analysis) as to examine the content of the messages transmitted. Even in the case of voice services, with free and popular services based on the VoIP protocol, a person who uses, for example, a French mobile number may actually be located anywhere in the world.

Hence, nowadays it is not possible to simply restrict the use of bulk measures by means of geographical criteria without a detailed analysis of the transmitted data. This is technically impossible, and even in cases where the prohibition of this type of data collection is established in legal regulations, its implementation consists of an attempt to filter out (delete) specific categories of data rather than establish technical measures to counteract (prevent) the collection of domestic data.

However, the domestic/foreign threat divide has also lost its relevance due to changing priorities in the area of national security, in which more and more attention has been paid to extremist or terrorist threats. Governments have used this argument to justify the need to deliberately implement bulk measures in relation to domestic communications. In fact, much of the discussion that has been ongoing over the years regarding the incompatibility of individual Member States' national retention laws with EU law concerns precisely the mass collection of metadata from electronic communications as a necessary measure to protect national security.[52] The need to apply untargeted surveillance within one's own country (in the form of bulk collection and making available of metadata from electronic communications) is one of the key arguments pointed out in the French Council of State's 2021 judgment.[53] While the Council acknowledged the incompatibility of the national legislation under review with EU law, at the same time it provided a detailed legal justification that opened up the possibility of using untargeted measures in the future.

The above leads to the conclusion that nowadays, both untargeted and targeted programmes are increasingly used to achieve the same objectives, but this is still done separately as a result of both their technical capabilities and the different entities entitled to use them. As indicated earlier, in theory any untargeted measure can be used in a targeted manner. However, this does not hold true the other way round. The reason is the completely different technical

52 Marcin Rojszczak, 'National Security and Retention of Telecommunications Data in Light of Recent Case Law of the European Courts' (2021) 17 *European Constitutional Law Review* 607.

53 Conseil d'État 21 April 2021, Case 393099, ECLI:FR:CEASS:2021:393099.20210421.

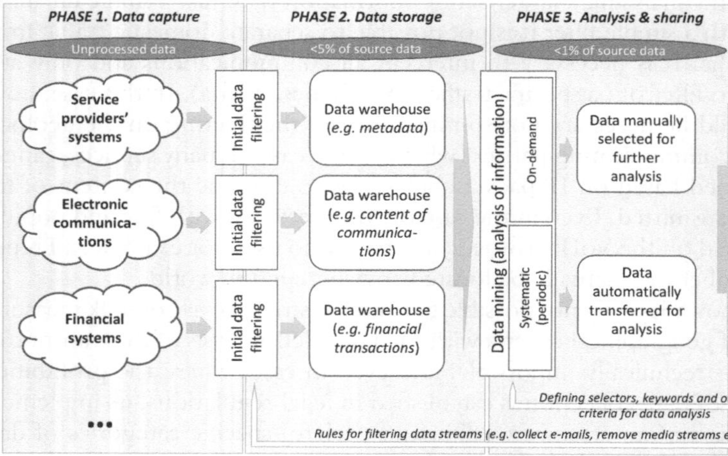

Diagram 1.1 The architecture of an untargeted surveillance system.

architecture of the two types of electronic surveillance systems. Today's targeted measures are sophisticated tools that allow the interception of different types of communications by, among other things, bypassing or breaching IT security. Hence, programmes such as Pegasus, Predator and Candiru, which have been gaining popularity in recent years and which are based on the distribution of malware (the so-called spyware), can be included in this group.[54] On the other hand, bulk surveillance systems are, in fact, large data warehouses that allow the analysis of very large data sets. An untargeted system is primarily an analytical tool, which makes it possible to carry out different types of analysis according to the criteria set (see Diagram 1.1). And, as with any other data warehouse, the effectiveness of untargeted systems depends not only on the quality of the data provided, but also on the quantity of the data.

This is why surveillance using untargeted means is often referred to as predictive (or preventive) surveillance.[55] This is because the idea behind it is that it should allow for the identification of previously unknown trends and non-obvious links between data.[56] Hence, the expectation of the proponents of this type of technology is that a system fed with sufficient data will be able to

54 Quentin Liger and Mirja Gutheil, 'The Use of Pegasus and Equivalent Surveillance Spyware' (PEGA Committee of the European Parliament 2023) <https://cli.re/o4ZRbp> accessed 6 September 2023.

55 For the distinction between predictive and preventive surveillance, see Albert Meijer and Martijn Wessels, 'Predictive Policing: Review of Benefits and Drawbacks' (2019) 42 *International Journal of Public Administration* 1031.

56 KA Taipale, 'Data Mining and Domestic Security: Connecting the Dots to Make Sense of Data' (2003) 5 *Columbia Science and Technology Law Review* 1.

identify serious security threats, such as terrorist risks, before knowledge of them is obtained by other, traditional means. The modus operandi of untargeted measures is, therefore, fundamentally different from that of targeted measures. In the case of the former, it is impossible to demonstrate that the criterion of necessity is met at the time of data collection. In other words, there is no certainty that the subsequent analysis of the data will reveal new knowledge and thus, in a way, confirm *ex post* the need for data collection.

Such "preventive" data collection in the case of targeted measures, leading to the surveillance of individuals who are not connected, even indirectly, with activities of interest to the state, would constitute a clear case of abuse of power. Thus, while the surveillance of random persons using targeted measures is, in principle, not acceptable in democratic states, a similar action using untargeted measures does not meet with an equal, unequivocally negative, reaction from either governments, the public, or the courts.

One of the sources of this phenomenon is a misunderstanding of the differences between the two categories of surveillance measures, as well as a misjudgement of the actual possibilities associated with using bulk surveillance. However, regardless of the assessment of the usefulness of each form of surveillance, it is true that today untargeted surveillance measures are increasingly used by actors and in areas hitherto reserved for targeted measures. As a result, untargeted surveillance is ceasing to be regarded solely as a means of gathering national security intelligence aimed, in particular, at identifying the most serious threats to the interests of the state, mainly beyond its borders.

1.5 Development of technical capabilities

It is true that without digitisation, the surveillance measures we know today would never have been developed. Although from the beginning of the development of analogue means of communication, mechanisms for eavesdropping on them were developed in parallel, for most of the 20th century they were not untargeted. This was primarily due to the very limited capabilities for the collection and subsequent analysis of communications intercepted. There were neither the means to eavesdrop on all transmitted communications nor, even more importantly, the possibility to rapidly process the communications recorded to provide information useful for intelligence.

It was not until the 1970s that computer systems capable of automatic (albeit a simplified and, by today's standards, primitive) analysis of a large data stream emerged. Despite their limited capabilities, these systems let analysts direct their attention to transmissions containing information of interest to the relevant services. At a later stage, they also allowed simple patterns (keywords) to be identified. However, these systems were implemented out of necessity: developments in data collection capabilities and the new means used for this purpose (including, for example, satellite intelligence), resulted in the collection of far greater volumes of data than the capacity to process them. continuing to keep traditional case files and analyse the data manually was not only too slow a solution, but above all did not allow related information to be quickly found in the already existing data banks.

The dynamic development of computing power and data storage capacity overcame the limitations involved in the processing of increasingly large electronic data sets. Not only did mass data processing become technically possible, but it was also becoming cheaper and cheaper every year. In the early 1990s, the cost of setting up a new computer centre by the German BND ran into hundreds of millions of marks.[57] At the same time, the US NSA spent sums many times greater on projects intended to increase its data processing capacity.[58] And as recently as 2012, it was estimated that acquiring and maintaining the technology needed to implement a bulk surveillance programme would cost a medium-sized European country a few tens of millions of dollars per year.[59] Viewed against the scale of a state's overall operations, this amount is almost imperceptible and corresponds to a tiny fraction of the police services budget, not to mention the funds allocated each year to defence. As a result, whereas only 30 years ago extensive electronic surveillance programmes were carried out mainly by developed, economically powerful states, today such systems can be implemented by almost any government, not excluding developing countries.

Democratisation in access to modern technology cannot per se be judged negatively. However, caution is required in the case of solutions that can clearly be used for anti-democratic transformations. Today, electronic surveillance systems are classified by many states in a manner similar to dual-use technologies, with the result that their marketing requires special export approvals.[60] This is how Israel controlled access to the Pegasus software, which is a modern targeted surveillance system.[61] In practice, oversight of access to surveillance technologies is not, and has never been, as rigorous as for classical means of warfare. As a result, export restrictions did not prevent Pegasus – treated as a "cyber weapon" in its country of origin[62] – from being sold to dozens of countries around the world, including many non-democratic ones and those

57 Schmidt-Eenboom (n 25) 162.

58 As a result, as early as the 1970s the NSA was described as "a several billion dollar a year corporation." Matthew M Aid, 'The National Security Agency and the Cold War' (2001) 16 *Intelligence and National Security* 27, 46.

59 Julian Assange and others, *Cypherpunks: Freedom and the Future of the Internet* (OR Books 2012) 38.

60 Sean D Kaster and Prescott C Ensign, 'Privatized Espionage: NSO Group Technologies and Its Pegasus Spyware' (2023) 65 *Thunderbird International Business Review* 355.

61 Patrick Howell O'Neill, 'The Man Who Built a Spyware Empire Says It's Time to Come out of the Shadows' *MIT Technology Review* (19 August 2020) <https://cli.re/PpY1yP> accessed 6 September 2023.

62 Thomas Brewster, 'Everything We Know About NSO Group: The Professional Spies Who Hacked iPhones with A Single Text' *Forbes* (25 August 2016) <https://cli.re/44x9Wq> accessed 6 September 2023.

suspected of serious human rights abuses.[63] Pegasus has been used for the surveillance of journalists in Mexico[64] and politicians in Poland,[65] as well as by Saudi Arabia in planning an assassination on the premises of its diplomatic establishment in Turkey.[66]

However, the objections to an overly broad access to modern surveillance measures are not exclusively related to the Pegasus system. Similar concerns were formulated many years ago in relation to the British company BEA, which supplied its surveillance technology to regimes in the Middle East.[67] But also during the Cold War, oversight of the marketing of surveillance systems did not protect against abuse. A case in point is the supply of the ADVOOKAT system to South Africa by the German conglomerate AEG Telefunken. Germany not only supplied the surveillance technology but also provided technical and training support – and this at a time when the South African regime was under UN sanctions.[68]

Increases in computing power and data storage capacity, as well as the growing popularity of the online services, have also resulted in transformations in data processing, including the spread of cloud computing and distributed computing. These changes have not been neutral from the perspective of the surveillance capacity of states. Indeed, they have led to the emergence of both new means of data collection, previously unavailable, as well as potential limitations to this process, such as those associated with the increasingly widespread use of transmission encryption.

Back in the first half of the 1990s, the natural limitation for conducting electronic intelligence activities was access to a transmission medium. To analyse data, it was first necessary to acquire them. Intercepting communications required access to the medium of transmission. Hence the crucial importance during the Cold War of SIGINT stations, which enabled data collection at a distance by capturing the entire spectrum of radio transmissions, including satellite communications. As late as the 1980s, due to technical limitations, the BND could only eavesdrop on one side of the transmission when intercepting satellite communications. If the entire conversation was to be recorded, it was

63 Bill Marczak and others, 'Hide and Seek: Tracking NSO Group's Pegasus Spyware to Operations in 45 Countries' (University of Toronto 2018) Citizen Lab Research Report No. 113 <https://cli.re/Bv3oDP> accessed 22 September 2020.

64 Jamie Wiseman, *Watching the Watchdogs: Pegasus Spyware and the Surveillance of Journalists* (International Press Institute 2020) <https://cli.re/YNVn8E> accessed 6 September 2023.

65 Stephanie Kirchgaessner, 'More Polish Opposition Figures Found to Have Been Targeted by Pegasus Spyware' *The Guardian* (17 February 2022) <https://cli.re/jpeo7a> accessed 6 September 2023.

66 Marko Milanovic, 'The Murder of Jamal Khashoggi: Immunities, Inviolability and the Human Right to Life' (2020) 20 *Human Rights Law Review* 1.

67 Jenna McLaughlin, 'BAE Systems Sells Internet Surveillance Gear to United Arab Emirates' *The Intercept* (15 June 2017) <https://cli.re/jpPpEE> accessed 6 September 2023.

68 Schmidt-Eenboom (n 25) 161–162.

necessary to interact with a SIGINT centre located close to the geolocation of the other side of the communication. As a result, for many years countries with extensive intelligence activities were also forced to maintain a global listening network and cooperate with each other in intercepting communications. The Internet and global digital services have de facto removed these limitations.

Although the general perception is that the Internet is a very loosely organised network based on the cooperation of many local telecommunications operators, in practice it is a hierarchical network. Individual telecommunications operators can be assigned different roles, depending on which level of network organisation they are at. As a general rule, each can be classified into one of the following tiers: Tier 1, Tier 2 or Tier 3. Tier 2/3 includes traditional ISPs, i.e. entities that provide services directly to the end-user and have interpretive agreements (that allow traffic exchange) with other operators. In contrast, Tier 1 includes entities that, using their own infrastructure and without incurring additional inter-operator costs, can provide global coverage with any other network connected to the Internet. In practice, Tier 2/3 operators use one or more of the so-called Internet exchange points (IXPs) through which they can route packets to other public networks. Tier 1 operators, on the other hand, are connected to multiple IXPs, which allows them to provide global coverage for their operations. Tier 1 operators must, therefore, have a geographically extensive telecommunications infrastructure, often covering thousands of kilometres of fibre-optic cables. Currently, depending on the definition adopted, around 20 entities are classified as Tier 1.[69] Hence, each of these entities mediates a significant proportion of Internet traffic, even though Internet users are not even aware of the existence of most of them. These entities play a key role in ensuring the efficiency and stability of network operations as well as the security of transmissions, including protection against unlawful surveillance.

Therefore in practice, regardless of how a user accesses the Internet and which telecommunications operator the sender and receiver of the data use, the transmission between them is, in many cases, carried out via the infrastructure owned by a Tier 1 operator.

Interfering with Tier 1 operators' infrastructure would potentially make it possible to intercept not only transmissions sent from or routed to a particular country, but also a significant proportion of global traffic exchanged on the Internet. Because of the way packets are routed, based on algorithms that minimise the cost of data transmission, transmissions between neighbouring countries can use infrastructure located on another continent. As a result, the monitoring of Tier 1 networks allows insight into a gigantic data stream and the interception of communications – including foreign communications – without the need to

69 See the ASRank ranking published by the Center for Applied Internet Data Analysis: <https://asrank.caida.org/>. Among the top 20 operators, US and European players dominate (16 positions).

expand the network of visible (and expensive) radio listening stations. Moreover, Tier 1 network operators are normal corporations with headquarters and boards of directors based in specific countries. These countries may use national law to oblige such operators to provide access to their telecommunications infrastructure. In effect, this creates the opportunity for public authorities to carry out global surveillance programmes by means of orders addressed to private (domestic) telecommunications operators, without developing advanced and transnational means for this purpose.

A similar effect can be achieved by monitoring communications at IXPs. IXPs usually have regional significance, so they allow for the interception of communications concerning a specific geographical area. At the same time, owing to technical reasons this solution is easier to apply and more difficult to detect than eavesdropping on fibre-optic communications (as in the case of eavesdropping on lines used by Tier 1 operators). This is because IXPs are, in principle, used to exchange traffic. They have high-capacity network equipment installed in them to enable appropriate packet routing. From the perspective of telecommunications operators, verification of unauthorised interference with transmission – including, for example, the copying of all or part of the data stream (e.g. by means of techniques such as port mirroring) – would require physical inspection of the infrastructure, which is not always possible or practical.

While the public has only scarce information on the scale and scope of electronic surveillance programmes, the information that has been disclosed confirms that both Tier 1 networks and IXPs are targeted for data acquisition in the course of surveillance programmes. In 2013, the documents published by Snowden revealed information on the cooperation between the NSA and the US company Level 3 (now Lumen Technologies), which involved the installation of eavesdropping devices on the fibre-optic infrastructure provided to technology companies (in this case, Google and Yahoo).[70] In turn, in 2015 the German media, citing testimony given before a Parliamentary Committee, reported that the BND had been monitoring the traffic handled by DE-CIX, Europe's largest IXP operator, since 2009.[71] DE-CIX has traffic exchange points not only in Germany but also in much of Europe, the United States, the Middle East, Russia and India. The details of the cooperation between the BND and DE-CIX remain secret, which makes it impossible to verify the media reports indicating that the BND was allowed unrestricted access to all traffic handled at the IXP node in Frankfurt, among others. The DE-CIX

70 Craig Timberg and Barton Gellman, 'NSA Paying U.S. Companies for Access to Communications Networks' *The Washington Post* (29 August 2013) <https://cli.re/97V1bb> accessed 6 September 2023.

71 Andre Meister, 'How the German Foreign Intelligence Agency BND Tapped the Internet Exchange Point DE-CIX in Frankfurt, Since 2009' *Netzpolitik.org* (31 March 2015) <https://cli.re/w34wND> accessed 6 September 2023.

operator took legal action to have the BND's surveillance measures declared unlawful. However, the Federal Administrative Court held that DE-CIX could not claim the protection of the constitutional right to secrecy of communications, as this right is vested in the parties to a communication, not in the intermediary, which has no influence on the content of the communications and is only performing the technical act of transmission.[72] In response, DE-CIX filed a constitutional complaint – which, however, was also dismissed.[73]

The globalisation of services provided over the Internet has also resulted in the need to develop new forms of data processing, such as cloud computing. This model involves the provision of a service using the service provider's computing power, also leading to the transfer of the user's data storage from their local computer to the service provider's remote infrastructure. An increasing number of popular services are provided in the form of cloud computing, ranging from email to office software (e.g. Office 365) and online storage (e.g. Dropbox) to specialised software for medical records or legal offices. In the cloud computing model, the user uses the online software to process their own data, but does so entirely remotely. For example, when a text document is created using a word processor and saved on a local computer, intercepting the content of the document would require access to the data storage device (the user's computer). In the case of using a cloud service, the document will also be saved on a remote network service, which means that it will first be uploaded to it and then stored on the provider's server. In this scenario, the content of the document can be captured not only on the user's terminal but also during transmission. Moreover, it can be retrieved (copied) directly from the service provider's servers. In practice, it is not easy to simultaneously monitor the activities undertaken locally by a large number of users on their private devices (e.g. computers, phones). This would require the installation of local monitoring agents, which is neither a simple nor an effective solution (for now leaving aside obvious questions about the legality of such an action). However, in the case of cloud computing, the same information can be accessed by intercepting data directly from the service provider's data centre, thus avoiding the problem of obtaining it from users' computers. In this way, it becomes possible to acquire information about all users of a given service (technology), and it can be done in a manner that does not require access to their devices or even control over the means of communication.

The spread of cloud computing has resulted in another, indeed more important, change in data availability. It resulted from the need for high availability of global services, which led to the redundancy of data centres and their even geographical distribution. As a result, the same service (e.g. Gmail) is provided using more than a dozen data centres around the world, located

72 BVerwG 30 May 2018, 6 A 3.16, ECLI:DE:BVerwG:2018:300518U6A3.16.0, para. 27–38.
73 BVerfG 5 December 2022, 1 BvR 1865/22, ECLI:DE:BVerfG:2022:rk20221205.1bvr186522.

in different places (countries). The decision as to which servers will handle a service request is solely dependent on network capacity and the decision of the service provider (Google), not the user's choice. Subsequent requests from the same user, residing in the same location and for the same service, may, due to different network loads, be handled by application servers located in different places. Ensuring service redundancy (fault tolerance) also requires data multiplication, i.e. simultaneous storage in several geographical locations. Furthermore, the proper functioning of such an extensive infrastructure, based on multiple data centres, obviously requires the provision of dedicated fibre-optic links, allowing rapid data transfer between individual computing centres. And it is precisely this type of network traffic, exchanged between the data centres of a single service provider, that was allegedly the object of surveillance carried out in collaboration with the Level 3 communications, as discussed above.

The fact that data from global online services are stored at the same time in many geographically dispersed locations means that potentially the same data can be intercepted in a similar way in several different locations. This opens up new opportunities for surveillance activities in countries with less restrictive laws related to access to data collected by online service providers. In practice, therefore, when talking about the surveillance potential of such global services, what matters is not only the regulations and laws specific to the user's location or the service provider's headquarters but, de facto, also the laws of each jurisdiction in which the service provider has a data centre dedicated to providing a specific service. This observation also explains why some electronic intelligence services establish and maintain permanent facilities in third countries.

In discussing the technological changes affecting the new possibilities of mass data collection, one cannot fail to address the oft-repeated argument that public authorities are unable to process the vast amounts of information they acquire, with the result that the actual severity of their surveillance activities from an individual rights perspective is low.[74] To put it in simpler terms: it is not the amount of information collected that matters, but the real capacity to analyse it. According to this view, if only a small proportion of Internet traffic can be processed, then the surveillance itself cannot per se be considered "mass." This argumentation also seems to be supported by the available statistics on the pre-filtering applied by individual electronic intelligence services, indicating that only a small proportion of the data are passed on for further analysis.[75]

The above conclusion is built on the assumption that the processing of data obtained from bulk surveillance is a centrally conducted process using

74 Richard A Posner, 'Privacy, Surveillance, and Law' (2008) 75 *University of Chicago Law Review* 245.

75 'Privacy and Security: A Modern and Transparent Legal Framework' (Intelligence and Security Committee of Parliament 2015) HC 1075 3.

mainframe computers. However, this is not the case. The modern data market also offers sophisticated means of distributed processing. Data can be analysed using a variety of mechanisms, including during the transmission itself. One of the significant technological breakthroughs in the telecommunications sector in recent years was the development and then dissemination of the DPI (deep packet inspection) technology.[76]

With the growth of the Internet, there was an increasing need to ensure that individual applications (services) had the necessary bandwidth for their proper operation (the so-called quality of service, or QoS). Typical examples of such services with high bandwidth requirements are streaming and telecommunications. The need to implement mass QoS services was the reason for the development of a new generation of network equipment, allowing real-time decisions on packet routing (i.e. transferring packets from the sender to the receiver) based not only on an analysis of network addresses (the locations of the sender and receiver of the data) but also on the substantive content of the message itself. It is this technology that is referred to as DPI. Its implementation in modern telecommunications equipment enables the smooth operation of streaming services (and, for example, VoIP) and allows for many other applications which were previously impossible.[77]

In the same way that DPI devices can give a higher priority to certain traffic (e.g. Netflix), they can also allow other packets to be blocked. Hence, DPI is one of the cornerstones of the modern online traffic moderation mechanisms.[78] It may be used for the real-time blocking of selected news outlets, social networks, or communication services.[79] DPI is also an excellent tool for passive surveillance (without directly modifying traffic), which makes the selective collection of a particular data stream possible in real time.

The use of DPI does not require gigantic data centres, as it is part of the functionality of high-performance network devices. Thus, instead of building one large data centre, it is possible to carry out real-time analysis, during transmission, using a large number of network devices.

76 Ralf Bendrath and Milton Mueller, 'The End of the Net as We Know It? Deep Packet Inspection and Internet Governance' (2011) 13 *New Media & Society* 1142.

77 Such as blocking peer-to-peer networks: Milton L Mueller and Hadi Asghari, 'Deep Packet Inspection and Bandwidth Management: Battles over BitTorrent in Canada and the United States' (2012) 36 *Telecommunications Policy* 462.

78 Sophie Stalla-Bourdillon, Evangelia Papadaki and Tim Chown, 'From Porn to Cybersecurity Passing by Copyright: How Mass Surveillance Technologies Are Gaining Legitimacy . . . The Case of Deep Packet Inspection Technologies' (2014) 30 *Computer Law & Security Review* 670.

79 See e.g. Mustafa Akgül and Melih Kırlıdoğ, 'Internet Censorship in Turkey' (2015) 4 *Internet Policy Review* <https://policyreview.info/node/366> accessed 6 September 2023; Feng Yang, 'The Tale of Deep Packet Inspection in China: Mind the Gap' in *2015 3rd International Conference on Information and Communication Technology (ICoICT)* (IEEE 2015) <http://ieeexplore.ieee.org/document/7231449/> accessed 6 September 2023.

An understanding of the way in which transmissions are organised in computer networks also gives a better understanding of the impact of encryption on the ability to conduct mass surveillance programmes on the Internet. In principle, data encryption – if implemented correctly – protects the confidentiality of the information thus secured from unauthorised access. Until 40 years ago, modern cryptographic measures were only applied by governments and international organisations. This is because they required the use of dedicated devices, access to which was controlled and supervised (see the comments on Crypto AG in section 1.2). It was only with the advent of software-based cryptographic tools that modern data encryption mechanisms became available to users.

As a general rule, most network protocols, including those fundamental to the operation of the Internet, were not designed to ensure the confidentiality of communications. It is only in recent years that more and more users have become concerned about privacy issues, and thus have chosen products that provide encryption for data transmitted over public networks.

However, in the vast majority of cases, transmission encryption only applies to the transport (e.g. SSL) or application (e.g. SFTP) layers, and therefore does not cover basic information about the source and purpose of the transmission, allowing these data to be freely accessed and collected. Furthermore, many applications use vendor-specific encryption mechanisms, not ones based on recognised industry standards or international norms. The quality of such encryption – and consequently the degree of security provided to the user – is unknown in many cases. As manufacturers do not disclose the cryptographic algorithms used, it is impossible to easily assess the level of security offered.

From the perspective of conducting mass surveillance programmes, the encryption of transmissions is obviously a factor that hinders the data collection process. Leaving aside the technical description of the popular algorithms in use today, it is generally accepted that the most popular block ciphers (such as AES-256) offer a high degree of protection. Encrypted data are also (to some extent) protected from DPI analysis.[80] While it is possible to use it to filter (block) traffic or determine the persons communicating with each other or using certain services, it is impossible to read the content of the (encrypted) communications. Hence, information security experts conclude that encryption mechanisms, if appropriately applied, significantly reduce the effectiveness of bulk programmes.[81] However, this view is not entirely true.

80 Mohammad Lotfollahi and others, 'Deep Packet: A Novel Approach for Encrypted Traffic Classification Using Deep Learning' (2020) 24 *Soft Computing* 1999.

81 See e.g. Mihir Bellare, Kenneth G Paterson and Phillip Rogaway, 'Security of Symmetric Encryption against Mass Surveillance' in Juan A Garay and Rosario Gennaro (eds), *Advances in Cryptology – CRYPTO 2014*, vol 8616 (Springer 2014) <http://link.springer.com/10.1007/978-3-662-44371-2_1> accessed 6 September 2023.

First, quite apart from the quality of the cryptographic mechanisms used, as a result of the restrictions on their legal use and the existence of legal regulations obliging service providers to cooperate in intercepting data, some transmissions simply cannot be encrypted. One example is mobile communications (GSM), including SMS messages, which use protocols that, for a long time, have not been considered secure.[82] Furthermore, there have been reports in the last decade about the cooperation of electronic intelligence services with leading technology companies in terms of weakening the cryptographic security measures offered by them.[83]

Second, as pointed out earlier, encryption in the vast majority of cases protects only a fragment of the transmission, rather than the whole of it. Some protocols do not even encrypt the entire content of user data. For instance, the S/MIME protocol, which supports encrypted emails, protects only the content of the message without encrypting the headers (including the sender and recipient fields).[84] Suffice it to say that, from the perspective of public authorities, the mere knowledge that certain individuals are communicating with each other or sending data of a certain size (e.g. large files) can often be useful.

Third, data encryption in transmission does not protect the information stored on a storage medium.[85] If a user uses webmail, messages stored on the email server will not be encrypted unless the service provider implements a suitable data encryption scheme. There are email service providers that allow users to define a separate key for encrypting the online mailbox, without which messages cannot be read.[86] In practice, however, this feature is used by a small percentage of users. The lack of encryption of stored data means that public authorities, rather than intercepting online transmissions, can access the same data through the surveillance of the service provider's infrastructure.

Fourth and finally, there is increasing regulatory pressure to restrict the use of cryptographic means or to introduce schemes for their use to allow

82 David Lisonek and Martin Drahanský, 'SMS Encryption for Mobile Communication' in *2008 International Conference on Security Technology* (IEEE 2008) <http://ieeexplore.ieee.org/document/4725375/> accessed 6 September 2023.

83 Aaron Pulver and Richard M Medina, 'A Review of Security and Privacy Concerns in Digital Intelligence Collection' (2018) 33 *Intelligence and National Security* 241, 242.

84 For more on email security in the context of the S/MIME protocol, see Jörg Schwenk, 'Email Security: S/MIME' in Jörg Schwenk (ed), *Guide to Internet Cryptography* (Springer International Publishing 2022) <https://link.springer.com/10.1007/978-3-031-19439-9_17> accessed 7 September 2023.

85 See also an introduction to data encryption scenarios available to users of online services: 'Guide for Data Protection: Encryption' (UK Information Commissioner's Office 2017) <https://cli.re/17kQra> accessed 7 September 2023.

86 This mechanism should not be confused with the so-called encryption at rest, which, in the case of cloud services, may involve encrypting data with a key generated by the service provider.

free access to encrypted data for public authorities.[87] Legislation of this type has been adopted in some countries,[88] and in others it has been debated for years.[89] In each case, the aim is to weaken the available cryptographic means, e.g. by obliging technology providers to include an additional cryptographic key at the disposal of the public authorities.[90] Significantly, steps taken in this direction are not exclusively the domain of non-democratic states, such as Russia or China. It could even be said that historically the forerunner of this regulatory direction was the United States, where in the 1990s there was a push for the widespread use of the Clipper chip, developed by the NSA and containing a backdoor giving the agency access to the data sent with its help.[91] Another example is the recently debated case of court orders issued at the request of the FBI requiring Apple to make changes to its iOS system which would allow access to encrypted data on specific iPhone devices.[92] The debate surrounding this case has also resulted in the proposal for a new regulation, the Lawful Access to Encrypted Data Act, requiring technology providers to intentionally weaken encryption mechanisms to allow access to data by public authorities.[93]

Against the backdrop of the discussion on the actual impact of data encryption mechanisms on the ability to conduct bulk surveillance, there is a concept – recently gaining popularity – for the application of a new type of surveillance, i.e. the so-called surveillance at source, also referred to as "client-side scanning."[94] It combines most of the mechanisms described earlier, in particular distributed computing and cloud services, with the aim to create an IT environment in which surveillance functions would, so to say, be embedded in the user environment. In such a view, the creation of surveillance mechanisms would be the responsibility of the technology (product/service) developer, while their use would be up to an authorised public authority. Currently, there

87 Nathan Saper, 'International Cryptography Regulation and the Global Information Economy' (2013) 11 *Northwestern Journal of Technology and Intellectual* 673.

88 Peter Alexander Earls Davis, 'Decrypting Australia's "Anti-Encryption" Legislation: The Meaning and Effect of the "Systemic Weakness" Limitation' (2022) 44 *Computer Law & Security Review* 105659.

89 Devansh Kaushik, 'Deciphering Encryption Rights in India: The Road Ahead' (2021) 2 *Global Privacy Law Review* 200.

90 OL Van Daalen, 'The Right to Encryption: Privacy as Preventing Unlawful Access' (2023) 49 *Computer Law & Security Review* 105804.

91 A Michael Froomkin, 'It Came from Planet Clipper: The Battle Over Cryptographic Key "Escrow"' (1996) University of Chicago Legal Forum 15.

92 Michael Hack, 'The Implications of Apple's Battle with the FBI' (2016) 2016 *Network Security* 8.

93 Draft of the Lawful Access to Encrypted Data Act, US Senate 23 June 2020 <www.congress.gov/bill/116th-congress/senate-bill/4051> accessed 6 September 2023.

94 See e.g. a discussion of new UK legislation regarding the obligation to scan encrypted chat messages on users' devices: Thomas Claburn, 'Signal Says It'll Shut down in UK If Online Safety Bill Approved' *The Register* (25 February 2023) <www.theregister.com/2023/02/25/signal_uk_online_safety_bill/> accessed 7 September 2023.

are no technical obstacles to implementing this type of measure.[95] The performance of consumer devices (e.g. laptops, mobile phones, tablets) is sufficient to carry out surveillance tasks in a way that would be imperceptible to the user (without a noticeable drop in performance). Accusations of the building in of such mechanisms have, in recent years, been levelled at Xiaomi, whose mobile phones, as alleged by the Lithuanian authorities, have mechanisms for blocking searches for certain categories of content on the Internet (these functions are inactive outside China).[96] On the other hand, in 2021 Apple proposed on its own initiative to introduce content filtering mechanisms into its IT product ecosystem; those would, however, be focused on identifying child sexual abuse.[97]

The technology of surveillance at source will be of considerable help in solving most of today's limitations on the use of untargeted surveillance. In such cases, monitoring mechanisms would cover all of a user's online activities, no matter what their geolocation is and regardless of the service used and the cryptographic transmission protection techniques applied.

1.6 Summary

Leaving aside the debate as to whether modern surveillance measures should really be called "mass surveillance" or rather "indiscriminate surveillance," there is no doubt that the possibilities of collecting and processing data, also using modern data mining systems, will continue to grow. The more people use digital services, the more data is created. The increasing quantity of data and the ease with which it can be obtained provide the impetus for creating new ways of collecting it, including for public purposes.

The well-documented – but also increasingly well-known to the public – invasion of privacy risks associated with mass surveillance have not contributed significantly to changes in user behaviour and preferences. The progressive "digital exhibitionism" is particularly noticeable (and worrying) in the case of young people, for whom electronic services are becoming the primary form of contact and relationship-building in their peer groups.[98]

In this respect, it is increasingly being pointed out that the acceptance of intrusive forms of monitoring is not due to a lack of knowledge or attention

95 L Geierhaas and others, 'Attitudes towards Client-Side Scanning for CSAM, Terrorism, Drug Trafficking, Drug Use and Tax Evasion in Germany' in *2023 IEEE Symposium on Security and Privacy (SP)* (IEEE Computer Society 2023) <https://doi.ieeecomputersociety.org/10.1109/SP46215.2023.00178>.

96 'Assessment of Cybersecurity of Mobile Devices Supporting 5G Technology Sold in Lithuania' (Lithuanian National Cyber Security Centre 2021) <https://cli.re/dNbm89> accessed 7 June 2023.

97 The plan to introduce the CSAM technology was later abandoned by the company: Jolynn Childers Dellinger and David Hoffman, 'You Are Being Scanned' (2022) 106 *Judicature* 68.

98 Mary Madden and others, 'Teens, Social Media, and Privacy' (Pew Research Center 2013).

on the part of users, but is evidence of a much deeper social change, leading to the creation of a new type of society referred to as a "surveillance society."[99] This term is used to describe a type of society which not only has implemented extensive surveillance mechanisms but actually functions thanks to these measures. Viewed in this light, surveillance does not merely serve as a means of gathering information about individuals or groups of individuals but is a two-way process of regulating social interaction.[100] Importantly, however, the idea of a surveillance society should not be exclusively associated with non-democratic states.[101]

This concept helps to explain why, despite the great attention paid to the protection of privacy, surveillance powers (including in democratic states) have been steadily expanded rather than reduced in recent years. As a result, the increasing availability of surveillance technologies has not been accompanied by a proportionate strengthening of control or oversight measures to limit the risk of abuse of power, a situation which can ultimately lead to the creation of quasi-democracies.

Modern electronic surveillance is not a mechanism external to the society it is intended to observe. Its use does not require the construction of large listening stations, extensive computing centres and the employment of many thousands of analysts. It can be implemented easily and cheaply because most of the technology needed to make it work is already present in the services and products widely used in the market. Its use is, however, not very visible or widely known, which does not mean that it is less intrusive. Moreover, the spread of technologies for rapid and mass processing of information also significantly facilitates the creation of new, previously unavailable, applications for surveillance measures. This issue will be discussed in more detail in the next chapter.

References

Ahmed M, 'GCHQ "Watched Millions of Yahoo! Customers on Their Webcams"' *The Times* (27 February 2014) <https://cli.re/rmBK3K> accessed 6 September 2023.

Aid MM, 'The National Security Agency and the Cold War' (2001) 16 *Intelligence and National Security* 27.

Aid MM and Wiebes C, 'Introduction on The Importance of Signals Intelligence in the Cold War' (2001) 16 *Intelligence and National Security* 1.

Akgül M and Kırlıdoğ M, 'Internet Censorship in Turkey' (2015) 4 *Internet Policy Review* <https://policyreview.info/node/366> accessed 6 September 2023.

Aldrich RJ, *GCHQ: The Uncensored Story of Britain's Most Secret Intelligence Agency* (Harper Press 2011).

99 David Lyon, *Surveillance Society: Monitoring Everyday Life* (Open University Press 2002).

100 In this respect, it is impossible to omit the links between a surveillance society and the concept of a 'disciplinary society' introduced by Foucault. Michel Foucault, *Discipline and Punish: The Birth of the Prison* (Second Vintage Books edition, Vintage Books 1995) 216.

101 Julie E Cohen, 'What Privacy is For' (2012) 126 *Harvard Law Review* 1904, 1914.

–, 'Operation Rubicon: Sixty Years of German-American Success in Signals Intelligence' (2020) 35 *Intelligence and National Security* 603.
Anderson D, 'Report of the Bulk Powers Review' (Independent Reviewer of Terrorism Legislation 2016) <https://cli.re/97RkoJ> accessed 9 June 2023.
Assange J and others, *Cypherpunks: Freedom and the Future of the Internet* (OR Books 2012).
'Assessment of Cybersecurity of Mobile Devices Supporting 5G Technology Sold in Lithuania' (Lithuanian National Cyber Security Centre 2021) <https://cli.re/dNbm89> accessed 7 June 2023.
Bamford J, *The Puzzle Palace* (Houghton Mifflin 1982).
Beach J and Bruce J, 'British Signals Intelligence in the Trenches, 1915–1918: Part 1, Listening Sets' (2020) 19 *Journal of Intelligence History* 1.
Bellare M, Paterson KG and Rogaway P, 'Security of Symmetric Encryption against Mass Surveillance' in Juan A Garay and Rosario Gennaro (eds), *Advances in Cryptology – CRYPTO 2014*, vol 8616 (Springer Berlin Heidelberg 2014) <http://link.springer.com/10.1007/978-3-662-44371-2_1> accessed 6 September 2023.
Bendrath R and Mueller M, 'The End of the Net as We Know It? Deep Packet Inspection and Internet Governance' (2011) 13 *New Media & Society* 1142.
Biermann K, 'Daten Abfischen Mit Lizenz Aus Dem Kanzleramt' *Zeit online* (4 December 2014) <https://cli.re/KDpWbJ>.
Brewster T, 'Everything We Know About NSO Group: The Professional Spies Who Hacked iPhones with a Single Text' *Forbes* (25 August 2016) <https://cli.re/44x9Wq> accessed 6 September 2023.
Bury J, 'Polish Codebreaking during the Russo-Polish War of 1919–1920' (2004) 28 *Cryptologia* 193.
Claburn T, 'Signal Says It'll Shut down in UK If Online Safety Bill Approved' *The Register* (25 February 2023) <www.theregister.com/2023/02/25/signal_uk_online_safety_bill/> accessed 7 September 2023.
Cohen JE, 'What Privacy is For' (2012) 126 *Harvard Law Review* 1904.
Crome H-H, 'The "Organisation Gehlen" as Pre-History of the *Bundesnachrichtendienst*' (2007) 7 *Journal of Intelligence History* 31.
Davis PAE, 'Decrypting Australia's "Anti-Encryption" Legislation: The Meaning and Effect of the "Systemic Weakness" Limitation' (2022) 44 *Computer Law & Security Review* 105659.
Dellinger JC and Hoffman D, 'You Are Being Scanned' (2022) 106 *Judicature* 68.
Ferris J, *Behind the Enigma: The Authorised History of GCHQ, Britain's Secret Cyber-Intelligence Agency* (Bloomsbury Publishing 2021).
Foucault M, *Discipline and Punish: The Birth of the Prison* (Second Vintage Books edition, Vintage Books 1995).
Froomkin AM, 'It Came from Planet Clipper: The Battle Over Cryptographic Key "Escrow"' (1996) University of Chicago Legal Forum 15.
Gallagher R, 'Inside Menwith Hill' *The Intercept* (6 September 2016) <https://cli.re/xz3xdJ> accessed 6 September 2023.
Gärditz K, 'Legal Restraints on the Extraterritorial Activities of Germany's Intelligence Services' in Russell A Miller (ed), *Privacy and Power* (Cambridge University Press 2017) <www.cambridge.org/core/product/identifier/9781316658888%23CT-bp-16/type/book_part> accessed 9 October 2020.
Geierhaas L and others, 'Attitudes towards Client-Side Scanning for CSAM, Terrorism, Drug Trafficking, Drug Use and Tax Evasion in Germany' in *2023 IEEE Symposium on Security and Privacy (SP)* (IEEE Computer Society 2023) <https://doi.ieeecomputersociety.org/10.1109/SP46215.2023.00178>.
Gellman B and Poitras L, 'U.S., British Intelligence Mining Data from Nine U.S. Internet Companies in Broad Secret Program' *The Washington Post* (7 June 2013) <https://cli.re/XAdAnp>.

Gellman B and Soltani A, 'NSA Surveillance Program Reaches "into the Past" to Retrieve, Replay Phone Calls' *The Washington Post* (18 March 2014) <https://cli.re/MAoXvn> accessed 6 September 2023.
Greenwald G, *No Place to Hide: Edward Snowden, the NSA, and the U.S. Surveillance State* (First Picador edition, Picador 2015).
'Guide for Data Protection: Encryption' (UK Information Commissioner's Office 2017) <https://cli.re/17kQra> accessed 7 September 2023.
Hack M, 'The Implications of Apple's Battle with the FBI' (2016) 2016 *Network Security* 8.
Jacobs B, 'Maximator: European Signals Intelligence Cooperation, from a Dutch Perspective' (2020) 35 *Intelligence and National Security* 659.
Jaycox MM, 'No Oversight, No Limits, No Worries: A Primer on Presidential Spying and Executive Order 12,333' (2021) 12 *Harvard National Security Journal* 58.
Kaster SD and Ensign PC, 'Privatized Espionage: NSO Group Technologies and Its Pegasus Spyware' (2023) 65 *Thunderbird International Business Review* 355.
Kaushik D, 'Deciphering Encryption Rights in India: The Road Ahead' (2021) 2 *Global Privacy Law Review* 200.
Kerbaj R, *The Secret History of the Five Eyes: The Untold Story of the International Spy Network* (Blink 2022).
Kirchgaessner S, 'More Polish Opposition Figures Found to Have Been Targeted by Pegasus Spyware' *The Guardian* (17 February 2022) <https://cli.re/jpeo7a> accessed 6 September 2023.
Kozaczuk W and Straszak J, *Enigma: How the Poles Broke the Nazi Code* (Hippocrene Books 2004).
Lewin R, 'A Signal-Intelligence War' (1981) 16 *Journal of Contemporary History* 501.
Liger Q and Gutheil M, 'The Use of Pegasus and Equivalent Surveillance Spyware' (PEGA Committee of the European Parliament 2023) <https://cli.re/o4ZRbp> accessed 6 September 2023.
Link D, 'Resurrecting *Bomba Kryptologiczna*: Archaeology of Algorithmic Artefacts, I' (2009) 33 *Cryptologia* 166.
Lisonek D and Drahanský M, 'SMS Encryption for Mobile Communication' in *2008 International Conference on Security Technology* (IEEE 2008) <http://ieeexplore.ieee.org/document/4725375/> accessed 6 September 2023.
Lotfollahi M and others, 'Deep Packet: A Novel Approach for Encrypted Traffic Classification Using Deep Learning' (2020) 24 *Soft Computing* 1999.
Lyon D, *Surveillance Society: Monitoring Everyday Life* (Open University Press 2002).
–, 'Situating Surveillance: History, Technology, Culture' in Kees Boersma and others (eds), *Histories of State Surveillance in Europe and Beyond* (Routledge, Taylor & Francis Group 2014).
MacAskill E and others, 'GCHQ Taps Fibre-Optic Cables for Secret Access to World's Communications' *The Guardian* (21 June 2013) <https://cli.re/3R3QwW> accessed 6 September 2023.
Madden M and others, 'Teens, Social Media, and Privacy' (Pew Research Center 2013).
Marczak B and others, 'Hide and Seek: Tracking NSO Group's Pegasus Spyware to Operations in 45 Countries' (University of Toronto 2018) Citizen Lab Research Report No. 113 <https://cli.re/Bv3oDP> accessed 22 September 2020.
Marklund A and Skouvig L (eds), *Histories of Surveillance from Antiquity to the Digital Era: The Eyes and Ears of Power* (Routledge 2022).
Matthews P, *SIGINT: The Secret History of Signals Intelligence 1914–45* (History Press 2013).
McLaughlin J, 'BAE Systems Sells Internet Surveillance Gear to United Arab Emirates' *The Intercept* (15 June 2017) <https://cli.re/jpPpEE> accessed 6 September 2023.
Meijer A and Wessels M, 'Predictive Policing: Review of Benefits and Drawbacks' (2019) 42 *International Journal of Public Administration* 1031.

Meister A, 'How the German Foreign Intelligence Agency BND Tapped the Internet Exchange Point DE-CIX in Frankfurt, Since 2009' *Netzpolitik.org* (31 March 2015) <https://cli.re/w34wND> accessed 6 September 2023.

Milanovic M, 'The Murder of Jamal Khashoggi: Immunities, Inviolability and the Human Right to Life' (2020) 20 *Human Rights Law Review* 1.

Mueller ML and Asghari H, 'Deep Packet Inspection and Bandwidth Management: Battles Over BitTorrent in Canada and the United States' (2012) 36 *Telecommunications Policy* 462.

O'Neill PH, 'The Man Who Built a Spyware Empire Says It's Time to Come out of the Shadows' *MIT Technology Review* (19 August 2020) <https://cli.re/PpY1yP> accessed 6 September 2023.

Posner RA, 'Privacy, Surveillance, and Law' (2008) 75 *University of Chicago Law Review* 245.

'Privacy and Security: A Modern and Transparent Legal Framework' (Intelligence and Security Committee of Parliament 2015) HC 1075.

Pulver A and Medina RM, 'A Review of Security and Privacy Concerns in Digital Intelligence Collection' (2018) 33 *Intelligence and National Security* 241.

Ratcliff RA, *Delusions of Intelligence: Enigma, Ultra and the End of Secure Ciphers* (Cambridge University Press 2006).

Rejewski M, 'Mathematical Solution of the Enigma Cipher' (1982) 6 *Cryptologia* 1.

'Report on the Democratic Oversight of Signals Intelligence Agencies' (Venice Commission 2015) CDL-AD(2015)011 <https://cli.re/ApE7Ad> accessed 6 September 2023.

Richards NM, 'The Dangers of Surveillance' (2012) 126 *Harvard Law Review* 1934.

Rojszczak M, 'National Security and Retention of Telecommunications Data in Light of Recent Case Law of the European Courts' (2021) 17 *European Constitutional Law Review* 607.

Saper N, 'International Cryptography Regulation and the Global Information Economy' (2013) 11 *Northwestern Journal of Technology and Intellectual* 673.

Schaller C, 'Strategic Surveillance and Extraterritorial Basic Rights Protection: German Intelligence Law After Snowden' (2018) 19 *German Law Journal* 941.

Schmidt-Eenboom E, 'The Bundesnachrichtendienst, the Bundeswehr and Sigint in the Cold War and After' (2001) 16 *Intelligence and National Security* 129.

Schwenk J, 'Email Security: S/MIME' in Jörg Schwenk (ed), *Guide to Internet Cryptography* (Springer International Publishing 2022) <https://link.springer.com/10.1007/978-3-031-19439-9_17> accessed 7 September 2023.

Sloan LD, 'Echelon and the Legal Restraints on Signals Intelligence: A Need for Reevaluation' (2000) 50 *Duke Law Journal* 1467.

Snowden EJ, *Permanent Record* (Metropolitan Books 2019).

Stalla-Bourdillon S, Papadaki E and Chown T, 'From Porn to Cybersecurity Passing by Copyright: How Mass Surveillance Technologies are Gaining Legitimacy . . . The Case of Deep Packet Inspection Technologies' (2014) 30 *Computer Law & Security Review* 670.

The Swiss Parliament, 'Case Crypto AG. Report of the Delegation to the Control Committee of the Federal Assembly' (The Swiss Parliament 2020) BBl 2021 156 <www.parlament.ch/centers/documents/de/bericht_gpdel_fall_crypto_d.pdf> accessed 6 September 2023.

Taipale KA, 'Data Mining and Domestic Security: Connecting the Dots to Make Sense of Data' (2003) 5 *Columbia Science and Technology Law Review* 1.

Timberg C and Gellman B, 'NSA Paying U.S. Companies for Access to Communications Networks' *The Washington Post* (29 August 2013) <https://cli.re/97V1bb> accessed 6 September 2023.

Van Daalen OL, 'The Right to Encryption: Privacy as Preventing Unlawful Access' (2023) 49 *Computer Law & Security Review* 105804.

Wegener J, 'Order and Chaos: The CIA's HYDRA Database and the Dawn of the Information Age' (2020) 19 *Journal of Intelligence History* 77.
Wiebes C, 'Dutch Sigint during the Cold War, 1945–94' (2001) 16 *Intelligence and National Security* 243.
Wiseman J, 'Watching the Watchdogs: Pegasus Spyware and the Surveillance of Journalists' (International Press Institute 2020) <https://cli.re/YNVn8E> accessed 6 September 2023.
Yang F, 'The Tale of Deep Packet Inspection in China: Mind the Gap' in *2015 3rd International Conference on Information and Communication Technology (ICoICT)* (IEEE 2015) <http://ieeexplore.ieee.org/document/7231449/> accessed 6 September 2023.

2 Sector-specific approach to bulk surveillance

2.1 Introduction

Electronic surveillance has traditionally been linked to eavesdropping on telephone conversations and, more broadly, the monitoring of transmissions. Both targeted and untargeted surveillance often aim to obtain information transmitted through specific communication channels. It is, therefore, not surprising that the vast majority of analyses of surveillance by public authorities, including abuses in this area, focus on cases of electronic communications monitoring.

As the use of digital services has rapidly evolved, the telecommunications market has also undergone a significant transformation in recent years. Various types of instant messaging have displaced traditional voice services. The mass popularity of social networking sites has, in turn, led to a gradual blurring of the boundary between what can be considered a communication service and services used for sharing information. Of course, these developments have not been without impact on surveillance law and practice. Indeed, it has turned out that, from the perspective of public authorities, the same information that was previously collected using sophisticated communications interception mechanisms can now be obtained directly from digital service providers. As a result, the boundary between the procedures applied to access data in transit and stored data has gradually begun to blur.

However, the era of widespread digitisation has resulted not only in easier access to various types of data but also, and perhaps above all, in the creation of new forms of data processing. The monetisation of data, which has been ongoing since the beginning of the 21st century, has led to the emergence of a global market of data brokers (i.e. companies professionally profiling users). These entities control huge databases, often containing information on hundreds of millions of people worldwide, and their capacity to obtain and process data exceeds that of most countries.

The same tools as those used by data brokers are also increasingly utilised by public authorities. Their use allows the creation of previously unknown surveillance systems, which make it possible to collect data on a large part of the population without the need to actively intercept electronic communications.

DOI: 10.4324/9781003449263-2

As a result, we are witnessing the disappearance of the paradigm according to which mass surveillance is synonymous with the surveillance of electronic communications. Indeed, as it turns out the abundance of available data sources – including publicly available ones – makes it possible to thoroughly monitor large groups of people without the need to resort to the means of intercepting electronic communications.

The aim of this chapter is to take a broader look at the different forms of indiscriminate surveillance. While Chapter 1 explored this issue from the perspective of the available technical capabilities, this chapter will discuss the areas in which these measures can be applied. Particular attention will be paid to new types of untargeted surveillance related to the monitoring of the financial market and public spaces. These will provide examples that will help understand how modern data analysis can lead to the creation of new surveillance techniques not known a dozen years ago or so. While users can influence the intensity and scope of their use of individual digital services (in extreme cases they can stop using them), protecting oneself against mass surveillance based on facial recognition and geolocation techniques would be impossible if these techniques were implemented on a large scale in public spaces. Therefore the conclusions presented will also serve as an introduction to the discussion on the standards of legal safeguards that should be applied in the area of electronic surveillance.

2.2 Electronic communications

Historically, the first – and to this day most frequently analysed – area in which untargeted means of surveillance are applied is electronic communications. It is commonly equated with eavesdropping on telephone conversations or, more broadly, the recording of communications transmitted among a limited group of recipients. In reality, however, the contemporary understanding of the term "electronic communications" has evolved considerably over the recent years, and even its legal definition today gives rise to much controversy.

These changes have led to a widening of the substantive scope of the term itself. While telecommunications services were initially associated only with voice services, gradually and with the development of technical possibilities as well as the spread of new types of services, the definition was extended to include text services, electronic mails, and then also certain types of modern digital services (e.g. instant messaging, online chat). Services included in the latter group are referred to as OTT (over the top) to emphasise that these services require access to the Internet to function properly.[1]

Market changes have also led to a blurring of the distinction between classic telecommunications services, provided to subscribers of telecommunications

1 'Report on OTT Services' (Body of European Regulators for Electronic Communications 2016) BoR (16) 35 <https://cli.re/ZZ4bny> accessed 30 October 2019.

networks, and complementary services, for the use of which it is enough to use, for example, to have an application installed on a mobile device. By the end of the first decade of the 21st century, tens of millions of Europeans were already using popular instant messaging services such as Skype or Viber. In individual countries, the number of users of OTT communication services has not only grown much more rapidly than that of the users of traditional telecoms services (landline and mobile) but has also represented an increasingly noticeable part of the market.[2]

However, whereas telecommunications services are provided using infrastructure located in the country where the user is residing when using a given service, in the case of OTT services these resources can be located de facto anywhere in the world. This, of course, has also created new opportunities for using surveillance measures, for it turned out that instead of relying solely, for example, on the interception of fibre-optic communications transmitted from a specific location, the same information could be obtained by monitoring communications directly at the service provider. This led to the development of programmes such as OPTIC NERVE, which allowed private video streams from the Yahoo! Webcam service to be captured.[3] Leaving aside purely technical differences, such as the location of the interception, surprisingly eavesdropping on OTT services (unlike classic telecoms services) did not violate EU telecoms secrecy laws. Aside from the fact that the OPTIC NERVE programme was run by intelligence services (and therefore not regulated under EU law; more on this later), it is worth examining this regulatory paradox. This first requires a discussion of how the so-called EU regulatory framework for the telecommunications market is defined.

In the EU legal order, the telecommunications sector had already become the subject of detailed regulation in the late 1980s.[4] However, it was only in the following decade that the first comprehensive rules for harmonising and liberalising telecommunications services were agreed upon.[5] Along with agreements on key aspects of the functioning of the market, such as the allocation of resources, access to infrastructure, or the principles of universal service provision, issues related to the security of transmission and the confidentiality of communications also received attention from the EU legislature. This led to the adoption of Directive 97/66,[6] in which for the first time in Community

2 Seongcheol Kim, Hyunmi Baek and Dam Hee Kim, 'OTT and Live Streaming Services: Past, Present, and Future' (2021) 45 *Telecommunications Policy* 102244.

3 More on OPTIC NERVE can be found in Chapter 1.

4 Joseph W Goodman, *Telecommunications Policy-Making in the European Union* (Edward Elgar 2006).

5 Martin Cave, Christos Genakos and Tommaso Valletti, 'The European Framework for Regulating Telecommunications: A 25-Year Appraisal' (2019) 55 *Review of Industrial Organization* 47.

6 Directive 97/66/EC of the European Parliament and of the Council of 15 December 1997 concerning the processing of personal data and the protection of privacy in the telecommunications sector, OJ 1998 L24/1; repealed.

law guarantees related to telecommunications secrecy were explicitly referred to, and issues concerning the processing of metadata (traffic data) were regulated.

Three regulations, which are still in force today in virtually unchanged form, are of particularly importance in this respect. The first of these, stemming from Article 4 of the Directive, referred to the so-called security of services and mandated the implementation by service providers and infrastructure operators of technical and organisational measures necessary to ensure the security of the services provided by them, taking into account technical feasibility, the costs of implementation, and the risks identified. The second norm (Article 5 of the Directive) obliged Member States to ensure, through national legislation, the confidentiality of communications transmitted via public networks and publicly available telecommunications services. In particular, this provision established a prohibition on listening, tapping, storage or other kinds of interception or surveillance of communications and related traffic data without the consent of the users concerned, except for legally permissible interference in pursuit of general security objectives (discussed further in section 5.2). Finally, the last of the provisions, Article 6 of the Directive, laid down an obligation to anonymise or delete, immediately upon termination of the call, traffic data related to users and collected and processed by the service or telecommunications infrastructure provider for the purpose of conveying the communication.[7]

Taken together, the three provisions referred to above (relating to service security, telecommunications secrecy, and limited metadata processing) set out the core of the obligations of telecoms providers to protect users from unauthorised interception of the content of communications or related data.

Importantly, however, these obligations were addressed only to certain entities that met the definitions introduced in the Directive, namely the so-called providers of publicly available telecommunications services and providers of public telecommunications infrastructure. And only to this extent did it protect users from the indicated forms of interference with their rights by the service provider, as well as by third parties and public authorities.

This means that the provision of services that did not meet the definition of a telecommunications service under Directive 97/66 was not covered by the guarantees/restrictions concerning the confidentiality of communications. Of course, such restrictions may have resulted from the national law (in particular, constitutional norms) of the Member States, but given the transnational nature of OTT services, this safeguard often created only illusory protection for the individual.

7 This restriction did not apply to the data processing necessary for the billing of services; this exemption became the basis for the mechanism called quick freeze, discussed in section 5.2, which aims to protect against the deletion of billing data by telecoms operators.

This problem was (partly) recognised in the reform of the EU telecommunications framework in 2002, leading to the adoption of the new Directive 2002/58 (e-Privacy Directive),[8] which replaced Directive 97/66 and is still in force today. While the basic obligations in terms of the security and secrecy of communications remained unchanged, they were referred to under the new term "electronic communications services." There is no doubt that in this way the legislature also intended to resolve the growing concerns about the overly narrow scope of application of EU e-privacy rules.[9] In reality, however, this goal was not achieved, as best evidenced by the ongoing debate 15 years after the adoption of the Directive as to whether an electronic mail service provided online (the so-called webmail) was an electronic communications service and, consequently, whether it was subject to the restrictions of the e-Privacy Directive. The issue was finally resolved by the CJEU only in 2019 in the *Gmail* case, with the Court finding that an online mail service is not an electronic communications service. The Court reached this conclusion by noting that a webmail service could not be considered to be consisting "wholly or mainly in the conveyance of signals on electronic communications networks" – which, as the law stood at the time, was a *sine qua non* for its recognition as an electronic communications service.[10]

In addition, in the *Gmail* judgment, the Court addressed only certain types of OTT services, leaving a number of unresolved concerns about other modern communication services. Some of these were the subject of the *Skype* case decided in the same year.[11] The Court ruled that OTT services that allow calls to be made to users using traditional telecoms services are electronic communications services for the purposes of EU law.[12] However, even the *Skype* judgment did not definitively resolve doubts about how to classify communication services that only allow messages to be transmitted to other users of the same service, i.e. instant messaging applications, including the most popular services used by hundreds of millions or even billions of users (e.g. WhatsApp, iMessage, Messenger).

The way in which modern communication services were classified was, in turn, crucial in determining whether their users could expect the same scope of protection as subscribers to standard telecommunications services.

This issue was also fundamental to the discussion on the scope of permissible surveillance by public authorities. The e-Privacy Directive not only

8 Directive 2002/58/EC of the European Parliament and of the Council of 12 July 2002 concerning the processing of personal data and the protection of privacy in the electronic communications sector, OJ 2002 L201/37.

9 See recital (6) of the e-Privacy Directive.

10 *Google LLC v. Bundesrepublik Deutschland* (C-193/18) EU:C:2019:498 at [37].

11 *Skype Communications Sàrl v. Institut belge des services postaux et des télécommunications* (C-142/18) EU:C:2019:460.

12 Marcin Rojszczak, 'OTT Regulation Framework in the Context of CJEU Skype Case and European Electronic Communications Code' (2020) 38 *Computer Law & Security Review* 105439.

established guarantees for the individual, but also set out the conditions for limiting these rights on the grounds of, *inter alia*, the pursuit of general security objectives.[13] The question, therefore, arose as to whether the exception provided for therein should by analogy be regarded as setting a limit to permissible interference in the case of the collection of data from OTT service providers. Furthermore, the different regulations on services that are functionally identical from the user's perspective also led to the risk of overly extensive interference with the content of communications by private parties (i.e. the service providers themselves). It is sufficient to recall the long-standing practice of Google, which, while offering the *Gmail* service free of charge, reserved the right to scan entire emails (and thus also their content) for marketing purposes, including behavioural advertising, in its terms of service.[14] It is difficult to imagine that telecoms providers could eavesdrop on the content of conversations or monitor text messages to profile the user and target them with relevant contextual advertising. And yet, this type of market practice was possible and used for years in the digital services market, leading to the creation by service providers of giant banks of information – something that has, of course, not gone unnoticed by states either.

Hence, it should come as no surprise that the NSA and GCHQ decided to set up surveillance programmes aimed directly at obtaining information from the data centres of major service providers such as Google and Yahoo. These aimed to intercept data streams exchanged directly within the data centres. Although the details of the individual programmes have not been disclosed, it is likely that in this way the security services gained access not only to the raw data collected by users, but also to the data banks (profiles) created by the individual service providers.

It was only in 2018, with the adoption of the new Directive establishing the European Electronic Communications Code (the EECC Directive),[15] that the EU legislature adopted solutions leading to OTT services being comprehensively covered by the obligations under the e-Privacy Directive, including those related to the security of the services provided and telecommunications secrecy. This was achieved by amending the definition of an electronic communications service to include a new category of the so-called interpersonal communications services. This concept was defined as including number-based interpersonal communications services (i.e. traditional telecommunications services, allowing the transfer of messages between subscribers to public telecommunications networks) and number-independent interpersonal communications services. The latter category also includes types of OTT services,

13 Art. 15(1) of the e-Privacy Directive.

14 Alex Hern, 'Google Will Stop Scanning Content of Personal Emails' *The Guardian* <https://cli.re/vNebeY> accessed 6 September 2023.

15 Directive (EU) 2018/1972 of the European Parliament and of the Council of 11 December 2018 establishing the European Electronic Communications Code, OJ 2018 L321/36.

i.e. services whose main element is a communication function allowing the transmission of messages between an identified group of recipients, but not allowing messages to be transferred to a public network.[16]

Although the 2018 reform of the EU regulatory framework for the telecoms sector is, in principle, assessed positively, it should be noted that some of its areas have not been finalised to date.

One relates to the unfinished work on a new regulation to replace the more than 20-year-old e-Privacy Directive. In fact, the Commission initially envisaged a comprehensive reform of data protection legislation that would result in the adoption of a data protection regulation (the GDPR,[17] replacing the earlier Data Protection Directive)[18] and precisely, a new e-Privacy Regulation to replace the e-Privacy Directive (Directive 2002/58).[19] Unfortunately, the work on the new e-Privacy Regulation has encountered a number of obstacles, mainly related to the lack of consent of Member States for what they view as the too far-reaching interference of the EU legislature with matters that should be subject to domestic laws. One of these areas was, in fact, issues concerning public authorities' use of surveillance measures, in particular, the principles of retention of telecommunications data (more on this in section 5.2).[20]

The second problem only became apparent once the national rules implemented to transpose the obligations under the EECC Directive began to be applicable. In the absence of a new regulation on e-privacy, the principles of the e-Privacy Directive – which did not distinguish between the obligations imposed on different types of obliged entities, thus including providers of all electronic communications services in its legal regime – had to continue to apply. This led to a situation where providers of number-independent interpersonal communications services were subject to the same prohibition on the collection and processing of the content of communications as other telecommunications service providers.[21] As a result, they were deprived of the possibility of using "voluntary techniques" to identify instances of service abuse. This

16 See Art. 2(7) of the EECC Directive.

17 Regulation 2016/679 of the European Parliament and of the Council of 27 April 2016 on the protection of natural persons with regard to the processing of personal data and on the free movement of such data, OJ 2016 L119/1.

18 Directive 95/46 of the European Parliament and of the Council of 24 October 1995 on the protection of individuals with regard to the processing of personal data and on the free movement of such data, OJ 1995 L281/31; repealed.

19 Giovanni Buttarelli, 'The Commission Proposal for a Regulation on ePrivacy: Why Do We Need a Regulation Dedicated to ePrivacy in the European Union Forewords' (2017) 3 *European Data Protection Law Review (EDPL)* 155.

20 Adam Juszczak and Elisa Sason, 'Recalibrating Data Retention in the EU : The Jurisprudence of the Court of Justice of the EU on Data Retention – Is This the End or Is This Only the Beginning?' (2021) eucrim – The European Criminal Law Associations' Forum <https://eucrim.eu/articles/recalibrating-data-retention-in-the-eu/> accessed 7 September 2023.

21 See the reasoning presented in the draft regulation on a temporary derogation from certain provisions of Directive 2002/58/EC as regards the use of technologies by number-independent

euphemistic term is to be understood to refer to the means of surveillance of users applied without external control, including, *inter alia*, the analysis of any part of communications (including their content) in search of instances of illegal activity, in particular those instances related to sexual abuse against children. While the fight against paedophilia is an important objective of public authorities, also considered in the context of the use of surveillance measures, a separate question is the extent to which such measures can be used by private actors and without state control. More broadly, this leads to another important question, namely whether the current trend of privatisation of security tasks may also lead to the transfer of the obligation of mass surveillance of users to private entities.[22] And if so, does this kind of surveillance, combined with the obligation to report the results to public authorities, not constitute a new, previously unknown, surveillance measure used in the interest of the state, albeit by private entities? This issue will be discussed in more detail later in the book (see section 6.6).

A final issue, and certainly not a side issue with respect to indiscriminate surveillance of electronic communications, concerns the collection and processing of metadata. Traditionally, this term is linked to the so-called traffic data, i.e. information transmitted with the communications but not comprising the content thereof. In particular, the term includes service usage data (billing data), such as information about the communicating parties, the duration of the connection, the amount of data exchanged and so forth.

As access to this type of information does not lead to the disclosure of the content of the communications, the prevailing view over the years has been that disclosure of metadata (or unauthorised processing of metadata) involves less severe consequences for the individual, including in terms of interference with their fundamental rights.[23] In some jurisdictions, metadata in general was excluded from the constitutional protection provided for the secrecy of correspondence. This is the case, for example, in the United States, where it has been recognised for years (under the so-called third-party doctrine) that the metadata related to electronic communications have been voluntarily entrusted by the individual to a third party (the telecommunications operator), and therefore the individual has no legitimate expectation of maintaining the confidentiality (privacy) of this type of information.[24] This position is prevalent in the US Supreme Court jurisprudence. For example, in the case of

interpersonal communications service providers for the processing of personal and other data for the purpose of combatting child sexual abuse online, COM(2020) 568 final.

22 Kaspar Rosager Ludvigsen, Shishir Nagaraja and Angela Daly, 'YASM (Yet Another Surveillance Mechanism)' (arXiv, 29 May 2022) <http://arxiv.org/abs/2205.14601> accessed 5 October 2022.

23 See e.g. the reasoning presented by the ECtHR in the *Uzun v. Germany* case, discussed in detail in section 4.4.

24 Neil Richards, 'The Third Party Doctrine and the Future of the Cloud' (2016) 94 *Washington University Law Review* 1441.

United States v. Ulbricht, the Court held that an individual could not point to an invasion of privacy where public authorities monitored IP addresses used in communications sent from their home router.[25]

This interpretation has enabled the creation of advanced surveillance programmes, allowing vast amounts of traffic data illustrating how Americans use telecommunications services to be collected without any external scrutiny (including judicial oversight), which is normally required for surveillance conducted within the United States.[26]

However, the concept of metadata does not refer only to voice communications or services provided by traditional telecommunications operators. The term also describes data accompanying other forms of electronic communication, such as emails or instant messaging. In this case, however, the range of information that can be defined as metadata is significantly broader. For example, an element of every email message is a rich set of headers that not only directly describe the parties to the communication but also provide detailed information about their identity (e.g. the time zone, sending server, intermediary servers and identifiers given to the message by different service providers). Email headers also contain information describing the content of the correspondence (including the code pages, referring to the natural language used, and DKIM data, which make it possible to confirm the integrity of the message, as well as information on attachments and their size). A standard email message is marked with a dozen or so SMTP headers[27] and, depending on the email service used, the type of antivirus software used and so on; a number of these may directly identify the user's terminal and even their identity. Moreover, unlike traditional telecommunications services (e.g. voice calls), the entire message is natively expressed in digital form (no transcoding is required to convey the content), which, combined with the lack of a clear separation between content and metadata (in the form of, for example, two separate data streams), may lead to cases of qualifying information that should be considered as the substantive content of the message as metadata.

Therefore depending on how the term "metadata" is defined in relation to an email message, it can, therefore, be considered that the essential part of an email message is not its content but the metadata. Alternatively, it could be argued that that all information transmitted, including all headers, is the content of the message. The resolution of this problem is not made easier by the fact that the terms "content" and "metadata" as used for regulatory purposes

25 *United States v. Ulbricht*, 858 F.3d 71 (2d Cir. 2017)

26 Laura Donohue, 'Bulk Metadata Collection: Statutory and Constitutional Considerations' (2014) 37 *Harvard Journal of Law and Public Policy* 757; Casey McGowan, 'The Relevance of Relevance: Section 215 of the USA Patriot Act and the NSA Metadata Collection Program' (2014) 82 *Fordham Law Review* 2399. For an in-depth analysis of US surveillance law, see also section 6.7.

27 The Simple Mail Transfer Protocol is a basic and most popular email protocol used on the Internet.

are alien to technical standards (see, for example, the definition of the *Content-Type* header in the SMTP standard).[28]

In the case of instant messaging, the situation appears even more complicated due to the lack of a standardised (open) format for transmitting such messages. Their transmission is based on communication protocols developed by the provider of a particular service, and in fact only the provider knows which part of the data stream relates to metadata and which to the actual content of the message. As the recently disclosed FBI analysis indicates, the scope of metadata collected from different OTT services varies from one provider to another, and as a result each provider applies different rules for making this type of information available in response to law enforcement requests.[29]

Therefore the discussion (including the legal debate) concerning the admissibility of different standards when it comes to access by public authorities to the content of a message and solely to the metadata associated with it must take into account the evolution of the term "metadata" itself. In particular, it should be noted that the term is used today to refer to a whole spectrum of information, not infrequently allowing a detailed description of both the nature of the communication and aspects of the communicating parties' private life.

Surveillance programmes dedicated to the collecting and processing of metadata have been developed in both the United States and Europe.[30] In addition, nowadays one of the central issues related to electronic surveillance is the admissibility of the so-called general data retention obligation, i.e. the duty to retain telecommunications data to make them available to public authorities at a later stage (more on this in section 5.2).

2.3 Web services and online data gathering

Notwithstanding the development of surveillance techniques aimed at extracting knowledge from electronic communications services, the surveillance potential associated with the mass profiling of users of digital services has also been growing for years. In fact, modern online services allow far greater opportunities to collect data on an individual's activities than measures based solely on the interception of electronic communications. The average smartphone user has dozens of applications on their device that they use in their

28 Hong Guo, Bo Jin and Wei Qian, 'Analysis of Email Header for Forensics Purpose' in *2013 International Conference on Communication Systems and Network Technologies* (IEEE 2013) <http://ieeexplore.ieee.org/document/6524415/> accessed 7 September 2023.

29 Leonny Correa, 'Data Can Be Obtained from Encrypted Messaging Apps as Shown by a Newly Discovered FBI Document' *Fordham Secure IT* (8 December 2021) <https://cli.re/mpNYY8> accessed 6 September 2023.

30 Bryce Clayton Newell, 'The Massive Metadata Machine: Liberty, Power, and Secret Mass Surveillance in the U.S. and Europe' (2014) 10 *Journal of Law and Policy for the Information Society* 481.

personal and professional lives.[31] The providers of these products collect information about the users and how they use the app, their interactions, the purchasing decisions they make and so on. This is a wealth of information that can then be used to create the user's digital profile. This makes it possible not only to draw inferences about their future decisions, but also to shape and thus influence their choices.[32]

An excellent example of the possibilities associated with user profiling – notably based on non-sensitive data – is the case of the US-based retail chain Target, a case which has been much discussed since 2012. For the purposes of its marketing campaigns, the company systematically collected information on individual customers' purchase histories so that it could offer them price promotions on products that, according to the algorithms used, might be of interest to those people in the future.[33] Thus, as a result of analysing shopping histories and comparing them with data on other customers, the algorithms used by Target determined that one of the chain's customers was in the early stages of pregnancy. This customer received a dedicated sales message containing a discount on products recommended during the first trimester of pregnancy. However, this information had reached her parents before they learned about their daughter's pregnancy. The Target case has been cited over the years to be an example of, on the one hand, the effectiveness of the analysis of large data sets, and on the other hand an obvious interference with the rights of the individual and the risk that information deemed sensitive from the individual's perspective will be revealed to others as a result of the analysis (research) of their daily activities.[34]

Significantly, the Target case concerned an entrepreneur that was not professionally involved in the creation and commercialisation of databanks and only processed information acquired on its own. Today, however, databases many times larger are held by each global digital service provider.

Much greater risks to individual privacy should be linked to the activities of professional data brokers, who maintain data banks that exceed even 1 billion user profiles (and thus a significant proportion of the world's population). Moreover, data brokers also hold very detailed data, describing an individual in multiple dimensions, which come from various sources, including publicly available information. To understand the surveillance potential associated with the activities of these actors, it is necessary to clarify the concept of a "data point." It is a single piece of information about an individual that has been obtained and describes a characteristic of that individual or the activities

31 'Something for Everyone: Why the Growth of Mobile Apps Is Good News for Brands' (Ipsos MORI 2017) <https://cli.re/kajqRY> accessed 6 September 2023.

32 Sha Zhao and others, 'User Profiling from Their Use of Smartphone Applications: A Survey' (2019) 59 *Pervasive and Mobile Computing* 101052.

33 Charles Duhigg, 'How Companies Learn Your Secrets' *The New York Times* (16 February 2012) <https://cli.re/3RqRxB> accessed 6 September 2023.

34 Stuart Sumner, 'Supermarkets and Data Brokers', *You: for Sale* (Elsevier 2016).

undertaken by them. More than 20 years ago, Latanya Sweeney showed that three data points (namely gender, zip code and age) were sufficient to establish the identity of 87% of the US population.[35] Data released by the FTC shows that data brokers surveyed in 2018 maintained profiles consisting of more than 1000 data points on average, describing aspects of life as diverse as wealth, online purchases, subscriptions, health, travel, addictions and so on.[36]

At this point, the legal basis for processing such large datasets requires further comment. In particular, after the entry into force of the GDPR, it has been pointed out that the maintenance of such information banks may demonstrate non-compliance with EU data protection rules.[37] This issue has been hotly debated, including with regard to the so-called territorial scope of application of the GDPR, enabling service providers (in the sense of the EU data protection law, "data controllers") to be covered by the EU rules even if they have their registered office and place of business in a third country (and thus outside the EU/EEA).[38]

The data brokers' market is growing not only in the United States but of course also in Europe. According to the data presented by one of its leaders in Poland, the source of the data acquired is 350,000 mobile applications and 17 million websites, which provide (or sell) information on user activity.[39] In other words, by installing the software, users of various types of (often *free*) mobile applications give these application providers permission to access certain categories of information (e.g. the user's email address, information on how the application is used). These data are then sold to data brokers. In effect, the data brokers market operates owing to the choices made by users themselves, who can take advantage of products provided to them for free on the condition that they consent to the use of their personal data for marketing purposes. This information, from a large number of such products, is then aggregated to form giant data banks, such as the one held by Axiom, which contains information on 2.5 billion people.[40]

The largest digital service providers, often referred to as *big tech*, are a special case in terms of data brokers. Although these companies are generally do not sell the user data they collect, due to the scale of their operations and the

35 Latanya Sweeney, *Simple Demographics Often Identify People Uniquely* (Carnegie Mellon University 2000).
36 'Data Brokers: A Call for Transparency and Accountability' (Federal Trade Commission 2014) <https://cli.re/PAWJPW> accessed 6 September 2023.
37 H Ruschmeier, 'Data Brokers and European Digital Legislation' (2023) 9 *European Data Protection Law Review* 27.
38 Paul de Hert and Michal Czerniawski, 'Expanding the European Data Protection Scope beyond Territory: Article 3 of the General Data Protection Regulation in Its Wider Context' (2016) 6 *International Data Privacy Law* 230.
39 See <https://selectivv.com/en/about-selectivv/> accessed 6 September 2023.
40 Justin Sherman, 'Data Brokers and Sensitive Data on U.S. Individuals' (Duke University Sanford Cyber Policy Program 2021) 4 <https://cli.re/p3x4zR> accessed 6 September 2023.

business model they adopt (which involves the commercialisation of data), the extent of the data they collect can create particular risks in terms of user surveillance. Examples include corporations such as Alphabet (Google) or Meta (Facebook, WhatsApp, Instagram), as well as numerous administrative decisions in which these entities have been fined for abusing user privacy.[41]

The mass collection of information on users by private parties is clearly not irrelevant to the ability of public authorities to conduct surveillance programmes.

First, instead of collecting the same information themselves (which would often be technically difficult, and in many cases even impossible), public bodies can oblige the service provider to transfer to them certain (or even *all*) information, thus gaining immediate access to it. Moreover, in many legal models access to electronic data is regulated in a different (less restrictive) way than access to transmitted data. Sometimes, in the former case, court approval is not even required,[42] or it is possible to waive the requirement by demonstrating the necessity of obtaining the requested information.[43] Second, the possibility for public authorities to gain access to private data banks (in particular from the big tech sector) significantly reduces the costs of running surveillance programmes because these are borne by the private entity. Additionally, it also increases their effectiveness. This is because the provider of the digital service has the fullest knowledge to optimise the effort spent on data collection while ensuring a sufficiently high quality of the data.

At the same time, this form of access to information does not give public bodies the opportunity to determine the scope of data collected. In this case, it is the technology companies that decide on the scope of data collected, are responsible for the legality of the process, and also determine the purpose of the processing. The purpose is to monetise the data, and not, for example, to meet public security objectives. Target's analyses, for example, identified pregnant women, not people who might be suspected of preparing a terrorist crime or money laundering. This leads to the (apparently accurate) conclusion

41 The highest fine to date was imposed on Meta by the Irish DPA in 2023 – see Naomi Nix, Annabelle Timsit and Cat Zakrzewski, 'E.U. Slaps Meta with Record $1.3 Billion Fine for Data Privacy Violations' *The Washington Post* (22 May 2023) <https://cli.re/zExzNv> accessed 6 September 2023. For an analysis of fines imposed in connection with GDPR violations, see Jukka Ruohonen and Kalle Hjerppe, 'The GDPR Enforcement Fines at Glance' (2022) 106 *Information Systems* 101876.

42 See e.g. Art. 236a of the Polish Code of Criminal Procedure. For other examples, see Sergio Carrera and Marco Stefan, 'Access to Electronic Data for Criminal Investigations Purposes in the EU' (Centre for European Policy Studies 2020) 2020–01 14 <https://cli.re/xPn7Eo> accessed 6 September 2023.

43 In the case of Polish legislation (see the previous comment), access to, for instance, emails stored on the service provider's servers does not require that the necessity condition be met. Confirmation of "relevance to ongoing proceedings" is sufficient. See Art. 218(1) of the Polish Code of Criminal Procedure.

about the limited usefulness of the data collected by big tech for law enforcement and secret service activities.

In recent years, however, there has been a legislative trend leading to the formation of a new category of obligations imposed on digital service providers. What they have in common is the aim to implement user surveillance measures aimed at identifying specific threats to public security, combined with the obligation to report the results obtained to state authorities. In effect, this type of legislation leads to the establishment of a new generation of surveillance programmes, carried out by private entities but based on a legal obligation imposed on them.

However, there are provisions in the EU legal order that appear to stand in the way of adopting such legal solutions. In particular, an element of the e-Commerce Directive,[44] introduced in 2000, is the prohibition under its Article 15(1) on the establishment of a so-called general monitoring obligation. This concept should be understood as the impermissibility for Member States to impose an obligation on a hosting provider to monitor all content made available (transmitted) by users to look for infringements. In other words, by shaping the obligations related to the responsibility of digital service providers (in particular, hosting services) for the actions taken by users, the EU legislature has clearly indicated the unacceptability of a situation in which the service provider (providing an intermediate digital service, i.e. a hosting service) would also act as a censor.[45]

Although the purpose of the measure was clear, its application has led to several ambiguities. These relate, in particular, to the interpretation of the general monitoring prohibition in the context of the objectives of the e-Commerce Directive as a whole, particularly with regard to the rules limiting intermediate service providers' liability. Indeed, the Directive provided that a service provider was exempted from liability for stored (shared) content if it had no knowledge of its unlawful nature. It was irrelevant how the knowledge of the "unlawfulness" in question was acquired; in particular, it could come from a user, a public authority or the service provider's own employees (e.g. content moderators). While there was no doubt that the service provider had an obligation to remove material that was explicitly identified as unlawful, doubts were triggered concerning the existence of an obligation to remove material with identical or similar content to statements previously identified as unlawful. If it were considered that the service provider also had an obligation to remove identical (similar) content, this would lead to the question of how

44 Directive 2000/31/EC of the European Parliament and of the Council of 8 June 2000 on certain legal aspects of information society services, in particular electronic commerce, in the Internal Market, OJ 2000 L178/1.

45 Toygar Hasan Oruç, 'The Prohibition of General Monitoring Obligation for Video-Sharing Platforms under Article 15 of the E-Commerce Directive in Light of Recent Developments: Is It Still Necessary to Maintain It?' (2022) 13 *JIPITEC* 176.

this obligation could be reconciled with the prohibition on imposing a general monitoring obligation.

This issue has been the subject of a number of rulings by the CJEU, the first of which were in cases concerning the protection of intellectual property. In the *L'Oréal* case the Court noted that national courts may issue judgments ordering the removal (blocking) of certain content and also impose obligations to prevent the occurrence of identical infringements in the future.[46] In this respect, according to EU law the measures applied must remain "fair and proportionate and must not be excessively costly."[47] In the Court's view, introducing a general monitoring obligation would not only be incompatible with the e-Commerce Directive, but would also be "dissuasive" and create a barrier to economic cooperation within EU's internal market.[48] This interpretation was also confirmed in subsequent cases. In *Scarlet Extended*, the CJEU aptly noted that obliging a service provider to identify infringements identical to those identified previously would de facto lead to the need to control all content published by users.[49] This would clearly lead to a requirement of "active observation of all electronic communications . . . and, consequently, would encompass all information to be transmitted and all customers using that network,"[50] which cannot be reconciled with the prohibition of imposing a general monitoring obligation. In a similar vein, the CJEU also alluded to the impermissibility of obliging a service provider to actively search for even a single file (a musical work) and thus require it to introduce a preventive mechanism to block the distribution of online content.[51] Indeed, in the Court's view ensuring the effectiveness of such a measure would require that verification of all material uploaded by users of the service in question be carried out.

However, in *Glawischnig-Piesczek v. Facebook*, decided in 2019, the Court reached a different conclusion. In considering a case concerning the protection of an individual against defamatory publications, the Court held that ensuring the effectiveness of judicial protection requires the possibility that an order to delete (block) data may also include an obligation to prevent future infringements of the same nature.[52] In this respect, the Court considered it legitimate to identify not only identical content but also "information with an equivalent meaning," which should be understood as publications that have been slightly altered, e.g. by a different choice of words or a transformation of an image.[53] The Court thus ruled that the service provider should block

46 *L'Oréal SA and Others v. eBay International AG and Others* (C-324/09) EU:C:2011:474.
47 Ibid. at [139].
48 Ibid. at [144].
49 *Scarlet Extended v. SABAM* (C-70/10) EU:C:2011:771.
50 Ibid. at [39].
51 *McFadden v. Sony Music* (C-484/14) EU:C:2016:689.
52 *Glawischnig-Piesczek v. Facebook* (C-18/18) EU:C:2019:821 at [41].
53 Ibid. at [39].

not only content (speech) identical to that previously deemed unlawful, but also statements substantively similar to it. In this regard, it also addressed the question of respect for the prohibition on imposing a general monitoring obligation, holding that the obligation of a digital service provider to search for certain information does not create a general obligation to search for all infringements. In the Court's view, the prohibition arising from the e-Commerce Directive should, therefore, not be interpreted as precluding the imposition of an obligation to analyse all content provided by users where specific, designated information is sought. In line with this interpretation, a general surveillance obligation concerns not the amount of data examined, but the amount of information sought.

The position set out in *Glawischnig-Piesczek v. Facebook* had the effect of sanctioning the use of so-called *upload filters*, i.e. measures to pre-emptively analyse all data submitted by users in search of unlawful information or, more broadly, information that violates the terms of service.[54] Bearing in mind that in the case of large service providers millions of publications may be subjected to such analysis every day, it is clear that this task must be performed automatically and using algorithmic systems. Thus, although the prohibition of a general monitoring obligation remains one of the founding principles of the EU regulation of the digital services market,[55] today it does not stand in the way of the increasing use of algorithmic and bulk processing of user data to identify infringements.

A prime example of this shift in EU regulatory policy is the provisions of the Terrorist Content Regulation, introduced in 2021.[56] This act establishes two new measures to counter the dissemination of extremist material. The first is directly and cross-border applicable removal orders. The second consists in the obligations to implement the so-called specific measures, in which the legislature may also include "technical means to identify and expeditiously remove or disable access to terrorist content."[57] From the beginning of the legislative work on the Terrorist Content Regulation, it was debated to what extent the mechanisms established in it could be reconciled with respecting the prohibition of a general monitoring obligation.[58] In particular, it was pointed out that a regulatory model would be created in which content providers, fearing

54 Daphne Keller, 'Facebook Filters, Fundamental Rights, and the CJEU's Glawischnig-Piesczek Ruling' (2020) 69 *GRUR International* 616.

55 FG Wilman, 'Two Emerging Principles of EU Internet Law: A Comparative Analysis of the Prohibitions of General Data Retention and General Monitoring Obligations' (2022) 46 *Computer Law & Security Review* 105728.

56 Regulation (EU) 2021/784 of the European Parliament and of the Council of 29 April 2021 on addressing the dissemination of terrorist content online, OJ 2021 L172/79.

57 Art. 5(2)(a) of the Terrorist Content Regulation.

58 Aleksandra Kuczerawy, 'General Monitoring Obligations: A New Cornerstone of Internet Regulation in the EU?' in Centre for IT & IP Law (ed), *Rethinking IT and IP Law: Celebrating 30 Years CiTiP* (Intersentia 2020).

the possibility of heavy financial penalties, would voluntarily implement overly extensive content filtering mechanisms.[59]

Also, the provisions of the Digital Services Act (DSA),[60] adopted in 2022, may, according to many experts, result in a further dilution of responsibility for the use of extensive content filtering mechanisms by hosting providers. The DSA introduces a reform of the liability framework for intermediary service providers and, in this respect, replaces the regulatory model introduced in the e-Commerce Directive. While the new act maintains, in principle, the prohibition on imposing a general obligation on service providers to monitor content, it adopts a number of provisions creating incentives for the implementation of such mechanisms on a voluntary basis. An example is Article 7 of the DSA, according to which service providers shall not be excluded from the benefit of limitation of liability if they, in good faith and on their own initiative, conduct "investigations into, or take other measures aimed at detecting, identifying and removing, or disabling access to, illegal content." It is noteworthy that the DSA also explicitly establishes obligations relating to the reporting to law enforcement authorities of the cases of abuse identified, or even suspicions thereof – in effect creating a framework for the use of voluntary surveillance, combined with mandatory reporting of its results to law enforcement.

Understanding the consequences of the gradual dilution of the protective function of the prohibition on imposing a general monitoring obligation requires consideration of the specificity of the entities that the prohibition should protect. Originally, it covered providers of hosting services, i.e. a specific category of providers of the so-called information society services. In EU law, information society services were often contrasted with electronic communications services. While the former concerned stored data (e.g. within hosting services), regulations under the EU telecommunications framework (in particular, the e-Privacy Directive) applied to electronic communications services (and thus data in transmission).

With the development of the digital market and the emergence of many modern services that also serve communication functions, this division often led to ambiguities, which were eventually addressed by the Court of Justice. The Court confirmed in its interpretation that the same service (or a separate part of it) can be classified as both an information society service as well as an electronic communications service at the same time.[61] In practice, more and more often classic information society services (hosting services) accompany communication services and are offered by the same service provider as part of a comprehensive set of products, and are also used by the same group of

59 More on the Regulation is set out in section 6.5.

60 Regulation (EU) 2022/2065 of the European Parliament and of the Council of 19 October 2022 on a Single Market for Digital Services, OJ 2022 L277/1.

61 *Skype Communications Sàrl v. Institut belge des services postaux et des télécommunications* (n 11) at [46].

users. For example, in the Facebook ecosystem, Messenger (a communication service) is an important element of the social network. Similarly, Google users use both classic information society services (such as YouTube) and communication services (Hangouts, Gmail). The two product groups are constantly intermingling, and manufacturers are trying to integrate their products as much as possible to create an interesting product set for the user, creating an "ecosystem" of applications and services in which users can freely manage their data within a single digital identity. Moreover, individual products are also evolving, and it is often increasingly difficult to draw a clear line between information society services and electronic communications services.

The development of the digital services market over the years does not seem to have been sufficiently recognised by legislators. Indeed, it is impossible to explain the persistence of separate privacy-related regulations for telecommunications services and for hosting services. This leads to paradoxes, such as the application of different control mechanisms depending on which service is used by the user, rather than what effect they intend to achieve. For example, currently (under EU law), a service provider can apply content analysis to all files uploaded by a user to an online drive they share with others (e.g. family). If the same file is sent using instant messaging or email, in most countries it will be illegal to monitor the transmitted content without court approval.

The erosion of the prohibition of a general monitoring obligation is also stimulating the development of increasingly sophisticated data analytics algorithms – admittedly used in a voluntary manner, but under the supervision of, or for the benefit of, public authorities. This issue will be discussed in more detail in Chapter 6.

2.4 Financial surveillance

The examples of the surveillance programmes discussed so far often refer to the long-standing division into stored data and transmitted data. As has been pointed out, this division is, first, increasingly difficult to define, and second, increasingly less useful in practice. Both data categories are processed similarly, often by the same technology companies, and transmitted using the same infrastructure. By eavesdropping on fibre-optic communications, it is possible to intercept at the same time information that a user writes (or reads) from their online service and the emails they send.

However, in recent years increasing attention has been paid to another category of information that allows detailed monitoring of user activity, even though it is not data intentionally produced by the user. These are the data that arise from an individual's use of various types of products or services. They are generated and usually controlled by the service provider, which means in particular that the individual does not have the possibility of managing (e.g. deleting) them. Depending on the definitions adopted, this category can also include metadata. Increasingly, however, a different term is being used to describe them, namely "transactional data."

Transactional data per se was a term used, among others, in the e-Evidence Regulation draft to describe information that, while not itself constituting content, provides context or additional information about the service provided.[62] Typical examples of transactional data include information on the progress of e-commerce orders or payment and billing information.

Unlike metadata, however, transactional data do not have to be linked exclusively to digital services. Electronic records are also created as traces of activity in a physical space, such as purchases made using cashless payments.

A particular area for creating large banks of information, which are a rich source of transactional data, is, of course, the systems used in the financial sector – particularly the clearing systems of banks and financial institutions. These databases can be a source of accurate information not only about activities – both professional and private – undertaken by individuals, but also about the relationships they build or sources of funding. What is more, due to restrictive sector regulations, these data are also of high quality.

Financial institutions play an important role in the procedures aimed at detecting and preventing serious crime, such as money laundering, arms trafficking, drug trafficking or terrorist financing. The monitoring of financial flows is also a valuable tool used in the prosecution of various types of cybercrime, and with the dynamic development of cryptocurrencies, it is a measure increasingly being applied to virtually *all* types of criminal activity.[63]

The transactional data held by financial institutions are also a helpful tool in identifying tax fraud cases, such as tax evasion or VAT carousel cases.[64] As a result, an increasing number of countries are choosing to implement special regulations aimed specifically at the financial sector to help tighten up the tax system and combat the most serious cases of crime.[65]

In general, regulations of this type can be divided into two categories depending on the entity responsible for carrying out the analysis to identify potential breaches of the law. The first group consists of mandatory transaction reporting schemes based on criteria set by public authorities, or resulting from the obliged institution's internal assessment system.[66] In particular,

62 See Art. 2(9) of the draft e-Evidence Regulation, COM(2018) 225 final. It should be noted, however, that this term was not included in the version of the Regulation adopted. Text adopted: Regulation 2023/1543 of 12 July 2023 on European Production Orders and European Preservation Orders for electronic evidence in criminal proceedings and for the execution of custodial sentences after criminal proceedings, OJ 2023 L191/118.

63 In this context, see Michael Fröwis and others, 'Safeguarding the Evidential Value of Forensic Cryptocurrency Investigations' (2020) 33 *Forensic Science International: Digital Investigation* 200902.

64 'Possible Solutions for Missing Trader Intra-Community Fraud' (CONT Committee of the European Parliament 2022) <https://cli.re/9ZpV7m> accessed 6 September 2023.

65 See e.g. Redmar Wolf, 'VAT Carousel Fraud: A European Problem from a Dutch Perspective' (2011) 39 *Intertax* 26.

66 In this context, see the requirements of Directive (EU) 2015/849 of the European Parliament and of the Council of 20 May 2015 on the prevention of the use of the financial system for the purposes of money laundering or terrorist financing, OJ 2015 L141/73.

transactions exceeding a certain amount, carried out between entities classified as high-risk (due, for example, to the frequent abuses taking place in a specific sector of the economy) or selected by the source of funds (e.g. payments from jurisdictions covered by domestic or international sanctions) may be subject to reporting. In each of these cases, only a certain amount of financial information, relating to customers and transactions that meet pre-determined criteria, is generally reported.[67]

At the same time, in recent years financial instructions have been legally obliged to significantly expand the KYC (*know your client*) procedures as part of, among other things, the AML system. As a result, banks collect very detailed information on customers, including the so-called beneficial owners, the source of funds, or the capital structures in which the various parties operate. These obligations extend equally to legal entities and individuals. The information obtained in this way is then used for the purposes of internal risk assessment – which is, in fact, a type of profiling (classification), except that it is aimed not at data monetisation (as in the big tech sector) but at identifying suspicious transactions.[68] However, in terms of technical capabilities these systems are not significantly different from the profiling measures used in other modern service sectors, e.g. by electronic service providers. They use similar data analysis mechanisms, increasingly based on machine learning algorithms, allowing knowledge to be built up based on different sources of information.[69]

A key difference between profiling by big techs and profiling by financial institutions stems from the fact that the latter are legally obliged to use such mechanisms as a *sine qua non* for banking activities. An example of such far-reaching legal requirements in terms of monitoring user activity is the EU Money Laundering Directive, which has been amended several times.[70] Similar legislation has also been introduced in other jurisdictions.[71] Furthermore, the European Union is also actively developing tools for Member State cooperation

67 For more on the effectiveness of these measures, see: 'David Chaikin, 'How Effective Are Suspicious Transaction Reporting Systems?' (2009) 12 *Journal of Money Laundering Control* 238. In this context, see also Nicholas Ryder, 'Is It Time to Reform the Counter-Terrorist Financing Reporting Obligations? On the EU and the UK System' (2018) 19 *German Law Journal* 1169.

68 Anthony Amicelle and Gilles Favarel-Garrigues, 'Financial Surveillance: Who Cares?' (2012) 5 *Journal of Cultural Economy* 105.

69 Roung-Shiunn Wu and others, 'Using Data Mining Technique to Enhance Tax Evasion Detection Performance' (2012) 39 *Expert Systems with Applications* 8769.

70 In this context, see the list of amendments presented in the consolidated text of the EU Money Laundering Directive (CELEX 02015L0849-20210630) <https://cli.re/JAZyq5> accessed 6 September 2023. See also Valsamis Mitsilegas and Niovi Vavoula, 'The Evolving EU Anti-Money Laundering Regime: Challenges for Fundamental Rights and the Rule of Law' (2016) 23 *Maastricht Journal of European and Comparative Law* 261; Patrícia Godinho Silva, 'Recent Developments in EU Legislation on Anti-Money Laundering and Terrorist Financing' (2019) 10 *New Journal of European Criminal Law* 57.

71 Ronald F Pol, 'Anti-Money Laundering: The World's Least Effective Policy Experiment? Together, We Can Fix It' (2020) 3 *Policy Design and Practice* 73.

in the area of anti-fraud, including those related to cross-border data analysis and exchange of information.[72]

Of course, the use of transaction monitoring systems can lead to abuse, e.g. resulting in a violation of the principle of proportionality, unlawful discrimination, or serving purposes other than those legally justified. However, this does not change the fact that such monitoring and reporting measures – as long as they do not allow for direct and bulk access by state authorities to the information held by financial institutions – do not create an obvious threat to the emergence of a mass surveillance system.

Data collected by financial institutions are of interest not only to law enforcement agencies but also to secret services. This is because they allow a better understanding of the funding mechanisms of international crime, including terrorism. This is how the German BND justified the purchase of a database of accounts held by a Liechtenstein bank for EUR 5 million.[73] This example confirms that detailed financial information that, notably, concerns an unspecified group of people can be a valuable source of intelligence. Moreover, its acquisition falls within the remit of intelligence agencies. The need for access to identical information collected by domestic institutions can, therefore, be argued for in the same way that the BND's purchase of a stolen financial database from a foreign financial institution was justified.

If it is considered that BND – and other public authorities – are able to analyse financial data more effectively, thereby revealing, among other things, serious threats to the interests of the state, then it would be reasonable to expect that instead of the many dispersed fraud identification systems implemented by financial institutions, there should be one central system, supervised by public authorities. In that case, financial institutions should be legally obliged to make available or periodically transmit the transactional data they hold to a designated public body, which would be responsible for the further processing of the data and reporting the results to authorised bodies, e.g. tax administration or law enforcement.

Systems of this type are already being developed. One example is the STIR system (the Clearing House ICT System), implemented in Poland and used for several years, to which information on all transactions carried out by entrepreneurs at all domestic financial institutions is sent every day. According to the available data, this amounted to more than 6 billion transactions in 2018–2019.[74] At the same time, complete information (as collected by the

72 'VAT Fraud: New Tool to Help EU Countries Crack down on Criminals and Recoup Billions' *European Commission Press Release* (14 May 2019) <https://cli.re/ZZj8Jy> accessed 6 September 2023.

73 Mark Hosenball, 'Should Intelligence Agencies Chase Tax Evaders?' *Reuters* (11 November 2011) <https://cli.re/m4yjXJ> accessed 6 September 2023.

74 For a more in-depth analysis of the STIR system, see: Marta Papis-Almansa, 'The Polish Clearing House System: A "Stir"ring Example of the Use of New Technologies in Ensuring VAT Compliance in Poland and Selected Legal Challenges' (2019) 28 *EC Tax Review* 43.

financial institution) is reported to the system, so the data is not aggregated or anonymised. As a rule, only information on business accounts is subject to mandatory reporting to STIR. Therefore data on personal accounts (maintained for natural persons) is not entered into the system. This is, however, only an apparent limitation, as first, natural persons may also conduct their own business activities (in Poland, ca. 2.5 million people in 2023);[75] and, second, financial institutions are obliged to report all financial transactions of entrepreneurs, regardless of whether the other party to the transaction is a legal person or a consumer. Thus, information about paying for a psychiatrist visit is provided to STIR as information concerning not the patient but the entrepreneur – a medical practice in this case.

STIR does not contain any limitation on the transactions subject to reporting, which would eliminate the risk of reporting low-value transactions, usually related to everyday activities. At the same time, access to the data by secret services bypasses the regulations stipulated for access to bank information and, therefore, does not require approval by either a court or a public prosecutor.[76]

The STIR example is not an isolated case. In 2023, the media revealed information regarding the Transaction Record Analysis Center (TRAC) programme, created as a result of a 2014 settlement made by, among others, Western Union, and which allowed US law enforcement and secret services extensive access to data on financial transaction details.[77] As part of TRAC, information was made available on transactions between the United States and designated third countries (including EU Member States, e.g. France). The database collected approximately 150 million transfers directed to or executed by persons residing in the United States. As with STIR, access to data in TRAC did not require court approval.[78]

However, in principle TRAC only collects information on foreign transactions carried out with selected countries and in a specific way (non-bank transfers). The scope of data collected is therefore clearly smaller than in the case of STIR. The latter de facto serves to collect and analyse a significant proportion of transactions carried out in the domestic banking system. This concerns both domestic and foreign transactions, irrespective of their amount (transfers of less than USD 500 are not recorded in TRAC).

Further differences between STIR and TRAC relate to the purpose of processing (STIR, detecting tax fraud; TRAC, countering terrorist financing), as

75 According to the official data presented on the <www.biznes.gov.pl/> website.

76 Marcin Rojszczak, 'Compliance of Automatic Tax Fraud Detection Systems with the Right to Privacy Standards Based on the Polish Experience of the STIR System' (2021) 49 *Intertax* 39.

77 Dustin Volz and Byron Tau, 'Little-Known Surveillance Program Captures Money Transfers Between U.S. and More Than 20 Countries' *The Wall Street Journal* (18 January 2023) <https://cli.re/74vqxX> accessed 6 September 2023.

78 Fikayo Walter-Johnson and Nathan Freed Wessler, 'How the Arizona Attorney General Created a Secretive, Illegal Surveillance Program to Sweep up Millions of Our Financial Records' *ACLU* (18 January 2023) <https://cli.re/rmdomA> accessed 6 September 2023.

well as the basic forms of data processing (STIR, automatic analysis; TRAC, making information available to authorised authorities).

However, in both cases similar allegations are made regarding the risk of abuse and excessive surveillance by public authorities. They are rooted in doubts about the lack of transparency of state actions, reinforced by the obvious disproportion between the objective declared and the means chosen to achieve it. Indeed, it is difficult to reasonably assume that all citizens can be suspected of tax evasion (STIR) or that every foreign transfer is linked to the financing of terrorism (TRAC).

At the same time, it is clear that public actors should not ignore the technological capabilities widely used in the private sector. Accepting that technology companies can monitor and profile hundreds of millions of users while prohibiting the use of such measures by public authorities would create a regulatory model in which big tech would be trusted more than the state. It also should be borne in mind that the usefulness of such mechanisms for counter-terrorism and fiscal crime is still being debated.[79]

Leaving aside questions about the proportionality and necessity of such measures (these issues will be further discussed in subsequent chapters of the book), bulk access to transactional data by public authorities illustrates that it is nowadays possible to build a mass surveillance programme without access to data from electronic communications. However, in the case of electronic communications or, more broadly, online services, the user has a choice and can (at least theoretically) opt out of certain types of services (e.g. email, instant messaging). Given the current direction of AML regulation, which assumes that an increasing proportion of transactions will be cashless and fosters cashless programmes, the threats associated with financial surveillance may come to the fore in the near future, creating, from an individual's perspective, an even greater risk of intrusion into their privacy than mass monitoring of electronic communications.

2.5 Public space surveillance

Monitoring of public spaces – including audio and video recording or tracking an individual's activity in a physical space – is not only a form of targeted surveillance that has been in use for decades, but also a useful means to increase citizens' sense of security and, moreover, expedite the identification of threats that require a response from security services.

Over the years, the very definition of a public space has also been subject to change, mainly as a result of urban development, but also due to changing

79 William Vlcek, 'Surveillance to Combat Terrorist Financing in Europe: Whose Liberty, Whose Security?' (2007) 16 *European Security* 99; Lucia Dalla Pellegrina and others, 'Organized Crime, Suspicious Transaction Reporting and Anti-Money Laundering Regulation' (2020) 54 *Regional Studies* 1761.

societal expectations regarding the effects that the legal model attaches to the various activities undertaken in it.[80] Hence, the historical understanding of a public space as a place open to the public was shaped by the image of the Roman *forum* – a space necessary for the functioning of social life and the conduct of political activities. Although it may seem distant and ill-suited to the challenges of the present day, the concept of the forum is still the source of the perception that public spaces are particularly important for ensuring freedom of expression.[81]

With the evolution of socio-economic realities, the concept of a public space as an area under the direct control of public authorities (public buildings, streets, parks) has gradually been extended to objects under private management but still accessible to the public (cinemas, museums or, today, shopping malls). Because of the different functions performed by the various facilities, not surprisingly their qualification as public spaces has also varied over time.

In many legal models, public authorities have specific powers – but also responsibilities – with regard to the organisation of public spaces, including in terms of ensuring the safety of those making use of them. A method that has been applied for years to meet the growing public expectations in this respect is the use of technical means, in particular video surveillance systems (CCTV). Nowadays, CCTV cameras have almost become the hallmark of modern urban spaces, and they remind residents of the constant presence of security monitoring – realising per se one of Foucault's postulates concerning "panopticism."[82] Foucault's reflections focused on exploring the impact of surveillance on an individual's behaviour. In this respect, as he himself emphasised, what was important for the effectiveness of surveillance was not whether the surveillance was actually carried out, but the constant conviction and reminder that it was in place. According to this conception, a CCTV camera affects an individual's behaviour even if no one is watching the image it records – and even if it is not actually working but the person being "watched" is unaware of that.

In practice, municipal CCTV systems are used not only for day-to-day security monitoring, but also to ensure the possibility of subsequently reconstructing the course of various types of incidents – criminal ones as well as those related to traffic collisions or the search for missing persons. As a result, in many large cities the number of CCTV cameras installed in public spaces reaches many thousands. In London alone, their number

80 Gregory Smith and Jan Gadeyne, *Perspectives on Public Space in Rome, from Antiquity to the Present Day* (Ashgate 2013).

81 Peter Marcuse, 'The Paradoxes of Public Space' (2014) 38 *Journal of Architecture and Urbanism* 102.

82 Michel Foucault, *Discipline and Punish: The Birth of the Prison* (Second Vintage Books edition, Vintage Books 1995) 201.

was estimated to have exceeded 900,000 devices in 2021,[83] and this figure should be considered an underestimate as it does not include devices used by private entities.

Even assuming that only a few thousand cameras observe the centre of any large city, it is obvious that the images that are being recorded by these devices cannot be analysed on an ongoing basis by a relevant group of operators. Thus, although the surveillance can be considered as an indiscriminate measure (monitoring/recording everything that happens in a given public space), the limited possibilities of processing the information so obtained mean that CCTV systems have not been classified as a useful source of data for mass surveillance systems to date.

This assessment has become partly obsolete with the advent of systems that allow real-time pattern recognition in the images being recorded. An example is license plate recognition systems, widely used today by parking operators and road administrators.[84] These systems can recognise passing vehicles in real time, which, combined with the large number of cameras deployed, potentially creates a mechanism for tracking a moving vehicle, as well as reconstructing the routes it has historically travelled. Importantly, this type of system has the potential to monitor (track) not just one specific vehicle, but all the vehicles that move within the CCTV system's range – no matter if there are five or 5 million of them. At the same time, the ability to continuously monitor all vehicles does not require large teams of analysts.

The case of license plate recognition systems also reveals significant differences between countries in treating this type of action as an interference with the right to privacy. Indeed, to assume that the recognition and recording of vehicle number plates does not affect an individual's rights would provide leeway to implement systems allowing the mass collection and analysis of this type of data without any legal restrictions established for interference with fundamental rights.

Although the case of automatic license plate recognition appears to be a very specific issue, drawing on this example makes it possible to build more general conclusions on the possibility of using CCTV as a mechanism for indiscriminate surveillance. However, to do so it is necessary to clarify two issues: first, whether it is legally permissible to restrict the possibility of observing events taking place in a public space; and second, whether – in the specific case of license plate recognition – the measure can be said to identify a specific individual and thus (potentially) invade their privacy.

83 This means that currently there is one CCTV camera for every 13 people. Jonathan Ratcliffe, 'How Many CCTV Cameras Are There in London?' *CCTV.co.uk* (18 November 2020) <https://cli.re/rmQynM> accessed 6 September 2023.

84 Linda M Merola and Cynthia Lum, 'Emerging Surveillance Technologies: Privacy and the Case of License Plate Recognition (LPR) Technology' (2012) 96 *Judicature* 119.

The first problem comes down to the question whether an individual can be prohibited from observing passing cars. If not, is it legally permissible to prohibit them from writing down in a notebook the license plate numbers of cars that travel along the road? While both questions may seem trivial and hypothetical, they actually reveal the essence of the problem that lies at the root of the dispute over the use of monitoring systems in public spaces: how far the right to use public spaces can be restricted in an attempt to protect the rights of others. Under US law, this raises the question of the existence of a reasonable expectation of privacy in the use of a public space.

In recent years, this issue has become of particular interest to both American and European courts. When discussing the permissibility to use video surveillance systems in the context of EU law, it is impossible not to refer to data protection legislation. The Court of Justice clarified as early as 2003 that the public dissemination of collected data does not fall within the boundaries of what can be considered "purely personal activity."[85]

In the *Ryneš* case, on the other hand, the CJEU clarified that the recording of images using outdoor home CCTV cameras which also cover public spaces does not constitute a purely private activity and thus does not fall under the exclusion of such activity from the scope of the data protection legislation.[86] This judgment has de facto made it necessary to recognise that any CCTV system that allows the recording of images of persons in public spaces – regardless of the party responsible for its installation and maintenance – "constitutes . . . the automatic processing of personal data."[87]

In this context, the Court also stressed that the mere possibility of recording images (e.g. using CCTV cameras) must always be assessed with regard to the purpose and proportionality of the use of such a measure, which predetermines that the recording of images per se constitutes an interference with the privacy of the persons recorded. This conclusion also remains valid if an event in a quasi-public space, such as common areas in residential buildings, is recorded.[88]

At this point, however, it is necessary to return to the question of whether the recording of number plates constitutes processing of personal data – that is, whether it is the processing of data about identified or identifiable natural persons.[89] It is clear that the plate number identifies the car, but not its user or passengers. However, in the same way, an IMEI number can be considered to identify a smartphone and not the subscriber using it, and a credit card number to identify a piece of plastic and not its holder. Unfortunately, this argument is not universally accepted in all Member States. While in most cases

85 *Criminal Proceedings Against Bodil Lindqvist* (C-101/01) EU:C:2003:596 at [47–48].

86 This proposal concerned the now defunct Directive 95/46 but remains relevant in today's legal environment. *František Ryneš v. Úřad pro ochranu osobních údajů* (C-212/13) EU:C:2014:2428 at [33].

87 Ibid. at [25].

88 *TK v. Asociația de Proprietari bloc M5A-ScaraA* (C-708/18) EU:C:2019:1064.

89 See the legal definition of personal data in Art. 4(1) of the GDPR.

courts and supervisory authorities take the view that the processing of plate numbers constitutes personal data processing,[90] in some Member States the opposite view prevails.[91]

In this regard, it is worth noting the position of the German Constitutional Court, which pointed out that the process of automatic analysis of number plates actually consists of two activities: the first is the algorithmic reading of the number; the second is its comparison with a database of vehicles sought or of interest to public authorities.[92] Each of these activities should be examined separately, as they constitute a separate interference with an individual's rights. In turn, this leads (in the Court's view) to the conclusion that reading the number plate, even if this information is not subsequently recorded in the police database, is an interference with the individual's right to informational self-determination.[93]

In the context of the earlier example concerning an observer noting down the plate numbers of passing cars, the position of BverfG predetermines that it is not only the recording of the numbers but already reading them – if this action is carried out by public authorities and is not of an incidental nature – that constitutes interference.[94]

Against this background, a discussion of the US perspective cannot be omitted. According to the standard of "reasonable expectation of privacy" cited earlier, an individual in a public space should understand that they may be observed by others and, consequently, cannot claim legal protection of their privacy to that extent. As a result, in most states there are no restrictions on using video and audio recording devices, including situations where their use is not clearly labelled.[95] However in some cases – including those where the intimacy of others was deliberately violated – US courts have ruled that covert surveillance in public places was inadmissible.[96]

90 This interpretation is also in line with the interpretation by the EU institutions – see and Council of Europe and others, *Handbook on European Data Protection Law – 2018 Edition* (Publications Office of the European Union 2018) 90. In this regard, it should further be noted that it also follows from the CJEU jurisprudence that identification numbers (in this case VINs) can be considered personal data – see *SS SIA v. Valsts ieņēmumu dienests* (C-175/20) EU:C:2022:124 at [36–37].

91 See the judgments of the Polish Supreme Administrative Court of 28 June 2019, I OSK 2063/17; of 14 May 2021, III OSK 1466/21.

92 BVerfG 18 December 2018, 1 BvR 142/15, DE:BVerfG:2018:rs20181218.1bvr014215 at [42].

93 Ibid. at [45].

94 However, it should be borne in mind that the example given focuses on commercial applications – not those of a purely personal nature. Thus, the use of a CCTV camera for a non-personal (i.e. commercial) purpose constitutes an interference with privacy, even if the numbers of passing cars are not stored in the database after the analysis is completed.

95 Jeremy Brown, 'Pan, Tilt, Zoom: Regulating the Use of Video Surveillance of Public Places Part V: Privacy: Section A: Notes' (2008) 23 *Berkeley Technology Law Journal* 755, 760.

96 Erin B Bernstein, 'Health Privacy in Public Spaces' (2015) 66 *Alabama Law Review* 989.

At the same time, however, US constitutional provisions set a more restrictive standard of protection in the case of surveillance conducted in a public place by public authorities. In this respect the interpretation of the application of the Fourth Amendment established in *Katz* applies, according to which the US Constitution "protects people, not places."[97] Interference by public authorities with an individual's privacy must, therefore, occur only in cases where there exists probable cause based on a court order – even when it consists of observation in a public space. At the same time, however, courts accept more extensive interference when, according to the test of "reasonable expectation of privacy," it is considered that the individual could have expected to be observed in the given situation. This leads to such surprising (from a European perspective) rulings as that in *Kyllo v. United States*, where it was held that the use of a thermal imaging device to observe details of activities undertaken in a home did not violate privacy because "the thermal imager did not expose any intimate details of the [suspect's] life."[98]

As a general rule, the American constitutional standard concerns targeted surveillance, i.e. surveillance conducted in relation to specific individuals. As in the European Union, it has also been debated in the United States whether vehicle monitoring is the same as surveillance of persons, and thus whether it requires the legal procedures mandated by the Fourth Amendment. Of note in this regard is the decision in *U.S. v. Jones*, in which the Supreme Court saw a link between the monitoring of vehicles' geolocation and the violation of a legitimate expectation of privacy.[99] This case is part of a broader discussion on the legitimate expectations of privacy of homeless people.[100] Indeed, if it were to be assumed, according to the prevailing view, that surveillance in a public place does not violate an individual's rights, this would mean that homeless people are, in fact, deprived of the possibility of protecting their privacy – and only because of their particular economic situation. This is a very important argument, the relevance of which should not be referred exclusively to the American legal model. The case of homeless people clearly demonstrates the flawed nature of establishing different (i.e. less tight) restrictions on the monitoring measures implemented in public spaces.[101]

97 *Katz v. United States*, 389 U.S. 347 (1967). 'A Reconsideration of the Katz Expectation of Privacy Test Notes' (1977) 76 *Michigan Law Review* 154.

98 *Kyllo v. United States*, 533 U.S. 27 (2001). See also Matthew Tokson, 'The Emerging Principles of Fourth Amendment Privacy' (2020) 88 *George Washington Law Review* 1.

99 David Reichbach, 'The Home Not the Homeless: What the Fourth Amendment Has Historically Protected and Where the Law is Going after Jones Comment' (2012) 47 *University of San Francisco Law Review* [i].

100 Wesley C Jackson, 'Life on Streets and Trails: Fourth Amendment Rights for the Homeless and the Homeward Bound Note' (2013) 66 *Vanderbilt Law Review* 933.

101 In this context, see also Nicole Jacoby, 'U.S. v. Jones Leaves Important Digital Privacy Questions Unanswered From the Committees' (2011) 37 *Litigation News* [vii].

In recent years, with the development of advanced facial recognition technology (FRT), new products that allow the instant identification of people in CCTV images have also appeared on the market. One of the more well-known solutions of this type is ClearView AI, developed in 2020 by a US technology start-up. The competitive advantage of the product lies not so much in the image processing and facial recognition algorithms themselves (based on machine learning systems), as in the massive database containing – as declared by the manufacturer – more than 20 billion images.[102] These images have been obtained from publicly available sources (mainly social media). In principle, ClearView AI was, according to the manufacturer, developed as a system to support the work of law enforcement and security services.[103] This information is corroborated by reports that the system is being used by Ukrainian services to identify perpetrators of war crimes during the war with Russia.[104]

As the data on which ClearView AI is based were collected without the consent of the individuals concerned, the legality of their processing is being challenged under EU law.[105] As a result, in February 2022 the Italian data protection authority was the first[106] to impose a hefty[107] financial penalty on the system manufacturer for violating data subjects' rights, invoking the extended, so-called territorial scope of EU data protection law.[108] However, key to the supervisory authority's decision was the confirmation that the operation of ClearView AI fell within the substantive scope of application of the GDPR, and thus that the service provider's activities could be considered personal data processing. The ClearView case also became one of the reasons for the European Parliament to include a prohibition on using biometric identification techniques by AI systems in the draft AI regulation.[109]

102 Jonathan Ames, 'Online Facial Images Were "Harvested"' *The Times* (24 May 2022) <https://cli.re/jpN1dM> accessed 6 September 2023.

103 Kashmir Hill, 'The Secretive Company That Might End Privacy as We Know It' *The New York Times* (18 January 2020) <https://cli.re/8zwAd3> accessed 6 September 2023.

104 Paresh Dave and Jeffrey Dastin, 'Ukraine Has Started Using Clearview AI's Facial Recognition During War' *Reuters* (14 March 2022) <https://cli.re/yw42KD> accessed 6 September 2023.

105 Isadora Neroni Rezende, 'Facial Recognition in Police Hands: Assessing the "Clearview Case" from a European Perspective' (2020) 11 *New Journal of European Criminal Law* 375.

106 Subsequent decisions were issued by the British (26 May 2022), Greek (13 June 2022), French (17 October 2022) and Austrian (9 May 2023) authorities. All the decisions – apart from the Austrian one – impose heavy financial penalties. The UK ICO also ordered ClearView AI to delete the data on UK residents.

107 In fact, this is the maximum penalty allowed under the GDPR – €20 million. See the justification for the amount in the French decision: Restricted Committee Deliberation No. SAN-2022-019 of 17 October 2022, Commission Nationale de l'Informatique et des Libertés, https://cli.re/wWBkRD> accessed 6 September 2023. English translation available at: <https://cli.re/j1djqe>.

108 See 'Hellenic DPA Fines Clearview AI 20 Million Euros' *European Data Protection Board* (20 July 2022) <https://cli.re/eryWp9> accessed 6 September 2023.

109 This topic is discussed in more detail in section 6.4.

Leaving aside the controversy over ClearView AI's compliance with EU data protection law, there is no doubt that the system is used by hundreds of police forces,[110] also outside the United States.[111] Moreover, bearing in mind the exclusion of national security from the scope of EU law, this solution can also be used by the secret services of EU Member States.[112]

ClearView is an interesting example also because it demonstrates how combining today's widespread access to large data sets with modern algorithms can create a new type of surveillance measure. ClearView resolves virtually all the limitations of standard CCTV systems. First, this type of technology allows hundreds of millions of people to be recognised in real time, far beyond the identification capabilities held by most countries (let alone specific police authorities). Second, its operation does not require large teams of people. A CCTV system consisting of thousands of city cameras does not need an equally large number of operators to identify and monitor people moving in public spaces. Third, ClearView also allows identification in conditions that go beyond the capabilities of the human eye (e.g. crowds, poor lighting conditions). Fourth and finally, in principle the system also does not require a great deal of work to create a reference database or to update the information collected. Identification takes place based on images that have been largely posted online by users themselves. And they continue to post them, constantly uploading new images to their social media profiles.

Hence, technology such as ClearView marks a shift from the previous paradigm that video surveillance systems, despite their high surveillance potential, do not constitute untargeted surveillance. The new generation of FRT not only enables the mass identification of individuals and the tracking of their activities, but in fact also extends the surveillance capabilities previously used in the digital sphere to the physical world. In this way, it complements other mass data collection techniques, increasing the quality of the information obtained and allowing new groups of people (including those not using digital services) to be monitored.[113]

Notwithstanding the success of the European Parliament's initiative to block the admissibility of measures such as those contained in ClearView within the

110 In the United States, it is estimated that over 600 services use ClearView. Rezende (n 105) 345.

111 Dallas Hill, Christopher D O'Connor and Andrea Slane, 'Police Use of Facial Recognition Technology: The Potential for Engaging the Public through Co-Constructed Policy-Making' (2022) 24 *International Journal of Police Science & Management* 325; Monika Zalnieriute, 'How Public Space Surveillance Is Eroding Political Protests in Australia' (2021) Verfassungsblog: On Matters Constitutional <https://intr2dok.vifa-recht.de/receive/mir_mods_00011558> accessed 8 September 2023.

112 Assuming this would be in line with national constitutional provisions and the ECHR.

113 For evidence regarding the use of FRT as a part of the state surveillance regime, see Karen Hao and Heidi Swart, 'South Africa's Private Surveillance Machine Is Fueling a Digital Apartheid' (2022) MIT Technology Review <https://cli.re/wPydyw> accessed 6 September 2023.

European Union, the technology has already emerged and will have a lasting impact on the assessment of the feasibility of bulk surveillance in public spaces.

2.6 Summary

Taking into account the development of technical capabilities (Chapter 1), as well as the way public authorities use them (Chapter 2), the following breakdown of the stages of development of indiscriminate electronic surveillance measures can be made:

1. pre-1960: the era of signals intelligence development, in which the ability to collect data outstripped the ability to analyse it quickly;
2. 1960–1990: development of computing capabilities combined with the construction of the first global electronic intelligence networks; creation of the first electronic databases and the digitisation of signals intelligence;
3. 1990–2000: gradual use of SIGINT capabilities for domestic tasks (identification of internal threats); expansion of capabilities for bulk interception of electronic communications as a result of the dynamic development of Internet services;
4. 2000–2015: after the rise in terrorist threats, the creation of many new surveillance programmes and instruments of international cooperation between intelligence services, and the widespread use of modern intrusive technologies explicitly developed for intelligence applications to monitor domestic events, a period of heightened public interest in the abuses of mass data collection and analysis in non-transparent surveillance programmes took place;
5. 2015–present: this period has been marked by the increased discussion on standards for the use of electronic surveillance, accompanied not only by the rapid development of new surveillance measures and techniques, but also by the ease with which they can be accessed; the emergence of companies that provide not only products but also services related to mass surveillance (the so-called *surveillance as a service*); and surveillance mechanisms built into consumer services and products that create previously unknown possibilities of the mass use of client-side scanning mechanisms.

Obviously, the above division serves to present the most important directions of the changes taking place, and the dates indicated therein provide only a rough guide. At the same time, however, the division allows one to see the dynamics of the changes taking place in the surveillance market. The advances in data collection and processing capabilities in recent years, as well as the ease of access to the necessary technologies, are unprecedented and create a major challenge for lawmakers to develop sufficiently effective and comprehensive legal safeguards to protect against potential abuse.

A distinguishing feature of the most recent (current) stage of development of the surveillance market is the emergence of multiple new solutions that allow for the bulk collection and analysis of information without the need for simultaneous electronic communications monitoring. These measures have an equally intrusive potential, but because of their more subtle implementation (which does not require, for example, eavesdropping on fibre-optic lines), they attract less attention and interest from the public. Importantly, despite having similar surveillance potential, the particular measures are regulated separately. The leading method of controlling surveillance activity is still the introduction of procedures for monitoring communications (data in transit) and stored data. This division, introduced decades ago, is losing relevance in today's world of global digital services.

The aforementioned case of ClearView, a service which, although widely used by SIAs, creates a major regulatory challenge for most European countries, proves the accuracy of this observation. Now public entities have been given the possibility of establishing the identity of any person without the need to create their own information banks. Everything is done for them by an external service provider operating in a foreign jurisdiction, subject to different regulations and different – foreign – supervision. From the perspective of public authorities, it is seemingly an ideal solution. It solves the problems of redundant data collection, and compliance with proportionality and necessity requirements. However, it is only *a façade of legality*, a kind of outsourcing of unlawful activity. If a public authority cannot carry out a certain activity itself, it seems clear that it cannot (at least in theory) legally use the results of the same activity carried out by third parties. Taking the opposite view is a straightforward way to legalise the admissibility of illegal evidence (e.g. obtained through torture) as long as the torture is used abroad.

The objective of a comprehensive regulation of surveillance measures should, therefore, be to establish standards or safeguards relating not to the technical means of obtaining the information, but to the purpose which the public authorities intend to achieve. Only in this way will it be possible to safeguard the individual's rights when new, as yet unknown, surveillance measures are used.

At the same time, one should not lose sight of the fact that the vast majority of the European acquis on electronic surveillance concerns cases involving the monitoring of electronic communications. This creates an additional difficulty in applying well-established legal concepts – such as the notion of strict necessity – to the new areas where surveillance measures are used.

References

Ames J, 'Online Facial Images Were "Harvested"' *The Times* (24 May 2022) <https://cli.re/jpN1dM> accessed 6 September 2023.

Amicelle A and Favarel-Garrigues G, 'Financial Surveillance: Who Cares?' (2012) 5 *Journal of Cultural Economy* 105.

Bernstein EB, 'Health Privacy in Public Spaces' (2015) 66 *Alabama Law Review* 989.

Brown J, 'Pan, Tilt, Zoom: Regulating the Use of Video Surveillance of Public Places Part V: Privacy: Section A: Notes' (2008) 23 *Berkeley Technology Law Journal* 755.

Buttarelli G, 'The Commission Proposal for a Regulation on ePrivacy: Why Do We Need a Regulation Dedicated to ePrivacy in the European Union Forewords' (2017) 3 *European Data Protection Law Review (EDPL)* 155.
Carrera S and Stefan M, 'Access to Electronic Data for Criminal Investigations Purposes in the EU' (Centre for European Policy Studies 2020) 2020-01 <https://cli.re/xPn7Eo> accessed 6 September 2023.
Cave M, Genakos C and Valletti T, 'The European Framework for Regulating Telecommunications: A 25-Year Appraisal' (2019) 55 *Review of Industrial Organization* 47.
Chaikin D, 'How Effective Are Suspicious Transaction Reporting Systems?' (2009) 12 *Journal of Money Laundering Control* 238.
Correa L, 'Data Can Be Obtained from Encrypted Messaging Apps as Shown by a Newly Discovered FBI Document' *Fordham Secure IT* (8 December 2021) <https://cli.re/mpNYY8> accessed 6 September 2023.
Dalla Pellegrina L and others, 'Organized Crime, Suspicious Transaction Reporting and Anti-Money Laundering Regulation' (2020) 54 *Regional Studies* 1761.
'Data Brokers: A Call for Transparency and Accountability' (Federal Trade Commission 2014) <https://cli.re/PAWJPW> accessed 6 September 2023.
Dave P and Dastin J, 'Ukraine Has Started Using Clearview AI's Facial Recognition during War' *Reuters* (14 March 2022) <https://cli.re/yw42KD> accessed 6 September 2023.
De Hert P and Czerniawski M, 'Expanding the European Data Protection Scope beyond Territory: Article 3 of the General Data Protection Regulation in Its Wider Context' (2016) 6 *International Data Privacy Law* 230.
Donohue L, 'Bulk Metadata Collection: Statutory and Constitutional Considerations' (2014) 37 *Harvard Journal of Law and Public Policy* 757.
Duhigg C, 'How Companies Learn Your Secrets' *The New York Times* (16 February 2012) <https://cli.re/3RqRxB> accessed 6 September 2023.
Europe and C of and others, *Handbook on European Data Protection Law – 2018 Edition* (Publications Office of the European Union 2018).
Foucault M, *Discipline and Punish: The Birth of the Prison* (Second Vintage Books edition, Vintage Books 1995).
Fröwis M and others, 'Safeguarding the Evidential Value of Forensic Cryptocurrency Investigations' (2020) 33 *Forensic Science International: Digital Investigation* 200902.
Goodman JW, *Telecommunications Policy-Making in the European Union* (Edward Elgar 2006).
Hao K and Swart H, 'South Africa's Private Surveillance Machine is Fueling a Digital Apartheid' (2022) *MIT Technology Review* <https://cli.re/wPydyw> accessed 6 September 2023.
'Hellenic DPA Fines Clearview AI 20 Million Euros' *European Data Protection Board* (20 July 2022) <https://cli.re/eryWp9> accessed 6 September 2023.
Hern A, 'Google Will Stop Scanning Content of Personal Emails' *The Guardian* <https://cli.re/vNebeY> accessed 6 September 2023.
Hill D, O'Connor CD and Slane A, 'Police Use of Facial Recognition Technology: The Potential for Engaging the Public through Co-Constructed Policy-Making' (2022) 24 *International Journal of Police Science & Management* 325.
Hill K, 'The Secretive Company That Might End Privacy as We Know It' *The New York Times* (18 January 2020) <https://cli.re/8zwAd3> accessed 6 September 2023.
Hong Guo, Bo Jin, and Wei Qian, 'Analysis of Email Header for Forensics Purpose' in *2013 International Conference on Communication Systems and Network Technologies* (IEEE 2013) <http://ieeexplore.ieee.org/document/6524415/> accessed 7 September 2023.

Hosenball M, 'Should Intelligence Agencies Chase Tax Evaders?' *Reuters* (11 November 2011) <https://cli.re/m4yjXJ> accessed 6 September 2023.

Jackson WC, 'Life on Streets and Trails: Fourth Amendment Rights for the Homeless and the Homeward Bound Note' (2013) 66 *Vanderbilt Law Review* 933.

Jacoby N, 'U.S. v. Jones Leaves Important Digital Privacy Questions Unanswered from the Committees' (2011) 37 *Litigation News* [vii].

Juszczak A and Sason E, 'Recalibrating Data Retention in the EU: The Jurisprudence of the Court of Justice of the EU on Data Retention – Is This the End or Is This Only the Beginning?' (2021) eucrim – The European Criminal Law Associations' Forum <https://eucrim.eu/articles/recalibrating-data-retention-in-the-eu/> accessed 7 September 2023.

Keller D, 'Facebook Filters, Fundamental Rights, and the CJEU's Glawischnig-Piesczek Ruling' (2020) 69 *GRUR International* 616.

Kim S, Baek H and Kim DH, 'OTT and Live Streaming Services: Past, Present, and Future' (2021) 45 *Telecommunications Policy* 102244.

Kuczerawy A, 'General Monitoring Obligations: A New Cornerstone of Internet Regulation in the EU?' in Centre for IT & IP Law (ed), *Rethinking IT and IP Law: Celebrating 30 Years CiTiP* (Intersentia 2020).

Ludvigsen KR, Nagaraja S and Daly A, 'YASM (Yet Another Surveillance Mechanism)' (arXiv, 29 May 2022) <http://arxiv.org/abs/2205.14601> accessed 5 October 2022.

Marcuse P, 'The Paradoxes of Public Space' (2014) 38 *Journal of Architecture and Urbanism* 102.

McGowan C, 'The Relevance of Relevance: Section 215 of the USA Patriot Act and the NSA Metadata Collection Program' (2014) 82 *Fordham Law Review* 2399.

Merola LM and Lum C, 'Emerging Surveillance Technologies: Privacy and the Case of License Plate Recognition (LPR) Technology' (2012) 96 *Judicature* 119.

Newell BC, 'The Massive Metadata Machine: Liberty, Power, and Secret Mass Surveillance in the U.S. and Europe' (2014) 10 *Journal of Law and Policy for the Information Society* 481.

Nix N, Timsit A and Zakrzewski C, 'E.U. Slaps Meta with Record $1.3 Billion Fine for Data Privacy Violations' *The Washington Post* (22 May 2023) <https://cli.re/zExzNv> accessed 6 September 2023.

Oruç TH, 'The Prohibition of General Monitoring Obligation for Video-Sharing Platforms Under Article 15 of the E-Commerce Directive in Light of Recent Developments: Is It Still Necessary to Maintain It?' (2022) 13 *JIPITEC* 176.

Papis-Almansa M, 'The Polish Clearing House System: A "Stir"ring Example of the Use of New Technologies in Ensuring VAT Compliance in Poland and Selected Legal Challenges' (2019) 28 *EC Tax Review* 43.

Pol RF, 'Anti-Money Laundering: The World's Least Effective Policy Experiment? Together, We Can Fix It' (2020) 3 *Policy Design and Practice* 73.

'Possible Solutions for Missing Trader Intra-Community Fraud' (CONT Committee of the European Parliament 2022) <https://cli.re/9ZpV7m> accessed 6 September 2023.

Ratcliffe J, 'How Many CCTV Cameras Are There in London?' *CCTV.co.uk* (18 November 2020) <https://cli.re/rmQynM> accessed 6 September 2023.

'A Reconsideration of the Katz Expectation of Privacy Test Notes' (1977) 76 *Michigan Law Review* 154.

Reichbach D, 'The Home Not the Homeless: What the Fourth Amendment Has Historically Protected and Where the Law Is Going after Jones Comment' (2012) 47 *University of San Francisco Law Review* [i].

'Report on OTT Services' (Body of European Regulators for Electronic Communications 2016) BoR (16) 35 <https://cli.re/ZZ4bny> accessed 30 October 2019.

Rezende IN, 'Facial Recognition in Police Hands: Assessing the "Clearview Case" from a European Perspective' (2020) 11 *New Journal of European Criminal Law* 375.

Richards N, 'The Third Party Doctrine and the Future of the Cloud' (2016) 94 *Washington University Law Review* 1441.

Rojszczak M, 'OTT Regulation Framework in the Context of CJEU Skype Case and European Electronic Communications Code' (2020) 38 *Computer Law & Security Review* 105439.

–, 'Compliance of Automatic Tax Fraud Detection Systems with the Right to Privacy Standards Based on the Polish Experience of the STIR System' (2021) 49 *Intertax* 39.

Ruohonen J and Hjerppe K, 'The GDPR Enforcement Fines at Glance' (2022) 106 *Information Systems* 101876.

Ruschmeier H, 'Data Brokers and European Digital Legislation' (2023) 9 *European Data Protection Law Review* 27.

Ryder N, 'Is It Time to Reform the Counter-Terrorist Financing Reporting Obligations? On the EU and the UK System' (2018) 19 *German Law Journal* 1169.

Sherman J, 'Data Brokers and Sensitive Data on U.S. Individuals' (Duke University Sanford Cyber Policy Program 2021) <https://cli.re/p3x4zR> accessed 6 September 2023.

Smith G and Gadeyne J, *Perspectives on Public Space in Rome, from Antiquity to the Present Day* (Ashgate 2013).

'Something for Everyone: Why the Growth of Mobile Apps is Good News for Brands' (Ipsos MORI 2017) <https://cli.re/kajqRY> accessed 6 September 2023.

Sumner S, 'Supermarkets and Data Brokers' in *You: For Sale* (Elsevier 2016).

Sweeney L, *Simple Demographics Often Identify People Uniquely* (Carnegie Mellon University 2000).

Tokson M, 'The Emerging Principles of Fourth Amendment Privacy' (2020) 88 *George Washington Law Review* 1.

'VAT Fraud: New Tool to Help EU Countries Crack down on Criminals and Recoup Billions' *European Commission Press Release* (14 May 2019) <https://cli.re/ZZj8Jy> accessed 6 September 2023.

Vlcek W, 'Surveillance to Combat Terrorist Financing in Europe: Whose Liberty, Whose Security?' (2007) 16 *European Security* 99.

Volz D and Tau B, 'Little-Known Surveillance Program Captures Money Transfers Between U.S. and More Than 20 Countries' *The Wall Street Journal* (18 January 2023) <https://cli.re/74vqxX> accessed 6 September 2023.

Walter-Johnson F and Wessler NF, 'How the Arizona Attorney General Created a Secretive, Illegal Surveillance Program to Sweep up Millions of Our Financial Records' *ACLU* (18 January 2023) <https://cli.re/rmdomA> accessed 6 September 2023.

Wilman FG, 'Two Emerging Principles of EU Internet Law: A Comparative Analysis of the Prohibitions of General Data Retention and General Monitoring Obligations' (2022) 46 *Computer Law & Security Review* 105728.

Wolf R, 'VAT Carousel Fraud: A European Problem from a Dutch Perspective' (2011) 39 *Intertax* 26.

Wu R-S and others, 'Using Data Mining Technique to Enhance Tax Evasion Detection Performance' (2012) 39 *Expert Systems with Applications* 8769.

Zalnieriute M, 'How Public Space Surveillance Is Eroding Political Protests in Australia' (2021) Verfassungsblog: On Matters Constitutional <https://intr2dok.vifa-recht.de/receive/mir_mods_00011558> accessed 8 September 2023.

Zhao S and others, 'User Profiling from Their Use of Smartphone Applications: A Survey' (2019) 59 *Pervasive and Mobile Computing* 101052.

3 Fundamentals of the European legal model

3.1 Introduction

This chapter presents the key legal concepts that form the regulatory background for the use of surveillance measures. The following sections discuss the most important legally permissible purposes for implementing surveillance measures; the impact of their use on individual fundamental rights; and the most significant criteria for assessing the permissibility of surveillance.

The first issue, which should be presented before constructing a common standard for the application of surveillance, is the interrelationship between the various human rights instruments in Europe. Indeed, the European human rights model should be understood not as a single set of regulations but as a set of interacting legal instruments based, in particular, on classical international law (the European Convention on Human Rights), EU law (the Charter of Fundamental Rights), and national law (the constitutional provisions of Member States). Therefore understanding the whole patchwork of different regulations setting standards for (and restrictions on) the use of bulk surveillance requires reference to each of these levels.

Significantly, the individual legal instruments introduce their own catalogues of (partly different) fundamental rights, and include definitions of the interrelationships between these rights and the principles of their application, limitation and derogation. Many of the fundamental rights are defined in an identical (or similar) manner in the ECHR, the Charter, and the constitutional laws. In reality, however, in several cases the respective instruments either directly introduce different definitions, or the interpretation by certain courts gives these rights a partially different meaning.

Despite a number of similarities between the EU Member States, attempting to treat all of them as operating under an identical legal order would lead to oversimplification. Different states have different capabilities and needs for using surveillance, including indiscriminate surveillance; are affected by different internal and external threats; and because of their own traditions and historical backgrounds give common legal concepts their own unique meaning.

Nowadays, the use of surveillance measures is most often associated with national security and the fight against serious crime. In practice, however, the

DOI: 10.4324/9781003449263-3

understanding of each of these concepts has changed significantly over the years, with the result that intrusive measures have increasingly been used also for other activities of public authorities that go beyond the narrowly defined national security objectives. Moreover, the assessment of the "intrusiveness" of surveillance itself has also changed considerably in recent years – mainly as a result of users' growing awareness of the risks associated with mass information processing. This has led to a situation where the same court, when assessing the compatibility of similar national laws, can come to conclusions diametrically opposed to those presented a decade earlier – mainly due to recognising that, as a result of technological change, the use of an identical surveillance measure could lead to a much more serious interference with individual rights than years ago.

The identification of the key elements of the standard for the use of electronic surveillance must, therefore, be based on the search for common concepts that are widely accepted at the European level. At the same time, it must also take into account that this standard is not only subject to constant change, but also that its current shape is often the result of a continuous dialogue among the ECtHR, the CJEU and the domestic high courts, as well as political compromises reached at the level of national governments.

3.2 Multilateral approach to the protection of human rights

While it is impossible to overestimate the influence of the ECHR on consolidating and strengthening the functioning of liberal democracies in Europe, it must be borne in mind that the Convention is de facto an instrument of classical international law. That is to say, it defines obligations addressed to states, thereby establishing guarantees for individuals in horizontal relations. There is no doubt that these are not only negative obligations (i.e. to refrain from unauthorised interference), but also positive ones (to introduce norms of national law protecting individuals from interference by other private actors). At the same time, however, the Convention does not explicitly impose restrictions on individuals or business entities, including technology corporations. Moreover, because the Convention is addressed to states, the obligations and guarantees thereunder must be interpreted with jurisdictional norms in mind. This has led to decades-long debates about the applicability of the ECHR to events occurring or individuals located outside the borders of a state party to the Convention.[1] These dilemmas are not exclusive to the ECHR but, in fact, apply to all international human rights mechanisms.[2]

1 See e.g. Michal Gondek, 'Extraterritorial Application of The European Convention on Human Rights: Territorial Focus in the Age of Globalization?' (2005) 52 *Netherlands International Law Review* 349; Cedric Ryngaert, 'Clarifying the Extraterritorial Application of the European Convention on Human Rights (Al-Skeini v. the United Kingdom)' (2012) 28 *Utrecht Journal of International and European Law* 57; Marko Milanović and Tatjana Papić, 'The Applicability of the ECHR in Contested Territories' (2018) 67 *International and Comparative Law Quarterly* 779.

2 Marko Milanović, *Extraterritorial Application of Human Rights Treaties: Law, Principles, and Policy* (1. publ, Oxford Univ Press 2011).

With regard to surveillance programmes – especially those that are cross-border in nature – this creates a whole range of ambiguities, from assessing whether the Convention provides safeguards for foreign nationals residing abroad (e.g. when their communications are intercepted on the territory of a state party to the Convention) to examining the legality of cross-border data exchange programmes carried out in cooperation with third countries, and to determining the permissibility of "outsourcing" the surveillance of a state's own citizens to foreign services and then transferring the processed results of such surveillance to the authorities of the ordering state.

At the same time, the ECHR does not contain a blanket exclusion of state activities undertaken in the field of national security, which means that surveillance programmes implemented in this area can also be assessed in terms of their permissibility and legality. Over the years, the Court has repeatedly evaluated domestic surveillance programmes, examining various aspects of the use of surveillance measures and, in some cases, analysing successive generations of surveillance legislation implemented in the same states.[3] As a result, its jurisprudence has fundamentally contributed to the development of a standard that is also applicable to the assessment of bulk surveillance measures.

In recent years, EU law has also increasingly been seen as a guarantor of fundamental rights. A key stage in the transformation of the European Union from an instrument of economic cooperation to an organisation built on shared values was certainly reaching an agreement on the Charter of Fundamental Rights, and subsequently (under the Lisbon Treaty) giving it the same force as that of the Treaties, which de facto rendered it a source of EU primary law.[4] In reality, however, the actual impetus for change in the field of the EU fundamental rights model came neither from the Member States nor even the CJEU, but from the German Federal Constitutional Court (BverfG) in its famous *Solange I* ruling.[5] It can be said that it was only the *Solange I* case that made it clear that in order for the project of building a European community to become a reality, it must be based on common values built on the recognition of the inviolability of human dignity. The BverfG aptly emphasised that tolerating the principle of the primacy of EU law required that the Union, as an international organisation, ensured the protection of fundamental rights at a level no lower than that resulting from the Member States' constitutional provisions. Otherwise, the supremacy of EU law could be called into question, and as a result the fundamental freedoms underpinning the internal market[6] could also be endangered.[7] In fact, the view that the protection of fundamental

3 A detailed analysis of ECtHR case law related to surveillance law will be presented in Chapter 4.

4 In fact, however, the way adopted in the Lisbon Treaty to give effect to the Charter is less clear than that proposed in the TCE and is still contentious and controversial today. PP Craig, *The Lisbon Treaty: Law, Politics, and Treaty Reform* (Oxford University Press 2010) 200.

5 BVerfGE 37, 291, 29 May 1974 (*Solange I*).

6 It should be noted though that today's concept of the European Union's internal market was shaped a decade after the *Solange I* case as a result of the work on the Single European Act of 1986.

7 Ulrich Scheuner, 'Fundamental Rights in European Community Law and in National Constitutional Law' (1975) 12 *Common Market Law Review* 171.

rights is a new (or additional) area of EU activity is therefore somehow misleading.[8] The protection of fundamental rights is a necessary element for the realisation of the idea of economic cooperation. The *Solange I* case is also an excellent example of how the dialogue between national constitutional courts and the CJEU shapes EU standards on the protection of fundamental rights.[9]

In discussing the impact of the rights and freedoms guaranteed by the Charter on the regulation of state surveillance activities, two considerations need to be borne in mind. First, EU primary law explicitly refers to the ECHR acquis and indicates that the guarantees under the Convention form part of EU law as general principles of law. Moreover, according to Article 52(3) of the Charter, to the extent that the Charter defines rights which correspond to those guaranteed by the ECHR, their meaning and scope are the same as those conferred by the Convention.[10] As a result, the body of ECtHR case law is of considerable relevance whenever the CJEU hears a case involving an individual's fundamental rights and freedoms. An example is the proceedings concerning the assessment of national legislation implementing surveillance programmes involving bulk and indiscriminate interception of data.

In reality, however, Article 52(3) of the Charter, cited above, sets a minimum standard for protection, which does not prevent the introduction of more far-reaching EU laws. An example of a difference between the standard under the Convention and the one in force in EU law is the authorisation required for the use of surveillance measures. According to the ECtHR, it can be granted not only by a court but also by an independent administrative authority, including *ex post* authorisation, whereas the CJEU accepts only judicial review applied *ex ante* (for more on this, see section 4.4.4).

When examining the relationship between the ECHR and the Charter, it is also important to bear in mind the limited scope of application of EU law, determined by the competences conferred on the European Union. As a general rule, the Charter's guarantees relate only to the performance of the Member States' obligations under EU law. Of particular importance in this case is the exclusion of tasks carried out in the field of national security. A typical example of the application of this exception are foreign intelligence activities carried out by a Member State's secret services. However, even such cases are

8 For more on the importance of shared values in the European integration project, see: Kiran Klaus Patel, *Project Europe: Myths and Realities of European Integration* (Meredith Dale tr, Cambridge University Press 2020) 146–174.

9 In the context of the BVerfG/CJEU dialogue, see Dieter Grimm, Mattias Wendel and Tobias Reinbacher, 'European Constitutionalism and the German Basic Law' in Anneli Albi and Samo Bardutzky (eds), *National Constitutions in European and Global Governance: Democracy, Rights, the Rule of Law* (TMC Asser Press 2019) <http://link.springer.com/10.1007/978-94-6265-273-6_10> accessed 8 September 2023.

10 This especially relates to the scope and meaning of the right to privacy as defined in Art. 7 of the Charter and Art. 8 of the ECHR: Explanations relating to the Charter of Fundamental Rights, OJ 2007 C303/17.

not entirely outside the scope of EU law. Indeed, if surveillance programmes are used to gather information about another Member State – in particular, to carry out mass surveillance of its citizens, to conduct economic intelligence operations, or to transfer the information gathered to a third country – this may jeopardise the project of building a European Union based on respect for common values and principles.

EU law may also have a significant impact on third countries (i.e. non-EEA countries). This is particularly the case when the European Union concludes international agreements or adopts other acts to regulate the flow of personal data – including within the framework of economic cooperation. The CJEU has, on several occasions, found such mechanisms to be incompatible with EU law precisely because of the lack of adequate legal safeguards in the third country's legal model.[11] In the *Schrems* case, it explicitly referred to the risk of the use of the data transferred in US-led electronic surveillance programmes.[12] Thus, while EU law – and by extension the CJEU's competence – are limited to the examination of certain types of surveillance used by Member State authorities, no such obstacle exists when assessing the permissibility of data transfers to a third country. In such a case, the EU law de facto creates the standard of review of the foreign legal model and that extends to all of its areas, including surveillance programmes carried out in the area of national security.

Of course, when discussing the foundations of the European system of human rights, the importance of the Member States' constitutional provisions cannot be overlooked. In this case, it should be borne in mind that the catalogue of fundamental rights introduced in the individual basic laws may be significantly different. Suffice it to say that the German constitution defines 18 rights and freedoms in the section on fundamental rights, while the Charter of Fundamental Rights defines more than 30 of them. A closer analysis reveals, however, that due to the different origins of the individual constitutional laws, the legislators often expressed the same rights and freedoms using different legal institutions to describe them. While the German constitution, referred to above, does not explicitly define the right to data protection, the German Constitutional Court inferred the existence of this right as early as in the 1980s in the precedent-setting judgment on the Census Act. There, it acknowledged that "the gathering and retention of data that has not been rendered anonymous for undefined or yet to be defined purposes would not be compatible" with the right to informational self-determination.[13] In this respect, it also included in the constitutional standard "independent data protection officers in order to ensure effective protection" of individual rights.[14]

11 See also sections 5.4 and 6.7.
12 *Maximillian Schrems v. Data Protection Commissioner* (C-362/14) EU:C:2015:650.
13 BVerfG 15 December 1983, 1 BvR 209/83 (*Census Act*) at [153].
14 Ibid. at [155].

In the Court's view, an infringement by the authorities of the individual's right to informational self-determination creates an obstacle to the development of their autonomy, thus jeopardising the establishment of proper social relations.[15] As a result, in Germany the right to data protection had been derived from constitutional guarantees more than 10 years before the first EU data protection act was established, and almost 20 years before the Charter of Fundamental Rights was drafted.

However, differences between national models of fundamental rights protection are more likely to manifest themselves in the scope of the limitation and derogation clauses in place. Indeed, the content of the right itself may turn out to be secondary if, based on the totality of the constitutional norms established, it is possible to introduce a more far-reaching interference with individual rights than is permitted in neighbouring states. Hence, although freedom of expression is defined in a similar way in all European (EU) states, the actual freedom to exercise this right may vary considerably due to the application of different limitation clauses.

The modern European legal system has been built on the same constitutional principles, among which – in addition to the rule of law, legalism, and the separation of powers – respect for fundamental rights is of utmost importance. The source of these rights is dignity, the protection of which is a fundamental task of public authorities. The inviolability of human dignity is guaranteed by the ECHR,[16] the Charter of Fundamental Rights,[17] and the constitutional provisions of the Member States.[18] However, dignity per se is not in every case defined as a kind of absolute right.[19] For example, in the German legal model dignity is fundamental and not subject to any limitations.[20] As a result, the German Federal Constitutional Court has held that even public security objectives do not justify measures that violate human dignity.[21] Moreover, it stressed that any law leading to an infringement of dignity must be declared unconstitutional.[22] On the other hand, the jurisprudence of the

15 Antoinette Rouvroy and Yves Poullet, 'The Right to Informational Self-Determination and the Value of Self-Development: Reassessing the Importance of Privacy for Democracy', in Serge Gutwirth and others (eds), *Reinventing Data Protection?* (Springer Netherlands 2009).

16 Sebastian Heselhaus and Ralph Hemsley, 'Human Dignity and the European Convention on Human Rights' in Paolo Becchi and Klaus Mathis (eds), *Handbook of Human Dignity in Europe* (Springer International Publishing 2019) <http://link.springer.com/10.1007/978-3-319-27830-8_47-1> accessed 9 March 2021.

17 Jackie Jones, 'Human Dignity in the EU Charter of Fundamental Rights and Its Interpretation Before the European Court of Justice' (2012) 33 *Liverpool Law Review* 281.

18 Aharon Barak and Daniel Kayros, *Human Dignity: The Constitutional Value and the Constitutional Right* (Cambridge University Press 2015).

19 For a comparative analysis, see Paolo Becchi and Klaus Mathis (eds), *Handbook of Human Dignity in Europe* (Springer International Publishing 2019).

20 Christoph Enders, 'Right to Have Rights – The German Constitutional Concept of Human Dignity' (2010) 3 *NUJS Law Review* 253.

21 BVerfG 31 January 1973 (2 BvR 454/71) at [30].

22 BVerfG 16 January 1957 (1 BvR 253/56) at [32].

Polish Constitutional Tribunal points out that while dignity is "inviolable, and the respect and protection thereof shall be the obligation of public authorities," it is not treated as a separate right, but rather as a kind of constitutional principle from which specific fundamental rights derive.

3.3 Legitimate objectives for implementing surveillance measures

3.3.1 National security

Security, like other terms relating to the activities of public authorities, does not have a closed and universally accepted definition. Depending on the era under study, the internal or external threats and the form of government being exercised, it is not only the perception of security but also the measures that can be taken to ensure it that undergo change.

Nowadays, national security is mainly associated with countering threats to the state's fundamental interests, including its territorial integrity, the protection of its constitutional order and its economic foundations. These tasks have traditionally been performed by secret services, including intelligence agencies and national security services.

However, with the end of the Cold War state security became less associated with external threats and increasingly identified with activities undertaken by national or international extremist groups or organised criminal groups. As a result, in contemporary national security studies threats emanating from *non-state actors* are one of the main areas of analysis.[23] Moreover, with the global coronavirus pandemic, it has become evident that some threats where no traditional actor can be identified at all (the so-called *actor-less threats*) can also significantly affect national security.[24]

The lack of clear definitional boundaries makes it difficult to indicate which state activities can be included in the area of national security. It should be borne in mind that different economic, political, or even geographical situations may affect the different priorities at the centre of a state's interests. Thus, while threats to sovereignty or basic economic interests may be considered to belong to the area of national security in most cases, including aspects of social,[25] environmental[26] or cultural[27] policies in this group may meet with less general approval.

23 'National Security Strategy and Strategic Defence and Security Review 2015' (HM Government 2015).

24 Shannon Havlicak Grondel, 'COVID-19, the Ubiquitous National Security Threat: Lessons Learned Around the Globe' (2021) 49 *International Journal of Legal Information* 66.

25 Mark Neocleous, 'From Social to National Security: On the Fabrication of Economic Order' (2006) 37 *Security Dialogue* 363.

26 Paul Ehrlich and Anne Ehrlich, 'The Environmental Dimensions of National Security' in Josef Rotblat and Vitalii I Goldanskii (eds), *Global Problems and Common Security* (Springer Berlin Heidelberg 1989).

27 Jeffrey S Lantis, 'Strategic Culture and National Security Policy' (2002) 4 *International Studies Review* 87.

Although the ECtHR has repeatedly referred to the notion of national security – including by introducing criteria for permissible interference with fundamental rights – its case law does not provide a clear definition of this concept.[28] Moreover, the Court itself has accepted the view that Contracting States should be granted a particularly wide margin of appreciation, allowing them to implement such measures as they deem necessary to protect their fundamental interests.[29] At the same time, however, it has emphasised that the performance of national security tasks must not lead to depriving an individual of protection against arbitrariness.[30] Hence, in examining the application of the national security clause the Court has focused on a detailed analysis of the necessity and proportionality of the measures taken.[31]

In the ECtHR jurisprudence, therefore, national security does not have an overriding importance.[32] In each case, invoking state security requires confirmation that the action taken by the public authorities is necessary to protect fundamental social needs or the democratic order of the state.[33] Thus, the ECtHR has, for example, held in its case law that disclosing information containing state secrets, whereby the public could learn about the scale of abuses related to surveillance activities carried out by the authorities, falls within the freedom of expression protected by the Convention.[34] The Court has also pointed out that national security cannot be treated as a blanket justification for actions by public authorities in respect of every breach of public order.[35] Even action against certain forms of serious crime, such as international drug trafficking – although clearly linked to general security objectives – has been deemed not related to the field of national security. Indeed, as the Court has pointed out, although the fight against drug trafficking requires decisive action, these crimes do not per se threaten the fundamental interests of the state.[36]

As a result, the lack of a closed definition of national security provides the necessary flexibility for the Convention, allowing the actions taken by authorities – including in the area of electronic surveillance – to be adapted

28 See generally Iain Cameron, *National Security and the European Convention on Human Rights* (Brill | Nijhoff 2000).

29 *Kaushal and Others v. Bulgaria* (1537/08) 2 September 2010 ECtHR at [28].

30 Ibid. at [29].

31 *Chahal v. the United Kingdom* (22414/93) 1 September 1994 ECtHR at [138]; *Grigoriades v. Greece* (24348/94) 4 September 1995 ECtHR.

32 The pursuit of national security objectives justifies limiting only certain rights guaranteed by the Convention – namely the right to a fair trial, the right to privacy, freedom of expression, assembly and association and freedom of movement. This means that it cannot justify derogation regarding other rights and freedoms, like freedom of thought – see *Nolan and K. v. Russia* (2512/04) 12 February 2009 ECtHR at [73].

33 *Klass and Others v. Germany* (5029/71) 18 December 1974 ECtHR at [42].

34 *Bucur and Toma v. Romania* (40238/02) 8 January 2013 ECtHR at [42].

35 *Akgün v. Turkey* (19699/18) 20 July 2021 ECtHR at [184].

36 *C.G. and Others v. Bulgaria* (1365/07) 24 April 2008 ECtHR at [43].

to new and evolving threats affecting state security. However, the above does not exclude the possibility of a judicial assessment of the admissibility of invoking the national security clause as a rationale for the limitation of fundamental rights. Thus, although the Court does not directly assess national security measures (e.g. it does not examine whether a particular surveillance programme has actually had an impact on the protection of the state against a particular threat), it can examine whether the very rationale for the establishment of a surveillance mechanism meets the criteria arising from the Convention – in particular, the standard of necessity in a democratic state under the rule of law.

The national security clause also has a specific role in EU law. Unlike the ECHR, which lacks such a general clause, it is enshrined in Article 4(2) of the TEU, which provides that national security is the exclusive competence of the Member States. Because the European Union, in accordance with the principle of conferral, exercises only the competences conferred upon it, the national security exception de facto excludes from the scope of EU law all activities undertaken by states in the area of state security. As a result, these activities are also outside the CJEU's competence. This is further reinforced in Article 276 of the TFEU, which excludes from the Court's jurisdiction the review of the validity and proportionality of actions taken by law enforcement and security services in the area of law and order, including internal security cases.[37]

Significantly, today's wording of the national security clause was only established in the Lisbon Treaty and is the result of discussions among Member States after the failed ratification of the Treaty establishing a Constitution for Europe (TCE).[38] The national security exception is, therefore, not a pillar of European integration. It is a relatively new institution, less than 15 years old in its current form.

Indeed, it was not until the draft TCE was prepared that the previously used term "internal security" was changed to "national security," whereby an explicit reference to the area of national security was for the first time introduced into the EU treaties.[39] However, the concept was already in use in EU law at the time. For example, the e-Privacy Directive,[40] which was in force at

37 Koen Lenaerts, 'Challenges Facing the European Court of Justice after the Treaty of Lisbon' (2010) 2 *Analele Universitatii din Bucuresti: Seria Drept* 1.

38 Treaty establishing a Constitution for Europe, OJ 2004 C310/1; not ratified. For a discussion, see Juliane Kokott and Juliane Kokott, 'The European Convention and Its Draft Treaty Establishing a Constitution for Europe: Appropriate Answers to the Laeken Questions?' (2003) 40 *Common Market Law Review* 1315; Jan Klabbers and Päivi Leino, 'Death by Constitution? The Draft Treaty Establishing a Constitution for Europe' (2003) 4 *German Law Journal* 1293.

39 See Art. I-5(1) of the TCE.

40 Directive 2002/58/EC of the European Parliament and of the Council of 12 July 2002 concerning the processing of personal data and the protection of privacy in the electronic communications sector, OJ 2002 L201/37.

the time of the development of the TCE, provided the possibility for Member States to adopt legislative measures restricting the rights and obligations set out therein as deemed necessary, appropriate, and proportionate to, ***inter alia***, safeguard national security objectives.[41]

In the current wording of Article 4(2) of the TEU, "maintaining law and order" and "safeguarding national security" are defined as separate essential functions of the state. This distinction is used both in the Treaties and in numerous secondary law acts. The Court's jurisprudence has clarified that a breach of public order encompasses such a disturbance of social order that, at the same time, involves "a genuine, present and sufficiently serious threat affecting one of the fundamental interests of society."[42] In explaining the notion of national security, on the other hand, the Court drew on its earlier interpretation of the term "public security."[43] The Court had referred that concept to both the internal and external security of a Member State, which it had linked to the protection of the functioning of the core public institutions and services and of the life of the population, as well as to the prevention of serious disturbances to foreign relations or to the peaceful coexistence of nations.[44] In more recent jurisprudence the Court, when examining the concept of national security, has clarified that it encompasses the essential functions of the State, as well as the prevention and prosecution of activities capable of seriously destabilising the fundamental constitutional, political or social structures of a country, and, in particular, of directly endangering the public or the population or the State as such, especially including terrorist activities.[45]

The exclusion of the area of national security from the scope of EU law creates the risk that individual states may deviate from the application of EU law (e.g. rules on the collection or sharing of electronic data) when it benefits them, which could clearly reduce the effectiveness of the EU legal model and hamper the unification of rules applied within the internal market. According to the well-established case law of the Court of Justice, limitations to rights and freedoms must be interpreted narrowly.[46] Furthermore, the power of a Member State to avail itself of a derogation provided for in the Treaties does not preclude judicial review of the measures taken under that derogation.[47]

41 A similar exemption was introduced in Art. 14(1) of Directive 97/66, a predecessor to the e-Privacy Directive.

42 *J. N. v. Staatssecretaris voor Veiligheid en Justitie* (C-601/15 PPU) EU:C:2016:84 at [65].

43 Ibid. at [66]. It should be recalled, however, that the European legislature does not treat both concepts as synonyms. For example, in Directive 95/46, in the catalogue of exemptions defined in Art. 13, national security and public security were listed separately. For more on these ambiguities, see also Iain Cameron, 'European Union Law Restraints on Intelligence Activities' (2020) 33 *International Journal of Intelligence and Counter Intelligence* 452.

44 *H. T. v. Land Baden-Württemberg* (C-373/13) EU:C:2015:413 at [41–44].

45 *La Quadrature du Net and Others v. Premier ministre and Others* (Joined Cases C-511/18, C-512/18 and C-520/18) EU:C:2020:791 at [135].

46 *IPI* (C-92/09) EU:C:2013:715 at [39].

47 *Van Duyn v. Home Office* (41/74) EU:C:1974:133.

Indeed, that is the only way to ensure that individual Member States do not unilaterally determine the meaning given to particular terms.[48] Importantly, the Court has also clarified that pursuing an objective relating to public order and national security does not justify measures resulting in a disproportionate interference with fundamental rights.[49] This means that a restriction on fundamental freedoms requires that a real and genuine link be demonstrated between the measure being implemented and the objectives pursued, and that those objectives cannot be attained by other, less restrictive, measures.[50] Thus, although Article 4(2) of the TEU does not explicitly provide for any limitation to the application of the national security clause and, in particular, does not require the condition of proportionality to be met, the need to do so arises from the interpretation of EU law provided by the Court of Justice.[51]

The above leads to the conclusion that the national security exception introduced in Article 4(2) of the TEU establishes a general derogation from EU law, but only to the extent of actions that necessarily respond to a real and present threat to state security.[52] However, also in this respect states may not take measures which are disproportionate or which infringe on rights guaranteed by EU law.[53]

3.3.2 Criminal investigations

In addition to pursuing national security objectives, the use of surveillance measures has traditionally also been linked to the needs of ongoing criminal proceedings. In fact, a significant part of the ECtHR's jurisprudence assessing the permissibility of secret surveillance has concerned criminal proceedings, and the aim of the complaints brought before the Court was to determine whether the manner in which the surveillance measure was ordered, and the legal safeguards implemented were adequate to the risks involved and did not constitute an abuse of power.[54]

As individual states are free to shape their criminal law, the way in which surveillance data are managed and subsequently used in criminal proceedings can vary significantly. However, as the ECtHR has pointed out, in each case communications interception leads to particularly serious interference with the right to privacy, so the measure must be used only in legally justified

48 *Omega Spielhallen- und Automatenaufstellungs* (C-36/02) EU:C:2004:614.
49 See e.g. *Commission v. Luxembourg* (C-51/08) EU:C:2011:336 at [124].
50 *Sayn-Wittgenstein v. Landeshauptmann von Wien* (C-208/09) EU:C:2010:806 at [90].
51 *H. T. v. Land Baden-Württemberg* (n 44) at [92]. It should be noted, however, that in this judgment the Court referred to the term "national security" to the extent that this concept was used in acts of secondary law.
52 Serena Crespi, 'The Applicability of Schrems Principles to the Member States: National Security and Data Protection within the EU Context' (2018) 43 *European Law Review* 669.
53 *LQN* (n 45) at [135].
54 See further in section 4.4.

circumstances.[55] For this reason, the Court has examined in its jurisprudence not only national surveillance laws but also the practice of their application. As a result, in *Iordachi v. Moldava* the Court observed that, during the period examined in the case, the national courts had approved almost all applications for the ordering of surveillance measures submitted by authorities. Taking this observation into account, the Court emphasised that the unusually high rate of approved applications might indicate that "the investigating judges do not address themselves to the existence of compelling justification for authorising measures of secret surveillance."[56]

The CJEU's jurisprudence, on the other hand, has in recent years developed the concept of "serious crime," according to which the degree of intrusiveness of the surveillance measures applied should be linked to the degree of harmfulness of the act whose detection or prosecution the measure is intended to serve.[57] In this way the Court recognised that different forms of surveillance entail different degrees of interference with individual rights – from which it concluded that measures leading to serious interference should only be used to combat crime also classified as serious.

As the Court of Justice aptly observed, "in accordance with the principle of proportionality, serious interference can be justified, in areas of prevention, investigation, detection and prosecution of criminal offences, only by the objective of fighting crime which must also be defined as 'serious'."[58] On this basis, it held that a surveillance measure allowing for serious interference with individual rights (in that case, general data retention) could be applied to "individuals suspected of planning, committing or having committed a serious crime or of being implicated in one way or another in such a crime."[59]

Moreover, such a measure may only be used if it genuinely serves the purpose of combating serious crime, and is not merely used an instrument for the performance of tasks indirectly related to that purpose. Therefore in the case of *Lietuvos Respublikos generalinė prokuratūra*, the Court held that this condition is not fulfilled in the case of access to retained telecommunications data motivated by the conduct of disciplinary proceedings related to suspected corruption of a public official (in the case at hand, a prosecutor).[60] In the Court's view, disciplinary proceedings, although they may lead to the initiation of criminal proceedings, are not such proceedings in themselves, and much less can they be considered to be related to the fight against serious crime.

55 In the context of criminal surveillance, see *Malone v. the United Kingdom* (8691/79) 2 August 1984 ECtHR at [81].
56 *Iordachi and Others v. Moldova* (25198/02) 10 February 2009 ECtHR at [51].
57 The term is also used in the ECtHR case law – see e.g. *M.K. v. France* (19522/09) 18 April 2013 ECtHR at [41].
58 *Ministerio Fiscal* (C-207/16) EU:C:2018:788 at [51].
59 *Tele2 Sverige* (C-203/15 and C-698/15) EU:C:2016:970 at [119].
60 *Lietuvos Respublikos generalinė prokuratūra* (C-162/22) EU:C:2023:631 at [43].

The criterion of "serious interference" used by the CJEU covers both quantitative and qualitative parameters of the surveillance applied. This leads to the conclusion that serious interference occurs not only when a large group of people is subjected to a surveillance measure (e.g. in the form of indiscriminate surveillance),[61] but also when measures are applied which allow the collection of detailed information on the private life of the persons subjected to surveillance.[62] Importantly, for the assessment of whether interference is serious, it does not matter how long a surveillance measure is applied if, even in a short period, it enables precise conclusions to be drawn about the private life of the data subject(s).[63]

It follows from the above that an example of a surveillance measure which, in the CJEU's view, does not lead to serious interference with individual rights – and which can, therefore, be used in relation to the fight against criminal offences in general – is the collection and making available to law enforcement authorities of information on the civil identity of users of electronic communications means.[64]

When looking for a legal definition of "serious crime" under EU law, one should first refer to the Treaty regulations. One of the tasks carried out by the Union, further strengthened by the Lisbon reform, is to ensure a high level of security by means of measures designed to prevent and combat crime.[65] As the CJEU has repeatedly emphasised in its case law, the fight against serious crime conducted with a view to ensuring public security constitutes an objective of general interest for the Union.[66] To that end, measures are put in place to approximate national criminal legislation,[67] to facilitate the collection and exchange of information by police and judicial authorities,[68] and to ensure the mutual recognition of judicial decisions.[69] The European Union's

61 *Prokuratuur* (C-746/18) EU:C:2021:152 at [40].
62 *G.D. v. the Commissioner of the Garda Síochána and Others* (C-140/20) EU:C:2022:258 at [47].
63 *Prokuratuur* (n 61) at [39].
64 *LQN* (n 45) at [157].
65 *See* Jacob Öberg, 'Union Regulatory Criminal Law Competence after Lisbon Treaty' (2011) 19 *European Journal of Crime, Criminal Law and Criminal Justice* 289; Tony Marguery, 'European Union Fundamental Rights and Member States Action in EU Criminal Law' (2013) 20 *Maastricht Journal of European and Comparative Law* 282; Valsamis Mitsilegas, *EU Criminal Law after Lisbon. Rights, Trust and the Transformation of Justice in Europe* (Hart Publishing 2018).
66 *Digital Rights Ireland* (Joined Cases C-293/12 and C-594/12) EU:C:2014:238 at [42].
67 See e.g. Directive 2011/36, Directive 2011/92, Directive 2014/62 and Directive 2018/1673.
68 See provisions related to the functioning of Europol (Regulation 2016/794) and Eurojust (Regulation 2018/1727). The importance and role of data sharing in the context of fighting serious crime are discussed in: Oldřich Bureš, 'Intelligence Sharing and the Fight against Terrorism in the EU: Lessons Learned from Europol' (2016) 15 *European View* 57.
69 See Regulation 1215/2012, Regulation 1896/2006, and Regulation 891/2007. For more on the mutual recognition of judgments, see: Jacob Öberg, 'Trust in the Law? Mutual

competence in the area of substantive criminal law concerns, in particular, acts of a cross-border nature and includes the introduction of standards for defining acts of serious crime as well as the setting of minimum sentences associated with each of these offences.[70] The category of cross-border serious crime includes a number of offences also related to the area of national security, such as terrorism, drug trafficking, arms trafficking and computer crime. For each of them, the European Union has introduced its own legislation.[71] As a result, the European Union not only adopts legislative measures approximating substantive criminal law in the area of combating serious crime, but also introduces mechanisms approximating national legislation on the collection of evidence or the exchange of information.

Although the Treaties use the term "serious crime," the concept has not been defined precisely, either through a closed list of offences or through some other criterion (e.g. a minimum or maximum penalty) to determine the range of acts that should be included in this category.

Moreover, the EU legislature appears to have defined the framework for serious crime differently for the purposes of different acts of secondary law. The Directive establishing the European Investigation Order (EIO) introduced a catalogue of 32 offences which – under additional conditions – may justify issuing a cross-border order for investigative measures. In addition to the offences overlapping with the types of "serious crime" listed in Article 83(1) of the TFEU, this catalogue defines a number of other offences, e.g. forgery of means of payment, trafficking in stolen vehicles, or arson. Although the legislature does not explicitly use the term "serious crime" in the EIO Directive, given the objectives of establishing the EIO such a qualification seems obvious, all the more so because the EIO can also be used to actively intercept telecommunications, and thus to implement surveillance measures. According to the CJEU's interpretation quoted above, the acts listed in the catalogue defined in the Directive must, therefore, be classified as *serious crime* because their prosecution may lead to the implementation of measures seriously interfering with fundamental rights.

The e-Evidence Regulation, on the other hand, introduced the requirement that one of the new measures provided for in this act, namely the European Production Order, can only be applied to acts that carry at least a 3-year maximum custodial sentence in the requesting state. According to the legislature, such a solution "will limit the scope of the instrument to more serious

---

Recognition as a Justification to Domestic Criminal Procedure' (2020) 16 *European Constitutional Law Review* 33.

70 Art. 83(1) of the TFEU. It should be noted that it is not the only provision defining EU competence in the area of criminal law. It defines, however, the legislative actions that can be taken under the ordinary legislative procedure.

71 Examples of such regulations are Directive 2013/40 (combating terrorism); Directive 2017/2103 (definition of drugs); and Directive 2013/40 (cybercrimes).

crimes."[72] As a side note, a similar requirement of carrying a custodial sentence was also introduced as one of the conditions for issuing an EIO.

The lack of a clear EU definition of "serious crime" means that the term can be – and is – defined differently in many Member States. Thus, in the United Kingdom the definition of serious crime requires finding that the offender "could reasonably be expected to be sentenced to imprisonment for a term of 3 years or more."[73] In Poland, on the other hand, the term is used to describe offences carrying a minimum (and not maximum, as in the case of the e-Evidence Regulation) sentence of 3 years' imprisonment.[74] At the same time, however, the Polish Criminal Code does not limit the use of surveillance measures only to this category of crimes.[75] In Germany, serious crimes (*Verbrechen*) are acts punishable by a minimum of 1 year's imprisonment.[76] In Spain, on the other hand, offences punishable by a minimum of 5 years' imprisonment are classified in this way.[77]

Moreover, many Member States lack a clear distinction of such most serious offences, which obviously makes it difficult to develop a single standard for the application of surveillance measures in criminal procedures and creates controversy regarding the correctness of the alignment of national legal orders with the interpretations of both the ECtHR and the CJEU.[78] Nevertheless, Member States have so far expressed no interest in resolving this problem by clarifying terms such as "serious crime" and "minor offences."[79]

3.4 Electronic surveillance and human rights

Although for years the use of surveillance measures was mainly identified with interference with individuals' privacy, this view should now be considered outdated. Modern surveillance measures, both targeted and untargeted, also have the potential to negatively affect a number of other basic rights without having a clear impact on the individual's privacy. Even assuming that the intention of using surveillance in a given case is to gather information, the knowledge gained may not be related to the person to whom the measures were applied. Suffice it to say that according to the information disclosed, BND has for many years been carrying out extensive industrial espionage programmes aimed at

72 Recital (31) of Regulation 2023/1543.
73 Art. 263(3) of the IPA 2016.
74 Art. 7(2) of the Polish Criminal Code.
75 Art. 237(3) of the Polish Code of Criminal Procedure.
76 Art. 12(1) of the German Criminal Code, www.gesetze-im-internet.de/englisch_stgb/englisch_stgb.html.
77 Art. 13(2)(b) of the Spanish Criminal Code.
78 Letizia Paoli and others, 'Exploring Definitions of Serious Crime in EU Policy Documents and Academic Publications: A Content Analysis and Policy Implications' (2017) 23 *European Journal on Criminal Policy and Research* 269.
79 Thomas Wahl, 'Future of EU Substantive Criminal Law' *eucrim* (10 September 2019).

gathering economic information on entities of interest to German authorities (or to German businesses).[80]

In an increasing number of cases, however, the ultimate goal of using surveillance measures is not to gather information about individuals but to influence them: to shape their worldview, change their behaviour, or impose on them a narrative pushed by those in power. Therefore surveillance systems have proven to be an effective means of controlling social unrest, as well as creating a chilling effect on the right to information or voting rights.

At the same time, one should not lose sight of the military applications of surveillance techniques. There is no reason not to believe General Michael Hayden, former head of the NSA and CIA, when he says, "We kill people based on metadata."[81] Targeted killing[82] and signature strike[83] programmes are examples of rapidly expanding areas in which surveillance is applied, including indiscriminate programmes (see e.g. the earlier comments on the GHOST-HUNTER programme).

This section discusses selected – and the best understood – aspects of the impact of surveillance measures on fundamental rights. The semantics of rights introduced in the ECHR has been used for this purpose, as it forms a common legal acquis of European states, protecting the values and guarantees on which modern democracies have been built. At the same time, however, it should be noted that the following overview discusses only a selection of the most perceptible risks associated with indiscriminate surveillance programmes.[84]

3.4.1 Right to privacy

When the risks associated with the use of electronic surveillance systems are considered, breaches of privacy are examined most frequently.[85] The increasing

80 Maik Baumgärtner and Martin Knobbe, 'Sonderermittler Spricht von Klarem Vertragsbruch Der NSA' *Der Spiegel* (30 October 2015) <https://cli.re/97VNQR> accessed 6 September 2023. These allegations eventually led to new safeguards being implemented in the amended BND Act – see section 6.2 for details.

81 Margaret Hu, 'Metadeath: How Does Metadata Surveillance Inform Lethal Consequences?' in Russell A Miller (ed), *Privacy and Power* (Cambridge University Press 2017).

82 Giuseppe Zappalà, 'Killing by Metadata: Europe and the Surveillance – Targeted Killing Nexus' (2015) 1 *Global Affairs* 251.

83 KJ Heller, '"One Hell of a Killing Machine": Signature Strikes and International Law' (2013) 11 *Journal of International Criminal Justice* 89.

84 The discussion omits, for example, the right to property, referred to by Patrick Brayer and later, more extensively, in the German Federal Administrative Court's judgment in DE-CIX. Patrick Breyer, 'Telecommunications Data Retention and Human Rights: The Compatibility of Blanket Traffic Data Retention with the ECHR' (2005) 11 *European Law Journal* 365, 374–375. BVerwG 30 May 2018, 6 A 3.16, DE:BVerwG:2018:300518U6A3.16.0.

85 However, more recently there have been a growing number of studies presenting a more holistic view of the impact of surveillance on individual rights; see e.g. Amy Stevens and others, '"I Started Seeing Shadows Everywhere": The Diverse Chilling Effects of Surveillance in Zimbabwe' (2023) 10 *Big Data & Society* 205395172311586.

understanding of the dangers of surveillance is certainly also a result of the growing public interest in the cases of serious abuses in this area, which have been widely discussed in recent years. The view pointing to the strong and negative impact of surveillance on the sphere of privacy is built on the conviction that the purpose of monitoring an individual's activities is to obtain information concerning them – and thus to *reveal* aspects of their private life. And although in recent years the right to privacy has become almost a buzzword, used with dozens of meanings and to describe the most diverse types of interference with personal rights,[86] it is, in fact, protection from surveillance that still marks the core or the essence of establishing the legal protection of privacy. At the same time, it is a relatively new institution, whose roots go back to the early 20th century[87] and which, in terms of international law, derives from the human rights protection systems established after the Second World War.

It was not until the tragic experience of fascism, and later communism, that a better understanding was achieved of the mechanisms of totalitarian regimes and the links between the total surveillance of the individual and the perpetuation of non-democratic models of government. The encirclement of an individual by those in power and stripping them of dignity, ultimately leading to the deprivation of subjectivity, would not have been possible without the involvement of an elaborate state apparatus focused on gathering knowledge about citizens. The purpose behind the creation of such an elaborate apparatus was, in fact, not so much to identify all instances of insubordination to the government as to collect any information that might prove useful to ensure obedience. Although under fascist rule there were no technical capabilities for indiscriminate surveillance as it is known today, there is no doubt that Nazi Germany created its own model of "mass surveillance," in which the intensity of surveillance, its omnipresence, and the belief in the complete visibility of the individual served the purposes of social control.

The need to implement legal mechanisms to protect privacy led not only to the explicit recognition of this right in the catalogue of fundamental rights, but also to its inclusion among the most important basic rights (the so-called first-generation human rights).[88] As a result, the right to privacy was taken into consideration in the drafting of the Universal Declaration of Human Rights and later became one of the fundamental guarantees established in the European Convention on Human Rights. Independently, the right to privacy was guaranteed in the constitutional provisions of EU Member States (or, more

86 In this context it is worth recalling the words of Tom Gerety who, when discussing the definition of privacy, noted: "A legal concept will do us little good if it expands like a gas to fill up the available space." Tom Gerety, 'Redefining Privacy' (1977) *Harvard Civil Rights-Civil Liberties Law Review* 233, 234.

87 Cf. Megan Richardson, *The Right to Privacy: Origins and Influence of a Nineteenth-Century Idea* (Cambridge University Press 2017).

88 O Diggelmann and MN Cleis, 'How the Right to Privacy Became a Human Right' (2014) 14 *Human Rights Law Review* 441.

broadly, European states). While in some cases this right was inferred from other constitutional norms (e.g. in Germany, from the so-called general right of personality),[89] in most cases it was derived from norms explicitly introducing guarantees concerning respect for private life.[90] These norms were often supplemented by additional regulations establishing specific guarantees in the area of secrecy of correspondence[91] or the principle of inviolability of the home.[92]

Although constitutional regulations were shaped at different times, one can easily find in them the drafters' ingrained conviction of the need to provide special protection for the individual against interference by public authorities. As a result, for almost the whole of the 20th century the legal protection of privacy was linked explicitly to protection from government interference. The focus on horizontal threats was not only due to the historical experience of authoritarian rule, but also because of the then limited data collection capacity available to private actors.

From the perspective of the ECtHR case law, the protection of privacy encompasses not only the spheres of life explicitly mentioned in the Convention, such as the secrecy of correspondence and respect for the home or family life, but also other activities which, as a result of social or economic changes, are recognised as constituting an element of private life. The Convention is a living instrument[93] and, as the Court has repeatedly emphasised, "must be interpreted in the light of present-day conditions" to ensure its effectiveness.[94] As a result, over the years the ECtHR has not only examined the permissibility of various forms of interference with the right to privacy, but also interpreted the right itself – often leading to an expansion of its substantive scope. For example, in the *Uzun* case, decided in the first decade of 21st century, the Court pointed out that the collection of metadata was less severe for the individual than the interception of information on the content of correspondence.[95] On this basis, it recognised the admissibility of less stringent legal safeguards for cases involving the collection of user geolocation data. Several years later, however, when examining the Bulgarian retention laws, the Court noted that "the acquisition of that [meta]data through bulk interception can therefore be just as intrusive as the bulk acquisition of the content of communications."[96] This

89 Art. 2(1) of the Basic Law.

90 David Erdos, 'Comparing Constitutional Privacy and Data Protection Rights within the EU' (University of Cambridge 2021) Faculty of Law Research Paper No. 21/2021 17–19 <https://doi.org/10.2139/ssrn.3843653> accessed 6 September 2023.

91 In the case of Germany, it is, among others, Art. 10(1) of the Basic Law.

92 See e.g. Art. 9(1) of the Greek Constitution.

93 George Letsas, 'The ECHR as a Living Instrument: Its Meaning and Legitimacy' in Andreas Føllesdal, Birgit Peters and Geir Ulfstein (eds), *Constituting Europe* (Cambridge University Press 2013).

94 *Tyrer v. the United Kingdom* (5856/72) 25 April 1978 ECtHR at [31].

95 *Uzun v. Germany* (35623/05) 2 September 2010 ECtHR at [66].

96 *Ekimdzhiev and Others v. Bulgaria* (70078/12) 11 January 2022 ECtHR at [394].

conclusion led to the recognition that access to metadata and to the content of communications by public authorities should be regulated in the same way and therefore be subject to the same legal safeguards.[97] The *Ekimdzhiev v. Bulgaria* judgment demonstrates the evolution of the Court's interpretation in assessing the permissibility of the same surveillance measures, which is due to the perception of social changes leading to the need to redefine (expand) the content of the right to privacy.

In recent years, the jurisprudence of the European courts has also made increasing use of the "reasonable expectation of privacy" test. Although this standard is most often linked to English and US law, the ECtHR also uses it to examine the need to extend the Convention's legal protection to new areas of an individual's activity.[98] Thus, in *Bărbulescu v. Romania* the Court confirmed that the term "private life" also covers an employee's electronic correspondence conducted from their workplace.[99]

Much of the misunderstanding about the European standard for the application of surveillance laws concerns not the detailed assessment of the measures applied, but the very moment from which one can speak of interference with the right to privacy. The Court has repeatedly pointed out that any collection of data on individuals in public databases constitutes an interference with their privacy,[100] and in this respect both the intended purpose of the processing and even the circumstance of whether public authorities used the collected data for the performance of their tasks are irrelevant.[101]

In this sense, interference is the very act of depriving an individual of control over information concerning their private life. Once the information is collected, it is the entity carrying out this activity that determines the purpose of the processing, and consequently it is up to this entity whether the data will be further processed at all, and if so, how. The Court, therefore, rightly links the threat to the individual's rights not to the *consequences* of the application of surveillance – understood as the actual use of the material collected – but to the very fact of its acquisition. This is an apt interpretation, conveying the essence of establishing the legal protection of privacy, namely the intention to protect the individual from an abuse of state power resulting in the collection of redundant information. The technical method of organising the data collection process is irrelevant to the occurrence of this interference. This makes it necessary to reject the arguments that information systems cannot invade

97 Ibid. at [395].

98 Eric Barendt, '"A Reasonable Expectation of Privacy": A Coherent or Redundant Concept?' in Andrew T Kenyon (ed), *Comparative Defamation and Privacy Law* (Cambridge University Press 2016) <www.cambridge.org/core/product/identifier/9781316402467%23CN-bp-6/type/book_part> accessed 10 September 2023.

99 *Bărbulescu v. Romania* (61496/08) 5 September 2017 ECtHR.

100 *Amann v. Switzerland* (27798/95) 16 February 2000 ECtHR at [70].

101 *Kopp v. Switzerland* (13/1997/797/1000) 25 March 1998 ECtHR at [53].

privacy because they process information automatically, and an individual's privacy can only be invaded by another person.[102]

In this way, the Court also makes it clear that the fundamental danger of surveillance is the infringement of an individual's informational autonomy, and thus on their right to informational self-determination. Informational autonomy in many constitutional systems is a guarantee derived directly from dignity, which imposes specific obligations on public authorities to protect it.[103] The link between respect for dignity and the right to privacy is also discernible in other legal systems.[104]

The inviolability of dignity is the source of other rights, including the right to privacy. Thus, in a democratic state governed by the rule of law, the right to privacy is protected not only in the interest of the individual, but also for the general good. Increasingly, therefore, intrusive surveillance measures are being examined in terms of their impact not only on the individual but also on society as a whole. In this sense uncontrolled surveillance, by distorting the ideas on which a democratic state under the rule of law was founded, threatens the sustainability of the state's political system. Already in *Klass v. Germany* the ECtHR saw that a secret surveillance system introduced to protect national security created the risk "of undermining or even destroying democracy on the ground of defending it."[105] This is a very interesting observation, as it partly undermines the prevailing view that it is non-democratic governments that resort to extensive surveillance measures. In fact, there is increasing evidence that nowadays the process also works the other way around, namely that it is the availability of surveillance systems that corrupts those in power, contributing to non-democratic regime transitions.[106]

3.4.2 *Data protection*

While the modern form of the right to privacy in Europe derives directly from the human rights systems established after the Second World War, the genesis of the legal protection of personal data must be linked to the era of dynamic computerisation of public institutions, which started in the 1970s. Notably,

102 Cf. Richard A Posner, 'Privacy, Surveillance, and Law' (2008) 75 *University of Chicago Law Review* 245.

103 See the *Census Act* judgment (n 13) and Gerrit Hornung and Christoph Schnabel, 'Data Protection in Germany I: The Population Census Decision and the Right to Informational Self-Determination' (2009) 25 *Computer Law & Security Review* 84.

104 Florent Thouvenin, 'Informational Self-Determination: A Convincing Rationale for Data Protection Law?' (2021) 12 *JIPITEC* 246.

105 *Klass and Others v. Germany* (n 33) at [49].

106 See e.g. Veronika Nagy, 'How to Silence the Lambs? Constructing Authoritarian Governance in Post-Transitional Hungary' (2017) 15 *Surveillance & Society* 447; Ozgun Topak, 'The Making of a Totalitarian Surveillance Machine: Surveillance in Turkey Under AKP Rule' (2017) 15 *Surveillance & Society* 535; Marcin Rojszczak, 'Surveillance, Legal Restraints and Dismantling Democracy: Lessons from Poland' (2021) 17 *Democracy and Security* 1.

data protection was for many years defined as a *lex specialis* in relation to the protection of privacy. Its purpose was to safeguard the interests of the individual in the area of automated information processing. Only recently has the right to data protection acquired the status of an autonomous subjective right, both under EU law and in the constitutional provisions of many EU Member States.[107]

Still, this right is not universally recognised and is largely linked to the European legal model. It is the EU data protection law that is considered to be the most extensive,[108] thus also providing a model for the introduction of similar national regulations in third countries (non-EU states).[109] At the same time, however, not even in all democratic countries are personal data subject to legal protection. An example is the United States, where due to a different constitutional model no general right to data protection – which would be a source of specific regulations on acquiring and processing data concerning natural persons – has been established so far (see also section 6.7).

Traditionally, the inclusion of data protection in the catalogue of EU fundamental rights is linked with the entry into force of the Lisbon Treaty, giving the Charter of Fundamental Rights the same force as that of the EU treaties. It is worth noting, however, that also before the Lisbon reform the CJEU had repeatedly commented on the role and importance of data protection,[110] as well as emphasising the need to respect fundamental rights as an impassable barrier defining the framework for the functioning of the European Union.[111] The ECtHR, on the other hand, has derived data protection obligations directly from privacy guarantees.[112]

However, it is only relatively recently that the CJEU has provided an interpretation that makes the essence of the two rights clearer and thus allows the differences between them to be pointed out and distinguished.[113] Indeed,

107 For the early history of data protection laws in Europe, see Gloria González Fuster, *The Emergence of Personal Data Protection as a Fundamental Right of the EU*, vol 16 (Springer International Publishing 2014) 55–74 <https://link.springer.com/10.1007/978-3-319-05023-2> accessed 22 September 2023.

108 JP Albrecht, 'How the GDPR Will Change the World' (2016) 2 *European Data Protection Law Review* 287.

109 Wolf Jürgen Schünemann and Jana Windwehr, 'Towards a "Gold Standard for the World"? The European General Data Protection Regulation between Supranational and National Norm Entrepreneurship' (2021) 43 *Journal of European Integration* 859.

110 Maria O'Neill, 'The Issue of Data Protection and Data Security in the (Pre-Lisbon) EU Third Pillar' (2010) 6 *Journal of Contemporary European Research* 211.

111 Antonio Tizzano, 'The Role of the ECJ in the Protection of Fundamental Rights' in Anthony Arnull, Piet Eeckhout and Takis Tridimas (eds), *Continuity and Change in EU Law* (Oxford University Press 2008).

112 Juliane Kokott and Christoph Sobotta, 'The Distinction between Privacy and Data Protection in the Jurisprudence of the CJEU and the ECtHR' (2013) 3 *International Data Privacy Law* 222.

113 Orla Lynskey, 'Deconstructing Data Protection: The "Added-Value" of a Right to Data Protection in the EU Legal Order' (2014) 63 *International and Comparative Law Quarterly* 569.

recognising that the right to data protection is an autonomous right requires confirming that, at least to some extent, it protects goods and values that go beyond the sole purpose of protecting the right to privacy – in other words, that it is possible to infringe the right to data protection without affecting the individual's privacy sphere.[114]

Surprisingly, this difference can be identified relatively easily by examining states' surveillance practices. It is clear that traditional surveillance programmes based on covert surveillance and information gathering are a typical example of interference with the right to privacy. Nowadays, however, gathering massive collections of information increasingly does not require covert surveillance or interception programmes, nor does it involve *revealing* any new information. As a result of a kind of information exhibitionism, an increasing amount of data can be obtained from public sources. Notably, in most cases this information is published by the data subjects themselves, for example through social media. This leads to the question of whether analysing data made public by an individual may violate their privacy.

The question essentially concerns how information autonomy should be understood in the third decade of 21st century. If autonomy is considered to protect an individual's freedom and right to decide how information concerning them is made available, it should also include the freedom to decide who has access to the information they have disclosed and for what purpose it may be further processed. In this view, the mere disclosure of information does not deprive the individual of the right to control the circulation of such information. This interpretation is prevalent in Europe and indeed directly follows from current EU data protection legislation. However, it is not a universally accepted view. For example, in the United States – under the third-party doctrine – an individual cannot expect legal protection when they have voluntarily entrusted information concerning them to a third party.[115] For this reason alone, the collection and processing of publicly available data by US entities (not only SIAs) does not lead to a violation of the constitutional right to privacy (to the extent guaranteed by the Fourth Amendment).[116]

The above demonstrates the need for a broader view of Informational autonomy, i.e. not only as a tool to protect privacy. Therefore the right to privacy could be defined as the protection of the confidentiality of the sphere

114 In this regard, see the critique of the Court's early position in: Jeanne Pia Mifsud Bonnici, 'Exploring the Non-Absolute Nature of the Right to Data Protection' (2014) 28 *International Review of Law, Computers & Technology* 131, 138.

115 For an ongoing discussion of the third-party doctrine, see Orin S Kerr, 'The Case for the Third-Party Doctrine' (2008) 107 *Michigan Law Review* 561; Erin Murphy, 'The Case Against the Case for Third-Party Doctrine: A Response to Epstein and Kerr Symposium: Security Breach Notification Six Years Later' (2009) 24 *Berkeley Technology Law Journal* 1239.

116 It should also be recalled that the Fourth Amendment has a vertical effect, so it only covers intrusions made by public authorities.

of private life, while the protection of personal data needs be understood as the realisation of the individual's informational self-determination.[117]

Analysis of publicly available data is a mechanism used in big data systems to reveal new information about an individual. As indicated earlier, using only publicly available information it is possible to build algorithmic inferences about individual characteristics, including those considered particularly sensitive (e.g. health status, sexual orientation, worldview). Knowledge of this type can then be used to make individual decisions. This creates a particular risk for an individual who first loses control over the information concerning them and then is deprived of any real possibility of controlling or influencing the accuracy of the information obtained through automated processing.

A separate problem concerns the purpose(s) of the use of the data acquired. It is not uncommon for abuses in the application of surveillance laws to arise not from excessive data collection, but from overly extensive use of the data – in particular in contravention of the original purpose or for a longer period than permitted. An example is databases maintained by public entities on the basis of legislation and containing information necessary for a specific public task, which over time are also used for additional public tasks not considered at the moment the information was collected.

Going further, the right to data protection may be interfered with not only by storing data for longer than legally permissible but also for longer than is necessary to achieve the intended purpose of the processing. As the CJEU pointed out in the *Ligue des droits humains* case, "the longer the period for the retention of PNR data, the more serious the resulting interference."[118] Consequently, extending the period of the retention of lawfully collected data – although per se it will not constitute an infringement of the right to privacy – may lead to an unwarranted interference with the right to data protection. Thus, overly extensive data retention regulations were the reason why the Court of Justice declared the EU-US economic data exchange mechanisms (Safe Harbour, 2014),[119] the proposed EU-Canada international agreement on PNR data exchange (2015),[120] and the EU PNR Directive (2022) to be incompatible with EU law.[121] In each case, the Court pointed to a breach of the right to data protection insofar as the regulations under review allowed access to, and processing of, data by authorities for longer than necessary to achieve the purpose for which the data were collected.[122]

117 JC Buitelaar, 'Privacy: Back to the Roots' (2012) 13 *German Law Journal* 171.
118 *Ligue des droits humains ASBL v. Conseil des ministres* (C-817/19) EU:C:2022:491 at [253].
119 *Maximillian Schrems v. Data Protection Commissioner* (n 12).
120 *Opinion on the EU-Canada PNR Agreement* (Opinion 1/15) EU:C:2016:656.
121 *Ligue des droits humains ASBL v. Conseil des ministres* (n 118).
122 More on international data exchange standards is contained in section 5.4.

3.4.3 Right to information

Unlike data protection, freedom of expression has been the subject of legal protection for centuries. The importance of free speech and the opportunity to freely obtain information for the formation of a democratic society is the reason why this right is commonly included in the catalogue of fundamental human rights. The views of John Stuart Mill, who in discussing the importance of freedom of expression observed that "no society in which these liberties are not, on the whole, respected, is free, whatever may be its form of government," have lost none of their relevance in this regard.[123]

Similarly to the right to privacy and personal data protection, freedom of expression is not an absolute right in the European legal model. It may, therefore, be subject to limitations (derogations), *inter alia*, to the extent that this is necessary to protect the rights of others. While the right to privacy – in its original conception – serves to protect the individual from interest from the outside world (the famous concept of the "right to be let alone"),[124] the right to information, in its very essence, protects the possibility of having access to the opinions and views of others. Nowadays, the right to information is defined as two complementary rights. The first is freedom of expression, protecting the ability to formulate and disseminate one's own opinions and beliefs; the second is the right to freely seek and learn about content of interest to an individual.

Although electronic surveillance systems are widely perceived as primarily a threat to individual privacy, in reality – with the spread of indiscriminate surveillance measures – this type of technology can have an equally negative impact on the free exercise of freedom of expression. Understanding this phenomenon first requires recalling the work of Michael Foucault and his vision of panopticism, a fundamental element of which was the establishment of mechanisms leading to self-control by the individual (and ultimately by society as a whole).[125]

This goal was to be achieved by ensuring the full visibility of the individual's activity, thus instilling in the individual the conviction that their life is constantly monitored. Foucault emphasised that to achieve this goal, it is not necessary for the monitoring mechanisms to function all the time, but they only need to create such a conviction. In his conception, constant observation is, therefore, not a condition for the success of the surveillance model. What is crucial is the individual's conviction that such supervision exists and that the actions the individual takes can be subject to constant scrutiny. The concept of

123 John Stuart Mill, *On Liberty, Utilitarianism, and Other Essays* (Mark Philp and F Rosen eds, New edition, Oxford University Press 2015) 15.

124 Samuel D Warren and Louis D Brandeis, 'The Right to Privacy' (1890) 4 *Harvard Law Review* 193.

125 Michel Foucault, *Discipline and Punish: The Birth of the Prison* (Second Vintage Books edition, Vintage Books 1995) 207.

panopticism also clarifies the real potential of modern surveillance measures. It manifests itself not in the mass collection of information intended to reveal to observers knowledge previously unknown to them, but in the change in an individual's behaviour that occurs because of the fear that all their actions are being monitored.[126]

The counterpart of the individual's self-control in legal science is the so-called chilling effect. This phenomenon consists of individuals' self-restraint in exercising their rights for fear of negative consequences from public authorities. The chilling effect is especially relevant to the exercise of fundamental rights, including in particular the right to information. Avoiding the search for content that is of interest to the individual for fear of a reaction from state authorities can lead to a restriction of freedom of expression, which in turn violates one of the constitutional foundations of a democratic state.[127]

The impact of the surveillance-related chilling effect on the right to information was confirmed by Jonathon Penney, who, based on information search statistics from the English-language version of Wikipedia, showed that the number of people reading entries about ongoing surveillance programmes had decreased, contrary to what one might have expected after Edward Snowden had revealed the scale of these programmes in 2013.[128] Penney explains this phenomenon by the fear of reaching out for content that, albeit concerned with issues at the centre of public debate, could – in the users' view – lead to negative actions by public authorities. This is an example of the self-control that Foucault wrote about, which, however, does not lead people to refrain from voicing their views, but discourages them from seeking information and, as a result, forming their own worldview.

Clearly, because surveillance can prevent users from obtaining information of interest to them, it also acts as a barrier against its further transmission, and therefore restricts the very essence of freedom of expression. In recent years journalists have also been accused of deliberately creating a threat to state security by publishing information about extensive surveillance programmes.[129] Of course, the very use of surveillance measures affects the freedom of the media too. This argument has been confirmed by Anthony Mills, who described numerous examples of the negative impact of public authorities' surveillance powers on the work of independent journalists in several countries, including European ones.[130]

126 Ibid. 201.

127 Daragh Murray and Pete Fussey, 'Bulk Surveillance in the Digital Age: Rethinking the Human Rights Law Approach to Bulk Monitoring of Communications Data' (2019) 52 *Israel Law Review* 31, 43–47.

128 Jonathon W Penney, 'Chilling Effects: Online Surveillance and Wikipedia Use' (2016) 31 *Berkeley Technology Law Journal* 117.

129 Geoffrey R Stone, 'Free Speech and National Security' (2009) 84 *Indiana Law Journal* 939, 956–957.

130 Anthony Mills, 'Now You See Me – Now You Don't: Journalists' Experiences With Surveillance' (2019) 13 *Journalism Practice* 690.

Electronic surveillance programmes negatively affect the freedom to speak out on important public issues not only in the case of journalists, but also in the case of social media users. This is the conclusion of Elizabeth Stoycheff's research, in which she demonstrated the impact of electronic surveillance programmes on user behaviour on Facebook. Stoycheff presented to respondents a non-existent post about an attack by US troops on ISIS positions, and then asked them to rate the likelihood that they would comment on, share or like the post, or create their own post on the same topic. The data obtained showed that one of the factors significantly influencing the behaviour declared by the respondents was their beliefs about the surveillance programmes in place. As Stoycheff pointed out, her findings "provide empirical evidence that the government's online surveillance programs may threaten the disclosure of minority views and contribute to the reinforcement of majority opinion."[131]

Criticism of the government by citizens is a natural and intrinsic part of any democracy. The introduction of measures that – even indirectly – may disrupt or impede this criticism must lead to reflection on the intentions of those in power.

In reality, demonstrating the negative impact of extensive surveillance measures on the right to information is not a simple task. Indeed, the essence of the chilling effect is that it triggers self-control, whereby individuals refrain from taking actions to which they are entitled. This concept is based on the creation in individuals of a belief in the possible negative consequences of their actions, but without the direct impact of restrictive legislation. Hence, it is not surprising that cases before the European courts concerning the illegality of bulk programmes primarily challenge infringements of the right to privacy, and freedom of expression is usually invoked as a supplementary ground.[132] Therefore to date neither the ECtHR nor the CJEU has undertaken a thorough examination of the impact of electronic surveillance programmes on freedom of expression. In this respect, the ECtHR's reasoning in *Weber and Saravia v. Germany* that indiscriminate surveillance did not lead to "particularly serious" interference with freedom of expression can hardly be considered as still valid.[133]

The situation is different in the American legal model. Due to the constitutional position of freedom of expression, specifically protected by the First Amendment, non-governmental organisations have argued in recent

131 Elizabeth Stoycheff, 'Under Surveillance: Examining Facebook's Spiral of Silence Effects in the Wake of NSA Internet Monitoring' (2016) 93 *Journalism & Mass Communication Quarterly* 296, 327.

132 In this regard, it is worth mentioning the case of *Privacy International v. the United Kingdom* (46259/16), which explicitly concerned a violation of Art. 10 arising from surveillance measures. However, the complaint was dismissed as inadmissible due to the non-exhaustion of domestic remedies.

133 *Weber and Saravia v. Germany* (54934/00) 29 June 2006 ECtHR at [151].

years that indiscriminate programmes are impermissible as they restrict free speech.[134] An example of this is the case of *Wikimedia Foundation v. NSA*, in which, however, the US courts found a lack of standing arising from a failure to show that the plaintiff had, in fact, been subjected to surveillance practices. As a result, the case was dismissed for failure to demonstrate a legal interest.[135]

3.4.4 Right to peaceful assembly

The same means that can be used to invade privacy or affect free speech can, in practice, be used to unlawfully interfere with freedom of assembly and association.[136]

As the ECtHR has pointed out, one of the reasons for the legal protection of freedom of assembly is to provide a forum for public debate and open expression of protest.[137] In this respect, a strong link is perceived between freedom of expression and freedom of assembly,[138] which leads to the conclusion that measures that threaten the former right can clearly also be regarded as restricting the free exercise of the latter. At the same time, however, the autonomous nature of freedom of assembly manifests itself by the fact that this right provides a venue for public debate and the free presentation and exchange of views.[139]

It is clear from the Court's well-established jurisprudence that although the right to assemble is subject to limitations, these should serve the purpose of ensuring the peaceful nature of the event and, in particular, protect the rights of others to prevent disorder.[140] Moreover, it is the duty of states not only to ensure respect for the right to assemble by refraining from unauthorised

134 Sunny Skye Hughes, 'US Domestic Surveillance after 9/11: An Analysis of the Chilling Effect on First Amendment Rights in Cases Filed against the Terrorist Surveillance Program' (2012) 27 *Canadian Journal of Law and Society* 399; Shane Kaminski Margot E Witnov, 'The Conforming Effect: First Amendment Implications of Surveillance, Beyond Chilling Speech' (2014) 49 *University of Richmond Law Review* 465.

135 *Wikimedia Foundation v. National Security Agency/Central Security Service*, No. 20-1191 (4th Cir. 2021). In February 2023, the US Supreme Court denied the petition for review of the case. See also Kevin A Diehl, 'Can the U.S. Government Legally Monitor Private Communications? If So, Given the U.S.'s Significant Protection of Privacy Rights, What Government Cannot?' (2017) 17 *Journal of Public Affairs* e1659.

136 Ilia Siatitsa, 'Freedom of Assembly under Attack: General and Indiscriminate Surveillance and Interference with Internet Communications' (2020) 102 *International Review of the Red Cross* 181.

137 *Stankov and the United Macedonian Organisation Ilinden v. Bulgaria* (29221/95 and 29225/95) 2 October 2001 ECtHR at [97].

138 *Ezelin v. France* (11800/85) 26 April 1991 ECtHR at [37].

139 *Kudrevičius and Others v. Lithuania* (37553/05) 15 October 2015 ECtHR at [86].

140 In this context, see e.g. *Sergey Kuznetsov v. Russia* (10877/04) 23 October 2008 ECtHR at [43].

interference, but also to implement national law and practice to counter infringements by others (as part of the so-called positive duties).[141]

Naturally, the mere exercise of surveillance measures does not predetermine that an interference with the right to peaceful protest is inadmissible. In particular, video surveillance systems are a standard means used by law enforcement agencies to document the organisation and course of events, as well as to record incidents that fall beyond the acceptable limits of a peaceful assembly. However, as experience from countries in which surveillance measures are used on a large scale demonstrates, "surveillance erodes trust, affecting individuals' ability to form and maintain relationships; negatively impacting on their ability to build networks and to organize politically; and directly undermining the right to freedom of assembly."[142]

The potential for abuse is clear in the case of untargeted surveillance systems. Such abuse arises not only from direct interference with the event, e.g. through the use of participant identification measures, but also in the event's preparation phase.

A long-standing method of avoiding identification used by participants in protests unfavourable to those in power use is to cover their faces. Ensuring the anonymity of participants is indicated by the Human Rights Committee as an important aspect of the exercise of freedom of assembly.[143] However, in the case of indiscriminate measures, the identification of users does not require image recording and can be carried out entirely by electronic means, e.g. IMSI catcher devices (such as Stingrays)[144] or the user geolocation data retained by telecoms operators. In the same way as data brokers analyse the purchasing preferences of the attendees of large public events (e.g. concerts), public authorities can identify individuals participating in peaceful protests. In turn, the use of modern facial recognition systems (see section 2.4) makes it possible to establish the identity of individuals even if they put on masks at some point to make their identification difficult.[145]

Surveillance systems can also be used to impede the organisation of protests, both at the stage of early preparations (e.g. by blocking access to electronic communications or by monitoring fundraising) and when the organisation of the event itself is in progress (e.g. by identifying groups heading to the venue). During the recent protests in China, security forces used information from

141 *Wilson, National Union of Journalists and Others v. the United Kingdom* (30668/96, 30671/96 and 30678/96) 2 July 2002 ECtHR at [41].

142 Daragh Murray and others, 'The Chilling Effects of Surveillance and Human Rights: Insights from Qualitative Research in Uganda and Zimbabwe' (2023) *Journal of Human Rights Practice* huad020, 13.

143 Ibid. at [60].

144 Paul F Scott, 'Secrecy and Surveillance: Lessons from the Law of IMSI Catchers' (2019) 33 *International Review of Law, Computers & Technology* 349.

145 Paul Mozur, Claire Fu and Amy Chang Chien, 'How China's Police Used Phones and Faces to Track Protesters' *The New York Times* (2 December 2022).

CCTV systems, telecommunications systems (information on users' mobile devices) and even electronic transaction clearing systems (determining the identity of metro ticket buyers).

Similar measures for the automated collection of information on protest participants are also used in democratic countries.[146] In addition to collecting data on actual participants in assemblies, public authorities also analyse social media data to study trends and public sentiment.[147] Information on protests is then processed in big data systems (e.g. Dataminr) to model risks to public security.[148]

Thanks to the possibility of using various databases, including those at the disposal of private actors, public authorities can easily break the apparent anonymity of protest participants and by presenting their technical capabilities simultaneously create a chilling effect on the rest of society, thus influencing future decisions on public expression. An example is the participants in the peaceful protests in Ukraine in 2014, who received a text message, "Dear subscriber, you are registered as a participant in a mass disturbance." According to the declarations of the main telecoms operators, they had not provided data on the geolocation of the phones of users participating in the protest, nor had they themselves sent this type of message.[149]

3.4.5 Right to a fair trial

According to data from the European Commission, more than 80% of criminal proceedings currently involve digital evidence, that is, data that were originally produced in electronic form.[150] The increasingly widespread use of electronic evidence concerns not only the area of cybercrime but also crimes unrelated to the use of new technologies. Invariably, one of the categories of evidence that stirs the greatest controversy is material obtained through surveillance measures. Particular attention is paid to questions of the legality and admissibility of evidence gathered in this way, especially where surveillance measures have been used in breach of the applicable legal framework.

146 Stephen Owen, 'Monitoring Social Media and Protest Movements: Ensuring Political Order through Surveillance and Surveillance Discourse' (2017) 23 *Social Identities* 688.

147 Brian Wheeler, 'Whitehall Chiefs Scan Twitter to Head off Badger Protests' *BBC News* (20 June 2013) <www.bbc.com/news/uk-politics-22984367> accessed 6 September 2023.

148 Teresa Scassa, 'Law Enforcement in the Age of Big Data and Surveillance Intermediaries: Transparency Challenges' (2017) 14 *SCRIPT-ed* 239.

149 Andrew E Kramer, 'Ukraine's Opposition Says Government Stirs Violence' *The New York Times* (21 January 2014) <https://cli.re/44mv9K> accessed 6 September 2023.

150 'Impact Assessment – e-Evidence – the Appointment of Legal Representatives for the Purpose of Gathering Evidence in Criminal Proceedings' (European Commission 2018) SWD (2018) 118 Final 33 <https://cli.re/yr2Yo5> accessed 6 September 2023. It should be noted, however, that the data presented were considered unverifiable – see Sergi Vazquez Maymir, 'Anchoring the Need to Revise Cross-Border Access to e-Evidence' (2020) 9 *Internet Policy Review* 1.

As a general rule, the ECtHR case law does not explicitly prohibit the use of illegally obtained evidence. The Court emphasises the importance of the fairness of the whole procedure, in which obtaining evidence is an important but not a decisive stage.[151] Therefore it should not come as a surprise that the ECtHR has accepted the possibility of using illegally obtained evidence to make further evidentiary findings (indirect evidence). Even the use of surveillance measures in a way that violates the fundamental right to privacy does not automatically result in a violation of the right to a fair trial.[152] Moreover, in the ECtHR's view, evidence obtained from defective surveillance may – once assessed by the national court – constitute the only evidence presented in the case, provided there is no doubt about the reliability and credibility of the information collected.[153]

As individual Member States are free to shape their own criminal procedures,[154] the way in which surveillance data are managed and subsequently used in criminal proceedings can vary significantly. As a result, national courts may also differently assess the implications of using flawed evidence with respect to the fairness of the proceedings. A recent example was the high-profile Irish case of Graham Dwyer, charged with murder and sentenced to life imprisonment in 2015.[155] As the evidence presented raised concerns about its legality, the defence successfully challenged the legality of the application of the domestic retention rules in a civil case.[156] The case was finally examined by the CJEU, which in 2022 found that the Irish national legislation did not comply with EU law because it resulted in a disproportionate interference with fundamental rights.[157] Moreover, the CJEU confirmed that it is not possible for a national court to delay the entry into force of a judgment declaring the contested legislation invalid as incompatible with EU law, as the judgment has an *ex tunc* effect.[158] This means the retention evidence presented in the Dwyer case had been collected de facto without a legal basis (based on an invalid national law). In 2023, however, the Irish Court of Appeal dismissed the application to reopen the criminal case, finding that although the original proceedings had been flawed, the retention evidence had not been crucial to the case.[159]

151 *Schenk v. Switzerland* (10862/84) 12 July 1988 ECtHR at [46].
152 *Khan v. the United Kingdom* (35394/97) 12 May 2000 ECtHR at [34–40].
153 Ibid. at [38].
154 Generally, this area is not subject to EU law harmonisation. Balázs Garamvölgyi and others, 'Admissibility of Evidence in Criminal Proceedings in the EU' (2021) *eucrim – The European Criminal Law Associations' Forum* <https://eucrim.eu/articles/admissibility-evidence-criminal-proceedings-eu/> accessed 11 March 2021.
155 For a discussion of the circumstances of the crime and the investigation, see: Paul Williams, *Almost the Perfect Murder* (Penguin 2016).
156 *Dwyer v. Commissioner of an Garda Síochána* ([2018] IEHC 685) 06 December 2018 Irish High Court.
157 *G.D. v. the Commissioner of the Garda Síochána and Others* (n 62).
158 Ibid. at [123].
159 Mary Carolan, 'Graham Dwyer Loses Appeal against Conviction for Murder of Elaine O'Hara' *The Irish Times* (24 March 2023) <https://cli.re/npxkmd> accessed 6 September 2023.

Another area of the potentially negative impact of the use of surveillance measures on the right to a fair trial is the interception of communications covered by the doctrine of legal privilege. Significantly, although the ECHR – unlike the constitutional provisions of Member States – does not explicitly guarantee the confidentiality of communications between lawyers and their clients, the Strasbourg Court has considered such protections as "the basic requirements of a fair trial in a democratic society."[160] A breach of legal privilege is therefore permissible only in extraordinary circumstances, and only to the extent that it does not lead to the complete abolition of the secrecy of lawyer-client correspondence.[161] In effect, as the Court emphasised, "the right to effective legal assistance must be respected in all circumstances."[162]

However, the very concept of untargeted surveillance cannot be reconciled with the above standard. Indeed, such measures involve the collection of *all* classes of information belonging to an unspecified group of persons. Information covered by legal privilege can only be removed at the stage of substantive analysis of the data, and notably through a manual content analysis. In other words, lawyers are, in principle, subject to indiscriminate surveillance programmes with the same intensity as the general public, which leads to the risk that data covered by legal privilege will be massively collected and analysed in the same fashion as other categories of information.

A separate area of the impact of indiscriminate surveillance on the right to a fair trial is related to the preventive nature of the activities carried out – aimed at uncovering facts and connections that *may* indicate criminal activity. A regular task of law enforcement is prevention, aimed at uncovering information about previously unknown crimes. The rules for carrying out such tasks are subject to detailed legal procedures, which, however, are not always explicitly included in criminal law (pre-trial investigations are generally not carried out in the context of specific criminal proceedings).[163] In any case, however, measures aimed at uncovering criminal activity – including with the use of surveillance tools – should be implemented based on verifiable justification, which can be subject to judicial review at a later stage.[164]

The above considerations can directly refer to the very essence of the operation of indiscriminate surveillance programmes. Building up expertise and knowledge in the area of public security to profile individuals with no connection to criminal activity seems incompatible with respect for one of the fundamental paradigms of a democratic state, according to which oppressive actions of the state should be limited to what is strictly necessary and justifiable.

160 *S. v. Switzerland* (12629/87 and 13965/88) 28 November 1991 ECtHR at [48].
161 *Lanz v. Austria* (24430/94) 31 January 2002 ECtHR at [52].
162 *Sakhnovskiy v. Russia* (21272/03) 2 November 2010 ECtHR at [102].
163 See e.g. Art. 20cb of the Polish Police Act, relating to the collection of data for the prevention or detection of criminal offences at the pre-trial stage.
164 *Karabeyoğlu v. Turkey* (30083/10) 7 June 2016 ECtHR at [103].

However, it should be borne in mind that according to the ECtHR's jurisprudence, the crime detection activities (i.e. those carried out before the stage of initiating criminal proceedings) which do not subsequently lead to the initiation of criminal proceedings and the bringing of charges are not covered by guarantees concerning the right to a fair trial.[165] This conclusion seems pertinent given that – in the event of the initiation of criminal proceedings – the evidence presented in the case will, in principle, be assessed before a court, which provides an opportunity to exclude material that was collected illegally. As a result, violations occurring before the formal initiation of proceedings are (at least in the ECtHR jurisprudence) not linked to the right to a fair trial and are assessed by the Court in the context of the standards developed in relation to violations of the right to privacy.[166]

The use of sophisticated surveillance tools to detect unknown breaches of the law has also come under scrutiny from national courts. An example is the case of the Palantir system, an extensive analytical tool also used by European law enforcement agencies.[167] In March 2023, the German Constitutional Court held that the use of this type of technology required the implementation of additional safeguards, the absence of which under German domestic law led to a violation of the constitutional right to informational self-determination.[168]

3.5 Proportionality and necessity of surveillance measures

In the European legal model, most individual rights and freedoms are not absolute. The guarantees stemming from the ECHR, EU law (the Charter of Fundamental Rights) as well as the constitutional provisions of Member States may be subject to limitations, the implementation of which must, after all, be necessary to achieve a legally justified objective of a democratic state.

Derived from the jurisprudence of the German Constitutional Court,[169] the principle of proportionality is nowadays a widely used and fundamental instrument for assessing the permissibility of limiting the scope of fundamental rights. The proportionality test is intended to ensure that the degree of interference with individual rights cannot exceed the value of the protected good.[170] The proportionality assessment has several steps: first, it requires confirmation

165 *Lenev v. Bulgaria* (41452/07) 4 December 2012 ECtHR at [158].

166 In this respect, however, it is important to bear in mind the "substantive," rather than "formal," way in which the ECtHR defines the term "criminal charge." *G.C.P. v. Romania* (20899/03) 20 December 2011 ECtHR at [38].

167 Andrew Iliadis and Amelia Acker, 'The Seer and the Seen: Surveying Palantir's Surveillance Platform' (2022) 38 *The Information Society* 334.

168 For a broader discussion of the judgment, see section 6.3.

169 M Cohen-Eliya and I Porat, 'American Balancing and German Proportionality: The Historical Origins' (2010) 8 *International Journal of Constitutional Law* 263.

170 Tor-Inge Harbo, 'The Function of the Proportionality Principle in EU Law' (2010) 16 *European Law Journal* 158.

that the measure being implemented pursues a legitimate aim. This is followed by verification that the measure under examination is adequate to achieve that aim and is necessary to achieve it – which means the impossibility of achieving the aim of the interference in a different, less intrusive way (the so-called least intrusive means test).[171] It is only in the final step that the balancing of rights takes place, and an assessment is made as to whether the degree of restriction on the rights of the person against whom the measure under examination is to be applied is counterbalanced by the benefits of protecting the rights and freedoms of others. In practice, this last step, often referred to as "strict proportionality," leads to the greatest difficulties in terms of the final assessment of the permissibility of a particular measure in a democratic state.

In practice, however, there are many definitions of proportionality. Not only have individual courts developed their own standards in this respect, but in some cases the same court may apply different principles to different categories of cases.[172] Moreover, in the case of the ECtHR, the (Convention-based) test of "necessity in a democratic society" is used instead of the classic proportionality test. As the Convention does not introduce a single limitation clause (along the lines of Article 52(1) of the Charter of Fundamental Rights or the constitutional provisions of most European states), the scope of permissible limitation is defined individually in relation to particular rights. This, in turn, leads to a situation where certain legal concepts applied by the ECtHR have different meanings depending on the fundamental right concerned. As a result, although the test of necessity in a democratic society is a *sine qua non* for the introduction of restrictions on, for example, the right to privacy or freedom of expression, the criterion of necessity is subject to a separate interpretation by the ECtHR with regard to each of these rights.[173]

The relationship between the necessity and proportionality tests has been the subject of much debate over the years.[174] In *Breyer v. Germany*, the Strasbourg Court itself clarified this relationship by pointing out that an interference can be considered "necessary in a democratic society" when it responds to a "pressing social need and if it is proportionate to the legitimate aim pursued."[175] However, in that judgment, the Court seems to have actually defined the relationship between necessity and proportionality in the strict sense (the balancing of rights).

The protection of the interests of state security and the fight against crime – or more broadly, for general security – are legitimate objectives of a democratic state. Public authorities not only can, but also are obliged to, take action in

171 Aharon Barak, 'Proportionality (2)' in Michel Rosenfeld and András Sajó (eds), *The Oxford Handbook of Comparative Constitutional Law* (Oxford University Press 2012).

172 *Gillow v. the United Kingdom* (9063/80) 24 November 1986 ECtHR at [55].

173 *Handyside v. the United Kingdom* (5493/72) 7 December 1976 ECtHR at [48].

174 J Gerards, 'How to Improve the Necessity Test of the European Court of Human Rights' (2013) 11 *International Journal of Constitutional Law* 466.

175 *Breyer v. Germany* (50001/12) 30 January 2020 ECtHR at [88].

these areas, effectively countering threats to public security.[176] Measures of covert surveillance certainly fall within the category of measures that may prove useful in this respect.[177] In practice, the last two steps of the proportionality test – that is, the existence of the necessity to implement surveillance and the balancing of whether the severity of the interference planned does not outweigh the benefits to be gained through it – require detailed assessment.

Indeed, it is these last two steps of the proportionality test that are most often problematic when assessing the legality of the use of surveillance measures. This is because, first, the *usefulness* of surveillance – understood as its usefulness from the perspective of the state authorities – does not predetermine the *necessity* of its use.[178] The assessment of the necessity of implementing a particular measure must also seek to achieve a fair balance between the intended purpose and the degree of interference with personal rights and freedoms.[179]

The Strasbourg Court has emphasised in its jurisprudence that states, in carrying out national security tasks, enjoy "a fairly wide margin of appreciation" in the selection of measures they deem necessary to achieve national security objectives.[180] This discretion, however, is not unlimited and is subject to judicial review, the purpose of which is to confirm that the way in which the surveillance is implemented, ordered and supervised will "keep the interference to what is 'necessary in a democratic society'."[181]

In criminal surveillance cases, on the other hand, the Court has noted that telephone tapping constitutes a very serious interference with an individual's rights, which can only be justified on very serious grounds based on a well-founded suspicion that the person is engaged in criminal activity.[182]

In this respect the Court has, therefore, clearly differentiated the standard of assessment of surveillance programmes according to the purpose they are intended to serve, leaving the margin of appreciation in relation to surveillance in criminal cases narrower than when the measure is intended to serve national security objectives.

Therefore, in *Szabo and Vissy v. Hungary*, the Court held that interference with individual privacy as a result of the implementation of modern surveillance programmes must meet a "strict necessity" test. This test requires, first, confirmation that the surveillance measure under examination is, in the general sense, necessary for the protection of the democratic system; and second,

176 *Ramda v. France* (78477/11) 19 December 2017 ECtHR at [96].
177 *Klass and Others v. Germany* (n 33) at [48].
178 *Dudgeon v. the United Kingdom* (7525/76) 22 October 1981 ECtHR at [51].
179 For other approaches to assessing the necessity test, see Steven Greer, *The European Convention on Human Rights: Achievements, Problems and Prospects* (Repr, Cambridge University Press 2008) 218–220.
180 *Weber and Saravia v. Germany* (n 133) at [106].
181 *Kennedy v. the United Kingdom* (26839/05) 18 May 2010 ECtHR at [154].
182 *Iordachi and Others v. Moldova* (n 52) at [51].

that in the circumstances of the case its use was necessary for the acquisition of "vital intelligence."[183] In the Court's view, any measure not fulfilling both criteria is open to abuse. In a similar vein, the ECtHR has emphasised the role of the least intrusive means test as a necessary condition for the permissibility of surveillance measures.[184]

Significantly, although over the years the ECtHR has examined the criterion of necessity (proportionality) of surveillance measures in great detail, the majority of the cases in question concerned instances of targeted surveillance. The interpretation of the criterion of necessity in a democratic society which was put forward in these cases was also applied to the examination of cases involving bulk surveillance. In this regard, as recently as 2008 the ECtHR did not find that "there is any ground to apply different principles concerning the accessibility and clarity of the rules governing the interception of individual communications, on the one hand, and more general programmes of surveillance, on the other."[185]

It was only with the rapid development of technical capabilities that it became clear that such an approach was inadequate to mitigate the risks associated with the use of modern indiscriminate surveillance measures. Moreover, the Court itself, in the *Mustafa Sezgin Tanrıkulu* case, recognised the dangers of using insufficiently precise statutory powers which, created for the implementation of targeted surveillance, could also be used to carry out mass surveillance.[186] As a result, in its subsequent case law the Court considered the question of the necessity (proportionality) of untargeted measures in more detail (this issue is further developed in section 5.3).

Notwithstanding the proportionality test, when discussing the permissibility of interference with fundamental rights, particular attention should be paid to confirming that the measure under examination does not affect the essence of the fundamental right – that is, the part of the right protected in any case.

As a general rule, the essence of a fundamental right may be defined in either a relative or absolute manner.[187] In the former sense, it is determined in the context of the factual situation under examination and is thus dependent on the circumstances of the particular case in which the interference is to occur (or has occurred). Hence, the relative concept is largely similar to the classical proportionality test. Under the absolute concept, on the other hand, the essence of a given right is immutable and thus sets an impassable limit for interference with the individual's right. As the drafters of the Charter defined the proportionality test and the condition of respect for the essence

183 *Szabó and Vissy v. Hungary* (37138/14) 12 January 2016 ECtHR at [73].
184 *Roman Zakharov v. Russia* (47143/06) 4 December 2015 ECtHR at [260].
185 *Liberty and Others v. the United Kingdom* (58243/00) 1 July 2008 ECtHR at [63].
186 *Mustafa Sezgin Tanrıkulu v. Turkey* (27473/06) 18 July 2017 ECtHR at [51–60].
187 Maja Brkan, 'The Concept of Essence of Fundamental Rights in the EU Legal Order: Peeling the Onion to Its Core' (2018) 14 *European Constitutional Law Review* 332.

of a fundamental right separately, it seems that they opted for defining the essence of fundamental rights in an absolute manner.[188]

Understood in this way, the purpose of protecting the essence of a fundamental right is to ensure that any measure that actually deprives an individual of a core part of the right guaranteed to them is considered unacceptable, without the need for carrying out a proportionality test, regardless of how important the objective it pursues may be. Koen Lenaerts rightly concluded that when examining restrictions to Charter rights, it is first necessary to confirm that the measure under examination does not violate the essence of a fundamental right. In this regard, one can therefore speak of a kind of "respect for the essence of a fundamental right" test, which precedes the proportionality test proper and is de facto a precondition for applying the latter.[189] The obligation to respect the essence of a fundamental right – i.e. to delimit a certain core of rights to which absolute protection should be granted – may also derive from the constitutional provisions of Member States, as well as from the ECtHR case law.[190]

Hence, a clear definition of the essence of a fundamental right is quintessential for assessing the permissibility of actions taken by public authorities. The EU Court of Justice addressed this issue when examining the Data Retention Directive, pointing out that the provisions under examination did not violate the essence of the right to privacy, as they did not allow the content of the electronic correspondence exchanged to be intercepted.[191] The CJEU thus indicated that the untargeted (bulk) collection of a large part (potentially, the entirety) of the content of electronic communications was a measure that could not be reconciled with respect for the Charter guarantees as it would lead to an infringement of the essence of the right to privacy.[192] With regard to the same regulations, the CJEU considered that there was no infringement of the essence of the right to the protection of personal data, because the service providers on whom the obligation to collect metadata from electronic communications had been imposed were required to comply with specific rules on the security of data processing. *A contrario*, it can be concluded that a violation of the essence of the right to data protection would occur if the processing of personal data was carried out in a way that failed to protect "against accidental or unlawful destruction, accidental loss or alteration" of that information.[193]

188 *Contra* Orlando Scarcello, 'Preserving the "Essence" of Fundamental Rights under Article 52(1) of the Charter: A Sisyphean Task?' (2020) 16 *European Constitutional Law Review* 647.

189 Koen Lenaerts, 'Limits on Limitations: The Essence of Fundamental Rights in the EU' (2019) 20 *German Law Journal* 779.

190 Sébastien Van Drooghenbroeck and Cecilia Rizcallah, 'The ECHR and the Essence of Fundamental Rights: Searching for Sugar in Hot Milk?' (2019) 20 *German Law Journal* 904.

191 *Digital Rights Ireland* (n 66) at [39].

192 See also *Maximillian Schrems v. Data Protection Commissioner* (n 12) at [94] and *Tele2 Sverige* (n 59) at [101].

193 *Digital Rights Ireland* (n 66) at [40].

In this way, the CJEU clarified that the purpose (essence) of the right to privacy is to protect the individual from a free and total insight into their personal affairs. Therefore no measure – even if it meets the criterion of proportionality – can be considered compatible with EU law if it introduces restrictions so far-reaching that the right to privacy becomes a mere mirage, a hollowed-out shell emptied of the freedoms available to the general public. With regard to the protection of personal data, on the other hand, the Court emphasised the importance of establishing elementary rules for data processing, limiting the risk of errors leading to damage or destruction of data. As pointed out earlier, in such a view a breach of the right to data protection (including also the essence of this right) might not result in any negative consequences at all in terms of individual privacy.[194] Moreover, the Court recognised – unfortunately in a residual way – the risk of extensive retention provisions infringing the essence of the right to freedom of expression. This issue has not yet been discussed more extensively in the case law.[195]

3.6 Summary

The European legal model is built on respect for human dignity and the fundamental rights associated with it. In a democracy, public authorities have only such powers that are necessary to perform the duties entrusted to them. And while there is no doubt that the pursuit of general security objectives – including protection against external as well as internal threats – is an important task of the state, not every action related to it can be considered acceptable. This is particularly the case for tasks undertaken in the field of national security, which are often covered by secrecy and are used to implement measures that go beyond the strictly understood definitions of necessity and proportionality. Although governments – while also pursuing their political agendas – have a great deal of discretion in setting national security objectives, such decisions may also be subject to subsequent judicial review. Also, under EU law, which explicitly exempts the area of state security from EU regulation, the national security exception does not constitute a carte blanche for those in power to take arbitrary actions at their unfettered discretion.

Both the CJEU and the ECtHR have established strict tests for assessing the permissibility of measures interfering with fundamental rights, in particular with respect to secret surveillance programmes. These involve the necessity criterion itself and the various stages of the proportionality test. As modern surveillance measures can be a tool that is used not only to collect information

194 More extensively, see: Maja Brkan, 'The Essence of the Fundamental Rights to Privacy and Data Protection: Finding the Way Through the Maze of the CJEU's Constitutional Reasoning' (2019) 20 *German Law Journal* 864.

195 *Tele2 Sverige* (n 59) at [101]. The essence of the rights to freedom of expression and information has been further elaborated in subsequent case law, but still without being explicitly defined – see *Poland v. Parliament and Council* (C-401/19) EU:C:2022:297 at [76–81].

on individuals but also to influence their decision-making or limit the choices available to them, only a careful assessment of the underlying assumptions of the surveillance programmes being implemented can help determine whether the mechanism in question is compatible with the values shared in a democratic state. Such an analysis should include, in particular, the declared purpose of implementing surveillance (the "pressing social need" criterion); the existence of a real and serious threat and the necessity of using surveillance to eliminate it (the "strict necessity" criterion); the impossibility of taking less intrusive measures (the "least intrusive measure" criterion); and the compliance of the surveillance measure in question with the strict proportionality test.

References

Albrecht JP, 'How the GDPR Will Change the World' (2016) 2 *European Data Protection Law Review* 287.

Barak A, 'Proportionality (2)' in Michel Rosenfeld and András Sajó (eds), *The Oxford Handbook of Comparative Constitutional Law* (Oxford University Press 2012).

Barak A and Kayros D, *Human Dignity: The Constitutional Value and the Constitutional Right* (Cambridge University Press 2015).

Barendt E, '"A Reasonable Expectation of Privacy": A Coherent or Redundant Concept?' in Andrew T Kenyon (ed), *Comparative Defamation and Privacy Law* (Cambridge University Press 2016) <www.cambridge.org/core/product/identifier/9781316402467%23CN-bp-6/type/book_part> accessed 10 September 2023.

Baumgärtner M and Knobbe M, 'Sonderermittler Spricht von Klarem Vertragsbruch Der NSA' *Der Spiegel* (30 October 2015) <https://cli.re/97VNQR> accessed 6 September 2023.

Becchi P and Mathis K (eds), *Handbook of Human Dignity in Europe* (Springer International Publishing 2019).

Bonnici JPM, 'Exploring the Non-Absolute Nature of the Right to Data Protection' (2014) 28 *International Review of Law, Computers & Technology* 131.

Breyer P, 'Telecommunications Data Retention and Human Rights: The Compatibility of Blanket Traffic Data Retention with the ECHR' (2005) 11 *European Law Journal* 365.

Brkan M, 'The Concept of Essence of Fundamental Rights in the EU Legal Order: Peeling the Onion to Its Core' (2018) 14 *European Constitutional Law Review* 332.

–, 'The Essence of the Fundamental Rights to Privacy and Data Protection: Finding the Way Through the Maze of the CJEU's Constitutional Reasoning' (2019) 20 *German Law Journal* 864.

Buitelaar JC, 'Privacy: Back to the Roots' (2012) 13 *German Law Journal* 171.

Bureš O, 'Intelligence Sharing and the Fight against Terrorism in the EU: Lessons Learned from Europol' (2016) 15 *European View* 57.

Cameron I, *National Security and the European Convention on Human Rights* (Brill | Nijhoff 2000).

–, 'European Union Law Restraints on Intelligence Activities' (2020) 33 *International Journal of Intelligence and Counter Intelligence* 452.

Carolan M, 'Graham Dwyer Loses Appeal against Conviction for Murder of Elaine O'Hara' *The Irish Times* (24 March 2023) <https://cli.re/npxkmd> accessed 6 September 2023.

Cohen-Eliya M and Porat I, 'American Balancing and German Proportionality: The Historical Origins' (2010) 8 *International Journal of Constitutional Law* 263.

Craig PP, *The Lisbon Treaty: Law, Politics, and Treaty Reform* (Oxford University Press 2010).

Crespi S, 'The Applicability of Schrems Principles to the Member States: National Security and Data Protection within the EU Context' (2018) 43 *European Law Review* 669.

Diehl KA, 'Can the U.S. Government Legally Monitor Private Communications? If So, Given the U.S.'s Significant Protection of Privacy Rights, What Government Cannot?' (2017) 17 *Journal of Public Affairs* e1659.

Diggelmann O and Cleis MN, 'How the Right to Privacy Became a Human Right' (2014) 14 *Human Rights Law Review* 441.

Ehrlich P and Ehrlich A, 'The Environmental Dimensions of National Security' in Josef Rotblat and Vitalii I Goldanskii (eds), *Global Problems and Common Security* (Springer Berlin Heidelberg 1989).

Enders C, 'Right to Have Rights – The German Constitutional Concept of Human Dignity' (2010) 3 *NUJS Law Review* 253.

Erdos D, 'Comparing Constitutional Privacy and Data Protection Rights within the EU' (University of Cambridge 2021) Faculty of Law Research Paper No. 21/2021 <https://doi.org/10.2139/ssrn.3843653> accessed 6 September 2023.

Foucault M, *Discipline and Punish: The Birth of the Prison* (Second Vintage Books edition, Vintage Books 1995).

Garamvölgyi B and others, 'Admissibility of Evidence in Criminal Proceedings in the EU' (2021) eucrim – The European Criminal Law Associations' Forum <https://eucrim.eu/articles/admissibility-evidence-criminal-proceedings-eu/> accessed 11 March 2021.

Gerards J, 'How to Improve the Necessity Test of the European Court of Human Rights' (2013) 11 *International Journal of Constitutional Law* 466.

Gerety T, 'Redefining Privacy' (1977) *Harvard Civil Rights-Civil Liberties Law Review* 233.

Gondek M, 'Extraterritorial Application of The European Convention on Human Rights: Territorial Focus in the Age of Globalization?' (2005) 52 *Netherlands International Law Review* 349.

González Fuster G, *The Emergence of Personal Data Protection as a Fundamental Right of the EU*, vol 16 (Springer International Publishing 2014) <https://link.springer.com/10.1007/978-3-319-05023-2> accessed 22 September 2023.

Greer S, *The European Convention on Human Rights: Achievements, Problems and Prospects* (Repr, Cambridge Univ Press 2008).

Grimm D, Wendel M and Reinbacher T, 'European Constitutionalism and the German Basic Law' in Anneli Albi and Samo Bardutzky (eds), *National Constitutions in European and Global Governance: Democracy, Rights, the Rule of Law* (TMC Asser Press 2019) <http://link.springer.com/10.1007/978-94-6265-273-6_10> accessed 8 September 2023.

Grondel SH, 'COVID-19, the Ubiquitous National Security Threat: Lessons Learned Around the Globe' (2021) 49 *International Journal of Legal Information* 66.

Harbo T-I, 'The Function of the Proportionality Principle in EU Law' (2010) 16 *European Law Journal* 158.

Heller KJ, '"One Hell of a Killing Machine": Signature Strikes and International Law' (2013) 11 *Journal of International Criminal Justice* 89.

Heselhaus S and Hemsley R, 'Human Dignity and the European Convention on Human Rights' in Paolo Becchi and Klaus Mathis (eds), *Handbook of Human Dignity in Europe* (Springer International Publishing 2019) <http://link.springer.com/10.1007/978-3-319-27830-8_47-1> accessed 9 March 2021.

Hornung G and Schnabel C, 'Data Protection in Germany I: The Population Census Decision and the Right to Informational Self-Determination' (2009) 25 *Computer Law & Security Review* 84.

Hu M, 'Metadeath: How Does Metadata Surveillance Inform Lethal Consequences?' in Russell A Miller (ed), *Privacy and Power* (Cambridge University Press 2017).

Hughes SS, 'US Domestic Surveillance after 9/11: An Analysis of the Chilling Effect on First Amendment Rights in Cases Filed against the Terrorist Surveillance Program' (2012) 27 *Canadian Journal of Law and Society* 399.

Iliadis A and Acker A, 'The Seer and the Seen: Surveying Palantir's Surveillance Platform' (2022) 38 *The Information Society* 334.

'Impact Assessment – e-Evidence – the Appointment of Legal Representatives for the Purpose of Gathering Evidence in Criminal Proceedings' (European Commission 2018) SWD (2018) 118 Final <https://cli.re/yr2Yo5> accessed 6 September 2023.

Jones J, 'Human Dignity in the EU Charter of Fundamental Rights and Its Interpretation Before the European Court of Justice' (2012) 33 *Liverpool Law Review* 281.

Kaminski ME and Witnov S, 'The Conforming Effect: First Amendment Implications of Surveillance, beyond Chilling Speech' (2014) 49 *University of Richmond Law Review* 465.

Kerr OS, 'The Case for the Third-Party Doctrine' (2008) 107 *Michigan Law Review* 561.

Klabbers J and Leino P, 'Death by Constitution? The Draft Treaty Establishing a Constitution for Europe' (2003) 4 *German Law Journal* 1293.

Kokott J and Kokott J, 'The European Convention and Its Draft Treaty Establishing a Constitution for Europe: Appropriate Answers to the Laeken Questions?' (2003) 40 *Common Market Law Review* 1315.

Kokott J and Sobotta C, 'The Distinction between Privacy and Data Protection in the Jurisprudence of the CJEU and the ECtHR' (2013) 3 *International Data Privacy Law* 222.

Kramer AE, 'Ukraine's Opposition Says Government Stirs Violence' *The New York Times* (21 January 2014) <https://cli.re/44mv9K> accessed 6 September 2023.

Lantis JS, 'Strategic Culture and National Security Policy' (2002) 4 *International Studies Review* 87.

Lenaerts K, 'Challenges Facing the European Court of Justice after the Treaty of Lisbon' (2010) 2 *Analele Universitatii din Bucuresti: Seria Drept* 1.

–, 'Limits on Limitations: The Essence of Fundamental Rights in the EU' (2019) 20 *German Law Journal* 779.

Letsas G, 'The ECHR as a Living Instrument: Its Meaning and Legitimacy' in Andreas Føllesdal, Birgit Peters and Geir Ulfstein (eds), *Constituting Europe* (Cambridge University Press 2013).

Lynskey O, 'Deconstructing Data Protection: The "Added-Value" of a Right to Data Protection in the EU Legal Order' (2014) 63 *International and Comparative Law Quarterly* 569.

Marguery T, 'European Union Fundamental Rights and Member States Action in EU Criminal Law' (2013) 20 *Maastricht Journal of European and Comparative Law* 282.

Milanović M, *Extraterritorial Application of Human Rights Treaties: Law, Principles, and Policy* (1. publ, Oxford Univ Press 2011).

Milanović M and Papić T, 'The Applicability of the ECHR in Contested Territories' (2018) 67 *International and Comparative Law Quarterly* 779.

Mill JS, *On Liberty, Utilitarianism, and Other Essays* (Mark Philp and F Rosen eds, New edition, Oxford University Press 2015).

Mills A, 'Now You See Me – Now You Don't: Journalists' Experiences with Surveillance' (2019) 13 *Journalism Practice* 690.

Mitsilegas V, *EU Criminal Law after Lisbon. Rights, Trust and the Transformation of Justice in Europe* (Hart Publishing 2018).

Mozur P, Fu C and Chang Chien A, 'How China's Police Used Phones and Faces to Track Protesters' *The New York Times* (2 December 2022).
Murphy E, 'The Case Against the Case for Third-Party Doctrine: A Response to Epstein and Kerr Symposium: Security Breach Notification Six Years Later' (2009) 24 *Berkeley Technology Law Journal* 1239.
Murray D and Fussey P, 'Bulk Surveillance in the Digital Age: Rethinking the Human Rights Law Approach to Bulk Monitoring of Communications Data' (2019) 52 *Israel Law Review* 31.
Murray D and others, 'The Chilling Effects of Surveillance and Human Rights: Insights from Qualitative Research in Uganda and Zimbabwe' (2023) Journal of Human Rights Practice huad020.
Nagy V, 'How to Silence the Lambs? Constructing Authoritarian Governance in Post-Transitional Hungary' (2017) 15 *Surveillance & Society* 447.
'National Security Strategy and Strategic Defence and Security Review 2015' (HM Government 2015).
Neocleous M, 'From Social to National Security: On the Fabrication of Economic Order' (2006) 37 *Security Dialogue* 363.
Öberg J, 'Union Regulatory Criminal Law Competence After Lisbon Treaty' (2011) 19 *European Journal of Crime, Criminal Law and Criminal Justice* 289.
–, 'Trust in the Law? Mutual Recognition as a Justification to Domestic Criminal Procedure' (2020) 16 *European Constitutional Law Review* 33.
O'Neill M, 'The Issue of Data Protection and Data Security in the (Pre-Lisbon) EU Third Pillar' (2010) 6 *Journal of Contemporary European Research* 211.
Owen S, 'Monitoring Social Media and Protest Movements: Ensuring Political Order through Surveillance and Surveillance Discourse' (2017) 23 *Social Identities* 688.
Paoli L and others, 'Exploring Definitions of Serious Crime in EU Policy Documents and Academic Publications: A Content Analysis and Policy Implications' (2017) 23 *European Journal on Criminal Policy and Research* 269.
Patel KK, *Project Europe: Myths and Realities of European Integration* (Meredith Dale tr, Cambridge University Press 2020).
Penney JW, 'Chilling Effects: Online Surveillance and Wikipedia Use' (2016) 31 *Berkeley Technology Law Journal* 117.
Posner RA, 'Privacy, Surveillance, and Law' (2008) 75 *University of Chicago Law Review* 245.
Richardson M, *The Right to Privacy: Origins and Influence of a Nineteenth-Century Idea* (Cambridge University Press 2017).
Rojszczak M, 'Surveillance, Legal Restraints and Dismantling Democracy: Lessons from Poland' (2021) 17 *Democracy and Security* 1.
Rouvroy A and Poullet Y, 'The Right to Informational Self-Determination and the Value of Self-Development: Reassessing the Importance of Privacy for Democracy' in Serge Gutwirth and others (eds), *Reinventing Data Protection?* (Springer Netherlands 2009).
Ryngaert C, 'Clarifying the Extraterritorial Application of the European Convention on Human Rights (Al-Skeini v. the United Kingdom)' (2012) 28 *Utrecht Journal of International and European Law* 57.
Scarcello O, 'Preserving the "Essence" of Fundamental Rights Under Article 52(1) of the Charter: A Sisyphean Task?' (2020) 16 *European Constitutional Law Review* 647.
Scassa T, 'Law Enforcement in the Age of Big Data and Surveillance Intermediaries: Transparency Challenges' (2017) 14 *SCRIPT-ed* 239.
Scheuner U, 'Fundamental Rights in European Community Law and in National Constitutional Law' (1975) 12 *Common Market Law Review* 171.

Schünemann WJ and Windwehr J, 'Towards a "Gold Standard for the World"? The European General Data Protection Regulation between Supranational and National Norm Entrepreneurship' (2021) 43 *Journal of European Integration* 859.
Scott PF, 'Secrecy and Surveillance: Lessons from the Law of IMSI Catchers' (2019) 33 *International Review of Law, Computers & Technology* 349.
Siatitsa I, 'Freedom of Assembly under Attack: General and Indiscriminate Surveillance and Interference with Internet Communications' (2020) 102 *International Review of the Red Cross* 181.
Stevens A and others, '"I Started Seeing Shadows Everywhere": The Diverse Chilling Effects of Surveillance in Zimbabwe' (2023) 10 *Big Data & Society* <https://doi.org/10.1177/205395172311586>.
Stone GR, 'Free Speech and National Security' (2009) 84 *Indiana Law Journal* 939.
Stoycheff E, 'Under Surveillance: Examining Facebook's Spiral of Silence Effects in the Wake of NSA Internet Monitoring' (2016) 93 *Journalism & Mass Communication Quarterly* 296.
Thouvenin F, 'Informational Self-Determination: A Convincing Rationale for Data Protection Law?' (2021) 12 *JIPITEC* 246.
Tizzano A, 'The Role of the ECJ in the Protection of Fundamental Rights' in Anthony Arnull, Piet Eeckhout and Takis Tridimas (eds), *Continuity and Change in EU Law* (Oxford University Press 2008).
Topak O, 'The Making of a Totalitarian Surveillance Machine: Surveillance in Turkey Under AKP Rule' (2017) 15 *Surveillance & Society* 535.
Van Drooghenbroeck S and Rizcallah C, 'The ECHR and the Essence of Fundamental Rights: Searching for Sugar in Hot Milk?' (2019) 20 *German Law Journal* 904.
Vazquez Maymir S, 'Anchoring the Need to Revise Cross-Border Access to e-Evidence' (2020) 9 *Internet Policy Review* 1.
Wahl T, 'Future of EU Substantive Criminal Law' *eucrim* (10 September 2019).
Warren SD and Brandeis LD, 'The Right to Privacy' (1890) 4 *Harvard Law Review* 193.
Wheeler B, 'Whitehall Chiefs Scan Twitter to Head off Badger Protests' *BBC News* (20 June 2013) <www.bbc.com/news/uk-politics-22984367> accessed 6 September 2023.
Williams P, *Almost the Perfect Murder* (Penguin 2016).
Zappalà G, 'Killing by Metadata: Europe and the Surveillance – Targeted Killing Nexus' (2015) 1 *Global Affairs* 251.

4 Shaping the European standard for electronic surveillance

4.1 Introduction

The permissibility of the use of various forms of electronic surveillance has for years been the subject of particular attention from both national constitutional courts and international courts. The multiplicity of the cases they've examined – reflecting the differences in respect of the legal models adopted, the areas in which surveillance is used, its intrusiveness, and the social acceptance of such measures – significantly influences the process of shaping the standards of minimum legal safeguards to limit the risk of abuse of power. This process is also considerably influenced by the different scopes of competence of individual courts as well as the different standards of review applied by them.

Therefore as of today there is no single comprehensive and universally accepted standard for assessing the legality of surveillance in the European legal model. Instead, in the European courts' jurisprudence several standards of review are applied, differing both in the degree of detail of the solutions adopted and in their scope of application. Given the special position of the European Convention on Human Rights, the Strasbourg Court's (ECtHR's) jurisprudence is of key importance for the unification of the interpretation applied. The ECtHR's jurisprudence should also be considered the richest, not only because of the number of cases that the ECtHR has decided but also due to their diversity – in terms of the purposes of the surveillance measures applied, their intrusiveness, and the different legal safeguards implemented in individual countries.

The principal aim of this chapter is to discuss the key legal safeguards that should be implemented to mitigate the risks associated with the use of electronic surveillance measures by public authorities. The starting point will be a discussion of the criteria of the accessibility and foreseeability of the law which set the framework for the ECtHR's review. One of the fundamental problems affecting judicial review of secret surveillance programmes is the lack of knowledge on the part of the individuals involved that their rights are being violated. Of course, in many cases secrecy is a necessary condition for the effectiveness of surveillance actions. At the same time, however, it can create an incentive to implement extra-legal measures or limit the effectiveness of external oversight.

DOI: 10.4324/9781003449263-4

Hence, one of the fundamental issues related to the ECtHR's jurisprudence is the concept of *in abstracto* review, which is of particular importance in the case of regulations applied in the area of state security.

This chapter will also present the most important evaluation criteria developed in the case law of the European courts. Historically, a significant proportion of the cases heard by them have concerned eavesdropping on communications in the context of criminal procedures. As a result, it is precisely the requirements defined for surveillance in criminal cases – first comprehensively discussed in *Huvig v. France* – that have been of particular importance in shaping the European standards. Interestingly, given the dynamic development of surveillance techniques, these criteria also had to be adapted relatively quickly to the peculiarities of programmes conducted in the area of state security and bulk surveillance measures.

Hence, it seems particularly interesting to present not only the interpretation of the individual elements of the *Huvig/Weber* test, but also the directions of its evolution, leading to the development of a framework for assessing cases of minor interference (*Uzun*) as well as a standard that takes into account the peculiarities of programmes involving bulk interception of communications (*Big Brother Watch*).

The chapter closes with a presentation of how the Strasbourg (ECtHR) acquis has been adopted in the CJEU's jurisprudence. While only a decade ago the role of the CJEU in shaping the Member States' legal framework for electronic surveillance was minor, today it is not an exaggeration to say that the Luxembourg Court's case law fundamentally influences the level of protection of individuals against extensive surveillance programmes carried out by public authorities. It is therefore clear that the EU Court of Justice not only builds on the legal concepts adopted in the Strasbourg jurisprudence, but also innovatively and inspiringly develops them, ultimately creating a coherent model for the protection of individual rights – a model which is considered by many to be more consistent than that resulting from the ECtHR case law.

In this respect, the considerations presented herein will also serve as a prelude to the next chapter, which will examine how the interpretation of the same requirements by the CJEU and the ECtHR has led to de facto different conclusions in the jurisprudence of the two courts regarding the conditions for the legality of indiscriminate surveillance programmes and their compatibility with the principles of a democratic state.

4.2 Secret surveillance programmes as interference with individual rights

As a general rule, judicial review of the actions of public authorities may be conducted *in abstracto* or *in concreto*, the latter taking into account the context of the circumstances of a specific case. The *in abstracto* type of scrutiny is usually associated with the jurisprudence of constitutional courts, and its purpose is to confirm that the legal provisions reviewed – which establish specific surveillance powers – comply with provisions stemming not only from the basic law but also from overarching international norms. The *in concreto* type of scrutiny concerns the way in which the powers of public authorities are exercised in a specific case, and thus allows both the legal safeguards established and the practice of their application by public authorities to be assessed.

Both types of review are exercised with regard to surveillance programmes. However, given the secret nature of surveillance activities, in many cases *in abstracto* review remains the only type of review available to protect the individual against overly extensive state powers. This is because the unavailability of this type of review would require the individual to demonstrate a legal standing in each case, i.e. to prove an actual interference with their rights. Only if the surveillance measure challenged were actually used in relation to the individual would the individual's right to judicial review of the action taken by the public authorities materialise. Obviously, such a review could only be *ex post* and would therefore be of limited use in protecting against future violations.

The possibility of abstract review – also with regard to potential violations – is particularly relevant for human rights systems. Yet as a general rule it follows from the well-established ECtHR case law that complaints concerning violations of Convention guarantees should not be of an abstract nature, which means, in particular, that the assessment of the compatibility of national practices with Convention obligations should be conducted in the circumstances of a particular case.[1]

Applying such an interpretation to surveillance programmes would, however, create the risk that due to the lack of transparency in the operation of secret services, judicial protection of the individual against the abuse of surveillance powers would de facto become illusory. Therefore it was in *Klass v. Germany* that the ECtHR held that the effectiveness of the Convention guarantees required *in abstracto* review of secret surveillance programmes.[2] In this regard, the Court pointed out that an individual could derive their legal interest (the victim status) from the mere existence of covert surveillance measures, without the need to prove that such measures had actually been applied to them.

However, abstract review thus defined has certain limitations. In particular, it cannot be conducted to assess national provisions unrelated to the circumstances of the case under examination.[3] Therefore, as a general rule, complainants may not seek recognition of hypothetical violations or violations that, in the circumstances of the case, could not have occurred.[4] Nor does the

1 *Roman Zakharov v. Russia* (47143/06) 4 December 2015 ECtHR at [164].

2 Janneke Gerards, 'Abstract and Concrete Reasonableness Review by the European Court of Human Rights' (2020) 1 *European Convention on Human Rights Law Review* 218.

3 *Taxquet v. Belgium* (926/05) 16 November 2010 ECtHR at [83].

4 *Tauira and 18 Others v. France* (28204/95) 4 December 1995 ECtHR.

Convention provide for *actio popularis* complaints. The hearing of a complaint should, therefore, not be of a wholly abstract nature, with the complainant challenging legislation solely based on its incompatibility with the guarantees under the Convention.[5] Thus, for example, in *Malone*, the Court indicated the possibility of an abstract review of the contested surveillance provisions, but at the same time stressed that the circumstances of the case showed that, having regard to the applicant's criminal past, the provisions under review "were liable to be employed."[6]

As a result, in cases involving surveillance in the context of criminal procedure, the Court carried out an abstract assessment subsidiarily, to the extent that the circumstances of the case so required.[7] As regards surveillance applied by security services, on the other hand, it has also accepted for examination more general complaints, the subject of which was, in fact, an assessment of the legality of the application of a particular legal regime rather than the practice of its application in relation to specific complainants.[8] In these types of cases, the Court indicated that a sufficient condition for recognising the victim of a violation status was the "very existence of legislation . . . permitting secret surveillance . . . under which all persons in the country concerned can potentially have their mail and telecommunications monitored."[9]

The Court has also accepted for examination complaints by persons indirectly affected by unlawful actions of public authorities. This also applies to instances of the use of surveillance measures where an indirect victim was defined as a person whose rights have been violated as a result of surveillance being applied in relation to a third party. Thus, in *Liblik and Others v. Estonia*, the applicants included two legal persons who indicated that their Convention guarantees had been violated as a result of wiretapping against a member of their supervisory body (the third applicant). Although the Court considered that eavesdropping on a member of a company's governing body did not automatically interfere with the legal person's right to privacy, it was nevertheless sufficient to recognise the admissibility of the applicant's complaint. In this respect, it was irrelevant that these companies had not been formally subjected to the surveillance activities and that no order for surveillance measures had been issued with respect to them.[10]

5 *Centre for Legal Resources on behalf of Valentin Câmpeanu v. Romania* (47848/08) 2 August 1984 ECtHR at [101]. Cf. William Schabas, *The European Convention on Human Rights: A Commentary* (First Paperback edition, Oxford University Press 2017) 782.
6 *Malone v. the United Kingdom* (8691/79) 2 August 1984 ECtHR at [64].
7 *Huvig v. France* (11105/84) 24 April 1990 ECtHR at [31]; *Kruslin v. France* (11801/85) 24 April 1990 ECtHR at [32]; *Goranova-Karaeneva v. Bulgaria* (12739/05) 8 March 2011 ECtHR at [47].
8 *Kennedy v. the United Kingdom* (26839/05) 18 May 2010 ECtHR at [124].
9 *Association for European Integration and Human Rights and Ekimdzhiev v. Bulgaria* (62540/00) 28 June 2007 ECtHR at [58–59].
10 *Liblik and Others v. Estonia* (173/15) 28 May 2019 ECtHR at [112].

The above conclusion has far-reaching implications for the ability to lodge a complaint about state surveillance activities. In fact, it predetermines the availability of legal recourse for persons whose data have been, or – adopting the criterion of reasonable likelihood discussed earlier – *may have been* intercepted as a result of surveillance activities targeting third parties. This opens up the possibility of challenging the unlawfulness of surveillance also in cases where there is no formal basis for the application of the available domestic judicial remedies. This conclusion is also in line with previous case law, in which the Court indicated that the application of surveillance measures to a lawyer led to an interference with the rights of the persons whose cases the lawyer was handling.[11] Obviously, this interference is separate and independent from the interference with the rights (e.g. the right to privacy) of the lawyer and – in the light of the ECtHR case law – can be asserted independently of the legal action taken by the person directly affected by the surveillance. In particular, even if that person does not take any action, this does not preclude those indirectly affected by the surveillance from taking legal remedies. This interpretation is clearly aimed at ensuring the full effectiveness of the Convention guarantees, which would not be possible if protection were denied to persons indirectly affected by state surveillance activities.

The above considerations should be referred to in cases where the surveillance targeted technology corporations (see the description of the OPTIC NERVE programme in section 1.2). Applying the same reasoning opens up the possibility for the users of digital services to seek protection if their data was (or could have been) intercepted and processed in one of the indiscriminate electronic surveillance programmes. Given the transnational nature of such services, this leads to the question of the possibility for foreigners – i.e. persons who are not subject to a particular state's jurisdiction – to complain about the national surveillance laws of that state. To put this simpler: can a French resident claim legal protection against the massive interception of their data at the DE-CIX by the German BND?[12] Because both France and Germany are parties to the European Convention on Human Rights, does defining obligations thereunder as including respect for the rights of a state's own citizens (residents) not negate the concept of ensuring the full effectiveness of the Convention in the (supranational) area of its application?

While there is no doubt that domestic surveillance programmes can be challenged using national law – and at a later stage, also before the ECtHR – it is unclear how such protection should be granted in the case of foreigners. This is a complex issue, which can be analysed both under the constitutional provisions of individual European states and under human rights instruments.

11 *Wieser and Bicos Beteiligungen GmbH v. Austria* (74336/01) 16 October 2007 ECtHR at [45].

12 DE-CIX, located in Frankfurt, is one of the main European Internet exchange points (IXP). See more in section 1.4.

In principle, the ECHR is an instrument of international law that imposes obligations on states parties to respect the rights of individuals under their jurisdiction. These guarantees, therefore, extend to persons under the effective control of government bodies. In practice, this protection is linked to possessing a citizenship status or residence in the territory of the state concerned or stems from some other connecting factor making it possible to show that the state's acts (or omissions) did, in fact, lead to a violation of a particular person's rights. Clearly, the purpose of the Convention is not to oblige the Contracting Parties to guarantee respect for the fundamental rights to persons located in other jurisdictions with no connection to a party to the Convention. Therefore the Court has indicated in its jurisprudence that the Convention is an instrument that must be considered in the context of the Contracting Parties' legal space and "was not designed to be applied throughout the world, even in respect of the conduct of Contracting States."[13] As a result, in its jurisprudence the Court uses the criterion of "effective control" as a condition for recognising a state's responsibility for activities outside its territory.[14]

Although the "effective control" test makes it possible to resolve doubts regarding the application of the Convention in many extraterritorial cases – especially those involving the use of armed forces beyond the national borders[15] – it is insufficient in cases involving modern means of electronic surveillance. Insofar as regards the earlier example concerning the DE-CIX surveillance practice, it is impossible to assume that it is the German state's role to ensure French citizens' privacy. Clearly, the German state does not exercise effective control that would allow French residents' rights to be protected. And because it does not exercise effective control, it cannot infringe rights that it did not guarantee in the first place.

However, the uncritical adoption of such an interpretation would lead to a situation where surveillance activities carried out by one state could not be legally challenged before the ECtHR by citizens (residents) of other states. Moreover, it would also hinder the development of a common, supranational, standard for the legal regulation of electronic surveillance. As a result, such an interpretation would also be incompatible with the principle of ensuring the full effectiveness of the Convention, as the actions of one state leading to a

13 *Banković and Others v. Belgium and Others* (52207/99) 10 May 2001 ECtHR at [80]; but *contra*: *Al-Skeini and Others v. the United Kingdom* (55721/07) 7 July 2011 ECtHR at [142].

14 'Guide on Article 1 of the European Convention on Human Rights' (European Court of Human Rights 2020) 1 <https://cli.re/JpwmZW> accessed 6 September 2023; Cedric Ryngaert, 'Clarifying the Extraterritorial Application of the European Convention on Human Rights (*Al-Skeini v. the United Kingdom*)' (2012) 28 *Utrecht Journal of International and European Law* 57.

15 Michael Duttwiler, 'Authority, Control and Jurisdiction in the Extraterritorial Application of the European Convention on Human Rights' (2012) 30 *Netherlands Quarterly of Human Rights* 137.

violation of the (Convention) rights of citizens of another party to the Convention would de facto remain outside the jurisdiction of the European Court of Human Rights.

This problem can be partly resolved by applying the so-called concept of preservation of legal space, introduced by the Court.[16] It applies in cases where one state party to the Convention undertakes actions resulting in the assumption of control over part of the territory of another state party to the Convention. According to the Court, such a case should be interpreted to secure for the persons under the occupying state's control all the rights vested in them under the Convention. This interpretation avoids a situation whereby these individuals would find themselves in a "legal void" in which their rights would be jeopardised because the home country would not exercise control over the area in which they are located.

One of the consequences of applying the concept of "legal space" to electronic surveillance programmes is the recognition that activities resulting in interference with the rights of persons under the jurisdiction of other states parties to the Convention are not excluded from the application of the Convention guarantees – including also when undertaken abroad. To date, however, this position has not been explicitly confirmed in the ECtHR's jurisprudence. It is therefore difficult to prejudge how the exercise of legal protection in such a case will look in practice. In particular, it seems that it should include granting citizens of other states parties to the Convention the possibility to avail themselves of adequate legal protection mechanisms that are at the disposal of a state's own citizens. Whether these must be identical measures remains an open question.

The issue of the cross-border use of surveillance programmes is also assessed by national constitutional courts. Noteworthy is the recent bVerfG ruling on the BND Act.[17] The subject matter of that case was whether German public authorities (in particular, the Federal Foreign Intelligence Service) remained bound by constitutional guarantees when carrying out intelligence operations abroad. The court aptly pointed out that in establishing an absolute obligation to respect human dignity, the German constitution does not impose any territorial or personal restrictions on applying this norm. This obligation therefore extends to all actions taken by public authorities, and thus prohibits the establishment and/or use of surveillance mechanisms that would lead to a violation of dignity, regardless of whether they concern persons under the effective control of the German authorities or foreigners with no ties to the German state. In this regard, bVerfG convincingly pointed out that the public authorities of a democratic state cannot consider that the obligation to respect fundamental rights extends only to persons under the jurisdiction of national laws. Interestingly, at the same time it emphasised that this conclusion does not prevent the

16 *Cyprus v. Turkey* (25781/94) 10 May 2001 ECtHR at [78].
17 BVerfG 19 May 2020 (1 BvR 2835/17) DE:BVerfG:2020:rs20200519.1bvr283517.

introduction of a different standard of legal safeguards applicable to electronic surveillance carried out abroad. The Court justified its position by pointing to the lower risk that foreign intelligence measures pose to the state's democratic system, as well as the lower possibility of the information obtained being used in a way that actually interferes with the rights of foreigners permanently residing outside the country.[18]

The interpretation provided by BVerfG must, of course, be read against the background of the German constitution, which contains particularly far-reaching guarantees regarding the inviolability of human dignity.[19] In comparison, the US Supreme Court has repeatedly indicated that the Fourth Amendment guarantees do not apply to foreigners outside the United States. The Court has explained that "[n]either the Constitution nor the laws passed in pursuance of it have any force in foreign territory unless in respect of our own citizens."[20] This view expresses the belief, still strong in American jurisprudence, that the purpose of adopting the Fourth Amendment was not to limit public authorities but to protect the rights of citizens.[21] Understood in this way, the protective function of the law must be linked to its applicability. In the US Supreme Court's view, not only is there no need for measures to limit the effectiveness of government action in an area outside US jurisdiction, but doing so may actually harm the interests of the state.[22] This interpretation of the law has also been confirmed in more recent case law, in particular in *Hernandez v. Mesa*, in which the Court held that actions by government agents conducted from within the United States whose effects materialise abroad do not violate Fourth Amendment guarantees.[23]

The difference between the European and US legal models also relates to the impossibility of an abstract review of the legality of surveillance programmes conducted in the United States. The federal courts, when examining the legitimacy of complaints brought before them, require that a legal interest (*locus standi*)[24] be demonstrated, which means showing that the plaintiffs were actually subjected to the challenged surveillance measures. Because of

18 Marcin Rojszczak, 'Extraterritorial Bulk Surveillance after the German BND Act Judgment' (2021) 17 *European Constitutional Law Review* 53; Katrin Kappler, 'Consequences of the German Constitutional Court's Ruling on Germany's Foreign Intelligence Service: The Importance of Human Rights in the Cooperation of Intelligence Services' (2022) 23 *German Law Journal* 173.

19 Christoph Enders, 'Right to Have Rights – The German Constitutional Concept of Human Dignity' (2010) 3 *NUJS Law Review* 253. See also the analysis presented in section 3.2.

20 *United States v. Curtiss-Wright Export Corp*, 299 U.S. 304 (1936).

21 *United States v. Verdugo-Urquidez*, 494 U.S. 259 (1990) at [260].

22 Ibid. at [273].

23 Alina Veneziano, 'Applying the U.S. Constitution Abroad, from the Era of the U.S. Founding to the Modern Age' (2019) 46 *Fordham Urban Law Journal* 602, 617.

24 In this context, see the analysis of the *Clapper v. Amnesty International USA* case presented in: Daniel J Solove and Paul M Schwartz, *Information Privacy Law* (Sixth edition, Wolters Kluwer 2018) 446–453.

the secrecy of surveillance activities and the possibility for the government to invoke the so-called state secrets privilege,[25] in practice it is virtually impossible to prove that the plaintiffs are claiming protection against actual abuse by public authorities.[26] This problem was made clear in *Clapper v. Amnesty International*, in which the US Supreme Court indicated that "respondents have no actual knowledge of the Government's [surveillance] targeting practices. Instead, respondents merely speculate and make assumptions about whether their communications with their foreign contacts will be acquired."[27] Moreover, because US SIAs can implement surveillance programmes on a variety of legal bases,[28] the Court pointed out that even if it were demonstrated that the complainants had been subjected to surveillance, it would remain an open question whether the surveillance practices used had been implemented under the contested legislation (in *Clapper*, it was the Foreign Intelligence Surveillance Act of 1978). In other words, given the peculiarities of US surveillance programmes, complainants should demonstrate not only the fact that public authorities have intercepted their communications but also the legal basis on which the interception was founded. In practice, this leads to the failure of subsequent lawsuits brought to federal courts by human rights organisations.[29]

The US example illustrates that were it not for the ECtHR's different interpretation of the admissibility of abstract review, the same difficulties that have been present in the United States for years could also limit the effectiveness of judicial review of the legality of surveillance programmes conducted in European countries.

4.3 Accessibility and foreseeability of the law

A preliminary step in the examination of the permissibility of domestic surveillance measures by the European Court of Human Rights is to assess whether the criterion of lawfulness arising from Article 8(2) of the Convention is met. By "in accordance with the law," the Court understands the cumulative fulfilment of three conditions. The first is of a substantive nature and requires that the scope and procedure for the use of surveillance be supported by national law. The second criterion relates to the accessibility of the law, i.e. the possibility for an individual to become familiar with the provisions that form the basis for the application of surveillance measures. The third criterion concerns the quality of the law – and, in effect, its foreseeability, which allows an individual to understand the circumstances in which an individual's activities may lead to

25 See e.g. the reasoning presented in *Jewel v. NSA*, 965 F. Supp. 2d 1090 (N.D. Cal. 2013).

26 Margaret B Kwoka, 'The Procedural Exceptionalism of National Security Secrecy' (2017) 97 *Boston University Law Review* 103.

27 *Clapper v. Amnesty Int'l USA*, 568 U.S. 398 (2013).

28 For a broader examination of the US legal framework for conducting indiscriminate surveillance, see section 6.7.

29 See e.g. the reasoning presented in *Klayman v. Obama*, No. 14-5004 (D.C. Cir. 2015).

intrusive surveillance measures being applied to them. The way in which the fulfilment of these requirements is assessed must make it possible to confirm that the legal model under scrutiny was in compliance with the principle of the rule of law, which in particular should entail mechanisms that protect the individual against the arbitrariness of the decisions taken and abuses of power.[30]

As a rule, the European Convention on Human Rights does not require that restrictions on rights are laid down solely in the form of a statute. Thus, although the ECtHR has repeatedly emphasised the importance of the criterion of the quality of the law, when examining national laws it has accepted that some aspects of surveillance procedures may be regulated by non-statutory law.[31] In this regard, the Court has emphasised the need to understand the term "law" in its substantive sense, covering also unwritten law, like established doctrines in common law.[32] However, even in such cases the lack of a statutory framework regulating the key aspects of the use of covert surveillance measures cannot be considered to be "in accordance with the law."[33]

The Court has recalled that irrespective of statutory law, an essential element of the application of the law is judicial interpretation – and the related margin of appreciation, which is an intrinsic element of the administration of justice. In this respect, it has affirmed that such interpretation may lead to the explanation (clarification) of the applicable laws, thereby influencing the practice of their application.[34]

The concept of law is similarly broadly understood under the Charter of Fundamental Rights. Significantly, in some editions of the Charter, the term "provided for by law" is also translated as explicitly requiring the introduction of a statutory law.[35] This is, however, due to referring the substantive compatibility criterion to the constitutional standard applicable in many states, which requires limitations to fundamental rights to be introduced in the form of a statute.

Although in its jurisprudence, the ECtHR defines the criterion of substantive legality by indicating that surveillance measures must have "some basis in domestic law,"[36] at the same time it emphasises that these regulations must be accessible and be formulated with sufficient precision. This condition is, therefore, not fulfilled by regulations which, although properly adopted, have not been published in a manner that is accessible to citizens.[37] However, in *Roman Zakharov v. Russia* the Court accepted the possibility of making legal

30 *Uzun v. Germany* (35623/05) 2 September 2010 ECtHR at [64].
31 *Malone v. the United Kingdom* (n 6) at [68].
32 *Sunday Times v. the United Kingdom* (6538/74) 26 April 1979 ECtHR at [48]. Bart van der Sloot, 'The Quality of Law' (2020) 11 *JIPITEC* 160, 164.
33 *Khan v. the United Kingdom* (35394/97) 12 May 2000 ECtHR at [28].
34 *Kopp v. Switzerland* (13/1997/797/1000) 25 March 1998 ECtHR at [62].
35 See e.g. the Polish ("*przewidziane ustawą*") translation of Art. 52(2) of the Charter.
36 *Amann v. Switzerland* (27798/95) 16 February 2000 ECtHR at [50].
37 *Shimovolos v. Russia* (30194/09) 21 June 2011 ECtHR at [59].

acts (implementing regulations) available in an official magazine published by the Ministry of Communications and distributed by subscription only.[38] In the above case, a regulation discussing the technical aspects of the use of surveillance measures had been published in this way. However, this regulation also contained aspects relevant from the perspective of the individual's rights, affecting the assessment of the intrusiveness of the measures applied.

This example points to an important problem: the degree of detail of the legal regulations adopted, understood as the transparency of the procedures established and their adequate precision. In discussing this condition, the ECtHR noted that national law should provide "adequate indication as to the circumstances in and conditions on which public authorities are empowered to resort to any such secret measures."[39] This requirement cannot, however, be interpreted as establishing a condition that the law should, in every case, exhaustively regulate all eventualities regarding the surveillance applied. Therefore the degree of detail in the legal regulation must depend on the purpose of its establishment, the essence of the measure in question, its intrusiveness, its scope of application, and the categories of information that can be collected with its use.[40] These criteria will not be met by regulations that leave too much discretion to the executive.[41] Moreover, leaving too much discretion to courts can also lead to a violation of the principle of the accessibility and foreseeability of the law.[42] While, as pointed out earlier, judicial interpretation is an important element in the administration of justice and also in adapting the legal model to changing social needs, it is unacceptable to allow courts complete discretion in their decision-making.[43] The purpose of ensuring the foreseeability of the law is, understood in this way, therefore to protect against abuses of power and not to provide an instrument for the individual to actually determine whether they are under surveillance in a given situation and whether they should adjust their conduct accordingly.[44]

In the case of criminal surveillance measures, the foreseeability of the law is therefore closely linked to the establishment of basic criteria for the use of surveillance – which include defining the categories of offences which may entail the authorisation of surveillance measures and the categories of persons who may be subjected to them (more on the basic legal safeguards are set out in the next section of this chapter). In that case, implementing surveillance mechanisms against a person who has no links to a specific type of criminal activity may constitute an abuse of power. This example simultaneously illustrates the

38 *Roman Zakharov v. Russia* (n 1) at [242].
39 *Halford v. the United Kingdom* (20605/92) 25 June 1997 ECtHR at [49].
40 *S. and Marper v. the United Kingdom* (30562/04 and 30566/04) 4 December 2008 ECtHR at [96].
41 *Hasan and Chaush v. Bulgaria* (30985/96) 26 October 2000 ECtHR at [84].
42 *Azer Ahmadov v. Azerbaijan* (3409/10) 22 July 2021 ECtHR at [71].
43 *Ahmet Yıldırım v. Turkey* (3111/10) 18 December 2012 ECtHR at [67–68].
44 *Vukota-Bojić v. Switzerland* (61838/10) 18 October 2016 ECtHR at [67].

difference between the criterion of foreseeability of the law and the proportionality of the measures adopted. A correctly adopted and published criminal statute allowing intrusive forms of surveillance to be ordered in relation to a criminal offence will meet the criteria of both substantive legality and foreseeability, whereas it may violate the condition of necessity insofar as it leads to a disproportionate interference with the right to privacy (for more on proportionality, see section 3.5). Consequently, the Court does not examine proportionality if it has already decided that the legislation under review infringes the principle of the foreseeability of the law.[45]

The link to the prevention of serious crime required for surveillance in criminal cases is not present in the case of measures applied in the area of state security. The condition of the foreseeability of the law requires, also with regard to national security purposes, that the regulations enacted be sufficiently precise to allow an assessment of whether surveillance is applied lawfully. However, in this regard the Court has pointed out that states cannot be obliged to enact legislation listing in detail all situations that may entail the implementation of covert surveillance operations. In particular, it considered that the criterion of the foreseeability of the law is met when the scope of surveillance is limited to cases of preventing acts of terrorism and undertaking rescue operations.[46]

At the same time, however, the Court has noted the risk that provisions which refer too broadly to the area of national security could be used for the surveillance of any individual, and potentially the whole society. These doubts have led to the question of whether mass surveillance activities could be considered to meet the foreseeability criterion. Thus, leaving aside the assessment of proportionality, whether the possibility of interception and analysis by public authorities of any electronic communications – if it is based on the applicable law – meets the condition of sufficient clarity and thus foreseeability.

This issue was addressed in detail in the case of *Big Brother Watch v. UK*, in which, among other things, the national legislation underpinning the GCHQ's implementation of electronic intelligence programmes was assessed.[47] According to the UK legislation under review,[48] the use of surveillance measures (an interception warrant) may be authorised where this is necessary, *inter alia*, to achieve state security objectives, to combat serious crime, or to protect the UK's economic interests.

In examining the foreseeability criterion, the Court pointed out that, in fact, all international communications that crossed UK borders fell within the scope of the regulation. However, considering the context of indiscriminate

45 *Valenzuela Contreras v. Spain* (58/1997/842/1048) 30 July 1998 ECtHR at [59–61].

46 *Szabó and Vissy v. Hungary* (37138/14) 12 January 2016 ECtHR at [64].

47 *Big Brother Watch and Others v. the United Kingdom* [GC] (58170/13, 62322/14 and 24960/15) 25 May 2021 ECtHR.

48 Sec. 5(3) of the Regulation of Investigatory Powers Act 2000.

surveillance programmes, the Court concluded that in practice, it was impossible to further clarify the scope of the measure *in abstracto*. As a result, it held that the UK legislation met the foreseeability test to the extent required to verify compliance with Article 8 of the Convention.[49]

The reasoning put forward above is questionable. This is because, on the surface, the Court departed from its earlier interpretation, in which it had emphasised the relationship between the foreseeability of the law and the protection against arbitrariness on the part of those in power. The essence of this protective mechanism is to provide the individual with a tool to assess the consequences of their actions and their relation to the use of intrusive surveillance measures. However, inasmuch as it is not possible to exhaustively describe all possible uses of surveillance measures, it is necessary to accept certain generalisations – but not in the nature of blanket norms. An element of the UK surveillance regime – in addition to the statutory provisions – is also the detailed regulations described in the Code of Practice, which has been formally approved and is binding on the executive.[50] This code describes in detail the legal safeguards implemented, explaining the procedures applied to the collection, processing, and use of electronic data. On this basis, the Court considered the UK regulations under examination to sufficiently fulfil the criterion of the foreseeability of the law.

It can thus be seen that the Court, in examining indiscriminate surveillance programmes, partly shifted the focus of the assessment of their permissibility by introducing, instead of a detailed test of foreseeability, a more rigorous analysis of the quality of the legal safeguards implemented. In doing so, the Court thus considered that bulk surveillance programmes, being of a different nature from the targeted measures applied in the context of criminal procedure, could not be effectively restricted *in abstracto*. This controversial approach leads to the acceptance of a deviation from the previously developed case law due only to differences in the technical architecture of a particular IT system. In the ECtHR's view, if the foreseeability of the law is an important criterion for examining the lawfulness of surveillance, the failure to meet this condition should in itself constitute a reason for a deeper analysis of whether the measure under examination can be reconciled with respect for fundamental rights. Unfortunately, such an analysis is lacking in the Court's most recent case law.

The arguments put forward in *Big Brother Watch v. UK* regarding the possibility of relating the foreseeability criterion to the reality of the operation of indiscriminate surveillance programmes can be contrasted with the conclusions of the *Centrum för rättvisa v. Sweden* case.[51] Its subject was the evaluation of Swedish surveillance legislation applied in the area of military

49 *Big Brother Watch and Others v. the United Kingdom* [GC] (n 47) at [376].
50 Ibid. at [366].
51 *Centrum för rättvisa v. Sweden* [GC] (35252/08) 25 May 2021 ECtHR.

intelligence. In this case, however, the domestic statute contained a more detailed – compared with the UK regulations – list of eight threats justifying the implementation of bulk surveillance measures. The list includes, *inter alia*, external military threats; the fight against international terrorism and other cross-border crime; the proliferation of weapons of mass destruction; serious threats to critical infrastructure; and foreign intelligence activities against Swedish interests.[52] Importantly, in defining the scope of the FRA's indiscriminate surveillance, the Swedish legislature did not use the general concept of "national security" at all.

An analysis of the Swedish legislation highlights the weakness of the British legislation, which entrusts the executive with overly broad powers, potentially leading to the risk of abuse of power. It is impossible not to get the impression that the Court, in its assessment, could (and should) have found the British regulations to be in breach of the foreseeability criterion, based on exactly the same reasoning it had used 2 years earlier in assessing the Hungarian legislation, when it had noted that "discretion granted to the executive in the sphere of national security [should not] be expressed in terms of unfettered power."[53] It is worth adding that doubts about how to interpret the foreseeability test in relation to indiscriminate surveillance programmes were also noted in the dissenting opinions to the *Big Brother Watch* judgment.[54]

4.4 Minimum legal safeguards and the intrusiveness of surveillance

A key step in the judicial assessment of surveillance legislation is to confirm that the regulations under examination contain adequate safeguards to minimise the risk of abuse of power. This adequacy should be examined taking into account not only the specifics of the legal system in question, but also the intrusiveness of the measures being implemented. As a result, the more serious the interference with individual rights, the more stringent and multifaceted the safeguards should be. An important element of this process is, of course, the assessment of proportionality – making it possible to finally decide whether the surveillance regime under examination can be reconciled with respect for the principles and values on which democratic states are built.

The European Convention on Human Rights does not contain a catalogue of detailed legal safeguards that would be mandatory when implementing electronic surveillance measures. Neither the Charter of Fundamental Rights nor the constitutional provisions of individual Member States contain such a catalogue. This is because the subject matter in question is regulated by ordinary

52 Art. 1 of the Swedish Act on Signals Intelligence Defence Activities, SFS 2008:717.

53 *Szabó and Vissy v. Hungary* (n 46) at [65].

54 *Big Brother Watch and Others v. the United Kingdom* [GC] (n 47) P. Lemmens, F. Vehabović and M. Bošnjak (concurring) at [12].

statutes, and the level of detail of the regulations adopted in this area varies greatly and depends on many factors, including historical ones or those related to the legal model in force. As a result, the process of shaping supranational standards for electronic surveillance was directly related to the jurisprudence of the ECtHR, which by examining the complaints submitted to it gradually developed its own standard of review, allowing it to assess the quality of the law examined. Importantly, this standard on the one hand had to ensure sufficient precision – to consolidate the most important control mechanisms throughout the Convention's territorial scope of application – and on the other hand could not be overly detailed, so that it could be implemented by states in which significantly different legal regulations were sometimes in place.

As a result, this process has led to the development of not one but several standards of legal safeguards – differing not only in the number of criteria for the assessment of national law but also in their restrictiveness and the margin of appreciation left to national legislatures.

4.4.1 Criminal surveillance – a Huvig/Weber *test and beyond*

For years, the key standard for legal safeguards was the *Huvig/Weber* test, developed on the basis of early ECtHR case law[55] and concerning cases of surveillance in criminal proceedings in which targeted means of interception of telephone communications were examined. Although from today's perspective this is a relatively narrow area of surveillance, cases of this type dominated applications submitted to the Court for many years.

In *Malone v. UK*, the Court noted that the phrase "in accordance with the law" – which is the Convention's condition for imposing restrictions on the right to privacy[56] – should be understood as requiring not only compliance with national law but also that the quality of the regulations be ensured.[57] Therefore, in the Court's view in relation to surveillance carried out in criminal cases, this requirement leads to the need not only to ensure the accessibility and foreseeability of the law (see earlier sections of this chapter) but also to establish an appropriate legal framework governing the manner in which the powers granted to the executive are exercised.[58] National legislation should

55 Of particular importance for the development of the European standard for the application of surveillance was the case of *Klass v. Germany*, which not only predetermined that abstract review of surveillance laws was possible (see section 4.2) but also established important criteria for the assessment of national law. See the impact of this case on national law in: Karen C Burke, 'Secret Surveillance and the European Convention on Human Rights' (1980) 33 *Stanford Law Review* 1113.

56 It should be recalled that the ECHR lacks a general limitation clause. As a result, different rights are accompanied by different sets of possible restrictions and rules for their implementation. In the context of national security, see the comments in section 3.3.

57 *Malone v. the United Kingdom* (n 6) at [67].

58 *Silver and Others v. the United Kingdom* (5947/72; 6205/73; 7052/75; 7061/75; 7107/75; 7113/75 and 7136/75) 25 March 1983 ECtHR at [68].

therefore include minimum safeguards affecting the key areas of surveillance use, thereby protecting surveillance practice from the risk of abuse of power.

In *Huvig v. France*, the Court defined such a minimum catalogue for the first time, but it described the safeguards indicated as exemplary.[59] It was only in the later case of *Weber and Saravia v. Germany* that this list was repeated and partly supplemented.[60] A catalogue of six legal safeguards was thus established and became, over the following decades, the benchmark for the review applied not only by the Strasbourg Court but also by the CJEU and the national courts of European states.

The so-called *Huvig/Weber* six included the following minimum legal safeguards:

1 the nature of offences which may give rise to an interception order;
2 a definition of the categories of people liable to have their communications intercepted;
3 a limit on the duration of interception;
4 the procedure to be followed for examining, using, and storing the data obtained;
5 the precautions to be taken when communicating the data to other parties;
6 the circumstances in which intercepted data may or must be erased or destroyed.

Although this standard was originally developed by the Court when examining surveillance provisions used in the context of criminal procedure, the ECtHR, both in *Weber and Saravia v. Germany* and later in *Roman Zakharov v. Russia*, confirmed its applicability also to cases of surveillance conducted in the area of national security.[61] Moreover, in *Liberty and Others v. the United Kingdom*, the Court recognised the adequacy of applying this standard also in bulk surveillance cases.[62]

According to the first condition of the *Huvig/Weber* test, the use of electronic surveillance measures should be limited to cases of fighting certain types of crimes. However, this requirement should not be interpreted as requiring a detailed list of offences that may lead to the imposition of a surveillance measure. Indeed, the Court has concluded that this criterion is satisfied if the national regulations define the types of offences using terminology precise enough to allow the individual to know the "conditions on which public authorities were empowered to resort to interception."[63] Therefore, in *Kennedy v. UK*, the Court considered it sufficient to link the possibility of

59 *Huvig v. France* (n 7) at [34].
60 *Weber and Saravia v. Germany* (54934/00) 29 June 2006 ECtHR at [95].
61 *Weber and Saravia v. Germany* (n 60) at [106]; *Roman Zakharov v. Russia* (n 1) at [232].
62 *Liberty and Others v. the United Kingdom* (58243/00) 1 July 2008 ECtHR at [63].
63 *R.E. v. the United Kingdom* (62498/11) 27 October 2015 ECtHR at [133].

using bulk measures to cases involving national security and the fight against serious crime.[64]

Although national legislatures have wide discretion as to how to define the acts that may involve the use of surveillance measures, this discretion is not unlimited. It is, therefore, unacceptable to transfer from the legislature to the judge the decision on the types of crime involving the possibility of using surveillance measures. This is because it would open up the possibility of using wiretapping whenever the judge considers the information thus gathered useful for the criminal proceedings being conducted.[65] The assessment of the necessity of surveillance in a given case must also consider the seriousness of the act the individual is charged with and be based on "facts and information capable of convincing an objective observer that the person concerned may have committed the offence in question."[66] And although this condition does not require the production of evidence of the same rank as that necessary to justify a conviction, the link between the specific person and the criminal act under investigation must be verifiable. This criterion is also similarly understood in relation to surveillance carried out in the area of national security.[67]

A further condition of the *Huvig/Weber* test relates to the identification of categories of persons to whom surveillance measures may be applied. Its establishment aims to clarify the circumstances in which intrusive forms of surveillance may be used. They can be defined by indicating the forms of communication subjected to surveillance, the identity of the communicating parties, or the types of activities undertaken.

In practice, national criminal laws most often require a surveillance order to identify the person or persons covered by it. This implies a prohibition of blanket surveillance, which should also be understood as defining its scope with terms that are vague or difficult to verify. Hence, in *Ekimdzhiev and Others v. Bulgaria*, the Court found the use of the imprecise concept of "object" in indicating the scope of surveillance to be defective.[68] Significantly, the Bulgarian legislation under examination defined in a detailed and exhaustive way the categories of persons who could be subjected to surveillance in the context of criminal procedure. However, in cases concerning national security, the regulations allowed surveillance to be ordered in relation to "persons or objects related to national security."[69] As the term "object" did not have a legal definition, this created the risk of arbitrarily extending the scope of surveillance, e.g. by indicating IT systems, which would de facto lead to circumvention of the

64 *Kennedy v. the United Kingdom* (n 8) at [159].
65 *Prado Bugallo v. Spain* (58496/00) 18 February 2003 ECtHR at [30].
66 *Karabeyoğlu v. Turkey* (30083/10) 7 June 2016 ECtHR at [103].
67 *Roman Zakharov v. Russia* (n 1) at [260].
68 *Ekimdzhiev and Others v. Bulgaria* (70078/12) 11 January 2022 ECtHR at [303].
69 Ibid. at [363].

legal restrictions established and prevent effective review of the surveillance action taken.

In the most typical case where surveillance is used to combat certain crimes, the category of persons covered should include only those associated with such acts.[70] In practice, however, a number of doubts also surround the permissibility of the use of surveillance in relation to a broader catalogue of persons, including those who, albeit unrelated to the crime, may possess information about it. While the Court has accepted this possibility in principle, it has also pointed out the link between the necessity of obtaining certain information and the actual purpose relating to the "prevention of disorder or crime."[71]

Significant doubts were also formulated when, due to the definitions used, the law allowed surveillance measures to be extended to de facto whole populations. Such a risk was perceived by the Strasbourg Court in the Hungarian legislation allowing surveillance measures to be implemented to prevent terrorist threats. The wording adopted enabled the issuance of an order covering not specific, identified individuals, but in fact anyone, which resulted from introducing the phrase "persons concerned identified . . . as a range of persons."[72]

In the case of indiscriminate surveillance measures, the definition of the categories of persons subject to surveillance was more problematic and was usually linked to the technical aspects of the data collection process (see also earlier comments on the foreseeability of the law). For example, in *Weber and Saravia v. Germany*, the scope of persons subject to surveillance was defined as users of international telecommunications services.[73] Due to the modus operandi of untargeted surveillance, all the data available in a given transmission medium may be collected at an initial stage. The initial definition of the categories of persons concerned by the application of such a measure is, therefore, problematic and in many cases impossible, given the way in which bulk surveillance operates.

In fact, similar concerns also emerge from the analysis of other safeguards described in the *Huvig/Weber* standard. For example, they relate to the limitation of the duration of surveillance and the obligation to establish detailed procedures for the use of the information obtained therefrom. The typical

70 See e.g. Art. 237(4) of the Polish Code of Criminal Procedure: "Surveillance and recording of the content of telephone conversations shall be permissible with regard to a suspected person, the accused, and with regard to the victim or another person who the accused may contact or who may be connected with the perpetrator or with an imminent offence." Equivalent regulations can be found in Art. 100a(3) of the German Code of Criminal Procedure. In this context, see also Francesca Galli, 'The Interception of Communication in France and Italy – What Relevance for the Development of English Law?' (2016) 20 *The International Journal of Human Rights* 666.

71 *Greuter v. the Netherlands* (40045/98) 19 March 2002 ECtHR.

72 *Szabó and Vissy v. Hungary* (n 46) at [38].

73 *Weber and Saravia v. Germany* (n 60) at [98].

solution used in criminal proceedings is to administer surveillance for a designated period of time, which can be extended where necessary.[74] As a general rule, in a democratic state surveillance cannot be carried out indefinitely, as this would mean, in essence, that it is implemented without any reason justifying its use. As a result, rather than protecting the democratic state it could pose a threat to its existence.[75] Therefore the very presence of a mechanism allowing surveillance to be repeatedly extended increases the risk of abuse of power. As a result, the law should define the criteria for setting the maximum duration of such measures. Namely, it should go beyond mere reference to the duration of the first surveillance order and indicate the total duration of all the measures applied in a given case.[76]

While in the cases of targeted surveillance the Court has repeatedly pointed out the impermissibility of surveillance for longer than necessary, the manner in which compliance with this criterion is assessed with regard to indiscriminate surveillance measures is problematic, to say the least. This problem is, in fact, a consequence of the mismatch between bulk surveillance and the aforementioned criterion of the *Huvig/Weber* test. Indeed, because a bulk surveillance regime is not applied to specific individuals but often to all users of a given means of electronic communication, it de facto serves the purpose of prevention (identification of unknown threats). It is therefore difficult to determine how long it would be applied. Theoretically, a solution to this problem could be the use of extensive judicial review procedures involving periodic re-certification of the rules governing indiscriminate programmes. Such a solution is used in the United States, among others.[77] However, it is difficult not to see that this review is *ex post* in nature, and therefore pursues a different objective than *ex ante* review, conducted at the time the surveillance is approved.

As regards the storage and further use of data, the Court's jurisprudence indicates the necessity to ensure the transparency of the actions taken, understood as access to a procedure describing the manner of "selecting for examination, sharing, storing and destroying intercepted material."[78] This condition

74 However, there is no standard across the Member States. For example, in France the maximum duration of the first interception order is 4 months (total duration of interception – 1 year) – Art. 100(1) of the Code of Criminal Procedure; in Germany, the initial duration of the first order is 1 month and can be extended – Art. 100e(2) of the Code of Criminal Procedure; in Spain, it is 3 months (the initial duration of surveillance) but not more than 18 months in total – Art. 588(b)(vii) of the Code of Criminal Procedure.

75 *Klass and Others v. Germany* (5029/71) 18 December 1974 ECtHR at [49].

76 See e.g. *Iordachi and Others v. Moldova* (25198/02) 10 February 2009 ECtHR at [45]; *Karabeyoğlu v. Turkey* (n 66) at [91].

77 See the so-called targeting, minimisation and querying procedures related to the Foreign Intelligence Surveillance Act, 'Release of Documents Related to the 2023 FISA Section 702 Certifications' Office of the Director of National Intelligence (21 July 2023) <https://cli.re/WMdWoB> accessed 6 September 2023.

78 *Liberty and Others v. the United Kingdom* (n 62) at [69].

is not fulfilled by establishing secret procedures of data processing, which in addition are not subject to any external review.[79] At the same time, however, this requirement does not imply an obligation to make available all regulations describing the manner of handling (processing) surveillance material. Transparency of the rules applied should concern those regulations that affect individual rights. It follows that ensuring compliance with this criterion does not necessitate publishing procedures of a purely technical or administrative nature which concern the manner in which the legal requirements are implemented.

Data obtained from surveillance should be processed for the time necessary to achieve the purposes for which they were legally collected.[80] Two conclusions emerge from this requirement. First, even a short time of the processing of irrelevant data (unrelated to the purpose of using surveillance) may violate the criterion of necessity.[81] Second, even relevant data cannot be processed indefinitely without an appropriate process for their regular evaluation – that is, in a way leading to the deletion of redundant information. Otherwise, data could, in fact, be stored indefinitely without any relation to the purpose for which they were collected, which cannot be considered necessary in a democratic state.[82] In this respect, the duration of data retention should also be defined taking into account the seriousness of the alleged infringement.[83]

Hence, satisfying the above conditions requires *a priori* that it be possible to link the information collected to a specific threat or a legitimate need for obtaining it. Only then is it possible to confirm that the further processing of this information meets the necessity requirement.

While this argument is implementable in the case of targeted measures, its reference to the specifics of bulk surveillance is at least problematic. The modus operandi of the latter presupposes the bulk collection of redundant data, which in the course of further analysis *may* prove useful for the pursuit of certain legitimate purposes. However, it is impossible to predict if and when such purposes may arise. As a result, there is no mechanism to determine whether data which is unnecessary today will turn out to be necessary tomorrow. This naturally leads to attempts to justify data collection in a way that violates the traditionally understood test of strict necessity (see further in section 3.5). In fact, however, these considerations did not affect the Court's assessment in *Weber and Saravia* that there was no risk of redundant data collection, and that it was sufficient for the German law to include a requirement to periodically review the usefulness of the data acquired as part of a strategic surveillance programme.[84]

79 *Zoltán Varga v. Slovakia* (58361/12) 20 July 2021 ECtHR at [169].
80 *Klass and Others v. Germany* (n 75) at [52].
81 *Roman Zakharov v. Russia* (n 1) at [255].
82 *Association "21 December 1989" and Others v. Romania* (33810/07) 24 May 2011 ECtHR at [174].
83 *Gaughran v. the United Kingdom* (45245/15) 13 February 2020 ECtHR at [94].
84 *Weber and Saravia v. Germany* (n 60) at [132].

In reality, the actual impact of legal safeguards on reducing the risk of abuse of power depends largely on the quality of the control mechanisms established. The role of external review is a key aspect affecting the ordering of surveillance, its conduct, and its termination.[85] It may therefore come as a bit of a surprise that this requirement was not addressed explicitly in the *Huvig/Weber* standard. In its early jurisprudence, the Court does not seem to have viewed independent judicial review as a necessary condition for the legality of surveillance activities.[86] However, this assessment changed in subsequent rulings, and the importance of external oversight was gradually reinforced.

The Court has consistently taken the view in its jurisprudence that oversight of state surveillance activities need not be exercised by courts.[87] As a result, the failure to establish such oversight mechanism – whether in the form of *ex ante* or *ex post* review – does not constitute an infringement of what may be considered necessary in a democratic society. An example of this is the German model of surveillance, in which *ex ante* review is carried out by an official with the qualifications required to hold the office of judge, while oversight over the use of surveillance measures is exercised by a special committee appointed by the parliament in accordance with a statutory procedure (the so-called G10 Commission).[88] Both bodies perform their functions completely independently and have sufficient powers and competences to exercise "an effective and continuous control" over the use of surveillance.[89]

However, the requirement of independence is not fulfilled when the process of reviewing or authorising surveillance is exclusively exercised by a representative of the government. This is also the case when a surveillance measure may be authorised by the public prosecutor if it follows from national law that the office of the public prosecutor is not independent from the executive.[90] Granting the power to administer surveillance to a political body, such as the Minister of Justice, creates a particular risk.[91] In practice, therefore, in each case the law should guarantee the possibility of subjecting the legitimacy of ordering surveillance to review by an independent body. In this respect, although the Court still considers it acceptable to entrust this role to

85 *Roman Zakharov v. Russia* (n 1) at [233].

86 *Huvig v. France* (n 7) at [33]: "The Court does not in any way minimise the value of . . . the need for a decision by an investigating judge, who is an independent judicial authority."

87 Gianclaudio Malgieri and Paul De Hert, 'European Human Rights, Criminal Surveillance, and Intelligence Surveillance: Towards "Good Enough" Oversight, Preferably but Not Necessarily by Judges' in David Gray and Stephen E Henderson (eds), *The Cambridge Handbook of Surveillance Law* (Cambridge University Press 2017) 510–511.

88 Russell A Miller, 'Intelligence Oversight – Made in Germany' in Zachary K Goldman, Jane Harman and Samuel J Rascoff (eds), *Global Intelligence Oversight* (Oxford University Press 2016) <https://academic.oup.com/book/4147/chapter/145922344> accessed 13 September 2023.

89 *Klass and Others v. Germany* (n 75) at [56].

90 *Dumitru Popescu v. Romania (no 2)* (71525/01) 26 April 2007 ECtHR at [71].

91 *Szabó and Vissy v. Hungary* (n 46) at [77].

independent administrative bodies, in more recent judgments it has emphasised that the fullest protection is afforded by the establishment of judicial review.[92] In each case, however, this review requires a genuine verification of the information provided and cannot be reduced to accepting the conclusions presented by authorised bodies without substantive analysis.[93]

Furthermore, an analysis of the ECtHR case law does not suggest that it is necessary to apply *ex ante* review in each and every case. The need to counter the most serious threats requires that authorised services have the competence to use such measures also in cases of urgency, for example when following the standard procedure might hinder the prevention of a crime. Therefore, as the Court has pointed out, although *ex ante* review provides the fullest protection against arbitrariness, its absence may be offset by *ex post* review, but with the understanding and assurance that it is not carried out in a piecemeal and random manner.[94] However, the Court has introduced exceptions to this rule, including, *inter alia*, surveillance concerning journalists or lawyers.[95] According to the Court, in such cases *post factum* review does not provide sufficient protection so as to effectively safeguard the trust necessary to properly exercise these professions.[96]

The purpose of applying *ex ante* review is to confirm that, in the circumstances of a given case, the application of a surveillance measure is necessary. This instrument cannot, therefore, be based on the issuance of blanket authorisations, where it is impossible to determine the limits of the consent granted. Also, an *ex post* examination of the reasons for ordering surveillance does not fulfil the objectives of *ex ante* review. It is clear that the assessment of the legitimacy of surveillance after it ends may be based on information and facts that were unavailable beforehand and thus could not have formed the basis for authorising the use of such surveillance.[97]

The issue of effective control over surveillance activities is also related to the assessment of the quality of the administration of justice (in this regard, see also section 3.4.5). When examining surveillance programmes in the area of criminal procedure, the Court has paid particular attention to the share of criminal cases in which evidence from covert surveillance was used and the total number of cases in which the use of surveillance measures was approved. In *Ekimdzhiev v. Bulgaria*, the Court noted that out of more than

92 *Kennedy v. the United Kingdom* (n 8) at [167].
93 *Zoltán Varga v. Slovakia* (n 79) at [156].
94 See *Szabó and Vissy v. Hungary* (n 46); see also *Centrum för rättvisa v. Sweden* [GC] (n 51) at [133]. However, the recent case law of the Court takes the view that both control measures (*ex ante* and *ex post*) should be applied cumulatively, see e.g. *Big Brother Watch and Others v. the United Kingdom* [GC] (n 47) at [319–320].
95 *Kopp v. Switzerland* (n 34) at [73–75].
96 *Telegraaf Media Nederland Landelijke Media B.V. and Others v. the Netherlands* (39315/06) 22 November 2012 ECtHR at [101].
97 *Liblik and Others v. Estonia* (n 10) at [141].

10,000 cases of ordering surveillance, only in fewer than 270 cases was the evidence obtained used in subsequent criminal proceedings related thereto.[98] Taking into account that Bulgaria's population was fewer than 8 million, the Court pointed out that the number of surveillance requests approved (with respect to the total population of Bulgaria) significantly exceeded the same percentage figures for other countries.[99] Similarly, in comparing analogous data on the number of approved requests in Moldova (with an average of about 2200 cases per year in 2004–2007 and a population of about 3.5 million), the Court concluded that "the system of secret surveillance in Moldova is, to say the least, overused, which may in part be due to the inadequacy of the safeguards contained in the law."[100]

A separate issue related to oversight over secret surveillance programmes, is the fulfilment of the notification obligation towards the person subject to surveillance. The need for notification mechanisms was not directly addressed in the *Huvig/Weber* standard, but in its subsequent case law the Court carefully examined the practice in this regard. Given the covert nature of surveillance and the purpose of its establishment, it is clear that the person subject to it cannot be informed of the action taken before it is completed. This, therefore, excludes the possibility of legal action by the person concerned at the stages of both ordering and implementing surveillance. Only notification after the end of surveillance allows the person concerned to challenge the legality of the measures implemented against them. In practice, however, informing the subject about surveillance upon its completion in every case could impede the purpose for which this measure was implemented. In some cases, the mere disclosure of the manner and forms of data collection could adversely affect the ability of the authorities to perform their tasks effectively.[101]

Therefore the Court accepts, in principle, that there is no obligation to notify every person subjected to surveillance.[102] However, in such a case – because of the lack of an effective remedy available to the person concerned – the Court points out that "the procedures in place should themselves provide adequate and equivalent guarantees for the respect of the rights of the individual concerned."[103] A similar position has also been put forward by the Venice

98 *Association for European Integration and Human Rights and Ekimdzhiev v. Bulgaria* (n 9) at [92].

99 The figure of approximately 10,000 approved surveillance applications relates to a 2-year period (1999–2000). For example, in *Malone v. the United Kingdom* (n 6), the Court indicated that in the 10 years analysed (1969–79), surveillance – involving the monitoring of telephone communications – was approved an average of 400 times, a figure that should be juxtaposed with the number of more than 26 million subscribers to telecommunications services.

100 *Iordachi and Others v. Moldova* (n 76) at [52].

101 *Cevat Özel v. Turkey* (19602/06) 7 June 2016 ECtHR.

102 *Weber and Saravia v. Germany* (n 60) at [135].

103 *Karabeyoğlu v. Turkey* (n 66) at [71].

Commission, which has stressed that "a general complaints procedure to an independent oversight body" can compensate for non-notification.[104]

At the same time, however, the adoption of a legal regulation completely eliminating the fulfilment of the notification obligation towards the targeted person – and this regardless of the circumstances of the particular case – goes beyond what can be considered compatible with the rule of law.[105] In particular, notification should be required if it does not jeopardise the purpose for which such surveillance was ordered.[106] This condition is not met by notifying only the persons in respect of whom surveillance is found to have been ordered unlawfully, for such a solution deprives the other persons under surveillance of their right to judicial review of the decisions taken in relation to them. For the same reason, the notification obligation should not be limited to a specific category of persons, e.g. by arbitrarily excluding legal persons from its scope.[107]

The ECtHR's position on notification rules is, in practice, difficult to interpret and, consequently, also difficult to apply. In reality, it is not the body ordering surveillance but the one carrying it out that has the necessary knowledge to assess whether the forms and means of surveillance used can be disclosed without prejudice to the interests of the secret service. This problem is particularly evident in the case of surveillance in the area of state security. In some legal models, the very information on the technical capabilities of secret services constitutes classified information and, as a result, is subject to legal protection.[108] Of course, the law may, in such a case, provide for a simplified form of notification, that is, communicating general information on surveillance measures ordered against a given person. Indeed, the very presence of such a mechanism would open up the possibility for the person concerned to initiate an independent review, in which the court, examining the entirety of the material collected, could assess the legality of the action taken.

Given the mass nature of interception in untargeted surveillance measures, implementing a notification process for such measures seems particularly complicated. Different jurisdictions have adopted different solutions in this regard. For example, in the German model (strategic surveillance), notification should be carried out after the end of the application of a surveillance measure, unless the purpose of the measure has not yet expired or "the occurrence of overarching disadvantages for the welfare of the Federation or a Land is foreseeable."[109] In such a case, it is possible to delay the fulfilment of the obligation to inform, or in an extreme case waive it, which, however, requires the approval of the competent oversight authority (in the case of German legislation, the so-called

104 'Report on the Democratic Oversight of Signals Intelligence Agencies' (Venice Commission 2015) CDL-AD(2015)011 6 <https://cli.re/ApE7Ad> accessed 6 September 2023.

105 *Szabó and Vissy v. Hungary* (n 46) at [86].

106 *Leander v. Sweden* (9248/81) 26 March 1987 ECtHR at [66].

107 *Ekimdzhiev and Others v. Bulgaria* (n 68) at [290].

108 See e.g. the judgment of the Polish Regional Administrative Court in Warsaw of 11 December 2015, II SA/Wa 1330/15.

109 Art. 12(1) of the German G10 Act.

G10 Commission).[110] Similar solutions have been adopted in the Swedish model.[111] However, as the Swedish DPA noted in 2010, the FRA had never carried out the notification obligation due to the premise of the secrecy of the operations conducted.[112]

In contrast, under the UK regime, classical notification is not used at all. Its role is fulfilled by the institution of a complaint, which makes it possible to check whether a person has been subjected to untargeted surveillance measures. A complaint of this type is investigated by a judicial body appointed for this purpose (the Investigatory Powers Tribunal). This model is, however, widely criticised as being highly reactive and based on a complaint of the person concerned, who after all does not necessarily have any suspicion that they have been subjected to extra-legal surveillance. Moreover, when filing the complaint the complainant must also indicate the public authority that they suspect of using surveillance measures – which, in practice, creates an illusory complaint mechanism, as it requires knowledge of not only the use of surveillance, but also of the circumstances of its implementation (more on notification in indiscriminate surveillance programmes in the following sections).

As a result, although the *Huvig/Weber* test remains the leading standard for assessing the permissibility of targeted forms of surveillance, especially those involving the interception of the content of communications (correspondence),[113] its utility for examining indiscriminate surveillance measures has for years remained problematic and provoked much interpretive controversy (see Table 4.1).[114]

4.4.2 A "less intrusive" Uzun*-based approach*

The *Huvig/Weber* test was created in response to the need to standardise a list of minimum safeguards applied in relation to surveillance involving the interception of communications. In the Court's view, the interception of the content of communications was an intrusion serious enough to require the establishment of particularly stringent mechanisms to protect individual rights.[115] Therefore this standard was also used in relation to other surveillance measures that made it possible to record communications.[116]

110 More on the G10 Commission in Miller (n 88) and section 6.2.

111 Art. 11b of the Swedish Signals Intelligence Act (n 52).

112 *Centrum för rättvisa v. Sweden* [GC] (n 51) at [60].

113 In the Court's view, the terms "correspondence" and "communications" – in the context of violations of Art. 8(2) – can be used interchangeably. See e.g. the *Dragoş Ioan Rusu v. Romania* case on violation of the secrecy of correspondence, which also applied the Huvig/Weber test: *Dragoş Ioan Rusu v. Romania* (22767/08) 31 October 2017 ECtHR at [35].

114 See e.g. Patrick Breyer, 'Telecommunications Data Retention and Human Rights: The Compatibility of Blanket Traffic Data Retention with the ECHR' (2005) 11 *European Law Journal* 365.

115 *R.E. v. the United Kingdom* (n 63) at [130].

116 For an analysis regarding the tapping of radio communications, see *Bykov v. Russia* (4378/02) 10 March 2009 ECHR at [79].

Table 4.1 The compatibility of the *Huvig/Weber* test with the characteristics of untargeted surveillance measures.

	Huvig/Weber test	*Compatibility with untargeted measures*
1	The nature of offences which may give rise to an interception order	*Minor/limited* Untargeted measures are not applied to specific individuals and are not used to gather information on specific acts. Untargeted measures are typically used to carry out tasks unrelated to criminal procedure. As a result, the scope of their use is not limited to the detection or prevention of specific types of crime and extends to, for example, the collection of information concerning the state's economic interests, the implementation of foreign policy and so on.
2	A definition of the categories of people liable to have their communications intercepted	*Minor/limited* All persons using specific communication channels can be covered by untargeted measures.
3	A limit on the duration of interception	*Minor/limited* Untargeted measures are generally not used to gather evidence on known risks; identification of unknown risks is not time-limited, although restrictions may be placed on this (e.g. periodic recertification of the use of designated keywords). *Ex ante* review, even if exercised, does not serve to confirm the necessity of applying surveillance to specific individuals in the case of indiscriminate surveillance measures. Nor does it indicate the duration of surveillance in relation to the persons to be targeted.
4	The procedure to be followed for examining, using and storing the data obtained	*Sufficient* The way in which data are collected and processed can be described in sufficient detail to allow this process to be audited. A potential difficulty may be the non-transparent mechanisms used to train the analytical models, making it difficult to verify how the data are used. Yet, even if that is the case, it is possible to subject this area to an independent *ex post* review.
5	The precautions to be taken when communicating the data to other parties	*Sufficient* There are no technical obstacles to restricting the rules on the distribution of, or access to, data from indiscriminate surveillance.
6	The circumstances in which intercepted data may or must be erased or destroyed	*Minor/limited* A key concern is to limit the duration of data retention and to ensure that this period is linked to the gravity of the violation, the counteracting of which was the reason the data were collected.

However, the Court considered it too far-reaching to extend the scope of this test also to cases involving other – in its view, less intrusive – forms of surveillance. An example is the monitoring of a person's geolocation in a public space, examined in *Uzun v. Germany*. The Court considered this measure to be less prone to abuse, as it did not allow detailed monitoring of various aspects of a person's private life, such as opinions and beliefs.[117]

These considerations led to the conclusion that in such cases, it would be sufficient to apply a less expansive standard, building on the earlier case law on violations of the right to privacy.[118] A new, simplified standard of safeguards was thus created, requiring four key areas to be defined in national law:[119]

1 the nature, scope and duration of the possible measures;
2 the grounds required for ordering them;
3 the identification of authorities competent to permit, carry out and supervise them;
4 the kind of remedy provided by the national law.

The move away from the stringent *Huvig/Weber* test to the *Uzun* standard also led to the abandonment of the strict necessity criterion as a requisite condition of the proportionality of the actions taken. Therefore the *Uzun* test is not only built of more general legal safeguards, leaving a greater margin of appreciation to public authorities, but it also requires a less rigorous compliance assessment than the *Huvig/Weber* test. While the two standards can be easily compared (see Table 4.2), in practice such a comparison does not provide an assessment of the quality of the safeguards themselves.

For example, under the *Uzun* model the use of a surveillance measure does not have to be limited to a catalogue of offences described in the law or to other legitimate purposes. While the legislature still has to define the criteria for ordering, carrying out, and supervising the use of surveillance, there is no requirement that the measures be time-limited in the same way as in *Huvig/Weber* or that the law should regulate in detail the handling of the information collected, including its retention.

Given the important differences between the two standards, it is first necessary to clarify the relevance and accuracy of the view that certain forms of electronic surveillance (in the *Uzun* case, geolocation monitoring) actually involve less interference with individual rights. Only if this is the case could the bifurcation of legal safeguard standards introduced by the Court be endorsed.

Tying the intrusiveness of surveillance to a particular scope of data gathered seems problematic. As explained earlier, nowadays it is not the technical method of acquiring the data, but the way they are processed and further used

117 *Uzun v. Germany* (n 30) at [52].
118 Ibid. at [66].
119 Ibid. at [63].

that reveals detailed information about the user.[120] While electronic communications are a valuable source of information, the observation of a person using modern CCTV systems can also lead to the disclosure of equally sensitive information about that person. Another obvious example is a mobile device user's geolocation data. It is impossible to accept the view that information concerning women visiting abortion clinics – which can be obtained by monitoring the geolocation of subscribers' devices – is, in each case, an invasion of privacy of a minor nature. Although in the *Uzun* case it was not a specific person who was directly monitored (e.g. the location of his smartphone) but the car in which he was travelling, this does not change the fact that detailed information of a strictly private nature can nowadays be revealed also by monitoring a vehicle's location and correlating the data thus acquired with other data sets.[121]

Although in the *Uzun* judgment the Court noted that technological developments have led to the need to adapt the existing legal framework to increasingly sophisticated surveillance measures,[122] it ignored the fact that already at the time of the judgment the risks of massive metadata processing were widely known and discussed in the case law of European courts. Suffice it to recall the bVerfG judgment on the German retention laws – handed down a few months before the *Uzun* ruling – in which the German Constitutional Court comprehensively explained why the collection of metadata (including location data) under the conditions of the modern information society lead to a far-reaching interference with the right to privacy.[123] This judgment was later largely confirmed by the Court of Justice in the precedent-setting *Digital Rights Ireland* ruling, which set the direction for the European debate on the legality of the use of untargeted surveillance measures for many years.

However, in *R.E. v. UK* – handed down in 2015 (thus after *Digital Rights Ireland*), the ECtHR linked the application of the *Huvig/Weber* test to cases of eavesdropping on the content of correspondence.[124] This position is explained by the reasoning in *Ben Faiza v. France*, where the Court differentiated the degree of interference depending on whether the surveillance device was used in a way that allowed the tracking of the user's location in real time, or *post factum*. The latter scenario concerned access to retained telecommunications data, by means of which the user's historical geographical location could be

120 See Chapter 1 for a discussion of user profiling based on publicly available sources.

121 In this regard see, for example, the details of *United States v. Jones* (see section 2.5), in which it was GPS monitoring of a vehicle that provided key investigative information (although all other available surveillance techniques were also used against the accused). See: Dorothy J Glancy, 'Privacy in Autonomous Vehicles' (2012) 52 *Santa Clara Law Review* 1171, 1212–1213.

122 *Uzun v. Germany* (n 30) at [61].

123 BVerfG 2 March 2010 (1 BvR 256/08) DE:BVerfG:2010:rs20100302.1bvr025608 at [211].

124 *R.E. v. the United Kingdom* (n 63) at [127].

reconstructed.[125] In the Court's view, this type of *post factum* surveillance leads to less interference with an individual's rights, because it serves to "establish facts" and not to monitor the activity of the person under surveillance on an ongoing basis.

This argumentation is hard to agree with, however. Indeed, it is not only internally incoherent (as discussed further below) but also completely ignores the previous case law on informational autonomy and the impact of the chilling effect on individual behaviour.[126] One of the key areas of privacy protection, related to the prevention of abuse by public authorities, concerns the limitations on building redundant, seemingly unnecessary, databases which, depending on the will of those in power, might later be used to interfere with personal rights. From the perspective of an individual's freedoms and liberties, it is irrelevant whether someone observes or can observe them in a situation where they have no tools to guard against or regulate this observation. By contrast, in *Ben Faiza v. France*, the Court held that active surveillance (combined with immediate data analysis) interfered with an individual's rights more than if the data in question were merely recorded by public authorities and used (or not) later.[127]

Such argumentation appears inconsistent also insofar as it omits an assessment of compliance with the necessity (proportionality) requirement. In *Ben Faiza v. France*, the applicants challenged not only the use of active geolocation data but also the acquisition of metadata from electronic communications by the police. In its analysis, the Court focused exclusively on the stage of accessing the metadata, without examining the lawfulness of their prior retention. In this respect, it found that *in the specific case* it was possible to demonstrate this necessity.[128] It is impossible to resist the impression that, using similar reasoning, the need to collect any data can be confirmed if, even to a residual extent, the information collected proves to be procedurally relevant at a later time. Such an interpretation is directly irreconcilable with the concept of strict necessity and, generally, the necessity test as such (for more on strict necessity and necessity in a democratic state in the Court's jurisprudence, see sections 3.5 and 5.3). Interestingly, in *Ben Faiza v. France* the Court referred to a definition of necessity which involves ensuring compliance with the condition of proportionality but did not actually conduct a detailed examination of this criterion.[129]

It was only in *Ekimdzhiev and Others v. Bulgaria* that the ECtHR more comprehensively considered the question of the compatibility with the

125 *Ben Faiza v. France* (31446/12) 8 February 2018 ECtHR at [74].
126 Daragh Murray and Pete Fussey, 'Bulk Surveillance in the Digital Age: Rethinking the Human Rights Law Approach to Bulk Monitoring of Communications Data' (2019) 52 *Israel Law Review* 31, 43–47.
127 *Ben Faiza v. France* (n 125).
128 Ibid. at [79].
129 Ibid. at [78].

Convention of a measure involving the bulk collection of traffic data (including location data). It first recalled that "all types of communications data at issue in the present case – subscriber, traffic and location data – can relate, alone or in combination, to the private life."[130] Building on the reasoning set out earlier in *Ben Faiza v. France*, the Court pointed out that collecting this type of information constitutes an interference with the secrecy of correspondence, guaranteed by Article 8 of the Convention. Significantly – and this is a novelty – the Court indicated that because "communications data can nowadays reveal a great deal of personal information . . ., the acquisition of that data through bulk interception can therefore be just as intrusive as the bulk acquisition of the content of communications."[131] In drawing such a conclusion, the Court considered it necessary to apply to the data retention regime the same safeguards as those applied in cases of covert surveillance of communications, i.e. the *Huvig/Weber* test rather than the *Uzun* test. Against this background, it is worth noting that in *Uzun v. Germany* the Court held that 3 months of surveillance using a GPS tracker did not amount to a serious interference with the user's privacy,[132] while in *Ekimdzhiev and Others v. Bulgaria*, it departed from differentiating the degree of interference by the duration of surveillance.[133]

However, it remains an open question to what extent the *Ekimdzhiev and Others v. Bulgaria* case demonstrates an evolution of the Court's standard and a departure from the application of the *Uzun* test, and to what extent its relevance is merely limited to a different assessment of cases of bulk collection of location data. In other words, does a single instance of the processing of location data (metadata) remain, in the Court's view, a "minor interference" and consequently justifies the application of the less restrictive *Uzun* test? In the *Ekimdzhiev and Others v. Bulgaria* judgment, there is no clear position in this regard, while the *Ben Faiza v. France* case implies that the monitoring of a specific person in a public space may constitute a lesser interference. Against this backdrop, however, noteworthy is the judgment in *Glukhin v. Russia*, in which the Court applied (although not directly) the *Huvig/Weber* test to assess the legality of a facial recognition system used with regard to persons recorded by a municipal CCTV system.[134]

According to the European Court of Justice, however, any processing of traffic data (including location) results in serious interference with the right to privacy, and therefore in accordance with the principle of proportionality, the use of such a measure should be limited only to cases of countering

130 *Ekimdzhiev and Others v. Bulgaria* (n 68) at [372].
131 Ibid. at [394].
132 *Uzun v. Germany* (n 30) at [80].
133 In this regard, see also *Centrum för rättvisa v. Sweden* [GC] (n 51) at [277].
134 *Glukhin v. Russia* (11519/20) 4 July 2023 ECtHR at [77].

threats that are also assessed as serious (for more on data retention, see section 5.2).[135] Moreover, the ECtHR cited this interpretation in *Breyer v. Germany* and followed the CJEU in finding that the collection of data on SIM card users' identities did not constitute a serious interference with the right to privacy.[136] Unfortunately, it is not clear from this judgment whether the collection of metadata should be defined as such interference. If this were so, it would result in a departure from the application of the *Uzun* test in the cases for which this test was developed – namely, the collection and processing of geolocation data.

Guidance on the scope of the *Uzun* test may also be provided by an analysis of the circumstances of cases in which this standard has been applied. It appears that in cases where surveillance measures have been applied to persons other than those suspected of serious criminal offences – such as journalists or participants in protests – the Court has emphasised the need for strict scrutiny to confirm that the scope of the measures taken did not go beyond what is acceptable in a democratic state. In doing so, it de facto excluded the possibility that such interference could be considered minor, which resulted in the application of the *Huvig/Weber* test to confirm its compliance with the Convention.[137]

It seems, therefore, that nowadays the practical relevance of the *Uzun* test remains limited. It should not be used to assess the permissibility of either eavesdropping on communications or on the bulk storage of data that can be used for profiling users. Instead, the standard can be used to test single cases of interference, but only if it does not appear from the circumstances of the case that the measure under examination was used to collect sensitive data, such as political views, for example.

4.4.3 From Huvig *to* Big Brother Watch*: aligning* Huvig/Weber *with indiscriminate surveillance*

Although the *Huvig/Weber* test was built for the purpose of assessing cases of targeted surveillance carried out in the context of criminal proceedings, in practice it has increasingly become referred to in surveillance measures involving bulk and indiscriminate interception of data. Indeed, the *Weber and Saravia v. Germany* case, from which this test takes its name, also examined an indiscriminate (or "strategic") surveillance (for a more extensive discussion, see section 1.2). However, it was only in the most recent cases, in which the complainants directly challenged the legality of the mass surveillance disclosed by Edward Snowden, that the Court had to address the issue comprehensively

135 *Ministerio Fiscal* (C-207/16) EU:C:2018:788 at [56]. Moreover, the *Ministerio Fiscal* judgment was noticed by ECtHR in the *Ekimdzhiev and Others v. Bulgaria* case (see n 68 at [241]).
136 *Breyer v. Germany* (50001/12) 30 January 2020 ECtHR at [94–95].
137 *Catt v. the United Kingdom* (43514/15) 24 January 2019 ECtHR at [114].

Table 4.2 Comparison of the *Huvig/Weber* and *Uzun* standards.

	Huvig/Weber test	*Uzun test*
1	The nature of offences which may give rise to an interception order	The nature, scope and grounds required for ordering surveillance measures
2	A definition of the categories of people liable to have their communications intercepted	
3	A limit on the duration of interception	The duration of the possible measures and the authorities competent to permit, carry out and supervise them
4	The procedure to be followed for examining, using and storing the data obtained	No detailed requirements; in this context, *Uzun* focuses on the quality of remedies provided by the national law
5	The precautions to be taken when communicating the data to other parties	
6	The circumstances in which intercepted data may or must be erased or destroyed	

while at the same time explaining how to apply the existing case law to the specifics of the contemporary forms of indiscriminate surveillance.

For years, it was pointed out that many of the *Huvig/Weber* requirements could not be easily applied to indiscriminate surveillance programmes (see Table 4.1). This led to a situation where on the one hand – also in the more recent case law – the Court emphasised the need to comply with *Huvig/Weber* for the sake of rigorous control of the use of surveillance, while at the same time accepting further derogations from this test regarding the most privacy-intrusive bulk surveillance measures.

An example is the judgment in *Centrum för rättvisa v. Sweden*, in which the Court first argues that the six safeguards of the *Huvig/Weber* test should be applied whenever electronic surveillance measures are implemented (i.e. not excluding indiscriminate measures), and then in a subsequent paragraph of the same judgment explains how this standard should be modified so that it can be applied to the assessment of indiscriminate surveillance programmes.[138] These conclusions were summarised by the Grand Chamber in *Big Brother Watch v. UK*, which led to the adoption of a modified legal safeguards standard dedicated to cases of bulk surveillance.[139] In the Grand Chamber's view, national law governing the use of untargeted regimes should specify, at a minimum:

138 *Centrum för rättvisa v. Sweden* [Chamber] (35252/08) 19 June 2018 ECtHR at [112–113].

139 For a legal and factual background regarding the *Big Brother Watch* case, see Bart van der Sloot and E Kosta, '*Big Brother Watch and Others v. UK*: Lessons from the Latest Strasbourg Ruling on Bulk Surveillance' (2019) 5 *European Data Protection Law Review* 252, 253–255.

1. the grounds on which bulk interception may be authorised;
2. the circumstances in which an individual's communications may be intercepted;
3. the procedure to be followed for granting authorisation;
4. the procedures to be followed for selecting, examining and using intercepted material;
5. the precautions to be taken when communicating the material to other parties;
6. the limits on the duration of interception, the storage of intercepted material, and the circumstances in which such material must be erased and destroyed;
7. the procedures and modalities for supervision by an independent authority of compliance with the above safeguards, and its powers to address non-compliance;
8. the procedures for independent *ex post facto* review of such compliance and the powers vested in the competent body in addressing instances of non-compliance.

Hence, the ECtHR considered that national legislation creating a framework for the use of bulk measures should, in addition to the requirements indicated in *Huvig/Weber*, lay down procedures for the authorisation of such measures and rules and for the exercise of oversight by an independent authority to ensure the lawfulness of surveillance activities and secure effective responses to abuses. Moreover, the Court emphasised the need for extensive *ex post* review mechanisms to ensure the so-called end-to-end control over the process of the use of surveillance measures by public authorities.[140]

The fundamental novelty of the *Big Brother Watch* standard is the de facto omission of reference to the requirement of strict necessity, understood as requiring that the need for the use of surveillance in the context of each individual case be demonstrated (see in more detail in section 3.5).[141] Moreover, the new standard departs altogether from the application of the first two *Huvig/Weber* requirements, i.e. to define the catalogue of offences to delimit the scope of surveillance and to clearly indicate the categories of persons to whom such measures may be applied.[142] As indicated earlier (see Table 4.1),

140 *Big Brother Watch and Others v. the United Kingdom* [GC] (n 47) at [350]. Bart van der Sloot, '*Big Brother Watch and Others v. the United Kingdom* & *Centrum För Rättvisa v. Sweden*: Does the Grand Chamber Set Back the Clock in Mass Surveillance Cases?' (2021) 7 *European Data Protection Law Review* 319, 323.

141 In the Grand Chamber's judgment (n 47), the term "strict necessity" was used exclusively in discussing the position of the Parties, the case law of the CJEU, and the dissenting opinions. By comparison, in *Szabó and Vissy v. Hungary* (n 46), the term was used on several occasions, including to justify why the measures implemented went beyond what is necessary in a democratic state.

142 *Big Brother Watch and Others v. the United Kingdom* [GC] (n 47) at [275].

both safeguards could not be easily implemented in the case of untargeted programmes. Therefore a new, less stringent requirement to indicate the circumstances justifying the interception of particular communications was introduced in place of the "categories of individuals concerned" requirement, but notably without reference to the notion of the *necessity* of that interception.

In practice, as indiscriminate programmes do not identify specific individuals to be subjected to surveillance, it is also problematic to verify the adequacy of the authorisation mechanisms implemented and independent control over the use of such surveillance. In the case of bulk surveillance, the counterpart of the surveillance subject is the list of selectors used. By limiting the list of selectors and ensuring their quality, it is possible to control the intrusiveness of the data collection process. This led to suggestion that authorisations for indiscriminate surveillance measures should include a list of permissible selectors – in the same way that orders for targeted surveillance include a list of individuals to be targeted. However, the Court considered that requiring a surveillance order to specify a list of selectors is too far-reaching and does not reflect the specifics of bulk programmes, the proper use of which requires a high degree of flexibility in the search criteria adopted.[143]

In so doing, the Court effectively accepted that, in the case of indiscriminate surveillance measures, *ex ante* review (whether judicial or otherwise) does not, in fact, have to restrict the scope of the use of surveillance through strict criteria, which would set an impassable limit to the lawful action of public authorities. At the same time, however, it recognised that such review must be applied when the so-called strong selectors are used, i.e. those which make it possible to identify a specific individual.[144]

The use of strong selectors allows an untargeted surveillance system to be used in a manner similar to targeted surveillance – that is, not to identify previously unknown threats but to collect information on specific individuals. Therefore the introduction of mandatory *ex ante* review with regard to strong selectors is intended to provide a level of protection of individual rights similar to that applicable to targeted surveillance (for an in-depth analysis, see section 6.1).

Taking into account the peculiarity of indiscriminate surveillance programmes also led the Court to modify (de facto, *relax*) the notification requirement. The Court correctly noted that the information obligation in the case of indiscriminate programmes is, in many cases, impossible to implement. Because the identities of the persons subjected to surveillance are not always known, it is impossible to inform them of the fact that they are covered by such measures. Even when their identity is known, these persons may be abroad, which creates further difficulties in informing them effectively. Moreover,

143 Ibid. at [354].
144 Ibid. at [425].

where surveillance is carried out in the area of state security, the exemption from notification on the grounds of protection of state secrecy is commonly used anyway (see earlier comments on this point in section 4.4.1 above). As a result, it is true that in many cases, basing the protection of the individual on the fulfilment of the notification obligation creates only an illusory protection of their interests. Therefore in more recent case law the Court has recognised that, in the case of indiscriminate measures, an alternative to notification may be the implementation of extensive *ex post* review procedures.[145] Moreover, it has emphasised that such measures may "even offer better guarantees of a proper procedure than a system based on notification."[146]

In this regard, it is worth comparing the conclusions of the three cases heard in recent years which examine and reviewed the surveillance laws in Hungary, Sweden, and the United Kingdom. The first of the cases, *Szabó and Vissy v. Hungary*, concerned de facto targeted surveillance that, in the absence of adequate safeguards, could be carried out in a manner involving any person or group of persons. In this case, the Court held that the failure to provide for any form of notification in the law could not be reconciled with the principle of the rule of law and, consequently, violated the Convention guarantees.[147] In contrast, in the Chamber's judgment in *Centrum för rättvisa v. Sweden*, the Court accepted the lack of notification combined with an *ex post* review mechanism.[148] In this regard, Swedish law provides for a specific remedy, which is the possibility for any interested party to lodge a complaint with SIUN, an independent body that exercises control over bulk surveillance regimes operated by the electronic intelligence service (FRA). SIUN is legally obliged to investigate the legitimacy of the complaint, including verification that there has been no abuse of power in an individual case.[149] However, the position expressed in the Chamber's judgment was partially modified by the Grand Chamber, which found that the institution of a complaint to SIUN was not per se sufficient for the *ex post* review process to be considered complete and independent in every case. Such an assessment by the Grand Chamber stems from the fact that SIUN, as the body that exercises oversight, functions in the process of applying surveillance and therefore cannot objectively supervise itself.[150]

In contrast, in the UK case – decided in parallel with the Swedish case – the complaints mechanism implemented by a specialised judicial body (IPT) was considered sufficient by the Grand Chamber, which led to the conclusion that this measure effectively replaced the complete absence of a notification

145 Ibid. at [358].
146 Ibid. See also *Centrum för rättvisa v. Sweden* [GC] (n 51) at [272].
147 *Szabó and Vissy v. Hungary* (n 46) at [86]. See also *Association for European Integration and Human Rights and Ekimdzhiev v. Bulgaria* (n 9) at [90].
148 *Centrum för rättvisa v. Sweden* [Chamber] (n 138) at [172].
149 See Art. 10a of the Swedish Act on Signals Intelligence Defence Activities, SFS 2008:717.
150 *Centrum för rättvisa v. Sweden* [GC] (n 51) at [359].

procedure. Against this background, however, it should be borne in mind that also in earlier case law (e.g. *Kennedy v. UK*) the Court had accepted the possibility of replacing the notification mechanism with an elaborate *ex post* review.[151] Although both *Kennedy* and *Big Brother Watch* examined the UK surveillance legislation, it was only in the latter case that the Court made it clear that an appropriately expansive *ex post* review could entirely replace the obligation to notify the person concerned.

The differences in the Court's interpretation of the standard of legal safeguards between the earlier cases applying the *Huvig/Weber* criteria and the more recent cases in which the Grand Chamber introduced the *Big Brother Watch* standard are also apparent with regard to the mechanisms established for dealing with the material collected. An example is the data retention requirement. Although, as indicated earlier, the Court repeatedly emphasised the importance of retaining surveillance data only for the time necessary to pursue legitimate purposes, the interpretation of this requirement in relation to indiscriminate surveillance measures was problematic. In their case, the "necessity of the processing" was often understood to mean that there was no certainty that the data were unnecessary.

In examining the modus operandi of signals intelligence, the ECtHR stressed that the intrusiveness of this form of surveillance increases with the degree of information processing. In other words, according to the Court it is the lowest at the initial stage of the bulk capture of transmissions. This observation led to the conclusion that a less stringent legal framework could be applied to data from bulk interception, allowing them to be retained for the time necessary for their processing.[152] The Court considered it acceptable for this period to be no more than 1 year. In such a view, it is only the processed information that should be assessed against the criterion established earlier in *Huvig/Weber*, according to which the duration of information storage should be linked to the need to achieve the purpose for which the data were originally collected. This interpretation thus implies not only that a separate retention period can be established for unprocessed data, but also that there is no obligation to demonstrate that the data originally collected as a result of the bulk interception of transmissions were actually necessary to achieve the legitimate purpose for which this measure was applied.

Rather than clarifying previous doubts, the Court's reasoning introduced a number of new ones. The very concept of "raw material" (or "unprocessed information") that was used by ECtHR is difficult to define. Contrary to popular opinion, bulk systems are not used to record all electronic communications. As explained in Chapter 1, selectors can be used as early as when filtering a data stream on network devices. In effect, what the Court calls

151 *Kennedy v. the United Kingdom* (n 8) at [167].

152 *Centrum för rättvisa v. Sweden* [Chamber] (n 138) at [146]; *Centrum för rättvisa v. Sweden* [GC] (n 51) at [340].

"raw material" is a collection of information that has already been subjected to automatic analysis and meets the initial search criteria set by the authorised bodies. Although the degree (depth) of such preliminary analysis may vary, in the absence of a transparent definition it is not clear when such a dataset should be considered already "processed" as interpreted by the ECtHR. It is possible that the criterion is subjecting it to manual analysis.[153] This, however, would lead to a situation where subjecting a dataset to advanced processing using big data algorithms would not mean that these data have been processed. Going further, if new facts were revealed as a result of such processing, the original data might de facto never be presented to the analyst and thus, in the above sense, would never become "processed."

It is also unclear how the Court concluded that a 12-month period of retention of unprocessed information does not, in principle, go beyond what can be considered necessary.[154] Such a long retention period creates an incentive to capture all information only to decide over a period of 1 year which information may have a value justifying its continued storage. Such an interpretation leads directly to condoning the existence of a system of permanent and widespread surveillance, during which the authorities can record any information. This reasoning appears to be manifestly incompatible with the Court's previous case law, which pointed to the impermissibility of subsequently justifying the necessity of surveillance orders that have already been executed.[155] It also appears that such a 12-month retention of "raw material" is exactly the measure that the Court defined as impermissible in its earlier case law, for it de facto leads to the collection of all data, including those unrelated to the purpose of applying surveillance.[156]

Thus, while the development of the *Big Brother Watch* standard certainly represents an important step in the evolution of the ECtHR's jurisprudence, thanks to which the risks associated with the use of untargeted measures are addressed more clearly, the Court's position remains insufficiently precise in many areas (see Table 4.3).[157] Moreover, given the short period that has elapsed since the Grand Chamber's judgment in *Big Brother Watch v. UK*, the actual usefulness of the standard set out therein has not yet been confirmed in any other case.[158]

153 *Centrum för rättvisa v. Sweden* [GC] (n 51) at [306]: "the processed information is analysed by an analyst in order to identify intelligence therein."

154 In fact, the Grand Chamber judgment lacks any in-depth analysis in this regard. This partly stems from the lack of sufficient information, which was also pointed out by the Court (see [343]).

155 *Liblik and Others v. Estonia* (n 10) at [141].

156 *M.K. v. France* (19522/09) 18 April 2013 ECtHR at [40].

157 Monika Zalnieriute, 'Procedural Fetishism and Mass Surveillance under the ECHR' (*Verfassungsblog*, 2 June 2021) <https://verfassungsblog.de/big-b-v-uk/> accessed 26 August 2022.

158 Yet, the standard of legal safeguards introduced in *Big Brother Watch* was referred to in *Ships Waste Oil Collector B.V. v. the Netherlands* (2799/16) 16 May 2023 ECtHR.

Table 4.3 Comparison of the *Huvig/Weber* and *Big Brother Watch* tests.

	Huvig/Weber test	*Big Brother Watch test*
1	The nature of offences which may give rise to an interception order	The grounds on which bulk interception may be authorised
2	A definition of the categories of people liable to have their communications intercepted	The circumstances in which an individual's communications may be intercepted
3	A limit on the duration of interception	The limits on the duration of interception, the storage of intercepted material and the circumstances in which such material must be erased and destroyed
4	The circumstances in which intercepted data may or must be erased or destroyed	
5	The procedure to be followed for examining, using and storing the data obtained	The procedures to be followed for selecting, examining and using intercepted material
6	The precautions to be taken when communicating the data to other parties	The precautions to be taken when communicating the material to other parties
7		The procedure to be followed for granting authorisation
8		The procedures and modalities for supervision by an independent authority of compliance with the above safeguards and its powers to address non-compliance
9		The procedures for independent *ex post facto* review of such compliance and the powers vested in the competent body in addressing instances of non-compliance

4.4.4 Adoption of the ECtHR standard by the CJEU

In discussing the impact of the Strasbourg standard on the CJEU's jurisprudence, it is important to bear in mind the significantly different scope of competence of the two courts in cases concerning surveillance measures implemented by public authorities. What is relevant in this respect is not only the Treaty exclusion of national security objectives from the scope of European Union law,[159] but also the limitations on the Luxembourg Court's competence to review the proportionality of measures used by national law enforcement authorities.[160]

Therefore it is the ECtHR that was traditionally seen as the supranational body for the protection of fundamental rights, and best placed to scrutinise

159 For more on the national security clause in EU law, see section 3.3.
160 See Art. 276 of the TFEU.

national surveillance programmes and, consequently, to set minimum standards for the legal safeguards applied in this area. It is only with the evolution of the EU telecommunications and digital services framework that questions about the legality of various forms of surveillance have been increasingly raised also in terms of the application of EU law.

Although the position presented in the CJEU's jurisprudence is often contrasted with the ECtHR's interpretation, in practice one cannot speak of a kind of jurisprudential parting of the ways between the two Courts.[161] The principle deriving from Article 52(3) of the Charter, that the way in which the rights guaranteed therein are applied must be consistent with the interpretation of the identical guarantees under the ECHR, also binds the CJEU. However, the ECtHR case law sets a minimum standard in this respect, creating space for establishing more far-reaching safeguards in relation to EU law.

Therefore it is not surprising that in the cases in which the Luxembourg Court examined national surveillance laws much of the reasoning presented was based on the interpretations previously provided by the ECtHR.[162] The EU Court of Justice– although not directly – also applied the criteria of the accessibility and foreseeability of the law established in the Strasbourg jurisprudence in the process of assessing surveillance measures.[163] Given the key role of proportionality as a necessary condition for the establishment of limitations to the rights guaranteed by the Charter, the CJEU in its jurisprudence applies the classical four-step proportionality test, whereby it assesses the various components of the surveillance provisions under review, also referring them to the standard introduced by the ECtHR. Even when the CJEU did not explicitly refer to the *Huvig/Weber* test, it did, in fact, invoke the same safeguards when examining successive areas of surveillance application.[164]

In doing so, the CJEU did not stop at interpreting the Strasbourg standard in the light of the norms of EU law, but – to ensure the full effectiveness of EU law – also identified additional requirements which, by setting a higher level of protection, sought to ensure the full effectiveness of the Charter's guarantees. In this way, the CJEU case law should be associated with the establishment of additional legal safeguards that expand on the ECtHR standards discussed earlier and bind the Member States, yet only to the extent that they apply European Union law.

161 Paul De Hert and Gianclaudio Malgieri, 'One European Legal Framework for Surveillance: The ECtHR's Expanded Legality Testing Copied by the CJEU' in Valsamis Mitsilegas and Niovi Vavoula (eds), *Surveillance and Privacy in the Digital Age: European, Transatlantic and Global Perspectives* (Hart 2021) 385–386.

162 *Digital Rights Ireland* (Joined Cases C-293/12 and C-594/12) EU:C:2014:238 at [54].

163 See e.g. Prokuratuur (C-746/18) EU:C:2021:152 at [49]; *G.D. v. the Commissioner of the Garda Síochána and Others* (C-140/20) EU:C:2022:258 at [62]; *SpaceNet* (Joined Cases C-793/19 and C-794/19) EU:C:2022:702 at [72].

164 *La Quadrature du Net and Others v. Premier ministre and Others* (Joined Cases C-511/18, C-512/18 and C-520/18) EU:C:2020:791 at [132]; 'LQN'.

According to the UK Investigatory Powers Tribunal, the group of requirements that go beyond the Convention standards includes:

1 a restriction on non-targeted access to bulk data;
2 a need for prior authorisation before data could be accessed;
3 provision for subsequent notification of those affected;
4 retention of all data within the European Union.[165]

However, it seems that, contrary to what the IPT has indicated, the first safeguard does not actually go beyond the ECtHR standard. Rather, it is the result of the application of the criterion of ***strict necessity*** – well-known from the Luxembourg standard – to the entire process of indiscriminate surveillance, that is, both at the data collection stage and with respect to the subsequent use of the data.[166]

As a result, the Court of Justice has consistently emphasised the need to demonstrate a close connection between the extent of the data processed and proceedings related to the prosecution of specific crimes or threats to public security.[167] At the same time, as in the ECtHR standard it is also important to examine whether the degree of interference with the individual's rights bears a relation to the gravity of the general interest for the pursuit of which the measure was established.[168]

In contrast, the differences between the CJEU and ECtHR jurisprudence are more pronounced with regard to the authorisation of the use of surveillance measures.[169] Like the ECtHR, the Luxembourg Court also accepts that the authorisation of surveillance can be entrusted to courts or other independent administrative bodies. However, unlike the Strasbourg standard the EU Court of Justice emphasises the importance of prior review as a necessary condition for the legality of the measures taken. The CJEU clarifies that, given the degree of interference with the rights of the individual involved in the use of electronic surveillance measures, *ex post* scrutiny, albeit an important safeguard, cannot replace prior review. Moreover, *ex ante* review must be carried out by a fully independent body, i.e. one that acts "objectively and impartially when carrying out its duties" and is "free from any external influence."[170] This excludes the possibility of entrusting the authorisation of surveillance orders to the public prosecutor's office if the law does not guarantee its full independence from the executive.

165 *Big Brother Watch and Others v. the United Kingdom* [GC] (n 47) at [235].
166 Which the ECtHR itself has de facto abandoned; see the analysis presented in section 5.3.
167 *Prokuratuur* (n 163) at [45].
168 *Ministerio Fiscal* (n 135) at [55] and *La Quadrature du Net and Others v. Premier ministre and Others* (n 164) at [131].
169 Valsamis Mitsilegas and others, 'Data Retention and the Future of Large-Scale Surveillance: The Evolution and Contestation of Judicial Benchmarks' (2022) European Law Journal 1, 28.
170 *Prosecutor's offices* (n 163) at [53].

The CJEU also stresses the importance of the notification obligation for the effective protection of rights of the persons concerned. As in the Strasbourg standard, the notification obligation should be fulfilled when it does not jeopardise the ongoing investigation.[171] At the same time, the CJEU points out the connection between the notification of persons subject to surveillance and the availability of judicial recourse. In doing so, it emphasises that

> legislation not providing for any possibility for an individual to pursue legal remedies in order to have access to personal data relating to him, or to obtain the rectification or erasure of such data, does not respect the essence of the fundamental right to effective judicial protection, as enshrined in Article 47 of the Charter.[172]

This leads to the conclusion that the lack of notification – if other redress mechanisms are not provided – constitutes a defect that renders the legislation under review incompatible with EU law.[173] However, the CJEU's position does not predetermine that it is impermissible to completely replace notification with the implementation of sufficiently elaborate *ex post* review measures, i.e. the solution explicitly advocated in the most recent ECtHR jurisprudence (*cf.* the earlier discussion of the *Big Brother Watch* standard).

The Luxembourg case law also imposes stricter limits on data retention procedures. Indeed, first of all it excludes the possibility of data transfer outside the European Union to ensure that the data collected will be permanently subject to the same legal protection. Moreover, while the CJEU – like the ECtHR – points out the need to store data only for the period needed to fulfil a legitimate purpose, it does not accept the possibility of collecting redundant data. According to the CJEU, any "legislation that provides for the retention of personal data must continue to satisfy objective criteria that establish a connection between the data to be retained and the objective pursued."[174] This leads to the conclusion that irrespective of the retention periods adopted, the retention of information unrelated to the purpose for which it was collected breaches the principle of proportionality and cannot therefore be reconciled with respect for Charter rights.[175] This conclusion is clearly difficult to reconcile with the permissibility of the storage of "raw material" arising from the most recent ECtHR case law.

4.5 Summary

Since the *Klass v. Germany* case – decided more than 40 years ago – the issue of the adequacy of the legal mechanisms established in the area of electronic surveillance has continuously been in the public spotlight, leading to

171 *Tele2 Sverige* (C-203/15 and C-698/15) EU:C:2016:970 at [121].
172 *Maximillian Schrems v. Data Protection Commissioner* (C-362/14) EU:C:2015:650 at [95].
173 *Opinion on the EU-Canada PNR Agreement* (Opinion 1/15) EU:C:2016:656 at [232].
174 *Ligue des droits humains ASBL v. Conseil des ministres* (C-817/19) EU:C:2022:491 at [118].
175 *Opinion on the EU-Canada PNR Agreement* (n 173) at [205].

numerous discussions and disputes. During this time, the ECtHR alone has decided dozens of cases in which complainants challenged various aspects of national surveillance regimes. There were often very significant differences between them concerning the purpose of surveillance, the manner in which it was established, the readability and accessibility of the regulations under scrutiny, and the procedures for legal protection. The development of technology has not only influenced the spread of new forms of surveillance but also significantly transformed the digital services market – changing public expectations of protection against unauthorised data collection and processing. Indirectly, it has also led to the evolution of legal safeguards standards, especially those responding to the increasing use of untargeted measures. Hence, based on the examination of the European case law, at least four major models for the legal regulation of surveillance measures can be identified:

1 *Huvig/Weber* – used in cases of individual surveillance, in cases of eavesdropping on communications, and in cases where surveillance has been applied to persons not connected (even indirectly) with criminal activity;
2 *Uzun* – established for the purpose of assessing cases of "minor" interference, in practice losing relevance from the perspective of assessing surveillance programmes conducted by public authorities;
3 *Big Brother Watch* – adapts the *Huvig/Weber* standard to the specifics of indiscriminate surveillance programmes;
4 *The CJEU standard* – which can be described as an extended ("enhanced") version of the *Huvig/Weber* standard used by the CJEU to assess electronic surveillance programmes conducted by public authorities. It remains partly incompatible with *Big Brother Watch*, which is interesting in that both standards build on *Huvig/Weber*.

The ECtHR's jurisprudence is, of course, of particular importance for surveillance practice. The Court's interpretation of concepts such as "strict necessity," "accessibility of the law" or "foreseeability of the law" has influenced the jurisprudence of European constitutional courts and has been permanently embedded in the EU legal order.

Although the ECtHR's extensive jurisprudence contains a number of guidelines clarifying how the legal safeguards and standards established relate to different forms of surveillance, in many cases these still prove to be insufficiently precise to definitively resolve the emerging ambiguities. This is partly the result of the wide margin of appreciation that the Court initially granted to states in shaping domestic criminal policy or in pursuing national security objectives. In recent years, the Court's position has also evolved in this respect, leading to a recognition that the more intrusive are the measures introduced into national legislation, the greater the limits to the states' discretion must be.[176]

176 Janneke Gerards, 'Margin of Appreciation and Incrementalism in the Case Law of the European Court of Human Rights' (2018) 18 *Human Rights Law Review* 495.

Against this background, even a preliminary analysis reveals differences between the interpretation of the same guarantees presented in the ECtHR and CJEU case law. Those differences have become particularly apparent in the last decade as both courts have dealt with assessing the admissibility of indiscriminate surveillance programmes, which cause the greatest concerns regarding not only interference with individual rights but also in terms of being a threat to the democratic system of the state.

It seems that understanding the reasons leading to the emergence of these differences is crucial to the discussion on the future shape of European electronic surveillance standards. Thus, this issue will be discussed in more detail in the next chapter.

References

Breyer P, 'Telecommunications Data Retention and Human Rights: The Compatibility of Blanket Traffic Data Retention with the ECHR' (2005) 11 *European Law Journal* 365.

Burke KC, 'Secret Surveillance and the European Convention on Human Rights' (1980) 33 *Stanford Law Review* 1113.

De Hert P and Malgieri G, 'One European Legal Framework for Surveillance: The ECtHR's Expanded Legality Testing Copied by the CJEU' in Valsamis Mitsilegas and Niovi Vavoula (eds), *Surveillance and Privacy in the Digital Age: European, Transatlantic and Global Perspectives* (Hart 2021).

Duttwiler M, 'Authority, Control and Jurisdiction in the Extraterritorial Application of the European Convention on Human Rights' (2012) 30 *Netherlands Quarterly of Human Rights* 137.

Enders C, 'Right to Have Rights – The German Constitutional Concept of Human Dignity' (2010) 3 *NUJS Law Review* 253.

Galli F, 'The Interception of Communication in France and Italy – What Relevance for the Development of English Law?' (2016) 20 *The International Journal of Human Rights* 666.

Gerards J, 'Margin of Appreciation and Incrementalism in the Case Law of the European Court of Human Rights' (2018) 18 *Human Rights Law Review* 495.

–, 'Abstract and Concrete Reasonableness Review by the European Court of Human Rights' (2020) 1 *European Convention on Human Rights Law Review* 218.

Glancy DJ, 'Privacy in Autonomous Vehicles' (2012) 52 *Santa Clara Law Review* 1171.

'Guide on Article 1 of the European Convention on Human Rights' (European Court of Human Rights 2020) <https://cli.re/JpwmZW> accessed 6 September 2023.

Kappler K, 'Consequences of the German Constitutional Court's Ruling on Germany's Foreign Intelligence Service: The Importance of Human Rights in the Cooperation of Intelligence Services' (2022) 23 *German Law Journal* 173.

Kwoka MB, 'The Procedural Exceptionalism of National Security Secrecy' (2017) 97 *Boston University Law Review* 103.

Malgieri G and De Hert P, 'European Human Rights, Criminal Surveillance, and Intelligence Surveillance: Towards "Good Enough" Oversight, Preferably but Not Necessarily by Judges' in David Gray and Stephen E Henderson (eds), *The Cambridge Handbook of Surveillance Law* (Cambridge University Press 2017).

Miller RA, 'Intelligence Oversight – Made in Germany' in Zachary K Goldman, Jane Harman and Samuel J Rascoff (eds), *Global Intelligence Oversight* (Oxford University Press 2016) <https://academic.oup.com/book/4147/chapter/145922344> accessed 13 September 2023.

Mitsilegas V and others, 'Data Retention and the Future of Large-Scale Surveillance: The Evolution and Contestation of Judicial Benchmarks' (2022) *European Law Journal* 1.

Murray D and Fussey P, 'Bulk Surveillance in the Digital Age: Rethinking the Human Rights Law Approach to Bulk Monitoring of Communications Data' (2019) 52 *Israel Law Review* 31.

'Report on the Democratic Oversight of Signals Intelligence Agencies' (Venice Commission 2015) CDL-AD(2015)011 <https://cli.re/ApE7Ad> accessed 6 September 2023.

Rojszczak M, 'Extraterritorial Bulk Surveillance after the German BND Act Judgment' (2021) 17 *European Constitutional Law Review* 53.

Ryngaert C, 'Clarifying the Extraterritorial Application of the European Convention on Human Rights (*Al-Skeini v. the United Kingdom*)' (2012) 28 *Utrecht Journal of International and European Law* 57.

Schabas W, *The European Convention on Human Rights: A Commentary* (First Paperback edition, Oxford University Press 2017).

Solove DJ and Schwartz PM, *Information Privacy Law* (Sixth edition, Wolters Kluwer 2018).

van der Sloot B, 'The Quality of Law' (2020) 11 *JIPITEC* 160.

van der Sloot B, 'Big Brother Watch and Others v. the United Kingdom & Centrum För Rättvisa v. Sweden: Does the Grand Chamber Set Back the Clock in Mass Surveillance Cases?' (2021) 7 *European Data Protection Law Review* 319.

van der Sloot B and Kosta E, '*Big Brother Watch and Others v. UK*: Lessons from the Latest Strasbourg Ruling on Bulk Surveillance' (2019) 5 *European Data Protection Law Review* 252.

Veneziano A, 'Applying the U.S. Constitution Abroad, from the Era of the U.S. Founding to the Modern Age' (2019) 46 *Fordham Urban Law Journal* 602.

Zalnieriute M, 'Procedural Fetishism and Mass Surveillance under the ECHR' (*Verfassungsblog*, 2 June 2021) <https://verfassungsblog.de/big-b-v-uk/> accessed 26 August 2022.

5 In search of a European consensus

5.1 Introduction

Although the permissibility of various forms of surveillance has been the focus of judicial attention for years, in practice it is only in the last decade that this issue has become the subject of many precedent-setting decisions. At least three main reasons that have contributed to the increased interest in judicial review of this area can be identified.

The first is the rapid development of surveillance capabilities, including those for mass information gathering and processing. This was a direct result of the 9/11 attacks on the World Trade Center (WTC) and the shift in the attention of SIAs to the identification of domestic threats. It is likely that had it not been for the attacks on the WTC (and subsequent ones in Madrid and London), many of the bulk NSA programmes later revealed by Edward Snowden would not have been created,[1] and the Data Retention Directive would not have been adopted in the European Union.[2] Disputes over the legality of data retention legislation led to a number of decisions by the highest judicial authorities of individual EU Member States, which ultimately came to be scrutinised by the CJEU and the ECtHR.

The second reason for the increased interest in judicial review of state surveillance activities is the increased public awareness of the intrusiveness of the measures employed, largely as a result of the information disclosed by Snowden in 2013. It is worth recalling that much of it had already been available (but not widely known) to the public earlier.[3] However, it was only the detail of the data provided by the former NSA analyst that revealed a fuller

1 Laura K Donohue, *The Future of Foreign Intelligence: Privacy and Surveillance in a Digital Age* (Oxford University Press 2016) 16–30.

2 See section 5.2.1.

3 The first information about STELLARWIND – the NSA-run metadata collection programme – was published by the New York Times back in 2005. See James Risen and Eric Lichtblau, 'Bush Lets U.S. Spy on Callers Without Courts' *The New York Times* (16 December 2005) <https://cli.re/A5byvJ> accessed 6 September 2023. G Alex Sinha, 'NSA Surveillance since 9/11 and the Human Right to Privacy' (2013) 59 *Loyola Law Review* 861.

DOI: 10.4324/9781003449263-5

picture of the reach of indiscriminate surveillance programmes. Largely as a result of Snowden's activity, a number of complaints were heard by the UK IPT, in which – not without some success[4] – various aspects of the UK's surveillance regime were challenged. Some of these cases eventually resulted in requests for a preliminary ruling to the CJEU and complaints to the ECtHR. In this way, the GCHQ's activities, which for years had escaped external oversight, came under scrutiny in cases such as *Privacy International* (CJEU, 2020); *Big Brother Watch v. UK* (ECtHR, 2021); and *Privacy International v. UK* (ECtHR, 2022). The importance of the information revealed by Snowden is also confirmed by the fact that it is essentially only the surveillance programmes run by the GCHQ that have been the subject of so many court complaints. The activities of the German BND, the French DGSE, and the Danish FE have not received so much public attention, mainly because information on the scale of the programmes conducted by these services has been largely based on media reports, often unverifiable.[5]

The third reason for the growing importance of judicial review of surveillance is related to the reluctance of some states to comply with the judicial interpretations provided in already decided cases. Suffice it to say that the CJEU has addressed the issue of data retention on eight occasions – not only because of ambiguities regarding various aspects of the application of data retention provisions, but also in response to legislative efforts to shape national legislation in such a way that would preserve the surveillance status quo while ostensibly aligning with the Luxembourg standard.

As a result, there have been a number of key judgments over the past decade or so that have assessed various aspects of the use of indiscriminate electronic surveillance measures. As similar surveillance regimes – and in some cases, even the same intelligence programmes – have been scrutinised by different courts, the consistency of the emerging line of case law has also become increasingly important. This issue has been of particular importance in relation to the two most important European courts, namely the CJEU and the ECtHR. Although they share the same legal concepts and standards as a source of interpretation, the arguments presented have in many cases led to different conclusions, potentially creating the risk of forming separate and (partly) incompatible lines of jurisprudence.

This chapter aims to discuss in more detail the similarities and differences in the current case law of the European Court of Justice and the European Court of Human Rights in key areas of the assessment of indiscriminate surveillance

4 See e.g. *Liberty & Others v. the Security Service, SIS, GCHQ* ([2015] UKIPTrib 13_77-H_2) 22 June 2015 Investigatory Powers Tribunal.

5 See e.g. Sébastian Seibt, 'How Denmark Became the NSA's Listening Post in Europe' *France24* (1 June 2021) <https://cli.re/vNxzdD> accessed 6 September 2023; Félix Tréguer, 'Major Oversight Gaps in the French Intelligence Legal Framework' *about:intel* (25 March 2022) <https://cli.re/XjMm1K> accessed 6 September 2023.

programmes. Therefore the CJEU's interpretation of the compatibility of untargeted surveillance measures with EU law will first be discussed using the example of EU and national telecommunications data retention rules. Next it will be explained why, when examining similar regulations, the ECtHR reached partially different conclusions in its recent case law. In this respect, particular attention will be paid to the differences concerning the interpretation of the concept of *necessity* in relation to bulk surveillance measures. The following section will present the differences in the assessment of the legality of international transfers of data obtained from bulk surveillance. The chapter will conclude by addressing the question of whether the partially different positions taken by the ECtHR and the CJEU result in strengthening or weakening the European legal model. In this regard, a proposal will also be presented for a new standard of legal safeguards, built on the best practices emerging from the jurisprudence of both Courts and aimed at ensuring fuller oversight over the modern forms of surveillance used by public authorities.

5.2 The CJEU perspective: a more than decade-long saga concerning a general data retention obligation

5.2.1 Origins of the legal regulation of data retention in EU law

A particular form of indiscriminate surveillance, and one which is also closely associated with EU law, is the so-called general data retention. This term is actually used to describe two measures that together form the legal framework for access by public authorities to retained telecommunications data.

The first is a general data retention obligation – i.e. a legal obligation for providers of electronic communications services to record all metadata originating from such services, combined with an obligation to retain the data for a specified period of time (usually 6–12 months). The second measure concerns procedures for access to retained data, indicating the circumstances and mode in which such metadata may be acquired by authorised public authorities (usually law enforcement authorities and secret services).

The genesis of the establishment of the EU data retention rules is linked to the discussion among Member States after the attacks of 11 September 2001, which highlighted the need to strengthen cooperation in the field of criminal law in relation to the collection and transfer of telecommunications data. According to some Member States, new cooperation mechanisms were needed to increase the effectiveness of actions taken against the most serious crimes – especially terrorist ones. It is worth recalling that one of the effects of the attacks on the WTC was the reorganisation of electronic intelligence structures by many states, which were then faced with more tasks related to identifying and combating internal threats. A response to these needs was increasing data collection and analysis capabilities, which also led to a new generation of surveillance programmes based on the mass interception of domestic electronic communications. This period also saw the development of programmes explicitly dedicated to the bulk collection and processing of metadata derived from electronic communications.[6]

A potential limitation to the effectiveness of the analytical systems being built was the lack of necessary data. Not only did different Member States regulate the area of access to telecommunications data differently, but they also applied different rules on the mandatory retention of such data. Hence, on the initiative of Ireland and France, among others, a new piece of legislation was drafted in 2014[7] and finally adopted as Directive 2006/24 (the Data Retention Directive [DRD]).[8] Its primary objective was to harmonise Member States' national laws with a view to establishing a legal obligation for telecommunications operators to collect the indicated categories of metadata. The measure was intended to help secure information not only for the purposes of proceedings conducted in a given Member State, but also for activities carried out by authorised bodies in other countries. Hence, the Data Retention Directive also created a general framework for future international cooperation in the area of the exchange of electronic evidence. Although this circumstance is often overlooked from today's perspective, it is worth recalling that the work on the DRD coincided with the turbulent period of the attacks in Spain and the United Kingdom. Indeed, in the course of the Council's work, the 2008 London bombings were explicitly identified as a circumstance leading to the intensification of efforts to rapidly adopt the Data Retention Directive, which was seen as an important mechanism in response to the growing terrorist threats at the time.[9] Already in the initial draft, it was pointed out that countering this type of threat required the establishment of far-reaching measures making use of untargeted data collection, thus moving away from the paradigm of collecting "specific data relating to specified individuals in specific cases."[10]

What is also important – and not without impact in today's discussion on data retention – is that the Franco-Irish proposal did not aim to adopt a directive but called for the adoption of a different type of EU legal act – namely a Council framework decision. Decisions of this type were, in the pre-Lisbon era, the appropriate instruments for action in the field of cooperation in criminal

6 See the STELLAR WIND programme referred to in n 3; the timeframe of the programme is presented in detail in: 'Report on the President's Surveillance Program' (Inspectors General of the DoD, DoJ, CIA, NSA and DNI 2009) <https://cli.re/VJnJ3P> accessed 6 September 2023.

7 'Draft Framework Decision on the Data Retention' (Council of the European Union 2004) 8958/04.

8 Directive 2006/24 of the European Parliament and of the Council of 15 March 2006 on the retention of data generated or processed in connection with the provision of publicly available electronic communications services or of public communications networks and amending Directive 2002/58/EC, OJ 2006 L105/54; repealed.

9 'Extraordinary Council Meeting Justice and Home Affairs' (Council of the European Union 2005) 11116/05 (Presse 187) <https://cli.re/n4Ev9d> accessed 6 September 2023.

10 See recital 6 in the 'Draft Framework Decision' (n 7).

matters. In the end, however, the new legislation was adopted based on the provisions on economic cooperation (harmonisation of national laws) under the general Article 112 of the TFEU (then Article 95 of the Treaty establishing the European Community). As it later turned out, this change was more far-reaching than initially envisaged by its drafters.[11]

The Data Retention Directive was, in principle, a *lex specialis* to the e-Privacy Directive, already in force at the time.[12] Its adoption also had the effect of limiting the ability of Member States to establish their own data retention rules based on Article 15(1) of the e-Privacy Directive. The Data Retention Directive thus led to full harmonisation within the scope of, and in relation to, data the retention of which was required under the Directive and for the purposes established by it.[13] This act then became the subject of transposition into national law,[14] leading to the adoption of provisions requiring telecommunications operators to retain metadata originating from electronic communications.

5.2.2 General obligation to retain data

From the beginning of the work on the Data Retention Directive, it was the subject of criticism. Both the formal basis for its introduction and the necessity in EU law of a measure such as a general obligation to retain data for crime-fighting purposes were questioned.[15]

In terms of its formal basis, as early as in 2009 the EU Court of Justice had to decide whether the EU institutions had exceeded their competences by introducing the Directive.[16] In the Irish government's view, a data retention directive introducing a measure to be used primarily for the prevention, investigation, detection and prosecution of crime should have been adopted through the legislative procedure dedicated to cooperation in criminal matters and not the ordinary legislative procedure typical for the harmonisation

11 The use of Art. 112 of the TFEU was intended to facilitate the procedure and adoption of the act without the need to ensure unanimity and in a way that covered the whole EU, including Ireland and Denmark.

12 However, it was not a *lex specialis sensu stricto*. Both acts were introduced on the same legal basis (harmonisation of the internal market) and worked independently.

13 See also Opinion of AG Saugmandsgaard Øe of 19 July 2016 *Tele2 Sverige* (Joined Cases C-203/15 and C-698/15) ECLI:EU:C:2016:572 at [113–115].

14 Which, however, was problematic from the start, leading to a series of disputes with the Commission, see Theodore Konstadinides, 'Destroying Democracy on the Ground of Defending It? The Data Retention Directive, the Surveillance State and Our Constitutional Ecosystem' (2011) 36 *European Law Review* 722, 734.

15 *Cf.* Marie-Helen Maras, 'From Targeted to Mass Surveillance: Is the EU Data Retention Directive a Necessary Measure or an Unjustified Threat to Privacy?' in Benjamin J Goold (ed), *New Directions in Surveillance and Privacy* (Willan 2013) <www.taylorfrancis.com/books/9781843927266> accessed 30 March 2021.

16 *Ireland v. Parliament and Council* (C-301/06) EU:C:2009:68.

of economic rules. If the Court had accepted that argument, the Member States could similarly demonstrate the lack of competence of the European Union to adopt other legislative measures having an indirect influence on the effectiveness of actions taken in the area of combating serious crime. Notably, one of the objectives of the Directive, explicitly mentioned in its wording, was the fight against terrorism,[17] which was a task also attributed to the area of national security. However, the Court did not share the applicants' position, pointing out that the analysis of the purpose of a measure such as a general data retention obligation must take into account the context of the entities obliged to apply it. Already in the *Promusicae* case, the Court had emphasised that national security, defence or public security were activities inherent to state authorities unrelated to the fields of activity of individuals.[18] The EU data retention rules imposed obligations on electronic communications services providers and did not regulate public authorities' use of such data. Having regard to this circumstance, the Court considered that the measure under review predominantly concerned the functioning of the internal market and that its adoption under the economic cooperation provisions had been appropriate.

With regard to the substantive scope of the provisions of the Directive, it was argued that the recording of all metadata on electronic communications without any connection with ongoing proceedings and in a generalised manner, in relation to all subscribers to telecommunications services, could not be reconciled with the principle of proportionality. Arguments formulated by national constitutional courts, which (to varying extents and degrees) drew attention to the disproportionality of unrestricted sharing of retained data with public authorities, were significant in this context.[19] Particularly influential in the evolution of the European jurisprudence was the 2010 judgment of the German Federal Constitutional Court (bVerfG), which found certain measures adopted in national law as a result of the transposition of the Data Retention Directive to be unconstitutional. The court aptly noted:

> The retained data has extensive informative value. Depending on how the affected persons use telecommunications services, the data may by itself already reveal profound insights into the social environment and the individual activities of individual citizens – this applies all the more if the data serves as a starting point for further investigations.[20]

17 See recital 9 of the Data Retention Directive.

18 *Promusicae v. Telefónica de España SAU* (C-275/06) ECLI:EU:C:2008:54 at [51].

19 Historically, the first judgment recognising the defectiveness of retention legislation was delivered by the Romanian Constitutional Court – see Adrian Bannon, 'Romania Retrenches on Data Retention' (2010) 24 *International Review of Law, Computers & Technology* 145.

20 BVerfG 2 March 2010 (1 BvR 256/08) DE:BVerfG:2010:rs20100302.1bvr025608 at [211].

On this basis, it pointed out that the analysis of retained telecommunications metadata – even if it does not include the content of correspondence – is sufficient to make detailed findings about an individual, including those related to their worldview, political opinions and personal preferences, as well as interests or vulnerabilities, "including those that fall within the intimate sphere."[21]

However the bVerfG, while ruling the German legislation unconstitutional, held that the 6-month data retention period "is not *per se* incompatible with Art. 10 of the Basic Law."[22] It pointed out that it was crucial to establish a link between retention and the actual necessity of obtaining certain information, in accordance with the principle of proportionality. Thus, although the Court's judgment is commonly cited as the first signal of the impermissibility of a general data retention obligation, the judgment per se did not reach such a conclusion. Moreover, the position presented by bVerfG at the time pointed rather to the possibility of implementing the Data Retention Directive in a manner consistent with the requirements under the German Basic Law.[23] Interestingly, a similar argumentation, focusing on the flaws in the data access procedures yet without directly questioning the legality of the data retention rules, can be found in a judgment of the Polish Constitutional Court passed 4 years later.[24]

The concerns raised by BVerfG were largely confirmed by the EU Court of Justice in the precedent-setting *Digital Rights Ireland* ruling. As recalled by the Court, respect for fundamental rights – including the right to privacy – requires that derogations from them be limited to what is strictly necessary.[25] This requirement cannot be fulfilled by a measure which permanently and in a generalised manner restricts the right to privacy of all users of electronic communications without any real connection with a necessity arising from the pursuit of public security objectives.[26] In this way, the Data Retention Directive transformed an exception – which is how interference with the rights of individuals should be treated – into a norm. As a result, the Court held that the act under review, due to the fact that it had established a measure

21 Ibid.

22 Ibid. at [205].

23 Anna-Bettina Kaiser, 'German Federal Constitutional Court: German Data Retention Provisions Unconstitutional in Their Present Form; Decision of 2 March 2010, NJW 2010, p. 833' (2010) 6 *European Constitutional Law Review* 503.

24 In this case, unlike in the BVerfG judgment, the Polish Constitutional Tribunal did not rule on the compatibility of data retention with national law, as this issue was outside the scope of the case. See Jan Podkowik, 'Privacy in the Digital Era – Polish Electronic Surveillance Law Declared Partially Unconstitutional: Judgment of the Constitutional Tribunal of Poland of 30 July 2014, K 23/11' (2015) 11 *European Constitutional Law Review* 577.

25 *Digital Rights Ireland* (Joined Cases C-293/12 and C-594/12) EU:C:2014:238 at [52].

26 Ibid. at [57–59].

violating the principle of proportionality, could not be reconciled with overriding norms of EU law and was therefore invalid.[27]

The Court's decision had the effect of eliminating the Directive itself from the EU legal system but did not directly affect the validity of the national provisions adopted to implement it. However, because the Court ruled on the incompatibility of a particular legal mechanism (a general data retention obligation) with EU law – and given the principles of cooperation and the primacy of EU law – it was obvious that Member States should immediately take action to withdraw any such contested provisions from their national legal orders. In some countries, this was accomplished both as a result of legislative intervention[28] and constitutional courts' decisions.[29] In many other countries, however, the allegedly flawed national provisions remained in force, mainly as a result of the unwavering belief that data retention was a measure genuinely necessary to protect the core state functions and counter cases of serious crime.

The *Digital Rights Ireland* judgment focused on assessing the permissibility of the application of general data retention insofar as this measure was provided for in the Data Retention Directive. At the same time, it also became the starting point for years of litigation, ultimately leading to a series of subsequent rulings in which the CJEU clarified its earlier position by explaining whether and in what respects the data retention mechanism could be considered compatible with the Charter.

A concept that was central to the Court's considerations was undoubtedly *strict necessity* – the need for which in assessing the permissibility of electronic surveillance stemmed directly from earlier ECtHR case law.[30] It was the test of strict necessity that stood in the way of accepting that the scope of data collected[31] (and, at the later stage, also made available)[32] did not have to be linked, even indirectly, to a genuine need justifying the pursuit of a legitimate aim (in this case, the fight against serious crime). In fact, contrary to

27 The Court pointed to violations of Art. 7 (the right to privacy), Art. 8 (the protection of personal data) and Art. 52(1) of the Charter of Fundamental Rights. See Tuomas Ojanen, 'Court of Justice of the European Union, Decision of 8 April 2014 in Joined Cases C-293/12 and C-594/12' (2014) 10 European Constitutional Law Review 528; Valerio Lubello and Arianna Vedaschi, 'Data Retention and Its Implications for the Fundamental Right to Privacy: A European Perspective' (2015) 20 *Tilburg Law Review* 14.

28 For example, legislative action was taken in Luxembourg. See a discussion of legislative action in individual EU Member States in 'National Data Retention Laws since the CJEU's Tele-2/Watson Judgment' (Privacy International 2017) <http://cli.re/68zdoe.> accessed 6 September 2023.

29 E.g. in the case of Austria, Belgium, Bulgaria, the Netherlands or Slovakia. For a broader discussion of the position of constitutional courts on the permissibility of data retention, see: Marek Zubik, Jan Podkowik and Robert Rybski (eds), *European Constitutional Courts towards Data Retention Laws* (Springer 2021).

30 *Digital Rights Ireland* (n 25) at [47].

31 Ibid. at [56].

32 Ibid. at [62].

what is often argued the Court did not consider generalised retention per se as incompatible with EU law. Instead, in its reasoning it pointed out that such a measure, to be lawful, required the principle of proportionality to be met, while bulk data collection, by its very definition, was not proportional. Leaving aside further considerations on *access* to data (discussed in the next section), in terms of data *collection* the Court emphasised in the *Tele2* case the need to define "clear and precise rules governing the scope and application of such a data retention."[33] At the same time, it explained that the substantive grounds that might justify preventive data retention ought to be based on the connection of the persons whose data were to be intercepted with serious crime, and "to contribute in one way or another to fighting serious crime or to prevent a serious risk to public security."[34] The Court pointed to the use of a geographical and/or temporal criterion (e.g. collection of data in locations particularly vulnerable to serious crime) as an example of grounds justifying the implementation of a data retention regime.[35]

In effect therefore, the CJEU argued that the data retention process itself could not cover all users of a particular service (in that sense, be "indiscriminate"), because in such a case it did not link the scope of the data collected to any verifiable criteria that would allow it to be considered limited to what was actually necessary. However – both in *Digital Rights Ireland* and in its subsequent case law – the Court did not require to establish a close link with specific criminal proceedings in every case of data collection. In this respect, the Court considered it sufficient to show that the procedures used differentiate, "in one way or another," the criteria used to determine the scope of data subjected to interception.[36]

The Court further clarified its position in the *SpaceNet* case by explaining that the retention of traffic data constituted a serious interference with individual rights regardless of the duration of the measure or the duration of subsequent data retention "when that set of data is liable to allow precise conclusions to be drawn concerning the private life of the person or persons concerned."[37] As the Court aptly pointed out, limiting the duration of the surveillance measure and the subsequent data retention time is not sufficient to negate the intrusiveness of such surveillance. Indeed, even if the data collected is subject to automatic processing and based on a small set of information, it is possible to infer specific characteristics of the persons subjected to such surveillance.[38] In this way, the Court referred to the increasingly debated idea that a general obligation to retain data could be considered acceptable if

33 *Tele2 Sverige* (C-203/15 and C-698/15) EU:C:2016:970 at [109].
34 Ibid. at [111].
35 *La Quadrature du Net and Others v. Premier ministre and Others* (Joined Cases C-511/18, C-512/18 and C-520/18) EU:C:2020:791 at [144, 150]; 'LQN'.
36 Ibid. at [144].
37 *SpaceNet* (Joined Cases C-793/19 and C-794/19) EU:C:2022:702 at [88].
38 For a broader discussion on this topic, see Chapters 1 and 2.

the information obtained were quickly processed. It is worth recalling that the *SpaceNet* case was decided in October 2022, thus already after the ECtHR's Grand Chamber judgment in *Centrum för rättvisa v. Sweden*. While the ECtHR accepted a 12-month retention period for "unprocessed data," the CJEU in the *Prokuratuur* case, that was decided in parallel, considered that any access to traffic data was a serious interference with individual rights.[39] In the *SpaceNet* case, it confirmed that the mere retention of the data also involved such interference.[40]

In terms of the link between retained data and ongoing criminal proceedings, in the *G.D.* case, the CJEU held that EU law

> does not make the possibility of issuing an order requiring a targeted retention subject to the condition either that the places likely to be the location of a serious crime or the persons suspected of being involved in such an act must be known in advance.[41]

The relevant criterion is a link connecting retained data in a genuine, objective and non-discriminatory manner with legitimate objectives of the authorities of a democratic state. Such a criterion may be met by identifying, for example, places at particular risk of serious crime.[42] Hence, it is worth emphasising that the CJEU's interpretation does not exclude the use of data retention in a preventive manner, which, at the same time, does not waive the obligation to respect the principle of proportionality.

This position has been and continues to be controversial. This is mainly related to the arguments, raised especially by Member States' secret services, pointing out that it is impossible to apply the aforementioned limitations to the data retention process, as in many cases user activity cannot be linked to a specific geographical area. According to this view, it should be possible to record entire metadata, while the fulfilment of the criterion of strict necessity should be assessed at the stage when the data are made available to approved authorities. Adopting such a position would, however, lead to the conclusion that the retention and subsequent sharing of data should be examined as a single interference with individual rights, which is not the case.

If all retained data were to be shared with law enforcement authorities, such a measure would be manifestly disproportionate and consequently unacceptable in a democratic state.[43] If, on the other hand, not all retained data were made available, then the two measures (retention and access) would have to be

39 *Prokuratuur* (C-746/18) EU:C:2021:152 at [39].

40 *SpaceNet* (n 37) at [88].

41 *G.D. v. the Commissioner of the Garda Síochána and Others* (C-140/20) EU:C:2022:258 at [75].

42 Ibid. at [79].

43 This is because it would require the assumption that any citizen could be suspected of involvement in criminal activity.

examined separately. Taking the opposite view would deprive the individual of legal protection in cases where retained data are not subsequently made available to the authorities. Both the ECtHR[44] and the CJEU[45] have emphasised in their jurisprudence that the mere collection of data on an individual already interferes with the right to privacy, and that it is irrelevant whether the data is subsequently used for any purpose.

When examining the retention provisions, the CJEU also made a clear distinction between the retention of data that allow details of private life to be ascertained and the collection of less sensitive data, the processing of which does not lead to the disclosure of such information. As a result, already in the *Ministerio Fiscal* case, it accepted the possibility of preventive retention of data relating to a user's civil identity. Because these data as such do not include information on the use of telecommunications services, they cannot be used to reveal detailed information about the user.[46] This position has been confirmed in later rulings.[47]

The Court has also applied this interpretation to other categories of data derived from electronic communications services. In principle, it stressed that the collection of data on the IP addresses of electronic services users constitutes a serious interference with their rights, as it "may allow precise conclusions to be drawn concerning the private life of the user of the means of electronic communication" and may also have a chilling effect on the right to information.[48]

At the same time, however, it noted that "the IP address might be the only means of investigation enabling the person to whom that address was assigned at the time of the commission of the offence to be identified."[49] The Court considered this circumstance to be of crucial importance, especially for the identification of the perpetrators of Internet crimes, including cases of serious crime (e.g. dissemination of child pornography). As the IP address does not in itself reveal the identity of the user, the Court considered that "a legislative measure providing for the general and indiscriminate retention of only IP addresses assigned to the source of a connection does not, in principle, appear to be contrary" to the guarantees under the Charter of Fundamental Rights.[50] In this respect, however, it pointed out the need for restrictive management of access to retained data, limiting their use solely to the fight against serious crime.

44 *Amann v. Switzerland* (27798/95) 16 February 2000 ECtHR at [70].
45 *Österreichischer Rundfunk and Others* (Joined Cases C-465/00, C-138/01 and C-139/01) EU:C:2003:294 at [75].
46 *Ministerio Fiscal* (C-207/16) EU:C:2018:788 at [60–61].
47 *LQN* (n 35) at [144, 157] and *G.D. v. the Commissioner of the Garda Síochána and Others* (n 41) at [71].
48 *G.D. v. the Commissioner of the Garda Síochána and Others* (n 41) at [73].
49 *LQN* (n 35) at [154].
50 Ibid. at [155].

In essence, therefore, in the *LQN* judgment the Court confirmed that it was possible to implement a measure based on the untargeted retention of telecommunications data in a manner compatible with EU law. This should, however, be limited to categories of data that do not allow disclosure of the user's identity and do not result in serious interference with the user's rights. The above leads to the important conclusion that the CJEU's interpretation of the impermissibility (disproportionality) of a general data retention obligation, while growing out of the concept of strict necessity, is at the same time contingent on the recognition that the criterion justifying serious interference with individual rights is met. Thus, general data retention that does not lead to such interference is not per se incompatible with the Charter guarantees.

Although this reasoning is clear and well-founded, it was built on the precarious assumption of the anonymity of a certain type of data associated with a user's online activities. It is worth recalling that several years ago the CJEU ruled that an IP address should be treated as personal data in specific cases.[51] A general obligation to retain data is imposed on providers of Internet access services. From the perspective of a service provider, an IP address that the provider itself has assigned to a specific user is not anonymous, in the same way that a telephone number is not anonymous to the telecoms operator that has assigned the number to a specific subscriber. Thus, using arguments similar to those that the Court put forward in finding the general retention of telecommunications data to breach the principle of proportionality, the conclusion can also be drawn that the retention of IP addresses is also impermissible.

It is worth recalling that the CJEU, in the *SpaceNet* judgment, confirmed that a general obligation to retain telecommunications data (traffic and location data) could not be reconciled with respect for the EU safeguards, even where the measure served the purpose of combating serious crime.[52] It is all the more difficult to understand why the recording of another category of data from electronic communications (IP addresses), allowing similar knowledge on the person under surveillance to be revealed, can be done in a generalised manner but subject to strict controls on its further sharing. The Court seems to have unnecessarily nuanced its position on this point, de facto to the detriment of the consistency of the case law on data retention.

5.2.3 *Criteria for lawful access to data*

The *Digital Rights Ireland* judgment, handed down in 2014, did not resolve a number of important concerns regarding the application of retention rules. Indeed, the Data Retention Directive did not regulate the rules on access to

51 *Breyer* (C-582/14) EU:C:2016:779 at [48].
52 *SpaceNet* (n 37) at [74].

retained data.[53] Its main purpose was to secure data availability so that national legislatures could adopt appropriate national legislation addressing the issue of the further sharing of the data.

The repeal of the Directive created a legal situation in which not only the national provisions implementing it, but also the national regulations on access to data from retention remained in force. Therefore the passing of the *Digital Rights Ireland* judgment sparked a discussion on the steps that Member States should take to comply with the interpretation provided by the Court of Justice. According to the most extreme position, national legislatures did not have to take any action. In this view, the effect of the repeal of the Data Retention Directive created a state of affairs in which the European Union no longer exercised the competences conferred on it, with the result that Member States became free to shape national data retention standards themselves.[54] There was also ambiguity regarding the data access procedures themselves. Indeed, repealing national data retention regulations would render the provisions setting standards for access to such data pointless.

The Court addressed some of these concerns in its judgment in the *Tele2 Sverige* case. The background of the case under examination was an assessment of the compatibility of the Swedish and UK data retention rules with EU law. The requests for a preliminary ruling formulated by the national courts sought not only to determine the possibility of establishing a general obligation to retain data, but also to identify the criteria for granting state authorities access to the information thus collected.

First, the Court determined that national legislation providing for "the general and indiscriminate retention of all traffic and location data of all subscribers and registered users relating to all means of electronic communication" could not be reconciled with the Charter of Fundamental Rights.[55] In this respect, it reiterated its reasoning from the *Digital Rights Ireland* judgment and held that the same reasons why the Data Retention Directive was incompatible with EU law made the counterpart national provisions also incompatible with it.

Second, the Court pointed out that irrespective of the scope of application of the obligation to retain data (and thus also in the case of targeted retention, applied in relation to specific individuals; see Diagram 5.1), respect for fundamental rights required that national legislation restrict access to the information collected to cases of fighting serious crime – and only subject to adequate legal safeguards.

53 See Art. 4 of the Data Retention Directive. Mark Taylor, 'The EU Data Retention Directive' (2006) 22 *Computer Law & Security Review* 309.

54 Niklas Vainio and Samuli Miettinen, 'Telecommunications Data Retention after *Digital Rights Ireland*: Legislative and Judicial Reactions in the Member States' (2015) 23 *International Journal of Law and Information Technology* 290, 303.

55 *Tele2 Sverige* (n 33) at [112].

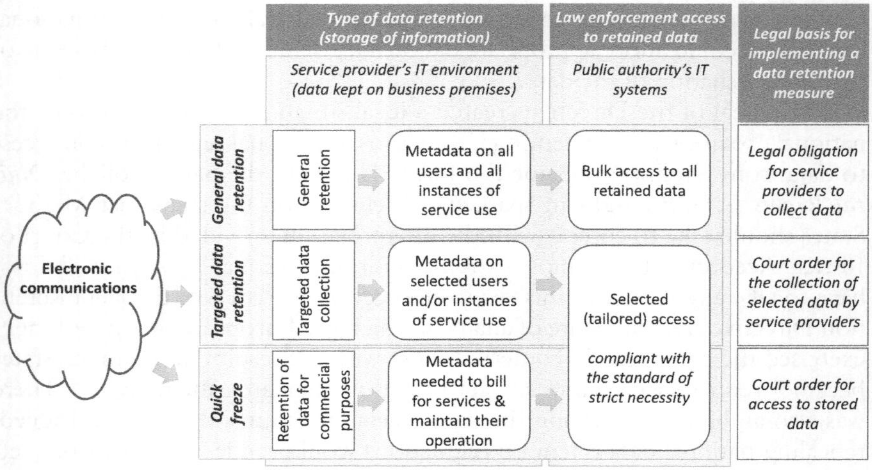

Diagram 5.1 Different types of data retention in EU law.

This requirement follows directly from the principle of proportionality, which (as understood by both the CJEU and the ECtHR) requires that the degree of interference with an individual's rights be in relation to the seriousness of the objective that the interference pursues. If the measure under examination leads to interference that is considered serious (for the reasons discussed previously), respect for the principle of proportionality requires that the scope of its use should be limited to cases of fighting crime that can also be considered serious.[56] Certainly, this condition is not met by acts which, although subject to disciplinary action, do not lead to criminal liability. It follows that it is not permissible to use retained data for disciplinary proceedings, including when investigating acts of corruption.[57]

On the other hand, with regard to the criteria justifying the granting of access to data, the Court – referring to the ECtHR's interpretation set out earlier in *Roman Zakharov v. Russia*[58] – pointed out that

> [such] access can, as a general rule, be granted, in relation to the objective of fighting crime, only to the data of individuals suspected of planning, committing or having committed a serious crime or of being implicated in one way or another in such a crime.[59]

56 *Ministerio Fiscal* (n 46) at [56].
57 *Lietuvos Respublikos generalinė prokuratūra* (C-162/22) EU:C:2023:631 at [43].
58 In its jurisprudence, the CJEU has reconstructed the *Huvig/Weber* standard, but without explicitly referring to the particular requirements previously established by the ECtHR.
59 *Tele2 Sverige* (n 33) at [119].

According to the CJEU, this criterion must be fulfilled before access is granted to the data in question, which implies that access to retained data must be preceded by *ex ante* review carried out by a court or an independent administrative authority (for more on this aspect, see section 4.4.4).

Against this background, it should be recalled that the interpretation of data retention rules discussed earlier left a certain margin that allowed for the collection of data in a preventive manner – i.e. in relation to persons of interest to law enforcement authorities because of, for example, their previous criminal history.[60] However, in terms of granting access to such data, the Court left no such margin of appreciation, which leads to the conclusion that, in any event, access to retained data must be granted only in relation to a specific and real threat to public security or be linked to the fight against serious crime.[61]

This observation helps explain why national rules allowing general access to any retained data are per se incompatible with the CJEU standard. While data retention rules may lead to the redundant collection of information (but gathered in accordance with the principle of proportionality), in the case of access to redundant data (unrelated to ongoing investigations), respect for the principle of strict necessity precludes such data from being made available to law enforcement authorities.[62]

The last issue that needs to be discussed in terms of access to retained data concerns the conditions that allow the so-called quick freeze (or expedited retention) mechanism to be applied in relation to the data stored by telecommunications operators. In addition to collecting data to comply with a legal obligation, telecommunications operators also collect and process data needed for the correct billing of services. These data, when no longer required according to national legislation (e.g. for the purposes of billing services, handling complaints or exercising claims), should be anonymised or deleted.[63] However, to prevent their permanent destruction, public authorities may use a specific legal mechanism in the form of a data preservation order that obliges the service provider to continue to store the data for the time necessary for an ongoing criminal investigation or other procedure justifying its storage to be completed. The issuance of a data preservation order is regulated by individual Member States' national laws, and its existence was also agreed upon in the Council of Europe Cybercrime Convention.[64]

60 *G.D. v. the Commissioner of the Garda Síochána and Others* (n 41) at [77].

61 Xavier Tracol, 'The Joined Cases of Dwyer, SpaceNet and VD and SR before the European Court of Justice: The Judgments of the Grand Chamber about Data Retention Continue Falling on Deaf Ears in Member States' (2023) 48 *Computer Law & Security Review* 105773.

62 Anja Møller Pedersen, Henrik Udsen and Søren Sandfeld Jakobsen, 'Data Retention in Europe – the Tele 2 Case and Beyond' (2018) 8 *International Data Privacy Law* 160, 168.

63 Such an obligation results from the e-Privacy Directive (for details, see section 2.1).

64 For a more detailed analysis, see Marcin Rojszczak, 'E-Evidence Cooperation in Criminal Matters from an EU Perspective' (2022) 85 *Modern Law Review* 847.

The quick freeze mechanism, therefore, does not oblige the service provider to collect new information, but only requires it to continue to store data already in its possession. It is, therefore, a measure distinct from a legal obligation to retain data. In this way, it avoids the problems associated with establishing a general data retention measure, in particular those related to the need to limit the scope of data collected to what is necessary to achieve a legitimate purpose. As a general rule, telecoms operators keep virtually the same dataset as that previously covered by retention rules but do so for their own purposes (billing of services) and without any connection to the objectives of fighting any crime. The quick freeze measure allows public authorities to access these data, including in a situation where no general data retention obligation has been established in national law.

The Court has, in principle, affirmed the possibility of using such orders to secure and subsequently access retained data. It has noted that once a preservation order is issued, the purpose of the further processing of the data changes. Therefore, bearing in mind that generally this is data identical to those previously retained under data retention provisions, the criteria for its lawful continued retention should be the same as those discussed earlier. As a result, according to the Court a measure such as quick freeze can only be used in the case of the fight against serious crime or the pursuit of overriding national security objectives, and that its use should be preceded by prior judicial review and last only for the time strictly necessary to achieve the purpose of its implementation.[65]

Importantly, however, the Court has noted that "such expedited retention need not be limited to the data of persons specifically suspected of having committed a criminal offence or acts adversely affecting national security."[66] This means that, as in the case of targeted retention, quick freeze may be used to secure information that is potentially related to an event under investigation or may lead to the disclosure of a crime or the circumstances of its commission. Therefore, according to the *G.D.* judgment, the use of this measure "need not be limited to the data . . . of persons specifically suspected of having committed a serious criminal offence or acts adversely affecting national security."[67]

As a result, taking into account the current CJEU jurisprudence it appears that a measure such as an expedited retention order is de facto capable of meeting the needs of law enforcement authorities in a manner similar to a general data retention obligation. At the same time, the application of this measure – as long as the criteria for access to data are observed – is not controversial in terms of its compliance with EU law. This observation explains why some Member States are exploring the possibility of remodelling national data retention legislation to eliminate a general data retention obligation and

65 *LQN* (n 35) at [163].
66 Ibid. at [165].
67 *G.D. v. the Commissioner of the Garda Síochána and Others* (n 41) at [75].

establish in its place two complementary mechanisms: targeted retention (for the collection of new data) and expedited retention (to secure data already in the possession of telecommunications operators).[68]

5.2.4 Data retention and national security

For many years the discussion on the permissibility of various forms of data retention focused on aspects related to the collection of data and their subsequent release to law enforcement authorities in the context of ongoing criminal proceedings. Suffice it to say that this issue has also been explored in the context of using evidence from telecommunications data retention failing to comply with EU law in a criminal trial – and thus in the context of respect for the right to a fair trial.[69]

Against the background of these discussions, however, another problem was increasingly becoming apparent: that of relating the Court's interpretation to cases of both the collection and sharing of retained data for national security purposes. This problem first required clarification as to whether the relevant provisions of EU law (in particular, the e-Privacy Directive) and the CJEU's interpretations concerning data retention applied to the area of national security at all. This was particularly relevant, bearing in mind the TEU's reservation of actions taken in the national security area to the exclusive competence of the Member States.[70] Only then was it necessary to clarify how the CJEU's interpretation should affect the practice of using retention measures in the sphere of national security.

The first problem outlined actually concerns the search for an interpretation of EU law that ensures its coherence. The starting point for understanding the source of the problem is the wording of the specific obligations under the e-Privacy Directive. This act continues to be one of the cornerstones of the EU regulatory model for the telecommunications market.[71] It is also not without significance that this directive was adopted during the Treaty of Amsterdam era, i.e. even before the Lisbon reform and the introduction of the national security exception in force today.[72] At the same time, the e-Privacy Directive – after the repeal of the Data Retention Directive – became the basis

68 For example, the German Minister of Justice, Marco Buschmann, favours *quick freeze* as a replacement for "unjustified data retention" regulations. 'ECJ Rules against Mass Data Retention in Germany' *Deutsche Welle* (20 September 2022) <https://cli.re/wPZW9X> accessed 6 September 2023.

69 In particular, see the *G.D. v. the Commissioner of the Garda Síochána and Others* case (n 41); also the *Prokuratuur* (n 39) judgment, detailing the requirements for independent oversight of surveillance powers.

70 Art. 4(2) of the TEU; see also section 3.3.

71 More on Directive 2002/95 and the EU regulatory framework for the telecoms market in section 2.1.

72 For more on the origins of the national security clause in EU law, see Marcin Rojszczak, 'National Security in a Digital Europe' (2023) 48 *European Law Review* 545.

for the adoption of national data retention legislation. Therefore the Court, in all judgments regarding data retention regimes has – in addition to compliance with primary law, in particular the Charter of Fundamental Rights – also examined the compatibility of national data retention legislation with the requirements under the e-Privacy Directive.

The historical background of the adoption of the e-Privacy Directive is relevant, as this act establishes, in Article 15(1), a derogation clause allowing Member States to adopt legislative measures restricting some of the rights and obligations set out therein if this proves necessary, appropriate and proportionate to, *inter alia*, safeguard national security objectives.[73] At the same time, the scope of application of the e-Privacy Directive (as indicated in its Article 1(3)) does not include "activities concerning . . . State security." Thus, in the same act the EU legislature simultaneously excluded the application of it as a whole to the subject matter of national security (replicating the Treaty provisions in force at the time, now Article 4(2) of the TEU) and established a specific norm (Article 15(1)) introducing a derogation from only certain provisions in the case of the performance of state security tasks.

Thus, because the EU legislature explicitly established a specific provision providing for the possibility of derogating from certain provisions of the Directive, subject to the conditions set forth therein, this means that in these cases, in principle the applicability of the Directive as a whole to the respective subject matter is not excluded. This observation, in turn, has led to obvious questions about the interplay of Article 4(2) of the TEU (i.e. the national security exception) with Article 15(1) of the e-Privacy Directive. Indeed, if the area of national security is considered to be excluded from the scope of EU law under Article 4 of the TEU, how should one interpret Article 15(1) of the e-Privacy Directive, which makes the applicability of the derogation motivated by national security objectives conditional on whether the measures taken prove to be "necessary, appropriate and proportionate within a democratic society"?

The CJEU analysed this issue as early as in the *Tele 2 Sverige* case, but the answer given at that time could not be regarded as fully exhaustive. The Court stated that, in principle, national measures adopted under the exemption provided for in the e-Privacy Directive (and thus measures adopted, *inter alia*, in the area of national security) fell within the scope of European Union law, as otherwise the provisions of the Directive in question would be of no practical application (it would be devoid of any effect [*effet utile*]). However, the Court's position did not provide a clear interpretation of the relationship between Article 15(1) of the Directive and Article 4(2) of the TEU.

At the same time, however, the Court signalled that in the case of pursuing national security objectives (such as the fight against terrorism), considerations

73 A similar exemption was introduced in Art. 14(1) of Directive 97/66, a predecessor to Directive 2002/58.

of fairness might lead to a different assessment of the proportionality of the data retention measures implemented. In this regard, it highlighted that in such cases it would be possible to provide public authorities with access also to data concerning persons not "suspected of planning, committing or having committed a serious crime or of being implicated in one way or another in such a crime." The Court thus accepted that, in special cases, it is possible to grant broader access to retained data, also covering persons unrelated to identified criminal activity – provided, however, that the data can contribute to countering threats to vital interests of national security, defence or public security in the specific case.[74]

Unfortunately, due to its vague language, the interpretation set out in the *Tele2 Sverige* case may be understood differently. Opponents of generalised forms of data retention have argued that its unlimited forms are unacceptable also in the area of state security. Its supporters have stressed that the Court indicated that more far-reaching measures could be established, and thus did not exclude general data retention per se. Yet others have continued to take the view that the Court's interpretation does not apply at all to the data retention provisions used by secret services, as this area falls, on the basis of Article 4(2), outside the scope of EU law.[75]

These ambiguities have led to a total of four references for a preliminary ruling to the CJEU from the French Council of State,[76] the Belgian Constitutional Court[77] and the UK Investigatory Powers Tribunal.[78] They aimed to clarify whether the same standard as that previously defined by the Court when examining the rules applied in the area of fighting crime should be applicable to data retention rules in the area of national security.

In examining these issues, the Court first addressed the relationship between the national security exception and the scope of application of the e-Privacy Directive. It recalled that national security remained the exclusive responsibility of each Member State.[79] This does not mean, however, that measures taken

74 *Tele2 Sverige* (n 33) at [119].

75 For different views on the Tele2 judgment and its applicability to national security cases, see Iain Cameron, 'Balancing Data Protection and Law Enforcement Needs: Tele2 Sverige and Watson' (2017) 54 *Common Market Law Review* 1467; E Kosta, '*United Kingdom SSHD v. Watson & Ors*: A "Thin" Nail on the Coffin of UK Data Retention Legislation' (2018) 4 *European Data Protection Law Review* 520; Xavier Tracol, 'The Judgment of the Grand Chamber Dated 21 December 2016 in the Two Joint Tele2 Sverige and Watson Cases: The Need for a Harmonised Legal Framework on the Retention of Data at EU Level' (2017) 33 *Computer Law & Security Review* 541.

76 Requests for a preliminary ruling referred by the *French Conseil d'État* (C-511/18 and C-512/18) 26 July 2018.

77 Request for a preliminary ruling referred by the *Belgian Cour constitutionnelle* (C-520/18) 19 July 2018.

78 Request for a preliminary ruling referred by the *UK Investigatory Powers Tribunal* (C-623/17) 31 October 2017.

79 *LQN* (n 35) at [135].

in this area are completely outside the scope of EU law.[80] Thus, the Court referred to its previous case law, in particular regarding the need to treat any limitation on rights and freedoms narrowly.[81]

With regard to the relationship between the scope of application of the e-Privacy Directive (Article 1(3)) and the content of the derogation clause provided for therein (Article 15(1)), the Court pointed out that, in principle, all the activities listed in the former provision belonged to the category of activities undertaken by public authorities and were alien to private actors. On this basis, it considered that the national security exception should be interpreted as applying only to activities undertaken directly by public authorities, and not by individuals performing a legal obligation imposed on them.[82] Adopting such an interpretation meant that activities undertaken directly by public entities, including secret services, in relation to national security objectives were excluded from the scope of EU law, including the e-Privacy Directive.

However, this exemption does not apply to the activities of commercial entities such as telecommunications operators. In their case, the obligation to retain data is part of the regulation of the telecommunications market, and thus a mechanism related to EU economic cooperation.[83] According to this position, a telecommunications operator, as a private entity, is not responsible for ensuring national security, and its activities cannot fall within the scope of the Treaty exemption laid down in Article 4(2).

The Court's position allows the scope of application of the national security clause to be clarified in a way that leaves secret services free to act – yet without the risk of different standards for the protection of electronic communications being adopted in each country under the pretext of ensuring national security.

Because the actions taken by telecoms operators do not fall under the Treaty exception of national security, they can be assessed in light of the requirements under EU law – including the e-Privacy Directive. This interpretation, therefore, focuses on the stage of data collection and not its subsequent release to public authorities. As a result, it is insufficient to conclude that access to retained data is not also exempted from EU law, including cases where it is gained by secret services. However, given that it is impossible to access data that have not been previously retained, this position significantly limits Member States' freedom to shape such data retention provisions that would violate the aforementioned CJEU standard, first presented in the *Digital Rights Ireland* judgment.

By applying the above interpretation to the circumstances presented in the *Privacy International* case, the Court declared the UK data retention

80 *Commission v. Portugal* (C-38/06) EU:C:2010:108 at [62].

81 *Privacy International v. Secretary of State for Foreign and Commonwealth Affairs and Others* (C-623/17) EU:C:2020:790 at [67] and the case law referred to therein.

82 Ibid. at [48].

83 See also earlier comments on the formal basis for the adoption of the Retention Directive.

regulations incompatible with EU law.[84] Indeed, the regulations under examination provided for the obligation of telecommunications operators to transmit all retained data to the UK SIAs on a permanent basis. The Court's reasoning in this regard is identical to that formulated earlier in relation to general retention used in the area of combating crime: the retention of data of all persons, including those without any connection with the activities of interest to secret services, clearly goes beyond what can be considered necessary in a democratic society.[85]

Against this background, it is worth noting the evolution of the Court's standard. While in earlier cases the collection and processing of bulk metadata had not been equated with other forms of electronic surveillance, in *Privacy International* the Court explicitly pointed out that metadata analysis could allow the disclosure of sensitive information and also enable "establishing a profile of the persons concerned," and thus concluded that metadata required the same protection as the content of communications.[86] This is an apt observation, which is also in line with the recent ECtHR case law, especially *Ekimdzhiev and Others v. Bulgaria* (see section 4.4.2).[87]

In the *LQN* judgment, the Court also clarified how to understand the argument presented in the earlier case law that it was possible to use measures leading to a more far-reaching interference with the individual's rights if they served *important* state security objectives. According to the Court, first of all the protection of national security goes beyond other objectives justifying the use of retained data, including the fight against crime, also serious ones, as well as the protection of public order.[88]

Hence, countering threats to state security may justify the implementation of data retention measures providing for the collection of data with regard to all users and, therefore, in an untargeted manner. However, a condition for compliance with EU law is to ensure that the manner in which such a measure is implemented does not go beyond what is *strictly necessary*.[89] As pointed out by the Court, it follows from this requirement that bulk data retention may be considered proportionate when it is limited in time and occurs in relation to a "genuine and present or foreseeable" threat to state security.[90]

The Court therefore made it clear that, due to the particular importance of the activities carried out in the field of national security for safeguarding the

84 *Privacy International v. Secretary of State for Foreign and Commonwealth Affairs and Others* (n 81) at [78].

85 Ibid. at [81].

86 Ibid. at [71].

87 *Ekimdzhiev and Others v. Bulgaria* (70078/12) 11 January 2022 ECtHR at [394]: "such data can be used to paint an intimate picture of a person."

88 *LQN* (n 35) at [136].

89 Ibid. at [137].

90 Ibid. In fact, however, a measure limited in this way would meet the definition of targeted retention, as the Court itself also notes in the same case (see [147]).

functioning of the state, they must be considered to be superior in their importance to public security activities in general and, consequently, in accordance with the principle of proportionality may justify the implementation of measures going even beyond those acceptable in the fight against serious crime.[91]

Against this background, however, a problem has emerged concerning the possibility of clearly distinguishing between tasks carried out in the area of state security and those related to the fight against serious crime (on this subject, see also section 3.3). For example, terrorist threats are classified in both categories, so theoretically they could justify the implementation of surveillance measures both in the area of state security (a broader scope of surveillance) and the fight against crime (a narrower scope), which could potentially lead to abuse of power.

In this regard, in the *G.D.* case the Court, summarising its earlier position expressed in *LQN*, confirmed that only "genuine and present or foreseeable"[92] threats could justify the implementation of undifferentiated and generalised data retention. Only in such a case would there be sufficiently concrete circumstances not only to justify the authorisation of this measure but also to allow the subsequent verification of the existence of grounds justifying its continued use. At the same time, it emphasised that the threat to national security could not be permanent – that is, related not to a specific threat but to a general risk of "the occurrence of tensions or disturbances, even of a serious nature."[93]

It follows from the above considerations that crime, even particularly serious ones, cannot be equated with a threat to national security. Equating them could result in the introduction of an intermediate category between national security and public security to apply to the latter the requirements inherent in the former.[94]

In practice, it also follows that data collected for national security purposes cannot be used in proceedings related to the fight against crime. However, this does not hold true for the reverse: data retained for the purpose of fighting serious crime may be made available for the carrying out of state security tasks. This is a direct consequence of the recognition that state security is linked to the protection of an overriding general interest, and therefore goes beyond the importance attributed even to the fight against serious crime.

Importantly, this interpretation – stemming from the CJEU's recent case law – in no way contradicts the position taken in earlier cases, according to which general data retention applied on a permanent and systematic basis without any connection to real threats cannot be reconciled with the principles of proportionality and strict necessity. Nor do national security considerations create a carte blanche for the unauthorised interference with individual rights. Unlimited data retention is permissible, but only to the extent necessary to counter serious threats to the state. Its use must be subject to judicial review

91 Valsamis Mitsilegas and others, 'Data Retention and the Future of Large-Scale Surveillance: The Evolution and Contestation of Judicial Benchmarks' (2022) *European Law Journal* 1, 8.
92 *G.D. v. the Commissioner of the Garda Síochána and Others* (n 41) at [58].
93 *SpaceNet* (n 37) at [93].
94 *G.D. v. the Commissioner of the Garda Síochána and Others* (n 41) at [94].

and limited in time. For this reason alone, it is a measure that is similar to targeted forms of data retention and does not transform a derogation from the protection of fundamental rights into their permanent restriction.

5.2.5 Algorithmic retention

In traditional telecommunications data retention regimes, data are first retained (a task carried out by telecommunications operators) and then made available (to varying extents) to authorised entities. As already determined by the Court in the *Digital Rights Ireland* case, these are, in fact, two separate intrusions that require independent assessment and are subject to different criteria of legality.

In principle, the conditions for lawful access to data are stricter than those for data retention. Indeed, the Court has accepted the possibility of establishing preventive data retention mechanisms, in which case it is sufficient to plausibly demonstrate that the scope of the data retained is related to the purpose for which the data are to be used later. In other words, a data retention regime may lead to the collection of a wider range of data than will later be made available to authorities. However, in the extreme case – that is, targeted retention – the data that may be retained are exactly the same as those provided later to public authorities. In this scenario, the problem of the preventive use of collected data, and therefore of assessing whether the manner of data retention does not breach the condition of necessity, does not arise at all. It should be noted, however, that while this case is the least cumbersome in terms of assessing its legality, it is also the least useful from the perspective of the purposes of data retention measures.

Member States invariably point out that data retention is useful for securing evidence relevant to establishing the circumstances of as yet undisclosed crimes and also for identifying new threats unrelated to the fight against crime. In the former case, a partial solution may be to implement the expedited retention (a quick freeze mechanism, discussed earlier). However, neither quick freeze nor, even less, targeted retention is sufficient for identifying new types of threats to general security.

Potentially, the so-called algorithmic retention, based on the selective collection of data based on the patterns (selectors) defined by authorities, could be a measure that both meets the needs of security services and remains in line with the standard set by the CJEU. Such a solution has been implemented in France and, according to the government, eliminates the need for general data retention. This is because only information meeting established criteria, and therefore of interest to secret services, can be recorded. With regard to these data, the condition required by the CJEU of linking the scope of the data collected to a specific and serious threat to state security is therefore met.[95]

95 These provisions had already been assessed by the French Constitutional Council, which recognised their compatibility with the Constitution. Conseil constitutionnel 23 July 2015 (2015-713 DC); English translation available at <https://cli.re/XjNE5q> accessed 6 September 2023.

Algorithmic retention can, therefore, be seen as a possible solution to disputes over the forms of general data retention. It allows the collection of data related to the activities carried out by law enforcement agencies and security services while not requiring the scope of persons or circumstances to be indicated precisely in a data retention order. Importantly, however, the measure's reliance on selectors de facto replicates the modus operandi of typical bulk surveillance systems, which, as explained in earlier chapters, also use the pre-filtering of data. Depending on how the keywords (search criteria) are defined, the extent of the data collected can vary and change over time (in this respect, see also the earlier discussion on "strong selectors").

In reality, therefore, algorithmic retention is a system of indiscriminate surveillance equipped with an additional process of pre-filtering information. Hence, it is already clear at this stage that the proportionality assessment in such a case should generally be focused on the process of defining the preliminary processing algorithms and the quality of the legal safeguards against the collection of redundant data.

In examining the compatibility of this measure with EU law, the Court first recalled that any operation on data is processing.[96] The processing carried out as part of the process of selecting the data to be retained is independent from the subsequent provision of access to data about the persons identified as a result of the automated analysis. Therefore the fact that only part of the information (meeting established criteria) is subjected to further processing (data access) does not diminish the scale of the original intrusion, which is still untargeted and envisages subjecting essentially *all* available data to processing.[97]

When examining the French regulations, the Court set out the requirements that should be met to assure that such automated processing does not infringe EU law. In the first place, it must comply with the general criteria for lawful access to data by public authorities as set out in the earlier case law. It must therefore take place based on a decision by a court or an independent administrative authority, so that it can be confirmed that the method of data filtering, its scope and the procedural safeguards implemented, are adequate and proportionate.[98] Subsequently, it is necessary to ensure that the processing is not carried out solely on the basis of characteristics classified as so-called sensitive data (special categories of data),[99] such as racial or ethnic origin, political opinions or religious beliefs.[100] In addition, it is necessary to implement measures to protect the individual against erroneous decisions, the occurrence of which is an inevitable consequence of large-scale automated processing. To

96 The legal definition of the processing of personal data is contained in Art. 4(2) of the GDPR.
97 *LQN* (n 35) at [172].
98 Ibid. at [179].
99 For the definition of special categories of personal data, see Art. 9(1) of the GDPR.
100 *LQN* (n 35) at [180].

this end, it is necessary to introduce a notification mechanism that provides for the possibility of reviewing the decisions taken, as well as to ensure periodic verification of the algorithms used in data processing.[101]

However, the Court recalled that such automated data retention

> is applied generally to all persons who use electronic communication systems, and consequently applies also to persons with respect to whom there is no evidence capable of suggesting that their conduct might have a link, even an indirect or remote one, with terrorist activities.[102]

Therefore the application of this measure, like others motivated by national security objectives, must be limited to situations where "a Member State is facing a serious threat to national security which is shown to be genuine and present or foreseeable."[103]

Hence, although algorithmic retention per se is not incompatible with EU law, the requirements imposed by the CJEU limit its use to emergency situations. In essence, therefore, all the limitations and caveats discussed earlier and formulated for cases of bulk data retention remain valid for this measure as well.

5.3 The ECtHR perspective: bulk surveillance in the light of the (strict) necessity test

Given the special position of the ECHR in the European legal model, this instrument seems to be best positioned to provide a comprehensive assessment of the permissibility of domestic surveillance measures. The ECHR's scope of application covers both targeted and untargeted surveillance programmes, including those applied in the area of the fight against crime and those related to state security. Moreover, special surveillance measures – such as those based on biometric techniques (e.g. facial recognition) or those involving general telecommunications data retention, discussed in the previous section – are also within the ECtHR's jurisdiction.

To date, the Strasbourg Court (ECtHR) has dealt explicitly with the examination of indiscriminate surveillance programmes on five occasions: *Weber and Saravia v. Germany; Liberty and Others v. the United Kingdom*; *Privacy International v. the United Kingdom*; *Centrum för rättvisa v. Sweden*; and *Big Brother Watch and Others v. the United Kingdom*. In addition, the issue of indiscriminate surveillance (also understood as blanket targeted surveillance) has also been addressed in a number of other judgments, discussed earlier in Chapter 4.

101 Ibid. at [182].
102 Ibid. at [174].
103 Ibid. at [177].

Although the ECtHR has developed its own assessment standard in these cases – in particular, the *Huvig/Weber* test, and subsequently also the *Big Brother Watch* test – the interpretation presented in these cases has often contrasted with the CJEU case law. The Luxembourg standard on indiscriminate surveillance programmes (in this case, general data retention) can be summarised in several points: (1) indiscriminate forms of surveillance involving bulk data collection lead, in principle, to a disproportionate interference with individual rights and are therefore incompatible with EU law; (2) given the particular importance of achieving national security objectives, states may use indiscriminate forms of surveillance where this is necessary to meet genuine state security needs; (3) in any case, data obtained in this way may not be stored outside the European Union.[104] It follows from the clear position set out in points 1 and 2 that using mass surveillance for purposes other than national security is unacceptable. In turn, it follows from condition 3 that it is impermissible to use such measures with the intention of transferring the data acquired to foreign partners. On the other hand, the Strasbourg standard does not appear to provide a straightforward answer to any of these issues.

The interpretation differences between the CJEU and the ECtHR are apparent even with regard to a fundamental issue, which is the manner in which the necessity of untargeted measures is examined. This observation may seem somewhat surprising, especially because the issue of necessity, or in relation to surveillance measures, *strict necessity*, has been the subject of interpretation by both courts for years. However, doubts as to how this concept should be interpreted have only arisen relatively recently and, it seems, are related precisely to the way indiscriminate programmes are assessed.

Already in *Weber and Saravia v. Germany*, the Strasbourg Court recognised that, in principle, the decision to use bulk surveillance measures fell within the wide margin of appreciation granted to states in the area of national security. Mass surveillance per se is, therefore, not impermissible. This position was confirmed by the court 15 years later in *Big Brother Watch and Others v. the United Kingdom*. Hence it follows from the interpretation provided by the ECtHR that, in its view, measures involving bulk and indiscriminate data collection do not per se go beyond what can be considered necessary in a democratic state. Thus, it is necessary to analyse how the Court understands this necessity and how it relates to the nature of the operation of untargeted surveillance measures.

The classic definition of necessity (see section 3.5) requires that the measure being implemented not only serves a legitimate aim but also must be needed to achieve it. This means that without the implementation of the mechanism

104 Marcin Rojszczak, 'National Security and Retention of Telecommunications Data in Light of Recent Case Law of the European Courts' (2021) 17 *European Constitutional Law Review* 607.

under examination, it would be impossible to achieve the set objective, in particular by less intrusive means.

It seems that this last condition – that is, necessity understood as the *effectiveness* of the measure in question combined with the absence of an alternative to its application – is the key to understanding the reasoning that led the ECtHR to the conclusion that it is possible to apply untargeted surveillance measures in democratic states.

As correctly recognised by the Court in *Weber and Saravia v. Germany*, before assessing the adequacy of the safeguards implemented, it is necessary to determine whether the measure under examination is proportionate to achieve the objective pursued. In fact, however, the Court did not carry out such an assessment, contenting itself with a discussion of the German government's declarations and assurances and the applicants' contrary position.[105] The judgment lacks a detailed explanation of the reasons why, in the circumstances of the case under examination, the bulk surveillance regime had to be implemented at all. Such an answer can be found in the subsequent case law, where the Court indicates that "bulk interception is generally directed at international communications."[106] As an example, it cites the German strategic surveillance programme, which was designed to intercept communications carried out between persons in the German territory and selected third countries. Based on its observation and assessment, the Court concluded that indiscriminate surveillance measures cover communications that could not normally be intercepted using another form of surveillance.

This is a surprising conclusion, clearly not borne out by the current technical possibilities (*cf.* Chapter 1). First, nowadays the interception of international traffic, even of a purely foreign nature, can be implemented using a number of different technical tools (e.g. malware, targeted eavesdropping on communication channels, securing data at the service provider). These capabilities are widely used by law enforcement and secret services, and they certainly lead to less intrusiveness than implementing a permanent mechanism for eavesdropping on all communications.

Second, there are no known instances of untargeted measures – including those geared towards the collection of foreign data (tapping on international communication channels) – that do not also record a large proportion of domestic traffic. Bulk surveillance has the purpose of monitoring *all* communications available in a particular medium. When the GCHQ intercepted nude photos from the mass surveillance of Yahoo! Webcam, it recorded intimate photos of not only foreigners but all users – and, therefore, British citizens, too.

105 *Weber and Saravia v. Germany* (54934/00) 29 June 2006 ECtHR at [108–112].

106 *Big Brother Watch and Others v. the United Kingdom* [GC] (58170/13, 62322/14 and 24960/15) 25 May 2021 ECtHR at [344].

In its reasoning, the ECtHR pointed to the example of Sweden – where the surveillance regime applied by FRA cannot by law cover data exchanged between users (the sender and the receiver) located within the national territory – as confirmation of the argument about the "international" nature of indiscriminate surveillance.[107] This is true – albeit with the proviso that the legal regulation cited should be read as prohibiting the *intentional* interception of purely domestic communications. However, as indicated earlier,[108] nowadays an email exchanged between users located in the same city can be carried out using infrastructure located on different continents. Moreover, regardless of the telecommunications infrastructure in place, these users can use email services provided from different countries. How would any intelligence agency, by pre-filtering the source data (without analysing it in detail), be able to determine the whereabouts of a particular user of the WhatsApp instant messaging service? Clearly, modern digital services do not work in the way assumed by the ECtHR. In most cases, data do not have a nationality. Only their subsequent analysis can reveal a user's location or identity.

At this point, it is also worth recalling the controversy over the so-called *about data collection* – a technique whose use is best documented in the case of NSA programmes[109] but which also relates to programmes run by other security services.[110] Its essence was the automatic (algorithmic) extension of data collection not only to persons/objects meeting the search criteria, but also to persons with whom the surveillance targets were in contact. Depending on the (covert) data collection criteria adopted, *about collection* led to the application of surveillance measures to a group of persons many times beyond the initial search criteria – and including, without exception, also domestic traffic.[111]

As a result, as Monika Zalnieriute aptly notes the ECtHR in *Big Brother Watch* in fact recognised the "inevitability" of the mass surveillance narrative by not questioning the effectiveness or proportionality of blanket surveillance

107 See Art. 2a of the Swedish Act on Signals Intelligence Defence Activities, SFS 2008:717.

108 See section 1.3.

109 In the case of US programmes, the issue of *about collection* is analysed almost exclusively in relation to the collection of data of Americans as part of foreign surveillance programmes. This practice was supposed to be discontinued in 2017, but it appears that this was so only in relation to certain surveillance programmes. See Ellen Nakashima, 'NSA Halts Controversial Email Collection Practice to Preserve Larger Surveillance Program' (28 April 2017) <https://cli.re/PpobVy> accessed 6 September 2023. For more on the differences between the European and US models of electronic surveillance, see section 6.7.

110 In fact, the term *about collection* is gradually being replaced by the more enigmatic phrase *incidental collection*. 'Developments in the Law – More Data, More Problems' (2018) 131 *Harvard Law Review* 1715, 1742.

111 Barton Gellman, Julie Tate and Ashkan Soltani, 'In NSA-Intercepted Data, Those Not Targeted Far Outnumber the Foreigners Who Are' *The Washington Post* (5 July 2014) <https://cli.re/dp2keR> accessed 6 September 2023.

regimes.[112] However, leaving aside the reasons why it considered indiscriminate surveillance indispensable (in the sense of *irreplaceable*), the Court came to an even more far-reaching conclusion in *Centrum för rättvisa v. Sweden*: it considered mass surveillance to be a measure of vital importance in identifying threats to national security.[113] The Grand Chamber confirmed this position by stating that "in present-day conditions, no alternative or combination of alternatives would be sufficient to substitute for the bulk interception power."[114]

Again, however, there is no evidence to support this argument by demonstrating not only the usefulness of using indiscriminate surveillance, but also the lack of an alternative to its application. The Court appears to have based its assessment – at least to some extent – on a belief in the ability of indiscriminate surveillance to detect *unknown* threats to public security. This characteristic, dubbed by the UK government as the ability to "discover 'unknown' unknowns," appears to be intended not only to justify the use of bulk surveillance, but also to predetermine the need for a particularly long retention period.

At the time of the *Big Brother Watch* judgement cited above (i.e. in 2021) a number of reports were available that called into question the real usefulness of measures based on the bulk collection and processing of information in terms of identifying previously unknown threats. In this regard, it is worth recalling the publications of the Privacy and Civil Liberties Oversight Board, an independent body set up by the US Congress to oversee the use the secret services' powers and to ensure that the actions taken by them do not lead to a violation of fundamental rights. The Board – after Snowden revealed the scale of the intelligence programmes conducted – published a report on telecommunications data retention programmes, in which it stated:

> We have not identified a single instance involving a threat to the United States in which the program made a concrete difference in the outcome of a counterterrorism investigation. Moreover, we are aware of no instance in which the program directly contributed to the discovery of a previously unknown terrorist plot or the disruption of a terrorist attack.[115]

Federal District Judge Richard Leon's opinion in *Klayman v. Obama* also reached similar conclusions: "The Government does *not* cite a single instance

112 Monika Zalnieriute, 'Big Brother Watch and Others v. the United Kingdom' (2022) 116 *American Journal of International Law* 585, 590.

113 *Centrum för rättvisa v. Sweden* [Chamber] (35252/08) 19 June 2018 ECtHR at [179];

114 *Centrum för rättvisa v. Sweden* [GC] (35252/08) 25 May 2021 ECtHR at [365].

115 'Report on the Telephone Records Program Conducted under Section 215 of the USA PATRIOT Act and on the Operations of the Foreign Intelligence Surveillance Court' (Privacy and Civil Liberties Oversight Board 2014) 11 <https://cli.re/83PVBx> accessed 6 September 2023.

in which analysis of the NSA's bulk metadata collection actually stopped an imminent attack, or otherwise aided the Government in achieving any objective that was time-sensitive in nature."[116] Besides, even the CJEU case law itself cites statistics casting doubt on the effectiveness of the collection and processing of bulk metadata as a necessary tool for identifying cases of serious crime and terrorism.[117]

In turn, the New America Foundation conducted an analysis of more than 200 cases of individuals suspected or convicted of terrorism-related offences by US authorities. The summary it published indicates that the NSA's electronic communications surveillance programme was the source of information for law enforcement agencies in only 1.8% of cases (four individuals). In comparison, traditional investigative techniques accounted for the initiation of 60% of the investigations examined.[118] Similar data were presented in a Danish Ministry of Justice report published in 2012, according to which "several years of collecting internet session data had not yielded any significant benefits for law enforcement – session data had played a minimal role in only one case."[119] This information questions the veracity of the thesis positing the usefulness of indiscriminate programmes for revealing ***unknown*** threats to state security.

The disproportion between the scope of data collected and their actual usefulness in the area of national security was also noted by Joseph Cannataci, UN Special Rapporteur on Privacy, who, in discussing the issue of mass electronic surveillance, stated that

> there is little or no evidence to persuade the Special Rapporteur of either the efficacy or the proportionality of some of the extremely privacy-intrusive measures that have been introduced by new surveillance laws in France, Germany, the United Kingdom and the United States.[120]

At the same time, however, in the view of the SIAs bulk surveillance measures "often form the backbone of investigative work," which can "help to better understand the risks surrounding [a secret service's] activities in order to protect the people it works with all over the world."[121] However, as indicated earlier the usefulness of a measure does not predetermine the necessity of its

116 *Klayman v. Obama*, 957 F. Supp. 2d 1 (D.D.C. 2013).

117 *Opinion on the EU-Canada PNR Agreement* (Opinion 1/15) EU:C:2016:656 at [55–56].

118 Peter Bergen and others, 'Do NSA's Bulk Surveillance Programs Stop Terrorists?' (New America Foundation 2014) <https://goo.gl/dpkEdC> accessed 6 September 2023.

119 'Liberty's Response to the Investigatory Powers Commissioner's Informal Consultation on Bulk Powers' (The National Council for Civil Liberties 2018) 6 <https://cli.re/RNXbYJ> accessed 6 September 2023.

120 'Report of the Special Rapporteur on the Right to Privacy' (UN Human Rights Council 2017) A/HRC/34/60 15.

121 David Anderson, 'Report of the Bulk Powers Review' (Independent Reviewer of Terrorism Legislation 2016) 111 <https://cli.re/97RkoJ> accessed 9 June 2023.

use. Interestingly, even in the report by the UK Independent Reviewer of Terrorism Legislation, the GCHQ assessed bulk powers as "used primarily to 'enrich' information that it had obtained through other means."[122]

The UK's involvement in bulk surveillance is particularly helpful here. After all, in the *Privacy International* case decided in 2022, the CJEU examined the regime of UK surveillance programmes. As a result, both the CJEU and the ECtHR assessed the necessity of surveillance measures in the same country at a similar time.[123] It is worth recalling that the Investigatory Powers Tribunal (IPT), in its request for a preliminary ruling, indicated that the use of bulk surveillance measures by the national secret services was "essential to the protection of the national security of the United Kingdom," making it possible to "discover previously unknown threats to national security." The IPT went on to stress that applying the interpretation set out by the CJEU in the *Tele2 Sverige* judgment "would frustrate the measures taken to safeguard national security by the SIAs, and thereby put the national security of the United Kingdom at risk."[124] Thus, in essence, by the very wording of the questions raised, the UK court sought to predetermine that indiscriminate surveillance was necessary to achieve national security objectives. However, as explained earlier the CJEU took a different view, according to which such a measure – although not per se incompatible with EU law – must, to comply with the criterion of strict necessity, be applied in response to a concrete and real threat to national security. This makes its implementation as a permanent mechanism of interference with fundamental rights impermissible.

This is an important difference in the positions of the two courts. Indeed, the ECtHR seems to accept that threats to national security can be of a permanent nature (e.g. a permanent threat from terrorist groups, as indicated in the case law of the French Council of State).[125] In contrast, the CJEU convincingly argues that threats to national security "can be distinguished, by their nature and particular seriousness, from the general risk that tensions or disturbances, even of a serious nature, affecting public security will arise."[126] This interpretation also explains why the UK government's way of defining necessity as "discovering 'unknown' unknowns"[127] cannot be reconciled with respect for the guarantees provided by the Charter. The detection of unknown threats, the nature of which the authorities cannot even specify (which, in turn, is supposed to justify an extended data retention period), is clearly not

122 Ibid. at [112].

123 However, it should be borne in mind that the *Privacy International* (CJEU) case dealt with the compliance of national retention laws with EU law, whereas the *Big Brother Watch* (ECtHR) case examined actions taken by the GCHQ.

124 *UK Investigatory Powers Tribunal* (n 78).

125 Conseil d'État 21 April 2021, Case 393099, ECLI:FR:CEASS:2021:393099.20210421.

126 *LQN* (n 35) at [136].

127 *Big Brother Watch and Others v. the United Kingdom* [GC] (n 106) at [422].

a means of responding to a "genuine and present or foreseeable" threat, as required by the CJEU standard.[128]

5.4 Cross-border data flows

An issue of significant importance for the discussion surrounding the future legal regulation of electronic surveillance is international cooperation in terms of data transfer. As the techniques used by signals intelligence developed, so did the importance of various forms of transnational cooperation between intelligence services. The best known example is the FVEY partnership, the reason for its creation being precisely cooperation on SIGINT.[129] Historically speaking, it was focused on the exchange of defence-related information and was closely associated with national security objectives. In reality, however, its tightening was also a result of the globalisation of the data market and the emergence of new forms of data processing. Over the years, computing power was not readily available and required financial outlays beyond the means of many countries. Therefore one element of the FVEY cooperation was to optimise the resources committed to SIGINT programmes, including their computing power and cryptanalysis capacities.[130]

Today, international cooperation on electronic surveillance can be conducted in several forms. The first focuses on the transfer (sharing) of the information collected with foreign partners. The second is related to obtaining such information from foreign sources. The third relates to gaining access to commercial data transferred under international data transfer agreements.

Although the first two cases seem closely related, they should in fact be examined separately. In the case of a transfer of data to a third country, the key issue is how to manage the risk of the data being further shared or used contrary to the original purpose. The sharing state de facto loses control over the data, which may result in the circumvention of the legal safeguards established to minimise the risk of abuse of power. In contrast, the receipt of data from external sources raises the question of the legality of its acquisition. Although many legislatures (and, as will be explained shortly, the courts as well) ignore this issue, the reality is that the examination of the permissibility of cross-border surveillance measures cannot omit the assessment of the mechanisms

128 *SpaceNet* (n 37) at [72].

129 Scarlet Kim and Paulina Perlin, 'Newly Disclosed NSA Documents Shed Further Light on Five Eyes Alliance' (*Lawfare*, 25 March 2019) <www.lawfareblog.com/newly-disclosed-nsa-documents-shed-further-light-five-eyes-alliance>. For more on the FVEY, see Chapter 1.

130 See e.g. 'U.S. Cryptologic Partnership with the United Kingdom' (National Security Agency 1997) <https://cli.re/VJVmqV> accessed 6 September 2023. More about the US-UK mutual cooperation regarding SIGINT in: Richard Kerbaj, *The Secret History of the Five Eyes: The Untold Story of the International Spy Network* (Blink 2022); Richard J Aldrich, *GCHQ: The Uncensored Story of Britain's Most Secret Intelligence Agency* (Harper Press 2011).

used to collect the data. Otherwise, an incentive is created for using international cooperation instruments to gain access to material that could not be legally obtained through domestic means. In the extreme case, this loophole opens up the possibility for secret services to outsource the surveillance of their own citizens to cooperating foreign services.

Before discussing the legal standards that should be applied in this area, it is necessary to explain the process of data sharing in the case of bulk surveillance measures. In targeted surveillance, the object of the transfer is data on specific individuals or concerning cases of interest to the cooperating services. This cooperation is therefore similar to the transfer of information in the form of traditional operational files – containing a set of information linked to a specific issue. The requesting service and the transferring service can, therefore, easily assess the compliance of the transfer with the legal requirements of the requesting and transferring states, respectively.

However, this model of cooperation does not apply to bulk surveillance measures. As explained in Chapter 1, an indiscriminate surveillance system is, in fact, a type of data warehouse – that is, an elaborate IT system that relies not only on large banks of information but also on sophisticated algorithms for processing it. The information obtained is processed in a mass manner, and the result of this processing is made available to analysts either directly or indirectly, e.g. by adding relevant keywords to the processed information so that it can be more easily retrieved in the future.

In such a data processing environment, "international cooperation" could, of course, consist of sharing the information resulting from the data processing process with foreign partners. Such transfers would be targeted and would essentially come down to sharing a specific set of information. However, the essence of many SIGINT cooperation agreements is not only to share information from each other's surveillance systems, but also to build common data collection and processing tools. These may include, for example, the creation of an analytical system that draws on multiple data sources (acquired by different intelligence agencies)[131] or the launch of a surveillance programme that transfers intercepted information in bulk to a foreign partner, e.g. in exchange for the ability to gain access to the analytical systems of the country with which the data are shared.

Cooperation in the field of indiscriminate surveillance is, therefore, much more complex both technically and organisationally. Above all, however, its effect is not the exchange of specific information but the building of common data collection and processing capabilities. This results in the creation of a new, transnational surveillance regime. An excellent example of this is the FVEY partnership cited earlier, which has implemented all the types of cooperation discussed above – from sharing databases with each other and

131 An example is the XKeyscore system, discussed in Chapter 1.

running "outsourced" surveillance programmes to developing analytical tools for common use.[132]

It is therefore not surprising that the issue of cross-border cooperation in the field of electronic intelligence has also become the focus of attention of both domestic and European courts. In this respect, it may come as a surprise that the ECtHR has only in recent years addressed this problem in more detail.

The Court has confirmed, in principle, that the decision to conclude an agreement on the exchange of information obtained from indiscriminate surveillance does not per se go beyond what can be considered necessary in a democratic state. As it pointed out, "international cooperation is crucial for the effectiveness of the authorities' efforts to detect and thwart potential threats to Contracting States' national security."[133] Such cooperation, according to the Court, can be undertaken for a variety of reasons, both as a response to identified threats and as part of joint operations to identify new threats.

At the same time, however, the lack of restrictions in the area of sharing a state's own datasets or obtaining information from foreign partners would create the risk of circumventing the Convention restrictions established to minimise the risk of abuse of power.[134] Therefore the Court first pointed out that a measure allowing surveillance material to be obtained from a third country must have an adequate basis in national law and meet the condition of the foreseeability of law (see section 4.3). Therefore the Court considered the instrument used to obtain the information as irrelevant for assessing compliance with human rights standards. Its collection by public authorities must be subject to appropriate restrictions. Hence, also in the case of acquiring information from a third country adequate safeguards must be implemented to protect against the risk of arbitrariness. This paves the way for applying in such cases the legal safeguards standards discussed earlier, particularly the *Huvig/Weber* scheme. In this way, the Court inferred the requirement to define in national law "the circumstances in which and the conditions on which the authorities are empowered to make" a surveillance request.[135] In doing so, it applied to an international cooperation regime a criterion which, although obvious in the case of targeted surveillance, appears difficult to use in relation to untargeted measures. In practice, a surveillance request referred to by the Court may concern not only acquiring specific information about an identified person, but also accessing a stream of raw intelligence data.

It is, therefore, unclear how the aforementioned condition is supposed to be met in such a case, especially because the Court itself recognises that the law cannot be expected to be so detailed as to define every case justifying the

132 Kerbaj (n 130) 309–311.

133 *Centrum för rättvisa v. Sweden* [GC] (n 114) at [321].

134 *Big Brother Watch and Others v. the United Kingdom* [GC] (n 106) at [497].

135 Ibid.

use of international data exchange measures.[136] Leaving aside this controversy, the interpretation provided by the Court also indicates that the practice of outsourcing surveillance to foreign partners must be carried out in the same way as if the surveillance were carried out using domestic means. It follows directly from this that there is a prohibition on the acquisition from foreign sources of material which would be impermissible to legally collect by domestic means.

Against this background, the Court's emphasis on the impossibility of assessing the activities undertaken by foreign intelligence services for their compliance with the Convention obligations raises serious doubts.[137] While according to the previously discussed interpretation of the scope of the Convention (the so-called effective control doctrine; see Chapter 4),[138] it is clear that the public authorities of a third country – acting outside the control of a state party to the Convention – are not covered by the obligations arising from the Convention; the results of their work affect the assessment of the compliance of the entire surveillance process. To assume that the collection of data by foreign bodies in a manner incompatible with the guarantees under the Convention does not prevent the use of such data by states parties to the Convention would render illusory the entire model of protection of fundamental rights. Hence, it is surprising that in the case of receiving foreign electronic surveillance material, the obligations of the receiving state – according to the Court – should focus on the further stages of the processing without the need to assess the legality of the process of obtaining this information.

In *Big Brother Watch v. the United Kingdom*, the Court also referred in detail to the standard of legal safeguards that should apply in the case of bulk sharing of data with foreign partners (in this case, transfers by the GCHQ to members of the FVEY agreement). In this regard, the Court held that such a transfer was permissible provided that the data had been collected and stored in a manner consistent with the requirements under the Convention (see the discussion of the legal safeguards standard in section 4.4) and upon its meeting additional safeguards strictly related to the transfer itself. That is:

1 the conditions for conducting it must be clearly set out in national law (the foreseeability of the law criterion);
2 ensuring that "safeguards capable of preventing abuse and disproportionate interference" are in place in the receiving state;
3 implementing tighter safeguards for the transfer of sensitive data, such as data concerning journalists;
4 subjecting the transfer mechanism to scrutiny by an independent body.[139]

136 *Centrum för rättvisa v. Sweden* [GC] (n 114) at [323].
137 *Big Brother Watch and Others v. the United Kingdom* [GC] (n 106) at [495].
138 See section 4.2.
139 *Big Brother Watch and Others v. the United Kingdom* [GC] (n 106) at [365].

Unfortunately, as in the case of other standards of legal safeguards related to electronic surveillance, the ECtHR's guidelines on data transfers are not particularly precise. Moreover, the Court itself, in its later case law, confirmed the possibility of taking a flexible approach to defining the requirements considered necessary in a given case.[140]

The doubts regarding the first criterion presented above were discussed earlier and stem from the Court's acceptance of the fulfilment of the foreseeability condition also when domestic law does not precisely indicate the grounds justifying the transfer of data to a foreign partner.[141] Such an interpretation increases the risk that the legal grounds will be defined too broadly, in effect violating the condition of the foreseeability of the law. This is what happened in the case of the Swedish legislation, which in the Grand Chamber's view defined the scope of intelligence cooperation too broadly, using the general term "international defence and security cooperation."[142]

However, even more controversy arises from the second condition, which concerns the legal safeguards in place in the state receiving the information. It is clear that the question of how the information is used is central to the effective protection of Convention rights. The question arises, however, as to how far the legal model of a third country may deviate from the Convention standard for such a transfer to be still considered permissible. In *Centrum för rättvisa v. Sweden*, the Court held that "the same or similar safeguards" should be expected.[143] By contrast, in *Big Brother Watch v. the United Kingdom*, decided a few months later, the Grand Chamber clarified that this requirement should not be understood as "comparable protection."[144] It is not clear how a state with "the same or similar safeguards" would at the same time fail to provide "comparable protection."

In its reasoning, the Grand Chamber appears to have indirectly referred to the standard applied by the CJEU, which under EU law has repeatedly indicated the necessity of ensuring *adequate* protection for data transferred to third countries (non-EEA) under economic cooperation instruments. The criterion of adequacy of safeguards is an explicit requirement of EU data protection law, designed to ensure that international transfers of personal data (outside the EEA) do not lead to a lowering of the level of protection under EU law.[145] However, it follows from the CJEU's case law that the adequacy

140 *Ships Waste Oil Collector B.V. v. the Netherlands* (2799/16) 16 May 2023 ECtHR at [46].
141 *Centrum för rättvisa v. Sweden* [GC] (n 114) at [323].
142 Ibid. at [318].
143 Ibid.
144 *Big Brother Watch and Others v. the United Kingdom* [GC] (n 106) at [365].
145 While this requirement derives from secondary legislation (see Art. 42(2) of the GDPR and Art. 35(1)(d) of the LED), the Court, in its interpretation, has linked the fulfilment of the adequacy condition to respect for the rights guaranteed by the Charter. In this regard, see the reasoning presented in *Schrems II* (C-311/18) EU:C:2020:559 at [182].

of safeguards may also be inferred from the interpretation of the Charter, and thus be based on EU primary law.[146]

The breach of the condition of adequate protection resulted in the CJEU declaring two important mechanisms for transatlantic cooperation on commercial data exchange with the United States to be invalid: the first in 2015, the *Safe Harbour* programme (the *Schrems* judgment);[147] and then in 2020, the *Privacy Shield* (the *Schrems II* judgment).[148] In both cases, the CJEU pointed out that federal law did not provide safeguards equivalent to EU law to ensure the protection of data subjects' rights against, *inter alia*, interference by US intelligence agencies carrying out bulk surveillance programmes.[149] In this regard, the CJEU emphasised that it was unacceptable to give a third country's national security objectives a higher priority than the protection of the rights of EU citizens.[150]

On the one hand, the CJEU's position clearly seeks to ensure the effectiveness of EU law insofar as it creates a supranational common data processing space. At the same time, however, the uncritical adoption of the concept of adequacy of safeguards – understood as their equivalence (but not identity)[151] – de facto imposes on foreign partners the need to adapt their legal models to the guarantees under EU law. Moreover, inasmuch as third countries are not members of the European Union, they cannot avail themselves of the Article 4(2) exemption in this respect. This leads to the conclusion that under EU law, the transfer of data obtained from electronic surveillance carried out between Member States may – under certain conditions – be exempted from the application of EU law, whereas the transfer of the same information between a Member State and a third country may only benefit from such an exemption if it is necessary to protect the national security of the transmitting (EU Member) State.[152]

Against this background, the ECtHR's position that there is no need for "comparable protection" in every case should be read as establishing a less restrictive, and thus more flexible, protection regime than that under EU law. Unfortunately, the Strasbourg Court has not explained how to assess whether the level of protection provided by a third country's legislation is sufficient to recognise the permissibility of the transfer. In this regard, it is also unclear how to reconcile this conclusion with the interpretation set out in *Centrum för rättvisa v. Sweden*, where the Grand Chamber indicated the need for an

146 *Opinion on the EU-Canada PNR Agreement* (n 117) at [134].

147 *Maximillian Schrems v. Data Protection Commissioner* (C-362/14) EU:C:2015:650.

148 *Schrems II* (n 145) at [180].

149 Ibid. at [180].

150 *Maximillian Schrems v. Data Protection Commissioner* (n 147) at [86].

151 Ibid. at [73].

152 Serena Crespi, 'The Applicability of Schrems Principles to the Member States: National Security and Data Protection within the EU Context' (2018) 43 *European Law Review* 669.

assessment of the necessity and proportionality of the transfer, taking into account "possible harm to the individual concerned."[153] It is also worth recalling here that one of the fundamental differences between the US and EU models for the use of electronic surveillance programmes in the area of state security relates precisely to the lack of consideration of the criteria of necessity and proportionality in the assessment of the legality of US services' surveillance programmes.[154]

In *Big Brother Watch v. UK*, the ECtHR also advocated that transfers of surveillance material to third countries should be subject to stricter requirements where the object is sensitive data. Information that could reveal journalistic sources was cited as an example, but the same criterion could also be applied to attorney-client privilege or other legally protected secrets. Insofar as concerns the practice of the UK services, the Court considered it sufficient that, in the case of transferring this type of information, "reasonable steps had to be taken to mark the information as confidential."[155] Unfortunately, it appears that also in this case the Court inappropriately applied its own standard of safeguards to the specifics of indiscriminate surveillance programmes. Without questioning the fact that the UK services use additional marking of the data being transferred, this is presumably the case when they have knowledge of the nature of the data. Bulk surveillance is based on large, unprocessed datasets. As indicated earlier, every hour the GCHQ (and other services running untargeted programmes) can intercept thousands of gigabytes of information and automatically transmit a large proportion of these data to foreign partners. Given that the material presented in the case showed that this practice was in place,[156] it is unclear why the Court did not undertake a deeper analysis as to how the GCHQ analysed such information in real time, and whether it did so thoroughly enough to mark, for example, the information covered by attorney-client privilege so that they could be appropriately flagged before being transferred to (shared with) foreign partners.

The differences between the standards on data transfers applied by the ECtHR and the CJEU not only concern the issue of the "adequacy" of safeguards. As in the case of the assessment of domestic surveillance programmes, the Luxembourg Court pays particular attention to the principle of strict necessity when addressing issues related to data transfers outside the EEA.[157] Hence, it scrupulously analyses not only the scope of the data to be transferred, but also the existence of legal mechanisms to ensure that the data will

153 *Centrum för rättvisa v. Sweden* [GC] (n 114) at [318].

154 See section 6.7 for more on this topic.

155 *Big Brother Watch and Others v. the United Kingdom* [GC] (n 106) at [397].

156 Ibid. at [362]: "it is now clear that some States are regularly sharing material with their intelligence partners and even, in some instances, allowing those intelligence partners direct access to their own systems."

157 *Opinion on the EU-Canada PNR Agreement* (n 117) at [141]; *Ligue des droits humains ASBL v. Conseil des ministres* (C-817/19) EU:C:2022:491 at [162].

not be used for any purpose other than a legally permissible one.[158] It further stresses the need to ensure adequate protection – equivalent to that laid down in the transfer agreement – in cases of the further transfer of the data to a third country's public authorities. It is also worth noting here that the problem of the further use of such information is an issue that has not been addressed in the ECtHR case law at all.

The requirements identified by the CJEU apply to cases of data transfers that are within the scope of EU law, i.e. concerning mainly economic cooperation but also police cooperation between Member States. One of the key criteria applied by the CJEU in the process of evaluating retention provisions is the requirement to keep the data within the territory of the European Union.[159] This condition aims to ensure the full effectiveness of EU law, including in particular the availability of judicial protection before an independent data protection authority, as provided for in Article 8(3) of the Charter. In this regard, the Court has emphasised that the scrutiny exercised by an independent authority is an essential element of respect for the right to the protection of personal data.[160]

Yet, the obligation to store data that come from telecommunications data retention within the European Union does not stand in the way of further transfers of such data to third countries. This kind of transfer (as well as making such data available to national authorities) should, however, be examined as a separate case of interference with fundamental rights and would therefore require a separate assessment of necessity and proportionality, as well as confirmation that appropriate legal safeguards have been implemented. In practice, however, if such a transfer is carried out within the framework of intelligence cooperation programmes, and thus by a public authority empowered to do so, this activity would clearly fall outside the scope of EU law.

5.5 Best of both worlds – a common legal framework for electronic surveillance

The noticeable differences between the CJEU and the ECtHR case law – leading to different legal qualifications and, consequently, different assessments of the permissibility of similar surveillance programmes – raise the question about the future of the European Union (or more broadly, European) standard for the use of electronic surveillance measures.

It should first be clarified whether such a standard is needed at all, and thus whether there is, in fact, an irreconcilable difference between the positions of

158 *Opinion on the EU-Canada PNR Agreement* (n 117) at [179–181].

159 *Tele2 Sverige* (n 33) at [122].

160 *Commission v. Germany* (C-518/07) EU:C:2010:125 at [23]. Alexander Balthasar, '"Complete Independence" of National Data Protection Supervisory Authorities. Second Try: Comments on the Judgment of the CJEU of 16 October 2012, C-614/10, with Due Regard to Its Previous Judgment of 9 March 2010, C-518/07' (2013) 9 *Utrecht Law Review* 26.

the two courts. Only then is it worth analysing what are the actual reasons (root causes) leading to the different interpretations of similar legal concepts. These considerations will finally make it possible to answer the question of whether the differences identified can and should be overcome in an effort to unify the case law of European courts, or whether the partially different positions presented by the ECtHR and the CJEU actually complement each other, strengthening rather than weakening the European legal model.

Both the Strasbourg Court and the Luxembourg Court are aware of the emerging jurisprudential differences. In the *SpaceNet* case the CJEU, addressing arguments that its interpretation of the permissibility of indiscriminate surveillance (data retention) was inconsistent with the views expressed by the ECtHR – in particular as set out in *Big Brother Watch v. UK* – pointed out that the Strasbourg standard applied, in principle, to the surveillance of international communications. The Court further stressed:

> The European Court of Human Rights did not rule, in those judgments, on the compatibility with the ECHR of a general and indiscriminate retention of traffic and location data on national territory or even a large-scale interception of those data for the purposes of the prevention, detection and investigation of serious criminal offences.[161]

It therefore considered that the ECtHR's interpretation did not apply to domestic surveillance measures used in the area of combating serious crime – and thus to such measures as general data retention. While this observation can be seen as just a convenient justification for the CJEU to introduce its own interpretation, it cannot be fully denied. Notably, the ECtHR did not apply its own *Big Brother Watch* test – dedicated to assessing indiscriminate surveillance – to the assessment of domestic retention laws examined in *Ekimdzhiev and Others v. Bulgaria*.

However, the Strasbourg Court (ECtHR) seems to overlook the distinction between international and national programmes, referring in detail to the CJEU's position on a general data retention obligation also in cases involving foreign surveillance in the area of state security. For example, in *Centrum för rättvisa v. Sweden*, the Court presented the conclusions of the *Privacy International* and *LQN* cases, while emphasising that EU law, in cases involving a genuine threat to national security, "did not preclude legislative measures requiring service providers to retain, generally and indiscriminately, traffic and location data for a period limited to what was strictly necessary."[162] Thus, it seems that each court was fully aware of the partially different interpretation presented by the other court, which, however, does not seem to have significantly affected the direction of each Court's own interpretation.

161 *SpaceNet* (n 37) at [125].
162 *Centrum för rättvisa v. Sweden* [GC] (n 114) at [129].

This leads to the question of whether the jurisprudential standards presented are truly different and, therefore, irreconcilable. The CJEU's position is clear and, in general, precludes the use of indiscriminate surveillance indefinitely and without connection to actual threats to important general security objectives. The Strasbourg Court, on the other hand, applies its own interpretation selectively without a clear indication as to whether the lack of reference to the previous standard is a permanent departure from it, or whether it is incidental and motivated by the consideration of the circumstances of the particular case under review. As a result, it is difficult to determine whether, and to what extent, the *Big Brother Watch* standard actually "replaces" *Huvig/Weber* in relation to particular forms of indiscriminate surveillance unrelated to the interception of electronic communications. Similar doubts concern the *Uzun* test and its usefulness, for example, in relation to surveillance programmes used in public spaces. The ECtHR emphasises the importance of the criterion of strict necessity in some cases – finding, based de facto on this criterion, the national legislation under examination to violate the guarantees under the Convention – only to fail to refer to this principle at all in subsequent judgments. It is noteworthy that in *Centrum för rättvisa v. Sweden* and *Big Brother Watch v. UK*, the only references to the "strict necessity" condition concerned the discussion of the CJEU standard and the parties' arguments. In its reasoning, the Grand Chamber did not refer at all – not even once – to the test of strict necessity, which it had in its earlier case law recognised as a key concept in setting the boundaries of lawful surveillance.[163]

The above leads to the question of why the ECtHR's interpretation is so unclear in many places, especially against the background of the CJEU's reasoning. Of course, the basic reason relates to the significant differences in the legal models under examination and the nature of the Convention – which is, after all, not an instrument for the harmonisation of national law. The legal space of the Council of Europe includes not only EU Member States but also countries often not counted among the established democracies. Suffice it to say that the view has been pushed over the years that the adoption by the ECtHR of overly stringent standards for the assessment of national laws could discourage some states from remaining within the Convention model. This was, therefore, a kind of strategy for "democratic consolidation" and promoting the protection of fundamental rights.[164] This reasoning could explain a situation where the Strasbourg Court's requirements applied to developing democracies would be less stringent than those applied to states with a long tradition of the rule of law. However, a different trend can be found in the ECtHR's jurisprudence, that of applying stricter scrutiny when examining complaints concerning surveillance in quasi-democratic states and less

163 See e.g. *Klass and Others v. Germany* (5029/71) 18 December 1974 ECtHR at [42].

164 Steven Greer, *The European Convention on Human Rights: Achievements, Problems and Prospects* (Repr, Cambridge University Press 2008) 105.

stringent requirements in the case of developed democracies. An example of this is the case of *Roman Zakharov v. Russia*, in which the Court aptly pointed out the flawed nature of Russia's surveillance laws, which could have been used to place any person under surveillance.[165] It is thus therefore all the more surprising that 4 years later the same Court, in assessing the UK regulations, accepted that the measures provided for therein could be used for the surveillance of any user using certain electronic communications channels.[166]

The accuracy of this (partly) critical assessment of the ECtHR jurisprudence is also confirmed by the separate opinions attached to particular cases. Similar arguments are repeated in them, related to the Court's overly vague interpretation,[167] acceptance of a departure from key legal concepts that underpinned earlier case law,[168] or failure to take a broader view of the context of the surveillance provisions under review, in particular by overlooking the need to establish stricter legal safeguards for indiscriminate surveillance measures.[169]

Against this background, the CJEU's standard appears simple and clear, and although some governments and even national courts contest it, the reason for the differences in the reception of the Court's position is not due to ambiguities in the interpretation presented, but a reluctance toward its practical application. To a large extent, the discrepancies between the interpretations by the CJEU and the ECtHR seem to stem from three fundamental differences: (1) the Strasbourg Court's attachment to the concept of strict necessity; (2) the recognition that respect for the essence of a fundamental right constitutes an insurmountable barrier to interference with individual rights; and (3) stronger safeguards for the right to data protection guaranteed in EU law than in the ECHR.

The first difference has already been discussed and is, in fact, related to the CJEU's application of the proportionality test, requiring that the degree of interference with individual rights must correspond to the importance of the protected value. Strict necessity precludes implementing measures that bear no real (even indirect or remote) relation to threats to public security, whether in terms of fighting crime or pursuing national security objectives. So it is this concept that, de facto, precludes the use of preventive surveillance to the same extent as that permissible in the ECtHR case law.

Equally relevant to the Luxembourg standard is the inviolability of the essence of a fundamental right, leading to the conclusion that certain forms of particularly intrusive interference are impermissible irrespective of the outcome of the proportionality test – and thus also where their implementation is

165 *Roman Zakharov v. Russia* (47143/06) 4 December 2015 ECtHR at [265].

166 *Big Brother Watch and Others v. the United Kingdom* [GC] (n 106) at [376].

167 Ibid. P. de Albuquerque (partly concurring and partly dissenting) at [2].

168 For example, in context of the foreseeability of a bulk surveillance regime, see *Big Brother Watch and Others v. the United Kingdom* [GC] (n 106) P. de Albuquerque (partly concurring and partly dissenting) at [16].

169 *Big Brother Watch and Others v. the United Kingdom* [GC] (n 106) P. Lemmens, F. Vehabović and M. Bošnjak (concurring) at [10].

motivated by particularly important and legitimate objectives of general security (see section 3.5). Hence, mass monitoring of electronic communications, which is considered to violate the very essence of a fundamental right, cannot per se be reconciled with EU law.[170] In such a view, the outcome of the assessment of the necessity of such a measure and the arguments – repeated by the ECtHR – that there is no alternative to its application, are irrelevant. Interestingly, the ECtHR jurisprudence also emphasises the importance of protecting the essence of a fundamental right, but unlike EU law the ECHR does not directly refer to this concept, making its relevance in the Strasbourg acquis contingent on the Court's (variable) interpretation.[171]

Also, the fact that EU primary law establishes separate privacy and data protection guarantees has the effect of setting clearer data protection standards than those applied under the ECHR.[172] As a result, the interpretation of EU law provided in the individual cases examined by the Luxembourg Court focuses on the assessment of respect for both the right to privacy and the right to data protection. The Charter of Fundamental Rights not only defines the subjective right to data protection itself, but also points to its most important components, which form the standard of review for the assessment of surveillance provisions. Hence the CJEU's attachment to examining the purpose of surveillance measures, as well as the availability of effective remedies for the persons concerned, including the possibility of the actual exercise of the rights of access and rectification. Of course, data protection is also an important element of the Strasbourg standard, but in this case it is also largely based on the Court's case law.[173] As a result, as in other instances the ECtHR invokes the data protection guarantees with varying intensity in different types of cases. This leads to a situation where it points out the impermissibility of a measure allowing the preventive collection of data on the whole population in one case[174] while accepting the use of an equivalent measure in another case.[175]

170 *Maximillian Schrems v. Data Protection Commissioner* (n 147) at [94–98].

171 Sébastien Van Drooghenbroeck and Cecilia Rizcallah, 'The ECHR and the Essence of Fundamental Rights: Searching for Sugar in Hot Milk?' (2019) 20 *German Law Journal* 904. For more on the essence of a fundamental right in EU law, see section 3.5.

172 At the same time, it should be borne in mind that the interpretation of the scope of Art. 8 of the ECHR has undergone a significant expansion over the years, and this process certainly cannot be considered completed. Maris Burbergs, 'How the Right to Respect for Private and Family Life, Home and Correspondence Became the Nursery in Which New Rights Are Born: Article 8 ECHR' in Eva Brems and Janneke Gerards (eds), *Shaping Rights in the ECHR* (Cambridge University Press 2014).

173 In the Council of Europe acquis, data protection guarantees – in addition to the ECtHR's interpretation of the right to privacy (Art. 8 of the ECHR) – also derive from Data Protection Convention 108. For more on the impact of surveillance on the right to data protection, see section 3.4.

174 *M.K. v. France* (19522/09) 18 April 2013 ECtHR at [40].

175 See the comments on the interpretation of the term "unprocessed information" in section 4.4.3.

Importantly, insofar as regards two of the three differences defined above, their source is not a different assessment of the facts of cases but a different legal framework set out in the enacted law. The Court of Justice cannot depart from the concept of the inviolability of the essence of a fundamental right, as it follows directly from the Charter of Fundamental Rights.[176] For the same reason, it cannot accept a measure allowing the processing of data by public authorities contrary to the purpose(s) for which the data were collected. The obvious conclusion follows that a proposal for a relaxation of (or partial departure from) the CJEU's interpretation to seek a common interpretation of the electronic surveillance standards would, de facto, require amending the EU treaties.

More importantly, however, the arguments that the CJEU's position is, in fact, too restrictive and thus impossible to apply, or that its application would expose Member States to increased risks in the area of the most serious threats, including terrorism, are not convincing. The CJEU has repeatedly emphasised that the protection of state security is a key public task and justifies the adoption of more far-reaching measures than those permissible in the fight against crime. In any case, however, access by public authorities to citizens' details must have a connection – even remote or indirect – with the threat due to which the data have been collected. Eavesdropping on nursery school teachers, doctors or housewives (i.e. members of the general public) not only does not help in the fight against terrorism but may reduce the effectiveness of the measures taken in this area, as it distracts the services by involving them in the analysis of useless information.[177]

Therefore it seems that it is the CJEU's interpretation that should be the foundation for the future standards of legal safeguards applied in the area of electronic surveillance. Actually, this is close to the ECtHR's early interpretation, as it de facto builds on the *Huvig/Weber* standard and extends it as far as necessary to take into account the specifics of the modern forms of surveillance.

By combining the conclusions drawn from the analysis of the case law presented above it is, however, possible to propose a more comprehensive list of safeguards that should be applied whenever the government of a democratic state decides to implement indiscriminate surveillance measures:[178]

176 Maja Brkan, 'The Essence of the Fundamental Rights to Privacy and Data Protection: Finding the Way Through the Maze of the CJEU's Constitutional Reasoning' (2019) 20 *German Law Journal* 864. For more on the essence of fundamental rights in the context of the CJEU case law, see section 3.5.

177 *Cf.* an alternative standard presented in: Paul Bernal, 'Data Gathering, Surveillance and Human Rights: Recasting the Debate' (2016) 1 *Journal of Cyber Policy* 243, 259.

178 Paul De Hert and Gianclaudio Malgieri, 'One European Legal Framework for Surveillance: The ECtHR's Expanded Legality Testing Copied by the CJEU' in Valsamis Mitsilegas and Niovi Vavoula (eds), *Surveillance and Privacy in the Digital Age: European, Transatlantic and Global Perspectives* (Hart 2021) 297.

1. *Accessibility of the law* – the need to ensure the secrecy of surveillance activities must not lead to the secrecy of the legal framework setting out the rules under which such activities are conducted.
2. *Foreseeability of the law* – the use of surveillance measures should be provided for by law, including the determination of all key aspects of ordering, implementing, and applying such measures.
3. *Principle of a specific purpose* – the legislature should indicate the specific reasons justifying the activation of untargeted surveillance measures, which should not be general clauses; it is also necessary to recognise the impermissibility of using data obtained by means of untargeted measures for other, less important public tasks.[179]
4. *Limitation of the scope of the data collected* – the scope of data collected should be related to the purpose for which the surveillance measure is to be used; the process of selecting communication channels and the use of selectors should be subject to real control by an independent authority; and the way in which the selectors are chosen and defined must allow for an assessment of the legality of the action(s) taken.
5. *Strict necessity as a condition for data access* – any access to data by public authorities must meet the condition of strict necessity; this excludes bulk access to, and bulk processing of, detailed data on individuals.
6. *Prior judicial review* – the choice of selectors and the procedures used at the data processing stage should be authorised by a court; in particular, the choice of strong selectors should be subject to the same procedure as the one used for targeted surveillance.
7. *Comprehensive ex post oversight* – oversight mechanisms should be built into every stage of the ordering and application of a surveillance measure; the way in which an untargeted surveillance regime operates, even if applied for a limited period, must be subject to systematic external scrutiny.
8. *Notification mechanism and judicial remedies* – allowing an individual to find out whether they have been put under surveillance and to subject the legality of the action taken against them to judicial review.
9. *Clear data retention periods* for each of the stages of the acquisition, processing and subsequent use of the information; for self-learning models, the mandatory use of anonymisation techniques to reduce intrusion into the rights of data subjects.
10. *International cooperation* – a statutory regulation of the acquisition and transfer of bulk data; establishing the requirement for comparable legal safeguards as a condition for transferring data abroad; subjecting the instances of acquiring data to procedures that are similar to those used for domestic surveillance.

179 In particular, this applies to the performance of the tasks listed in the ECtHR's limitation clauses – i.e. to tasks carried out not only for crime-fighting purposes but, for example, also for the protection of health or the economic well-being of the country.

11 *Establishing prohibitions in relation to certain subject-matter and persons* – extending the prohibition of the deliberate collection of sensitive data and data containing legally protected secrets to indiscriminate programmes; introducing additional safeguards for the construction of systems based on the bulk interception of publicly available data (both in public spaces and on the Internet).

In analysing the above list, one can easily identify references to the existing interpretations applied in electronic surveillance cases. This proposal has been drafted in such a way as to address, as comprehensively as possible, the problems that have already been recognised and discussed for years, as well as those that are yet to be analysed in detail (e.g. surveillance based on biometric systems).

An alternative to the above list is the proposal – discussed almost a decade ago[180] – to create a new legal instrument in the form of a legally binding international agreement establishing minimum legal safeguards and cooperation mechanisms in the field of electronic surveillance. This instrument could be available to all interested states, regardless of whether they belong to the same economic organisation or human rights system. Such a solution would also make it possible to create a transnational secure data processing space, in which states would apply the same rules on access to private data by public authorities. At the same time, this could help address the problem of ensuring the adequacy of safeguards for data transfers in the field of economic cooperation.[181]

Leaving aside the feasibility of implementing the standards presented above, there is no doubt that each of the issues they relate to should be given detailed attention in the discussion on the European model of electronic surveillance. Moreover, the omission of even one of these areas de facto undermines the effectiveness of all others – in the extreme case, creating an illusion of the protection of and respect for fundamental rights.

5.6 Summary

Despite the number of precedent-setting judgments issued in recent years, the problem of developing a common European standard for the use of electronic

180 'Working Draft Legal Instrument on Government-Led Surveillance and Privacy' (UN Special Rapporteur on the Right to Privacy 2018) <https://cli.re/GJD2JB> accessed 6 September 2023.

181 The Parliamentary Assembly of the Council of Europe has also presented its own initiative to develop an international treaty setting standards for the use of electronic surveillance (the so-called intelligence codex) – see Resolution 2045 (2015) <https://cli.re/1PY7bD> accessed 6 September 2023. However, this proposal did not gain the approval of the Committee of Ministers – see Reply to Recommendation 2067 (2015) 'Committee of Ministers' (14 October 2015) <https://cli.re/vPdM3k> accessed 6 September 2023.

surveillance measures is still far from being resolved. Part of the reason for this is the divergences emerging between the interpretations applied by particular courts. These differences not only pertain to the European courts, but also are equally pronounced at the national level. Suffice it to mention the diametrically opposed reactions of national courts to the CJEU judgment in the *LQN* case. Although the French Conseil d'État, the Belgian Cour constitutionnelle and the UK Investigatory Powers Tribunal did not explicitly challenge[182] the CJEU's core arguments, their analysis of the judgment led them to different conclusions. Thus, the Cour constitutionnelle found the Belgian retention regulations in the area of state security to be invalid.[183] The Investigatory Powers Tribunal also applied the CJEU's interpretation directly, finding that the contested provisions of the Telecommunications Act of 1984 were incompatible with EU law.[184] The French Conseil d'État, on the other hand, presented an elaborate argumentation aimed at demonstrating that an untargeted surveillance regime may be applied in the specific emergency situations that France has been facing for years.[185]

In fact, developing a coherent framework for the use of surveillance is a task that goes far beyond the judiciary. New legislative initiatives and the desire to develop a political consensus at both the EU and international levels play an important role in this regard.

One of the unfinished pieces of EU data protection law reform is the new e-Privacy Regulation.[186] This act is intended to replace the more than 20-year-old e-Privacy Directive discussed earlier. Its adoption is also crucial in view of the need to ensure consistency in the EU's regulatory framework for the telecoms market. The discussion on the shape of the new regulation has been ongoing since 2017, and despite initial optimism,[187] the negotiations were not concluded quickly.[188] One of the problem areas was precisely the retention provisions, in particular the content of the derogation clause authorising states

182 This risk was particularly associated with the proceedings before the Council of State, as the French government requested that the *LQN* judgment be recognised as *ultra vires*. Francesco Martucci, 'Primacy, Identity and Ultra Vires: Forging the Union through the Law without Foregoing the Rule of Law' (2021) 3 *RED* 19.

183 Cour constitutionnelle 22 April 2021 (57/2021) at [B.18].

184 It should be noted, however, that in this case the domestic legislation in question was no longer in force when the judgment was handed down. Investigatory Powers Tribunal 22 July 2021 [2021] UKIPTrib IPT_15_110_CH.

185 Conseil d'État 21 April 2021 (393099) FR:CEASS:2021:393099.20210421 at [44].

186 Proposal for a Regulation concerning the respect for private life and the protection of personal data in electronic communications and repealing Directive 2002/58/EC, COM/2017/010 final.

187 Giovanni Buttarelli, 'The Commission Proposal for a Regulation on ePrivacy: Why Do We Need a Regulation Dedicated to ePrivacy in the European Union Forewords' (2017) 3 *European Data Protection Law Review (EDPL)* 155.

188 Luca Bertuzzi, 'Leading MEP Enraged by Swedish Presidency's Neglect of ePrivacy Regulation' *Euroactiv* (8 March 2023) <https://cli.re/KJbEn1> accessed 6 September 2023.

to introduce national data retention rules.[189] As a result of the CJEU's unambiguous interpretation, some Member States are calling for amendments to the draft regulation to reopen the way for the use of indiscriminate data retention in Member States.[190] However, it seems that these attempts are doomed to failure. Although the CJEU, in examining retention regulations, analysed the obligations under the e-Privacy Directive, it derived the impermissibility of general retention directly from the provisions of the Charter. Changing secondary legislation in this regard – e.g. by drafting the new e-Privacy Regulation accordingly – will not change the interpretation of the Charter and, therefore, will not affect the validity of the CJEU's existing interpretation.[191] In practice, however, if such legislative action(s) were taken, they would certainly result in further doubts as to the permissibility of the new retention regime, leading to further cases ultimately being decided by the CJEU.

Given the cross-border nature of the data market, it seems that it may be particularly important to draw on international law instruments to develop common criteria for the use of electronic surveillance. Basing standards solely on regulations of a regional scope – whether derived from European Union law or the acquis of the Council of Europe – will have little impact on the practice of using surveillance in third countries. This observation is corroborated by the discussion in Europe concerning US surveillance programmes, which has been ongoing for years.[192]

The global data market means that the same data can be intercepted in multiple locations simultaneously. The lack of a supranational surveillance regulation not only creates the conditions for the development of elaborate means of mass surveillance, but also encourages the adoption of legally dubious schemes for the cross-border exchange of the data acquired. In this respect, it is impossible to agree with Niels Annen, German Minister of State at the Federal Foreign Office, who has stated that "the Federal Government does not see any gap in international law in this area."[193] Not only do the German SIAs themselves carry out extensive surveillance programmes, the legality of which has been repeatedly questioned in recent years,[194] but they have also been very actively cooperating with foreign partners in terms of sharing and extracting

189 Adam Juszczak and Elisa Sason, 'Recalibrating Data Retention in the EU : The Jurisprudence of the Court of Justice of the EU on Data Retention – Is This the End or is this Only the Beginning?' (2021) eucrim – The European Criminal Law Associations' Forum <https://eucrim.eu/articles/recalibrating-data-retention-in-the-eu/> accessed 7 September 2023.

190 'The issue of data retention in the proposal for ePrivacy Regulation – discussion paper', Council of the European Union (14 February 2019).

191 Marcin Rojszczak, 'The Uncertain Future of Data Retention Laws in the EU: Is a Legislative Reset Possible?' (2021) 41 *Computer Law & Security Review* 105572.

192 This topic is discussed in more detail in the next chapter (section 6.8).

193 Stefan Talmon, 'No Need for Legal Instrument on Electronic Surveillance and Privacy' *German Practice in International Law* (5 June 2018) <https://cli.re/23aKvx> accessed 6 September 2023.

194 For recent examples, see the BND Act case of 2020 (BVerfG 1 BvR 2835/17), the BKA surveillance case of 2016 (BVerfG 1 BvR 966/09) and the DE-CIX case of 2018 (BVerwG 6 A 3.16).

information. It seems, therefore, that the German government (in fact, like many others) not so much fails to understand the need for legally binding instruments in this area as it does not itself need such regulation.

Viewed against this background, a particularly interesting case is that of Poland, where as of 2023 a general data retention obligation is still in place and special services and the police have direct access to retained data, without any *ex ante* control and in an automated manner, and the use of the data is not limited to cases of fighting serious crime (or even any crime at all). It is, therefore, an almost complete ***anti-model*** compared with the standards set by the CJEU. Going further, in the area of electronic intelligence the Polish legislature has contented itself with a general (blanket) standard according to which the Intelligence Agency and the Military Intelligence Service are authorised to "conduct electronic intelligence."[195] This is a complete statutory regulation, consisting of exactly three words. The legislature has not introduced any rules, boundaries, or procedures establishing any legal framework for the exercise of this power. This is another kind of anti-model, this time in terms of the foreseeability and accessibility of the law. The Polish law is thus clearly incompatible with the ECtHR's interpretation – and not only that presented in the most recent judgments but even the requirements indicated in the 1978 case of *Klass v. Germany*. And all this concerns a state which is both a party to the European Convention and an EU Member State.

Similar reservations can also be raised with regard to other Member States. Suffice it to mention the recent reform of the Italian retention law, aimed at ***extending*** (to 6 years) rather than shortening the data retention period.[196] These examples clearly show that the establishment of appropriate standards does not resolve the question of the legal regulation of electronic surveillance, which also requires that the application of such standards be ensured – a task that, in turn, requires the cooperation of all branches of government, not only the judiciary but also the legislature and, of course, the executive.

Therefore in the foreseeable future it is to be expected that the problem of setting limits to the use of electronic surveillance will not cease to be the subject of heated debates at the political, legislative and judicial levels. It is worth noting that further cases on this very issue are pending before the ECtHR alone, including those challenging the French[197] and Polish[198] surveillance laws.

References

Aldrich RJ, *GCHQ: The Uncensored Story of Britain's Most Secret Intelligence Agency* (Harper Press 2011).

Anderson D, 'Report of the Bulk Powers Review' (Independent Reviewer of Terrorism Legislation 2016) <https://cli.re/97RkoJ> accessed 9 June 2023.

195 Art. 6(1)(8) of the Polish Act of 24 May 2002 on the Internal Security Agency and the Intelligence Agency.

196 'National Data Retention Laws since the CJEU's Tele-2/Watson Judgment' (n 28) 28.

197 *Association confraternelle de la presse judiciaire v. France et 11 autres requêtes* (49526/15).

198 *Pietrzak v. Poland* (72038/17) and *Bychawska-Siniarska and Others v. Poland* (25237/18).

Balthasar A, '"Complete Independence" of National Data Protection Supervisory Authorities. Second Try: Comments on the Judgment of the CJEU of 16 October 2012, C-614/10, with Due Regard to Its Previous Judgment of 9 March 2010, C-518/07' (2013) 9 *Utrecht Law Review* 26.

Bannon A, 'Romania Retrenches on Data Retention' (2010) 24 *International Review of Law, Computers & Technology* 145.

Bergen P and others, 'Do NSA's Bulk Surveillance Programs Stop Terrorists?' (New America Foundation 2014) <https://goo.gl/dpkEdC> accessed 6 September 2023.

Bernal P, 'Data Gathering, Surveillance and Human Rights: Recasting the Debate' (2016) 1 *Journal of Cyber Policy* 243.

Bertuzzi L, 'Leading MEP Enraged by Swedish Presidency's Neglect of ePrivacy Regulation' *Euroactiv* (8 March 2023) <https://cli.re/KJbEn1> accessed 6 September 2023.

Brkan M, 'The Essence of the Fundamental Rights to Privacy and Data Protection: Finding the Way Through the Maze of the CJEU's Constitutional Reasoning' (2019) 20 *German Law Journal* 864.

Burbergs M, 'How the Right to Respect for Private and Family Life, Home and Correspondence Became the Nursery in Which New Rights Are Born: Article 8 ECHR' in Eva Brems and Janneke Gerards (eds), *Shaping Rights in the ECHR* (Cambridge University Press 2014).

Buttarelli G, 'The Commission Proposal for a Regulation on ePrivacy: Why Do We Need a Regulation Dedicated to ePrivacy in the European Union Forewords' (2017) 3 *European Data Protection Law Review (EDPL)* 155.

Cameron I, 'Balancing Data Protection and Law Enforcement Needs: Tele2 Sverige and Watson' (2017) 54 *Common Market Law Review* 1467.

Crespi S, 'The Applicability of Schrems Principles to the Member States: National Security and Data Protection within the EU Context' (2018) 43 *European Law Review* 669.

De Hert P and Malgieri G, 'One European Legal Framework for Surveillance: The ECtHR's Expanded Legality Testing Copied by the CJEU' in Valsamis Mitsilegas and Niovi Vavoula (eds), *Surveillance and Privacy in the Digital Age: European, Transatlantic and Global Perspectives* (Hart 2021).

'Developments in the Law – More Data, More Problems' (2018) 131 *Harvard Law Review* 1715.

Donohue LK, *The Future of Foreign Intelligence: Privacy and Surveillance in a Digital Age* (Oxford University Press 2016).

'Draft Framework Decision on the Data Retention' (Council of the European Union 2004) 8958/04.

'ECJ Rules against Mass Data Retention in Germany' *Deutsche Welle* (20 September 2022) <https://cli.re/wPZW9X> accessed 6 September 2023.

'Extraordinary Council Meeting Justice and Home Affairs' (Council of the European Union 2005) 11116/05 (Presse 187) <https://cli.re/n4Ev9d> accessed 6 September 2023.

Gellman B, Tate J and Soltani A, 'In NSA-Intercepted Data, Those Not Targeted Far Outnumber the Foreigners Who Are' *The Washington Post* (5 July 2014) <https://cli.re/dp2keR> accessed 6 September 2023.

Greer S, *The European Convention on Human Rights: Achievements, Problems and Prospects* (Repr, Cambridge University Press 2008).

Juszczak A and Sason E, 'Recalibrating Data Retention in the EU: The Jurisprudence of the Court of Justice of the EU on Data Retention – Is This the End or Is This Only the Beginning?' (2021) *eucrim – The European Criminal Law Associations' Forum* <https://eucrim.eu/articles/recalibrating-data-retention-in-the-eu/> accessed 7 September 2023.

Kaiser A-B, 'German Federal Constitutional Court: German Data Retention Provisions Unconstitutional in their Present Form; Decision of 2 March 2010, NJW 2010, p. 833' (2010) 6 *European Constitutional Law Review* 503.

Kerbaj R, *The Secret History of the Five Eyes: The Untold Story of the International Spy Network* (Blink 2022).

Kim S and Perlin P, 'Newly Disclosed NSA Documents Shed Further Light on Five Eyes Alliance' (*Lawfare*, 25 March 2019) <www.lawfareblog.com/newly-disclosed-nsa-documents-shed-further-light-five-eyes-alliance>.

Konstadinides T, 'Destroying Democracy on the Ground of Defending It? The Data Retention Directive, the Surveillance State and Our Constitutional Ecosystem' (2011) 36 *European Law Review* 722.

Kosta E, '*United Kingdom SSHD v. Watson & Ors*: A "Thin" Nail on the Coffin of UK Data Retention Legislation' (2018) 4 *European Data Protection Law Review* 520.

'Liberty's Response to the Investigatory Powers Commissioner's Informal Consultation on Bulk Powers' (The National Council for Civil Liberties 2018) <https://cli.re/RNXbYJ> accessed 6 September 2023.

Lubello V and Vedaschi A, 'Data Retention and Its Implications for the Fundamental Right to Privacy: A European Perspective' (2015) 20 *Tilburg Law Review* 14.

Maras M-H, 'From Targeted to Mass Surveillance: Is the EU Data Retention Directive a Necessary Measure or an Unjustified Threat to Privacy?' in Benjamin J Goold (ed), *New Directions in Surveillance and Privacy* (Willan 2013) <www.taylorfrancis.com/books/9781843927266> accessed 30 March 2021.

Martucci F, 'Primacy, Identity and Ultra Vires: Forging the Union through the Law without Foregoing the Rule of Law' (2021) 3 *RED* 19.

Mitsilegas V and others, 'Data Retention and the Future of Large-Scale Surveillance: The Evolution and Contestation of Judicial Benchmarks' (2022) *European Law Journal* 1.

Nakashima E, 'NSA Halts Controversial Email Collection Practice to Preserve Larger Surveillance Program' (28 April 2017) <https://cli.re/PpobVy> accessed 6 September 2023.

'National Data Retention Laws since the CJEU's Tele-2/Watson Judgment' (Privacy International 2017) <http://cli.re/68zdoe.> accessed 6 September 2023.

Ojanen T, 'Court of Justice of the European Union, Decision of 8 April 2014 in Joined Cases C-293/12 and C-594/12' (2014) 10 *European Constitutional Law Review* 528.

Pedersen AM, Udsen H and Jakobsen SS, 'Data Retention in Europe – the Tele 2 Case and Beyond' (2018) 8 *International Data Privacy Law* 160.

Podkowik J, 'Privacy in the Digital Era – Polish Electronic Surveillance Law Declared Partially Unconstitutional: Judgment of the Constitutional Tribunal of Poland of 30 July 2014, K 23/11' (2015) 11 *European Constitutional Law Review* 577.

'Report of the Special Rapporteur on the Right to Privacy' (UN Human Rights Council 2017) A/HRC/34/60.

'Report on the President's Surveillance Program' (Inspectors General of the DoD, DoJ, CIA, NSA and DNI 2009) <https://cli.re/VJnJ3P> accessed 6 September 2023.

'Report on the Telephone Records Program Conducted under Section 215 of the USA PATRIOT Act and on the Operations of the Foreign Intelligence Surveillance Court' (Privacy and Civil Liberties Oversight Board 2014) <https://cli.re/83PVBx> accessed 6 September 2023.

Risen J and Lichtblau E, 'Bush Lets U.S. Spy on Callers Without Courts' *The New York Times* (16 December 2005) <https://cli.re/A5byvJ> accessed 6 September 2023.

Rojszczak M, 'National Security and Retention of Telecommunications Data in Light of Recent Case Law of the European Courts' (2021a) 17 *European Constitutional Law Review* 607.

–, 'The Uncertain Future of Data Retention Laws in the EU: Is a Legislative Reset Possible?' (2021b) 41 *Computer Law & Security Review* 105572.
–, 'E-Evidence Cooperation in Criminal Matters from an EU Perspective' (2022) 85 *Modern Law Review* 847.
–, 'National Security in a Digital Europe' (2023) 48 *European Law Review* 545.
Seibt S, 'How Denmark Became the NSA's Listening Post in Europe' *France24* (1 June 2021) <https://cli.re/vNxzdD> accessed 6 September 2023.
Sinha GA, 'NSA Surveillance since 9/11 and the Human Right to Privacy' (2013) 59 *Loyola Law Review* 861.
Talmon S, 'No Need for Legal Instrument on Electronic Surveillance and Privacy' *German Practice in International Law* (5 June 2018) <https://cli.re/23aKvx> accessed 6 September 2023.
Taylor M, 'The EU Data Retention Directive' (2006) 22 *Computer Law & Security Review* 309.
Tracol X, 'The Judgment of the Grand Chamber Dated 21 December 2016 in the Two Joint Tele2 Sverige and Watson Cases: The Need for a Harmonised Legal Framework on the Retention of Data at EU Level' (2017) 33 *Computer Law & Security Review* 541.
–, 'The Joined Cases of Dwyer, SpaceNet and VD and SR before the European Court of Justice: The Judgments of the Grand Chamber about Data Retention Continue Falling on Deaf Ears in Member States' (2023) 48 *Computer Law & Security Review* 105773.
Tréguer F, 'Major Oversight Gaps in the French Intelligence Legal Framework' *about:intel* (25 March 2022) <https://cli.re/XjMm1K> accessed 6 September 2023.
'U.S. Cryptologic Partnership with the United Kingdom' (National Security Agency 1997) <https://cli.re/VJVmqV> accessed 6 September 2023.
Vainio N and Miettinen S, 'Telecommunications Data Retention after *Digital Rights Ireland*: Legislative and Judicial Reactions in the Member States' (2015) 23 *International Journal of Law and Information Technology* 290.
Van Drooghenbroeck S and Rizcallah C, 'The ECHR and the Essence of Fundamental Rights: Searching for Sugar in Hot Milk?' (2019) 20 *German Law Journal* 904.
'Working Draft Legal Instrument on Government-Led Surveillance and Privacy' (UN Special Rapporteur on the Right to Privacy 2018) <https://cli.re/GJD2JB> accessed 6 September 2023.
Zalnieriute M, 'Big Brother Watch and Others v. the United Kingdom' (2022) 116 *American Journal of International Law* 585.
Zubik M, Podkowik J and Rybski R (eds), *European Constitutional Courts towards Data Retention Laws* (Springer 2021).

6 Emerging challenges of bulk surveillance

6.1 Introduction

Despite the wealth of case law and the unprecedented public interest in recent years in the problem of control over public authorities' surveillance powers, a consensus on the legal standards to be applied in this area is still far from being reached.

Thus the final chapter of this book aims to explore issues that are often omitted from the mainstream discussion on the future legal regulation of surveillance, the importance of which seems set to grow exponentially in the years to come. These include issues such as the increasing use of machine learning systems; new forms of surveillance related to content monitoring at source; and the progressive privatisation of surveillance in multiple areas. What these issues have in common is that understanding them requires rejection (at least in part) of the assumptions that have been made for years and on which the existing legal safeguards models have been built.

Of course, the evolution of legal safeguards and standards is neither a new nor a unique process observed only in the case of electronic surveillance. Suffice it to say that the first of the standards developed by the ECtHR (i.e. *Huvig/Weber*) was and still is successfully applied in cases of targeted surveillance. It was only the proliferation of untargeted surveillance systems that has revealed its limitations, ultimately leading to the need for additional safeguards explicitly limiting the risks associated with bulk information collection and processing.

At the same time, the standards for indiscriminate surveillance are not perfect, as they are largely based on outdated assumptions about the design and operation of such systems. The blurry distinction between the stages of collecting information and its subsequent analysis, an issue which comes up again and again in the case law of the European courts, is increasingly of historical interest only. Modern indiscriminate surveillance can be carried out without the need for covert data acquisition, i.e. solely as an elaborate analytical system based on information that the public administration already has or can obtain from publicly available sources (e.g. social networks). Advanced IT systems that help make fuller use of information already in public data warehouses are being more and more often implemented, including in European countries.

DOI: 10.4324/9781003449263-6

Moreover, modern forms of data processing allow untargeted surveillance systems to be used in ways that are increasingly similar to targeted systems. However, as bulk surveillance is usually regulated separately (and less restrictively) than targeted surveillance, this creates a risk that bulk systems will be used to obtain information that could not be legally collected using targeted surveillance measures. This problem has been known for years and has led many jurisdictions to establish additional restrictions on the use of the so-called strong selectors. At the same time, there is no widespread acceptance that such a practice of using untargeted surveillance measures should per se be prohibited. Moreover, the increasing use of advanced algorithmic systems leads to definitional problems regarding the term "strong selector." In turn, data repositories at the disposal of law enforcement and secret services allow for the detailed profiling of individuals in a way similar to the profiling carried out by data brokers in relation to commercial data. Therefore when discussing standards related to electronic surveillance, more and more attention should be paid to overseeing the use of existing information banks.

A separate issue is the impact of the increasing use of machine learning (AI) systems on surveillance regulation. Such solutions have the potential to overcome many technological limitations and can, in effect, lead to the creation of a new class of surveillance systems. In the case of AI systems, it will be possible to replace classical selectors (data filtering mechanisms) with implicit and non-transparent algorithmic decisions. However, the use of AI in the area of electronic surveillance will not just improve the existing forms of data collection and processing, but will also bring about the development of completely new solutions – with no equivalents today. As a consequence, the proliferation of these types of systems may result in the need to revise the existing legal safeguards and standards, which are partly unsuited to the capabilities offered by AI – much like the standards for targeted surveillance, as discussed earlier, proved inadequate for controlling bulk surveillance risks.

The final issue analysed in this chapter concerns the controversy over US surveillance programmes, a controversy that has been growing in recent years. From the European perspective, it appears that this issue may be fundamental to the proper shaping of relations with a leading economic partner. The application of different – and apparently incompatible – rules for the use of electronic surveillance not only causes many tensions in the global digital market, but also creates barriers to the development of cooperation between public authorities.

6.2 Mass surveillance as a targeted measure

One of the key problems with indiscriminate surveillance measures is the risk that they will be used for targeted surveillance, i.e. to gather information on specific individuals or events. As indicated earlier,[1] any untargeted surveillance system can be utilised in this way. To do so, it is enough to use the so-called

1 See section 1.3.

strong selectors. This term should be understood as the implementation of mechanisms to filter data based on keywords that directly identify a specific individual.

While the use of targeted surveillance measures usually requires compliance with strict procedural safeguards, the use of strong selectors allows, at least in theory, the same information to be obtained while subject to the less stringent safeguards established for indiscriminate surveillance.

This risk is involved not only in the data collection stage. A potentially much bigger problem is the lack of control over the analysis of the data already collected in public databases. This is because the selectors used in bulk surveillance programmes serve to pre-filter the stream of information being intercepted. The data that meet the criteria described in the selectors are then stored and made available for further analysis. However, this analysis is not carried out just once or only within the scope of the criteria described in the keywords. As a result, it is possible, for example, to use overly general selectors, allowing the recording of data of persons only remotely related to the events being investigated by secret services to obtain detailed information on a specific person at the data analysis stage. Indeed, such capabilities were offered by systems such as xKeyscore, developed by the NSA. They made it possible to quickly access information of interest stored in many extensive databases. Importantly, these searches could be carried out on data that were already held and therefore did not require modification of the data collection process, including a change in the selectors used. This example illustrates that, surprisingly, untargeted measures can be used to conduct targeted surveillance not only based on strong selectors, but also because of overly general search criteria. In the latter case, a lot of redundant information will be collected, potentially allowing surveillance to be extended to persons outside the interest of authorities.

The above risks can be mitigated in several ways. First, identical legal safeguards can be established for both surveillance regimes. Second, the legal framework for indiscriminate surveillance can be supplemented by detailed procedures related to the use of different categories of selectors. Third, the risk of abuse can be mitigated by establishing a set of evidentiary rules preventing the use of information derived from indiscriminate surveillance in criminal proceedings.

The first proposal is the solution that most fully eliminates the risk of abuse of bulk measures for targeted surveillance, yet at the same time, it is the most difficult one to apply in practice. Leaving aside the need for political will to establish stricter oversight mechanisms for bulk surveillance measures, it is also true that their modus operandi is different from that of targeted measures. Bulk data capture and analysis are techniques that are expected to go beyond the capabilities of targeted surveillance measures, in particular by identifying links between data that point to new, previously unrecognised, types of threats. However, regardless of the amount of source data (and therefore how effectively the filtering mechanisms will be applied), it is clear that to look for new links in the information base, these data must first be collected – something that would be impossible if the criteria inherent in targeted surveillance measures were strictly applied. In other words, it seems that separate legal regimes for targeted and indiscriminate surveillance are a necessity arising from both the different modus operandi of each of these measures and from the purposes of their application.

Therefore in recent years most attention has been focused on the second of the regulatory strategies mentioned above: that of placing restrictions on the way selectors are defined. This issue is most often associated with the adoption of a stricter regime for the approval of strong selectors. A model example of this regulatory direction is the Swedish legislation on surveillance by FRA. The Act on Signals Intelligence in Defence Intelligence Activities provides for the mandatory use of keywords in the processes of collecting data for indiscriminate surveillance programmes. The set of selectors to be used is included in a surveillance request, which is subject to review and authorisation by a specialised court (the Swedish Defence Intelligence Court, *Försvarsunderrätt elsedomstolen*).[2]

In Article 3 of the Act, the legislature introduced a general principle that keywords that allow a specific natural person to be identified may only be used if such a measure is of particular importance to the secret service. At the same time, it is impermissible to make a surveillance request based solely on strong selectors ("the search terms or categories of search terms . . . cannot relate only to a specific natural person"). Therefore both mechanisms are intended to counteract the possibility of conducting overly detailed data searches using untargeted surveillance measures. In turn, the risk of collecting redundant data is mitigated by requiring the Intelligence Court to examine whether "the purpose of the collection cannot be met in a less intrusive manner."[3] However, the Swedish act does not require the use of further instruments, including an *ex post* evaluation, to confirm whether the data actually collected are used in accordance with the original purpose for which they were obtained. Also, the control over keywords only covers the information collection stage, that is the process of acquisition of information by FRA. The Act does not regulate how the data are then used – and therefore does not restrict the use in the data analysis process of terms or keywords other than those specified in the court order. However, this was not an oversight on the part of the legislature, but an intentional solution – which also extends to the possibility of indicating in the order not specific selectors but categories of them. At the same time, the Act does not define "categories of search terms," which leaves this issue to the discretion of the Intelligence Court.

While the Swedish regulations apply only in the area of military intelligence, the counterpart German regulations have a broader scope of application. In the German legal model, there are currently de facto two statutes establishing

2 See Art. 4a(3) of the Swedish Act on Signals Intelligence Defence Activities, SFS 2008:717.
3 Ibid., Art. 4a(5)(2).

the legal framework for the conduct of indiscriminate surveillance programmes by BND. The first is the so-called G10 Act, which concerns surveillance measures interfering with the constitutional right to communicate, as defined in Article 10 of the Basic Law (hence its common name, *Artikel 10-Gesetz*).[4] The other is the BND Act, which forms the basis for the implementation of foreign surveillance programmes.[5] This statute was amended in 2022 in response to objections raised by bVerfG.[6] As highlighted by the Federal Constitutional Court, the obligation to respect dignity sets an impassable barrier to all activities of German state authorities, including the intelligence service. The Court derived from this the need to establish minimum legal safeguards also for surveillance programmes of a so-called purely foreign nature.[7]

As a result, the procedure provided for in the G10 Act is applied to domestic surveillance measures (as well as quasi-foreign surveillance, such as the strategic surveillance programme),[8] while the procedure described in the BND Act applies only to programmes under which information on German residents is not collected. Both statutes establish separate restrictions on the use of specific types of selectors.

The strategic surveillance programme is conducted based on approvals granted by the executive, i.e. the Federal Minister of the Interior, upon seeking a mandatory opinion of the G10 Commission, an independent administrative body.[9] A surveillance order indicates both the keywords as well as the permitted method of data collection. Unlike in the Swedish model, the G10 Act requires an indication in the order of what proportion of available traffic may be intercepted, which cannot exceed 20% for untargeted surveillance measures.[10] This means that irrespective of the selectors adopted, BND may

4 Gesetz zur Beschränkung des Brief-, Post- und Fernmeldegeheimnisses [en: German Federal Law on the Restriction of Letter, Post and Telecommunications Secrecy], BGBl. I 1254; 2298; referred to as the 'G10 Act'.

5 Gesetz über den Bundesnachrichtendienst [en: Law on the Federal Intelligence Service], BGBl. I 2954, 2979; referred to as the 'BND Act'.

6 BVerfG 19 May 2020 (1 BvR 2835/17) DE:BVerfG:2020:rs20200519.1bvr283517.

7 Marcin Rojszczak, 'Extraterritorial Bulk Surveillance after the German BND Act Judgment' (2021) 17 *European Constitutional Law Review* 53; Katrin Kappler, 'Consequences of the German Constitutional Court's Ruling on Germany's Foreign Intelligence Service: The Importance of Human Rights in the Cooperation of Intelligence Services' (2022) 23 *German Law Journal* 173.

8 The surveillance programme which involved the interception of communications in which one of the parties was on German territory. The strategic surveillance programme was analysed both by BVerfG (1 BvR 2226/94-1 BvR 2420/95-1 BvR 2437/95) and by the ECtHR (*Weber and Saravia v. Germany*). For details, see section 1.2.

9 As the statute requires 3 of the 5 members of the Commission to be qualified to hold the office of a judge, the mandatory approval of surveillance requests fulfils the same role in the German model as judicial review in other countries' legal systems. However, the G10 Commission is not formally a court.

10 Art. 10(4) of the G10 Act.

not record more than 20% of the data transmitted over the communication channels subjected to surveillance.

With regard to the choice of selectors, the Federal Intelligence Service may only use keywords which are "intended and suitable for the clarification of facts about the danger area designated in the order."[11] At the same time, the use of terms containing identifiers resulting in "targeted detection of specific telecommunications connections" or relating to the collection of information about a "core area of private life" is not permitted.[12] The latter condition refers to a concept characteristic of German law (but also found in other jurisdictions, e.g. Polish law) and excludes the collection of information of a strictly private nature.[13]

It is worth noting that the G10 Act also introduces an interesting definition of "strong selectors," the essence of which is not the identifiability of a particular person but the uniqueness of the identifier used in a given communication channel. This is a narrower definition than, for example, the one found in the Swedish legislation cited earlier. In this sense, an identifier from an instant messenger would be an impermissible selector, but this is not the case with, for example, a person's identity document number. In practice, however, it appears that the mechanism discussed effectively counteracts the use of bulk programmes for targeted surveillance, as it stands in the way of intercepting the entire communication of a specific user.

Targeted surveillance is regulated differently in the provisions of the BND Act. In fact, in foreign applications the German legislature explicitly allowed targeted surveillance to be implemented as one of the ways of using bulk powers.[14] This solution should not come as a surprise, especially bearing in mind that the risk of abuse associated with the use of indiscriminate surveillance against specific individuals increases if the material collected can later be used in domestic operations. With regard to foreigners residing outside the country's own jurisdiction, the risk of such abuse appears to be significantly lower.

Foreign surveillance, like strategic surveillance, must be carried out based on keywords. However, the BND Act does not provide for specific limits on the amount of information obtained, nor does it set any limitations related to the use of overly detailed identifiers. Moreover, the Act introduces different procedures for authorisation and review in relation to untargeted and targeted surveillance activities.

While targeted surveillance using untargeted measures is explicitly allowed under the BND Act, a number of restrictions have been established regarding

11 Art. 5(2) of the G10 Act.
12 Ibid.
13 Edward J Eberle, 'Observations on the Development of Human Dignity and Personality in German Constitutional Law: An Overview' (2012) 33 *Liverpool Law Review* 201. On the absolute nature of human dignity, see also Chapter 3.
14 Art. 23(5) of the BND Act.

the categories of persons and data excluded from such surveillance. Namely, as in the case of domestic measures the collection of data of a strictly private nature is not permitted,[15] and similar prohibition applies to the targeted collection of data exchanged with members of the clergy, lawyers, and journalists.[16] The legislature also provided for a more restrictive regime for the targeted collection of data on the institutions of the European Union and on the public bodies of other Member States;[17] this was clearly a response to media reports on the abuse of power by BND for the surveillance of allies.[18]

Undoubtedly, a major problem with the regulatory model introduced in the BND Act is the assumption that domestic and foreign traffic can be separated. In practice – as has been pointed out on several occasions in this book – this is not a technically straightforward task. It is possible to introduce data filtering mechanisms based on the information about the geolocation of the communicating parties, the IP addresses used, or other network identifiers. However, given the nature of global IT services, these mechanisms seem to be far from sufficient, leading to the risk of traffic between domestic users being classified as foreign communication. This does not, however, change the fact that the BND Act is one of the few European examples of legislation that clarifies the scope, forms, and means of indiscriminate surveillance of a so-called purely foreign nature.[19] Indeed, it is difficult to criticise the German law, bearing in mind that in neighbouring countries the same issues are subject to residual statutory regulation.[20]

The French amendment to the Internal Security Code adopted in 2015 is far from the German model. The purpose of adopting the new legislation was to establish a more coherent framework for the use of surveillance measures by secret services. Previously, surveillance powers had been the subject of regulations scattered across several acts. As a result of the reform, the Internal Security Code became a supplement to criminal legislation, setting out the procedures for surveillance in the area of state security, as however broadly defined.

The new legislation was also the French authorities' response to the 2015 attacks in Paris – hence the desire to expand the state's surveillance capabilities, which is noticeable in the wording of the regulation. Unlike the German legislation, the Internal Security Code establishes procedures to be applied in cases of

15 Art. 22(1) of the BND Act.
16 Art. 21(1) of the BND Act.
17 Art. 20(1) of the BND Act.
18 Maik Baumgärtner and Martin Knobbe, 'Sonderermittler Spricht von Klarem Vertragsbruch Der NSA' *Der Spiegel* (30 October 2015) <https://cli.re/97VNQR> accessed 6 September 2023.
19 But not the only one. The UK regulations introduced in the IPA 2016 are also noteworthy against this background.
20 See the comments on the Polish legislation applicable to foreign surveillance the summary of Chapter 5.

both domestic surveillance and programmes of a purely foreign nature. However, in neither area does it place restrictions on the selectors used. This means that French law does not establish an obligation to use selectors in indiscriminate surveillance programmes at all. Moreover, it does not provide any restrictions on the quality of the selectors used or the criteria for declaring them unacceptable. In the French model, these issues are subject to the executive's decisions, and their determination falls within the prime minister's competence.[21]

The rules on foreign surveillance are also exceptionally general in the French legislation, despite the fact that the previously applicable regulations were overturned by the Constitutional Court on the grounds that, *inter alia*, they were too blanket in nature.[22] The Internal Security Code defines domestic communications as those carried out using "subscription numbers or identifiers traceable to the national territory."[23] Only communications meeting this condition cannot be subject to targeted surveillance measures that bypass the procedures inherent in domestic surveillance. In any other case, the scope and forms of surveillance activities are not subject to statutory restrictions, but only to the conditions set out in the authorisation issued by the prime minister. Although France has established an independent body to oversee the exercise of surveillance powers (the National Commission for the Control of Intelligence Techniques [CNCTR]), obtaining its consent is not a mandatory step in the process of authorising foreign surveillance.

Against the backdrop of the continental regulations, British legislation is also noteworthy. The surveillance regime applied in the United Kingdom has been modified several times in recent decades. It has been shaped in a special way, with extensive powers to run indiscriminate surveillance programmes granted to the executive. This model reflects the times when electronic surveillance was not subject to statutory regulation at all, or was regulated only to a limited extent.[24] It is only in recent years that successive laws, adopted in the wake of the evolution of the jurisprudential standards on electronic surveillance, have clarified the scope and forms of surveillance, also establishing increasingly detailed legal safeguards. The UK model separates the requirements associated with the stages of data collection (acquisition) and subsequent data use (analysis of the information collected). In theory, this provides more complete safeguards against the risk of data being used contrary to the purpose for which they were collected. However, unlike the continental regulations discussed earlier, the provisions of the Investigatory Powers Act 2016 do not introduce additional restrictions concerning the choice of strong selectors. In this respect, they merely require that the selection of material for

21 In the context of foreign intelligence, see Art. L854-2 of the Internal Security Code.
22 Conseil constitutionnel 23 July 2015 (2015-713 DC).
23 Art. L854-1 of the Internal Security Code.
24 Phil Glover, *Protecting National Security: A History of British Communications Investigation Regulation* (Routledge 2022) 79–110.

further analysis take into account the criteria of proportionality and necessity.[25] This assessment, however, is not made by a court but by an SIA analyst, who should not only verify the fulfilment of both conditions but also record the justification, thus enabling a subsequent review of the legality of the action taken.

This is an atypical solution because, as indicated earlier, the assessment of the criteria of proportionality and necessity in relation to the use of surveillance measures is a complex problem that requires extensive legal expertise. Therefore this assessment is usually made by courts and not by intelligence analysts. All the more so because – as will be shown in the following sections – these analysts may de facto be subcontractors entrusted with technical data processing tasks. In this respect, it is therefore not surprising to see the relatively high number of errors that, according to the 2021 Investigatory Powers Commissioner's report, characterise this process. As indicated in the report, "41% of the statements sampled failed to address either necessity or proportionality in sufficient detail and 8% failed to address both."[26] This means that in more than one-third of the cases analysed the selection of material (and, therefore, the search criteria used) did not comply with the provisions arising from the IPA 2016.

Significantly, all the examples of legal mechanisms for controlling the use of overly detailed – as well as overly general – keywords discussed above relate to surveillance systems applied to electronic communications. Indeed, the attention of legislators in this regard focuses exclusively on this one area of applying surveillance, i.e. electronic communication systems. However, as pointed out earlier, mass surveillance is a measure that is increasingly being used outside the field of telecommunications as well. For example, the provisions governing the STIR system, implemented in Poland, do not contain any restrictions concerning automatic data analysis whatsoever. The system collects a large amount of financial information (including data on accounts and financial transactions), and its use by the tax administration is intended to help identify cases of tax evasion or tax offences (e.g. VAT carousel fraud).[27] The data collected are subject to systematic analysis (carried out on a daily basis) according to patterns that are unknown and not verified by a court (or any other independent institution). As a result, the way the system operates is beyond any external control, which also means that no one, apart from the tax administration staff, verifies whether the analysis conducted in STIR is not of an individual nature (and therefore focused on the financial surveillance of specific individuals).[28]

25 Art. 152(5) of the IPA.

26 'Annual Report of the Investigatory Powers Commissioner 2021' (Investigatory Powers Commissioner 2021) 54.

27 For an analysis of the STIR case, see section 2.3.

28 Marta Papis-Almansa, 'The Polish Clearing House System : A "Stir"ring Example of the Use of New Technologies in Ensuring VAT Compliance in Poland and Selected Legal Challenges' (2019) 28 43; Marcin Rojszczak, 'Compliance of Automatic Tax Fraud Detection Systems

Therefore while controlling the scope of data collected is a task that can be precisely regulated by law, far more problems arise when it comes to controlling the subsequent use of these data. There is no doubt that the dynamic nature of the threats that SIAs and law enforcement agencies have to counter requires that adequate flexibility of action be ensured. Hence, expecting a surveillance order to specify a closed list of keywords in every case seems impossible. On the other hand, bearing in mind that untargeted surveillance measures are applied to an unknown group of persons, largely unconnected with activities of interest to state authorities, the failure to set a verifiable framework for the selectors used significantly increases the risk of arbitrariness in the decisions taken. A solution to this problem may be the third strategy presented earlier, i.e. excluding the possibility of using data obtained from indiscriminate surveillance in criminal proceedings. Such a solution has been used for years in the United Kingdom, with some limitations.[29] However, it is rare among other democratic states, including EU Member States. In most countries, indiscriminate surveillance material may be transmitted to other public entities, including law enforcement. Individual legislatures define their own substantive and procedural rules for such transfers. For example, in the case of the BND Act, the Federal Intelligence Service may transfer certain data obtained from untargeted surveillance measures to law enforcement agencies when the information is related to one of more than 20 types of crime.[30] And this is not an extraordinary situation. In this regard, it should be borne in mind that while the mere provision of data does not predetermine the permissibility of their use in criminal proceedings,[31] such a solution certainly increases the risk that systems originally implemented in the area of state security will, over time, begin to support other tasks that those currently in power classify as particularly important. This, in extreme cases, could also lead to attempts to use them for such controversial applications as monitoring abortion clinics[32] or public health risks.[33]

---

with the Right to Privacy Standards Based on the Polish Experience of the STIR System' (2021) 49 *Intertax* 39.

29 Sec. 56 of the IPA 2016 excludes from legal proceedings both material obtained under an interception warrant and anything tending to suggest that the conduct covered by such a warrant has occurred or is going to occur. This is, however, subject to the limited exceptions contained in Schedule 3 to the IPA.

30 See Art. 29(3) of the BND Act. For the list of criminal offenses, see Art. 100b(2) of the German Code of Criminal Procedure.

31 For a detailed comment, see section 3.4.5.

32 Natasha Singer and Brian X Chen, 'In a Post-Roe World, the Future of Digital Privacy Looks Even Grimmer' *The New York Times* (13 July 2022) <https://cli.re/VJxBq8> accessed 6 September 2023.

33 Yael Keshet, 'Fear of Panoptic Surveillance: Using Digital Technology to Control the COVID-19 Epidemic' (2020) 9 *Israel Journal of Health Policy Research* 67; Lorie Donelle and others, 'Use of Digital Technologies for Public Health Surveillance during the COVID-19 Pandemic: A Scoping Review' (2023) 9 *Digital Health* <https://doi.org10.1177/205520762311732>.

6.3 Future use of surveillance data warehouses

The discussion on the legal regulation of electronic surveillance largely focuses on the data acquisition stage. However, without diminishing the importance of control over the process of gaining access to information, one should not lose sight of the fact that nowadays it is possible to build surveillance systems based solely on publicly available data. In such a case, mass surveillance does not require any covert data capture. After all, the analysis of publicly available – or, more broadly, commercially acquired – data is a primary technique used by data brokers, i.e. entities that on daily basis create data banks containing information on hundreds of millions of individuals.

Widespread access to large datasets is creating pressure to develop techniques to process them efficiently. It is, therefore, not surprising that security services, as well as law enforcement agencies, are increasingly keen to implement solutions with the fundamental aim of making fuller use of the data they already possess. This is not only about IT tools in a strict sense. An example of an organisational solution in this area is the so-called fusion centres, i.e. dedicated units for sharing information held by secret services and police authorities.[34] Although most units of this type have been established in the United States, this form of national security cooperation is also used in Europe.[35] An example is France, where the basis for the organisation of such data-sharing centres was introduced in the Internal Security Code, discussed earlier.[36]

On the one hand, the fusion centre concept helps make better use of the information already acquired by authorities; but on the other hand it makes it significantly more difficult to control whether these data are being processed solely for the purpose(s) for which they were collected. Against this background it is worth recalling the recent controversy over the work of the US-based centres. According to the information revealed by a major data leak,[37] many of these centres have for years been collecting massive datasets with no clear connection to the fight against terrorism and serious crime, i.e. the very purpose for which they were established. Moreover, many of the fusion centres actually focus on collecting all kinds of data on minorities, even "targeting their places of worship and community activity."[38]

34 Thomas Nolan, 'Fusion Centers' in David Gray and Stephen E Henderson (eds), *The Cambridge Handbook of Surveillance Law* (Cambridge University Press 2017) <www.cambridge.org/core/product/identifier/9781316481127%23CN-bp-6/type/book_part> accessed 24 September 2023.

35 Renske van der Veer, Walle Bos and Liesbeth van der Heide, 'Fusion Centres in Six European Countries: Emergence, Roles and Challenges' (International Centre for Counter-Terrorism 2019) <https://cli.re/838YPz> accessed 6 September 2023.

36 See Art. L863-2 of the Internal Security Code.

37 Frank Bajak, 'Germany Seizes Server Hosting Pilfered US Police Files' (9 July 2020) <https://cli.re/7EVbvX> accessed 6 September 2023.

38 Jonathan Hafetz, 'Homeland Security's Fusion Centers Show the Dangers of Mission Creep' *The Hill* (19 March 2019) <https://cli.re/PAM5eE> accessed 6 September 2023.

In this regard, it should be recalled that in *M.D. v. Spain*, the ECtHR held that the use of data contrary to the purpose for which they were collected, without legal grounds and solely based on a "police report in issue, which was drafted in respect of individuals whose behaviour did not imply any criminal activity," constituted an unlawful interference with the right to privacy.[39]

The creation of an overly flexible (i.e. unaccountable) mechanism for sharing surveillance data is an incentive to use this information for any public task. Although most European fusion centres were created in response to the 9/11 attacks and the growing terrorist threat, their organisation and modus operandi vary. In some cases (in Germany, for example),[40] they were set up directly within the structures of national security services and perform a coordinating function for the services, rather than operating as a separate centre of competence. In contrast, the Belgian Coordination Unit for Threat Analysis was established as a centre responsible for conducting strategic analysis concerning threats stemming from terrorism or extremism.[41] The centre prepares its reports based on data made available by the services required to do so, but does not have access to the source data and uses only the information that has already been processed. The UK's Joint Terrorism Analysis Centre (JTAC) has a broader remit. Although it operates within the structures of the National Intelligence Service (MI5), it is treated as a separate structure within the UK intelligence community.[42] What the European fusion centres fundamentally have in common is that their purpose is to facilitate access to data and to break down barriers to information-sharing between different services. but not to share raw intelligence. As a result, the fusion centre concept is also actively employed as a tool for implementing the European Union's common security and defence policy.[43]

A separate trend leading to an increase in the quality of analysis of the data already at the disposal of public authorities is the expansion of analytical capabilities by individual services. To this end, they are increasingly turning to modern algorithmic systems. One example is the French Internal Security Service (DGSI), which for several years has been running an extensive project to build a next-generation analytical system,[44] intended to allow advanced data

39 *M.D. and Others v. Spain* (36584/17) 28 June 2022 ECtHR at [64].

40 This is the case in Germany for example, where there are two centres: GTAZ and GETZ. The former is coordinated and operates within the structures of BfV; and the latter within the structures of BKA.

41 Art. 3 of Wet betreffende de analyse van de dreiging [en: Threat Analysis Act].

42 Bradley Bamford, 'The United Kingdom's "War Against Terrorism"' (2004) 16 *Terrorism and Political Violence* 737.

43 Artur Gruszczak, 'Intelligence Fusion for the European Union's Common Security and Defence Policy' (2022) 19 *Politeja* <https://journals.akademicka.pl/politeja/article/view/4784> accessed 19 September 2023.

44 Damien Leloup, 'Palantir, l'embarrassant Poisson-Pilote Du Big Data' *Le Monde* (9 October 2018) <https://cli.re/KDYevQ> accessed 6 September 2023.

analysis, including targeted re-evaluation of the information that has already been processed previously. Interestingly, DGSI initially announced a partnership with Palantir Technologies Inc., whose product is to be eventually replaced by a national solution.[45]

Palantir is a powerful analytical tool that is widely used by many secret services and law enforcement agencies in both the United States and Europe.[46] A lot of attention has recently been attracted by the German bVerfG's ruling which challenged the possibility of using this product for preventive criminal database analysis. The case addressed by the Federal Constitutional Court concerned the hessenData system (based on the Palantir technology), implemented by the police in the German state of Hessia.[47] The case is interesting in that it was the first time that the intrusiveness of the use of algorithmic data analysis (big data) in the area of electronic surveillance had been explicitly considered by a European constitutional court. The case was not about the legality of collecting certain data, but about the effects of applying new forms of data processing to data previously acquired. In essence, the Court examined whether the use of more technically advanced processing tools could per se affect the assessment of the degree of intrusiveness or of interference with fundamental rights. This is a very interesting problem which, unfortunately, has not been addressed in detail in the ECtHR's jurisprudence to date.

The bVerfG, while recognising the opportunities associated with the use of machine learning systems in the area of electronic surveillance (discussed in more detail in the next section), noted that the use of systems based on pre-defined patterns "can be complex and largely beyond scrutiny for users and affected persons alike."[48] This is because these systems allow new facts that go beyond the initial dataset to be revealed. An example of this is algorithmic risk analysis, which not only enables the identification of locations associated with higher crime levels but also reveals the factors that influence the level of crime. At the same time, analyses revealing sensitive data or explicitly targeting specific individuals can be performed in the same way. The disclosure – in an algorithmic manner – of new data links does not remain neutral from an individual rights perspective. As the Court aptly pointed out, "connections

45 Mathieu Rosemain, 'A French Alternative to Palantir Would Take Two Years to Make, Thales CEO Says' *Reuters* (23 October 2020) <https://cli.re/372ezq> accessed 6 September 2023.

46 In the United Kingdom alone, the media report that Palantir handles "several" contracts for the UK government, including MI6: Ali Mitib, Lucas Amin and Jenna Corderoy, 'Ex-MI6 Chief Put US Firm on Path to £27m Border Software Contract' *The Times* (5 September 2023) <https://cli.re/ax22xQ> accessed 6 September 2023. For more on Palantir, see: Andrew Iliadis and Amelia Acker, 'The Seer and the Seen: Surveying Palantir's Surveillance Platform' (2022) 38 *The Information Society* 334.

47 Johanna Sprenger and Dominik Brodowski, ' "Predictive Policing", "Predictive Justice", and the Use of "Artificial Intelligence" in the Administration of Criminal Justice in Germany' (2023) *e-Revue Internationale de Droit Pénal* 5, 13–16.

48 BVerfG 16 February 2023 (1 BvR 1547/19) DE:BVerfG:2023:rs20230216.1bvr154719 at [101].

are only established during the data processing stage itself, and there is an increased risk of persons being included in further police measures despite not having provided any grounds for suspicion through actions that are attributable to them."[49]

This leads to the conclusion that the degree of intrusiveness of surveillance depends not only on the extent of the data acquired, but also on how they are processed. In particular, if the forms of data processing offer access to detailed information which permits the reconstruction of the behaviour, preferences or worldview of specific individuals, the intrusion should be regarded as particularly serious. Therefore bVerfG held that in such a case an assessment of the implementation of algorithmic systems as lawful "may only be justified subject to the strict requirements that apply to intrusive covert surveillance measures generally."[50]

At the same time, however, the bVerfG judgment does not rule out the use of systems such as Palantir in the area of public security, although it points out that the implementation of such solutions must be preceded by a careful analysis of their possible impact on the rights of those whose data will be processed. This should result in the establishment of an appropriate regime of legal safeguards defining acceptable error rates, permissible categories of information processed, as well as restrictions excluding certain areas from analysis (e.g. special categories of data, including information on health, sexual orientation, religion), and establishing safeguards against discrimination.

The position set out in the hessenData case also helps to clarify how to assess the permissibility of surveillance systems built on publicly available data (or data obtained from commercial sources). Also in this case, the use of algorithmic processing may significantly increase the degree of interference with individual rights, making it necessary to adopt higher standards of proportionality and necessity.

It is to be expected that in the years to come the collections of information held by security authorities will not only grow but also increase in quality. The processing of this information using new computing models can significantly increase the intrusiveness of surveillance from an individual's point of view. The merging of multiple databases, including those publicly available, as well as the use of new means of obtaining information may lead to a drastic reduction in an individual's informational autonomy.

A measure to reduce the risk of this scenario is the development of a new category of rules setting standards for the lawful processing of large datasets for public purposes.[51] The emphasis here should be not only on the lawfulness of obtaining the information, but also on the necessity of the processing

49 Ibid. at [94].
50 Ibid. at [104].
51 For more about the European Big Data regulatory strategy, see: Paul De Hert and Vagelis Papakonstantinou, 'Framing Big Data in the Council of Europe and the EU Data Protection

techniques implemented. In part, mechanisms of this type are already present in the EU legal order and are related to data protection legislation (in particular, the GDPR and the LED). However, bearing in mind that an important part of the work of SIAs and law enforcement agencies related to the use of surveillance measures concerns the area of state security, the scope of application of EU law in this case may be significantly limited as a result of the national security exception (discussed in detail in section 3.3).

6.4 AI-based surveillance

An inherent feature in the use of bulk surveillance measures is the collection of vast amounts of information that is not useful for achieving the surveillance objective. Analyses of the programmes conducted by the GCHQ have indicated that the "vast majority" of data are removed at the first stage of filtering.[52] Only a small proportion of the data stream is subjected to further analysis, including using selectors, which leads to a further reduction in the (removal of) redundant information. Ultimately, only about 1% of the data have been archived, allowing them to be easily processed in the future, including by means of tools such as the xKeyscore system developed by the NSA.[53] Similar algorithms are used by BND, which according to available information means that only about 1% of the 220 million metadata collected each day are subject to long-term, in-depth analysis.[54]

Data filtering is therefore a multi-stage process, and its use is not motivated by a desire to comply with the legal requirements, but by the existing technical limitations involved in capturing and processing large datasets. Information disclosed in 2013 shows that the GCHQ was developing technical capabilities to achieve a capacity to process 10 gigabits of data per second. Today, such capacity characterises the fibre-optic links used even in the SOHO sector. In 2021, Google commissioned a transatlantic fibre-optic link (12 fibre pairs) with a maximum capacity of 250 terabits per second – which is 25,000 times greater than that which was being deployed by the GCHQ a decade earlier. To put this figure into perspective: assuming that a typical user has 50 GB of their private data, Google's fibre-optic link (one of 19 similar ones in operation) allows all the information belonging to over 500 people to be transmitted every second (or 1.8 million people every hour).

Given the massive increase in the popularity of bandwidth-intensive digital services (e.g. streaming media) and the development of broadband Internet

Law Systems: Adding "Should" to "Must" via Soft Law to Address More than Only Individual Harms' (2021) 40 *Computer Law & Security Review* 105496.

52 'Privacy and Security: A Modern and Transparent Legal Framework' (Intelligence and Security Committee of Parliament 2015) HC 1075 32.

53 More on XKeyScore in section 1.3.

54 Kai Biermann, 'BND Stores 220 Million Telephone Data – Every Day' *Die Zeit* (2 February 2015) <https://cli.re/XA7j4Y> accessed 6 September 2023.

access, covering an increasing number of end users (including wireless access, i.e. the 5G network), it is clear that this rapid growth in telecommunications bandwidth will be maintained in the years to come.

The possibilities of data processing are growing as intensely as the possibilities of transmitting them. Leaving aside the purely technical limitations, it should also be recalled that surveillance data are subject to manual analysis sooner or later. Even if only a small percentage of the data are ultimately made available to analysts, the number of personnel employed between 2013 and 2023 would have had to increase proportionally to the volume of data transmitted. In other words, to maintain the proportion resulting from the increase in data volume, secret services would need tens of thousands of new staff to analyse the data received from untargeted surveillance systems in the same way, even after pre-filtering.

The above problem clearly points to the need to look for new, previously unused data analysis tools, enabling the quality of automated analysis to increase without creating thousands of new jobs. A technology that seems to offer such possibilities is artificial intelligence systems.

Although the term AI is commonly used today to describe elaborate algorithmic systems, in fact there is no universally accepted legal definition of the term.[55] Most often, AI systems are combined with machine learning systems, which make it possible to identify previously unknown relationships between data. Such *knowledge*, however, should not be confused with *facts*. Hence, in the case of algorithmic systems, it is important to assess the accuracy indicators of the conclusions presented, usually described by the *false positive* and *false negative* measures. The former indicator, a false positive, is used to show how many of the analysis results were wrongly classified as meeting given criteria (e.g. an algorithm identifying cancerous lesions classified healthy tissue as a lesion). A false negative, on the other hand, is an indicator to assess the number of cases missed, i.e. those that were not considered to meet the search criteria (using the earlier example, failure to identify a cancerous lesion and considering such lesioned tissue to be healthy). Of course, both measures are applicable irrespective of the domain in which the algorithm is used – and therefore also apply to assessing the quality of algorithms used for public security purposes.[56]

What significantly differentiates machine learning systems from the earlier generation of algorithmic systems is the ability of the former to go beyond the original programming and to establish their own patterns for solving a

55 Francesco Corea, 'Introduction to Artificial Intelligence' in Francesco Corea (ed), *An Introduction to Data*, vol 50 (Springer International Publishing 2019) <http://link.springer.com/10.1007/978-3-030-04468-8_3> accessed 18 September 2023.

56 In this context, see the relationship between both indicators and the generation of biased results: Anthony W Flores, Kristin Bechtel and Christopher T Lowenkamp, 'False Positives, False Negatives, and False Analyses: A Rejoinder to Machine Bias: There's Software Used across the Country to Predict Future Criminals. And It's Biased against Blacks' (2016) 80 *Federal Probation* 38.

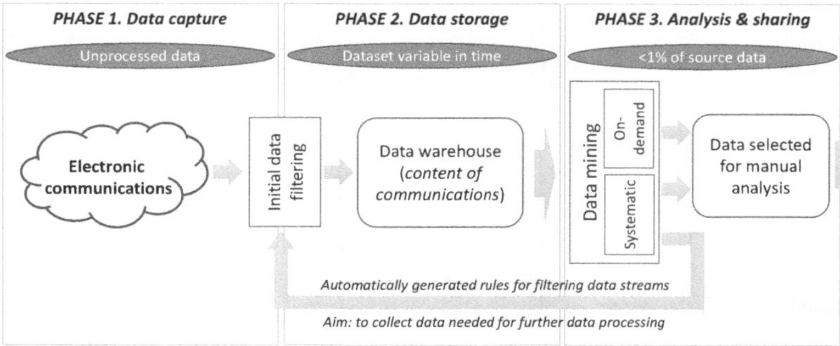

Diagram 6.1 Model of an AI-driven bulk surveillance system.

problem they have been given. In other words, machine learning systems can reveal a previously unknown data link through which they are able to classify new cases, e.g. events associated with a major public security threat, more efficiently (with a higher level of confidence). This means (at least in theory) that the use of AI in the area of electronic surveillance could lead to a new generation of systems in which traditional selectors (keywords or regular expressions) would be no longer needed as a prerequisite for data analysis. In contrast to the data analysis systems in use today, AI-based systems will be hybrid, combining features of indiscriminate surveillance (access to bulk amounts of information) with targeted analysis (an identifiable algorithmic justification for the processing of particular types of data).

This means that the boundary between the data collection and subsequent analysis stages in AI-based surveillance systems could become blurred. The analysis stage may lead to an automatic change in the criteria associated with information collection (see Diagram 6.1). On the one hand, this feedback loop may make it possible to reduce the severity of the surveillance measure, while on the other hand it may lead to the emergence of new threats not present in classical surveillance systems. The potential benefit is related to the continuous verification of data collection criteria and the possibility of reinterpreting previous results (see Diagram 6.1). This leads to the minimisation of the information stored and the possibility of automatically anonymising it to the extent needed to improve the computational models used. If it were possible to achieve the first of the benefits described – i.e. the restriction of the data collected to cases of interest (even distant ones) to authorities – this would already be a real breakthrough for the untargeted surveillance systems used today. At the same time, the use of AI in the area of electronic surveillance also presents new risks. Understanding them, however, requires a closer discussion of how such systems work.

As a rule, self-learning algorithms are trained to solve a specific analytical problem, in many cases, boiling down to the appropriate classification

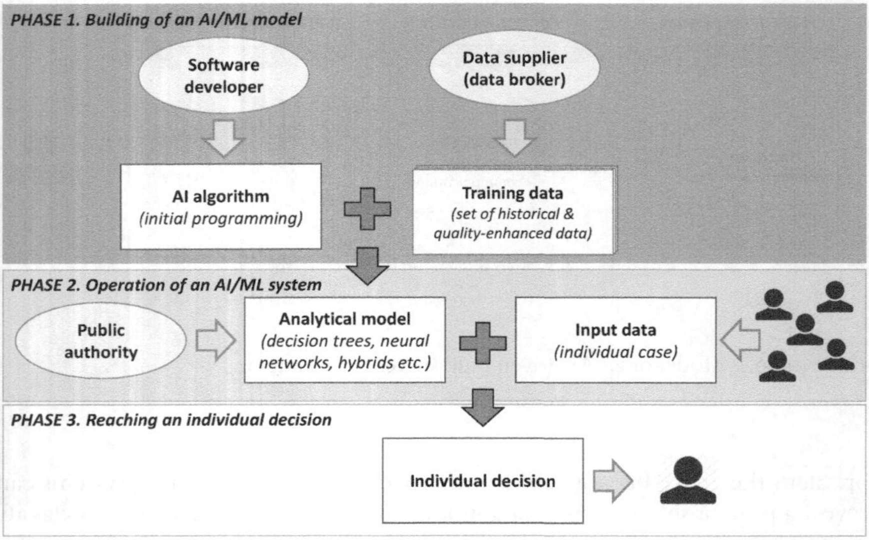

Diagram 6.2 Scheme of an AI/ML decision-making process.

(sorting) of input data.[57] This sorting can concern, for example, a creditworthiness assessment (an AI system used in the financial sector); music tastes (an AI system used in streaming media); or identification of suspected tax evaders (a system used by tax administration).

The first of the problems associated with the use of AI in the field of public security concerns the learning process itself. The quality of the results generated by AI directly depends on the quality of the data used to train the model. The process of implementing a machine learning system takes place in several stages, with the training stage being the key one. It can be conducted in several ways, in particular as supervised or unsupervised learning.[58] In both cases, the aim is to create a decision-making model based on the analysis of test (training) data. These data are, in essence, a properly prepared set of information describing historical cases and the decisions made in them. If, therefore, past decisions were subject to errors (e.g. reflecting the biases of those who made them), it can be expected that the analytical model built on the analysis of these data will also replicate these "erroneous" decisions.[59] In general,

57 Ethem Alpaydin, *Machine Learning: The New AI* (MIT Press 2016) 55–60.

58 Wolfgang Ertel, 'Machine Learning and Data Mining' in Wolfgang Ertel (ed), *Introduction to Artificial Intelligence* (Springer 2011) <https://link.springer.com/10.1007/978-0-85729-299-5_8> accessed 18 September 2023.

59 For more about AI biases, see: Sina Fazelpour and David Danks, 'Algorithmic Bias: Senses, Sources, Solutions' (2021) 16 *Philosophy Compass* e12760.

therefore, an AI system may malfunction not because it was badly programmed but because it was trained on data that contained errors.[60] In fact, the problem of bias in automatic decisions has been one of the criticisms levelled against the Compass system, which has been used for years in the United States in the area of parole application assessment.[61]

The second feature associated with self-learning models is the so-called incremental effect, increasing the usefulness of algorithmic analysis but at the same time standing in the way of reducing the size of redundant data. The incremental effect can be defined as the possibility of establishing different conclusions when re-analysing the same data. Depending on the design decisions taken during the implementation of a machine learning system, the system may continue to learn after the initial programming stage (and thus improve with the analysis of subsequently processed information), or its development may be halted so that the cases analysed later will not influence the decision model that is being used. In the former scenario, the acquisition of new sets of information may alter the previous analysis results. For example, the same system may – when reconsidering the same set of information intercepted from electronic communications – come to a different conclusion, in effect identifying specific persons as suspects of extremist activities. The reason for this change in the system's decision is the new knowledge that the system acquired between the first and the subsequent analyses, resulting in a reinterpretation of the data acquired previously. Importantly, the different assessment may be influenced not so much by the particular situation of the individual whose data are being analysed, but by knowledge from the analysis and decisions made in other similar cases. This leads to the fundamental conclusion that in the analysis of large datasets by means of self-learning algorithms, an individual decision depends not only on the information examined in a given case (in particular, information that is influenced by the individual) but also on the conclusions from similar cases which, according to the algorithm, are close enough to justify making a similar decision. Therefore an AI algorithm's decision is not necessarily fixed over time and can be justified by arguments that do not relate to the specific case under examination. In other words, a person previously considered not to be a threat to public security may, upon reassessment, be deemed to be prone to extremism – even though the set of data analysed has not changed. What changes, however, is the context of the analysis, which is beyond the control of this individual.

This reveals a third important feature of AI systems, which is the lack of transparency of inferences that characterise some types of algorithms. This is a

60 Sandra G Mayson, 'Bias in, Bias Out' (2018) 128 *Yale Law Journal* 2218.

61 Flores, Bechtel and Lowenkamp, 'False Positives, False Negatives, and False Analyses' (n 56). See also Julia Angwin and others, 'Machine Bias' *ProPublica* (23 May 2016) <https://cli.re/mp8mRz> accessed 6 September 2023.

much-discussed problem of the "explainability" of AI decisions.[62] In general, it is often presented as characterising only systems based on artificial neural networks, but – as we have shown with Jarek Gryz[63] – even moderately complex models based on decision trees suffer from the same drawback. The inability to explain the reasons for the decisions made by a large proportion of AI algorithms also leads to calls for the use of this class of systems to be abandoned in cases where important individual interests are decided (e.g. regarding fundamental freedoms or rights).[64]

The lack of explainability clearly limits the possibility of judicial review of the decisions made. If an AI-based algorithm determines that a particular person (visible on a recording) is the perpetrator of a certain crime, such knowledge – although useful in secret services' work – may not be sufficient as evidence in criminal proceedings. Depending on the applicable conditions for the admissibility of evidence, the recognition by an AI algorithm of the perpetrator in the recording may per se be inadmissible evidence or, in general, lead to the invalidity of the entire proceedings conducted based on such evidence.[65] Hence, the permissibility of the use of the results of AI algorithms as "probable cause" in the context of criminal proceedings is already being debated today in the United States.[66]

Given the above features of AI systems, it is highly doubtful that the use of this class of solutions will actually make it possible to ensure the proportionality of indiscriminate electronic surveillance and, as a result, eliminate the controversy regarding the permissibility of this type of surveillance in the European legal order. Above all, the expectation that AI systems will set the criteria for data filtering on their own, as it were, and thus ensure that the data collection process consistently complies with the criterion of necessity in a democratic state under the rule of law, stems from a misunderstanding of how the technology currently in place works. In the course of building an analytical model, the algorithm independently creates a set of patterns (parameters) that play a role similar to that of classical selectors. However, it should be borne in mind that this stage first requires the collection of large amounts of

62 Andrew D Selbst and Julia Powles, 'Meaningful Information and the Right to Explanation' (2017) 7 *International Data Privacy Law* 233; Margot E Kaminski, 'The Right to Explanation, Explained' (2019) 34 *Berkeley Technology Law Journal* 189.

63 Jarek Gryz and Marcin Rojszczak, 'Black Box Algorithms and the Rights of Individuals: No Easy Solution to the "Explainability" Problem' (2021) 10 *Internet Policy Review* <https://policyreview.info/articles/analysis/black-box-algorithms-and-rights-individuals-no-easy-solution-explainability> accessed 28 November 2021.

64 Cynthia Rudin, 'Stop Explaining Black Box Machine Learning Models for High Stakes Decisions and Use Interpretable Models Instead' (2019) 1 *Nature Machine Intelligence* 206.

65 Gabrielle M Haddad, 'Confronting the Biased Algorithm: The Danger of Admitting Facial Recognition Technology Results in the Courtroom Notes' (2020) 23 *Vanderbilt Journal of Entertainment & Technology Law* 891.

66 Michael L Rich, 'Machine Learning, Automated Suspicion Algorithms, and the Fourth Amendment' (2015) 164 *University of Pennsylvania Law Review* 871.

redundant data (for the purpose of the training and further development of the analytical model). Furthermore, the parameters created by the algorithm (quasi-selectors) are often incomprehensible to humans. They describe statistical relationships between the data under study, which – although helpful for algorithmic decision-making – may not have any meaning in natural language. As a result, any assessment of the validity of the use of these parameters (as selectors) would de facto be impossible, and the oversight over the entire surveillance process would be based mainly on a statistical analysis of the quality of data processing, without the possibility of verifying the necessity of instances of individual data collection.

This issue was recognised in the *Ligue des droits humains* judgment, in which the CJEU examined the permissibility of the application of the Belgian – and more broadly the European Union – rules on retention of PNR data.[67] As PNR data were processed in Belgium using an AI system, the questions posed by the national court in a request for a preliminary ruling also concerned the impact of the use of this technology on the protection of fundamental rights. The CJEU first noted that "given the opacity which characterises the way in which artificial intelligence technology works, it might be impossible to understand the reason why a given program arrived at a positive match."[68] In turn, the lack of transparency of the decision taken deprives individuals of the right to judicial review thereof, "in particular in order to challenge the non-discriminatory nature of the results."[69] The Court thus recognised the link between the use of AI systems and the protection of Charter guarantees. This judgment, however, does not predetermine the complete impossibility of a lawful use of algorithmic systems based on machine learning in the field of public security. More and more systems of this type are being designed in such a way that the decision-making paths can be traced. In contrast, in the case of systems using opaque logic, the problem of the lack of explainability of decisions can be addressed by subjecting the decisions to additional human control.[70]

Hence, in the newly proposed Artificial Intelligence Act, the EU legislature has strengthened the regulations for the supervision of the functioning of AI-based algorithmic systems. The draft regulation distinguishes a specific category of products – the so-called high-risk systems – including, *inter alia*, systems that process biometric data to identify individuals, and systems used

67 A passenger name record (PNR) is personal information provided by passengers and collected by air carriers. In line with the legal requirements introduced after 9/11 in the United States and European Union, PNR data are also transferred to public authorities as part of anti-terrorism measures.

68 *Ligue des droits humains ASBL v. Conseil des ministres* (C-817/19) EU:C:2022:491 at [195].

69 Ibid.

70 Evelien Brouwer, 'Ligue Des Droits Humains and the Validity of the PNR Directive: Balancing Individual Rights and State Powers in Times of New Technologies' (2023) 60 *Common Market Law Review* 839.

in law enforcement and the administration of justice.[71] Extensive requirements have been introduced for this category of systems with regard to the quality, reliability, and transparency of processing. In particular, products of this type "shall be designed and developed in such a way to ensure that their operation is sufficiently transparent to enable users to interpret the system's output and use it appropriately."[72] Moreover, high-risk systems must operate in a human-supervised environment. In particular, where biometric identification is used, the draft regulation requires mandatory verification by two persons before further action is taken against an individual based on the outcome of the processing.

Due to the unique nature of the AI Act – de facto the first regulation introducing legally binding requirements for the use of AI systems – the legislative work received, from the very beginning, a great deal of attention from the public and various interest groups. One area of particular focus concerned the use of biometric systems and, more broadly, AI systems in the field of public security. The backdrop to the ongoing discussion was the growing popularity of ClearView[73] and concerns that the proliferation of such systems would usher in the demise of privacy in public spaces.[74]

Hence, an amendment was introduced during the work in the European Parliament to establish a ban on the use of "AI systems that create or expand facial recognition databases through the untargeted scraping of facial images from the internet or CCTV footage."[75] It is worth noting that an earlier draft presented by the Commission had already contained the same prohibition of untargeted real-time biometric identification of persons for public security tasks;[76] however, this prohibition had not included *post factum* identification, for example in relation to footage from CCTV or UAV systems.

Against the backdrop of the discussion on the effects of adopting the AI Act, the controversy over the scope of the national security clause also resurfaced. As in other cases in which secret services use cutting-edge technologies, it was debated to what extent the prohibitions and restrictions laid down in the regulation (including those concerning the processing in the field of combating crime) would apply in the area of national security. Interestingly, the drafters – unlike, for example, in the telecommunications legislation discussed earlier – provided for an exclusion of only the area of military uses of AI from the application of the regulation. Thus the draft lacks an explicit exclusion of the area of national security, which obviously does not limit or affect the interpretation of the clause provided for in Article 4(2) of the TEU. However,

71 See Annex III to the draft EU AI Act, COM/2021/206 final.
72 Art. 13(1) of the draft EU AI Act.
73 More on ClearView in section 2.4.
74 European Parliament resolution of 6 October 2021 on artificial intelligence in criminal law and its use by the police and judicial authorities in criminal matters (2020/2016(INI)).
75 See Art. 5(1)(d b) of the EU AI Act as proposed by European Parliament, P9_TA(2023)0236.
76 Art. 5(1)(d) of the draft EU AI Act.

it seems that issues of national security – including the use of AI systems, e.g. in the area of electronic surveillance – will not be entirely outside the scope of the AI Act.[77]

Doubts about the actual impact of the AI Act on the surveillance activities of states are being discussed in relation to the French statute, adopted in 2023 and introducing specific measures related to the Olympic and Paralympic Games in Paris in 2024.[78] The provisions of the law establish a legal framework for the implementation of an extensive video surveillance system covering both the Olympic area as well as the means of public transport. To this end, there are plans to install a system of dedicated cameras as well to use UAVs. The system is to operate on a temporary basis until 31 March 2025 for the sole purpose of ensuring the security of the sporting events. Importantly, the current regulation stipulates that the video surveillance system will not be used to identify individuals or to process biometric data (including facial recognition).[79] Critics of the law point out that the French authorities are using the organisation of the Olympics as a pretext to test an intrusive AI surveillance technology.[80] They also point to the risk that the measures implemented will not be temporary and will continue to be used even after the sporting events. The controversy over the new law led to a complaint being filed to the Constitutional Council, which found the video surveillance regulations to be in line with the Basic Law.[81] In the Council's view, the regulations reviewed do not significantly increase the risk to individuals, as "algorithmic processing proceeds exclusively with an attention signalling, strictly limited to the indication of the predetermined event or events that they have been programmed to detect."[82] The Council also noted the quality of the legal safeguards established, in particular the prohibition of the processing of biometric data and the constant human oversight over the operation of the algorithms.[83]

In reality, however, the French case is the first such extensive implementation of an AI system for the monitoring of physical space in Europe. Leaving aside the assessment of whether the system being implemented in France is at all within the scope of EU law, the experience of its application will certainly be used in further discussions on the future of AI-based surveillance in the European Union.

77 See e.g. the powers of the competent authorities as indicated in Art. 70 of the draft EU AI Act.
78 Art. 10 of Loi no 2023-380 du 19 mai 2023 relative aux jeux Olympiques et Paralympiques de 2024 et portant diverses autres dispositions.
79 Ibid., Art. 10(IV).
80 'Les Mesures de Vidéosurveillance Algorithmique Introduites Par La Loi JO 2024 Sont Contraires Au Droit International' *Le Monde* (6 March 2023) <https://cli.re/4Rodb3> accessed 6 September 2023.
81 Conseil constitutionnel 17 May 2023 (2023-850 DC).
82 Ibid. at [43].
83 Ibid. at [45].

6.5 Automatic content control and electronic surveillance

The general perception is that electronic surveillance measures used by public authorities are primarily a tool for obtaining information in a covert manner to reveal previously unknown information about the persons under scrutiny.

Chapter 2 explained that this way of defining electronic surveillance is outdated, as it ignores the growing field of application of user monitoring mechanisms implemented by digital service providers.[84] On the one hand, these mechanisms may be used exclusively for commercial purposes. On the other hand, the need to implement them is increasingly driven by the need to comply with legal or regulatory requirements. A particular case in point concerns the obligations related to online content filtering, which have been expanding for years. The main purpose of using such mechanisms is to prevent digital services from being used to distribute unlawful content.

The first question to be resolved is whether algorithmic content analysis aimed at identifying infringements should, in fact, be classified as a surveillance measure at all. Doubts in this case seem to arise from the belief that, first, the author intends the content posted on the Internet to be publicly available anyway, which means it is not private in nature; and second, that the degree of intrusiveness of content moderation depends on the identity of the entity performing it, and in particular that content moderation by private actors (service providers) is not surveillance, as it does not lead to the acquisition of knowledge about an individual by public authorities.

Both views indicated above are built on false assumptions. Not all content published on social media is made available publicly. Many of the popular online services can also be used for correspondence or the exchange of views among closed groups. Therefore if a public authority were to set up a mechanism to analyse every communication exchanged on a social media platform (e.g. Facebook), then – leaving aside the definition of a digital service adopted[85] – the common perception of such an action would be that it constitutes a form of covert observation of user activity and would, therefore, be a surveillance measure. If such a measure were applied to the entirety of content (speech) posted by all users, it would be untargeted. This is exactly how automatic content filtering mechanisms work – the difference being that, in their case, the surveillance mechanism is implemented by a service provider, albeit in performance of a legal obligation and de facto for the purposes of a public task.

84 Stanisław Tosza, 'Internet Service Providers as Law Enforcers and Adjudicators. A Public Role of Private Actors' (2021) 43 *Computer Law & Security Review* 105614.

85 As indicated in Chapter 2, information society services and electronic communication services are defined separately in EU law. In the case of, for example, Meta services, a user using the same website may submit a comment either via an information society service (in which case it will be subject to content filtering mechanisms) or via a communication service (in which case it will be subject to the protections provided for telecommunications secrecy).

Because content moderation serves a public purpose, the assessment of the legality of actions taken in this regard should also be carried out using the standards developed for other cases of interference with individual rights by state authorities.

In recent years, there has been a systematic and steady trend toward weakening the legal safeguards built into EU law to prevent public authorities from using digital services as tools for establishing permanent mechanisms to monitor user behaviour. In particular, this problem relates to the interpretation of Article 15(1) of the e-Commerce Directive (now Article 8 of the Digital Services Act), which stands in the way of establishing a so-called general monitoring obligation (see section 2.2 for a detailed analysis). The erosion of this safeguard is a consequence of the legislative action taken by both EU Member States and the European Union, as well as the interpretation presented by the Court of Justice.

When the German government pushed for the adoption of the Network Enforcement Act in 2017 (NetzDG),[86] the problem of the distribution of hateful content and incitements to violence had already been the subject of European debate for years.[87] Yet, there were no effective legislative solutions to respond in a timely manner to emerging violations while at the same time protecting freedom and diversity of expression. At the time of the work on NetzDG, the Court of Justice had not yet ruled on the *Glawischnig-Piesczek v. Facebook* case, in which it later addressed the question of whether it was compatible with EU law to apply content removal orders also covering future publications, including those with an "equivalent meaning."[88] At the same time, the implications of the ECtHR's high-profile ruling in the *Delfi* case were still being debated. In that case, the Court had held that service providers should respond to ***manifestly unlawful*** content, i.e. content whose "unlawful nature did not require any linguistic or legal analysis."[89] The Strasbourg Court's position was built on the correct assumption that a state of affairs in which a service provider can limit its liability for publishing illegal content in situations where its unlawful nature is manifest is unacceptable. Therefore, given the professional nature of its business, if a service provider does not react to cases of obvious abuse even without being separately notified, it is liable for the infringement that occurs. Although the *Delfi* and subsequent cases heard by the ECtHR dealt explicitly with instances of hate speech, they also had a significant impact on the way of defining the scope of liability of service providers for cases of publication of any illegal content.

86 Netzwerkdurchsetzungsgesetz vom 1. September 2017, BGBl. I S. 3352; referred to as 'NetzDG'.

87 William Echikson and Olivia Knodt, 'Germany's NetzDG: A Key Test for Combatting Online Hate' (Centre for European Policy Studies 2018) 2018/09 <https://cli.re/Bvv1Zx> accessed 6 September 2023.

88 The case of *Glawischnig-Piesczek v. Facebook* is discussed more extensively in section 2.2.

89 *Delfi AS v. Estonia* (64569/09) 16 June 2015 ECtHR at [117].

Enacted in such a regulatory environment, the German NetzDG law established the (then innovative) fast-track procedures for blocking and removing unlawful content. Significantly, NetzDG in its original form did not per se require the use of any proactive mechanisms, i.e. mechanisms aimed at analysing newly published content for its legality. The essence of the law was to establish expedited procedures for removing the content reported to the service provider. In particular, service providers (meeting the statutory conditions) were obliged to block obviously unlawful material within 24 hours of receiving a complaint; for all other material (i.e. material whose unlawfulness was not obvious), the provider should respond without undue delay, but no later than 7 days after receipt of the complaint.[90]

In principle, NetzDG did not introduce its own definition of unlawful content, relying in this respect on existing German regulations, e.g. regarding hateful or discriminatory speech; content violating human dignity or inciting violence; and content related to the dissemination of propaganda and symbols of terrorist organisations or organisations whose functioning is prohibited by the German Basic Law.[91] However, the short response time allotted to the service provider (24 hours), combined with high financial penalties and possible criminal liability, created a clear incentive for service providers to implement automatic scanning mechanisms to identify questionable material.[92]

The entry into force of NetzDG also marked a turning point in the European debate on the use of extensive content filtering measures by service providers. Similar legislative action was taken in France,[93] Austria,[94] the United Kingdom,[95] and Poland[96] in the following years. The adoption of NetzDG also gave impetus to EU legislative work, especially related to the Digital Services Act. Within a short period, the German legislation became a model for dozens of similar laws adopted outside Europe. Therefore many point out that NetzDG has become the model for a new censorship regime on the Internet.[97]

90 Art. 3(2) of NetzDG.

91 See the definition of illegal content introduced in Art. 1(3) of NetzDG.

92 For a broader analysis of the impact of NetzDG on digital services, see: Amélie Heldt, 'Reading between the Lines and the Numbers: An Analysis of the First NetzDG Reports' (2019) 8 *Internet Policy Review* <https://policyreview.info/node/1398> accessed 7 June 2022.

93 Loi n° 2020-766 du 24 juin 2020 visant à lutter contre les contenus haineux sur internet [en: Act n° 2020–766 of 24 June 2020 Aimed at Combating Hateful Content on the Internet].

94 Bundesgesetz über Maßnahmen zum Schutz der Nutzer auf Kommunikationsplattformen [en: Federal Law on Measures to Protect Users on Communication Platforms].

95 Online Safety Bill, version of 13 September 2023 <https://cli.re/D8Zqyd> accessed 6 September 2023.

96 Projekt ustawy o ochronie wolności słowa w internetowych serwisach społecznościowych [en: Draft Act on the Protection of Freedom of Expression on Online Social Networks].

97 Jacob Mchangama and Natalie Alkiviadou, 'The Digital Berlin Wall: How Germany (Accidentally) Created a Prototype for Global Online Censorship – Act Two' (Justitia 2020).

The French law, on the other hand, was repealed almost in its entirety by the Constitutional Court shortly after its adoption.[98] However, the French legislation stipulated a more far-reaching requirement for service providers, one that obliged them to remove certain content categories within 60 minutes.[99] The main objection raised in the judgment was that this interference was disproportionate, creating the risk of a significant restriction on freedom of expression. The short response time on the part of a service provider prevented not only a reasonable review of the notification received, but also legal action by the author of the contested content. However, it is worth recalling that a similarly short time limit (60 minutes) was also later introduced in the EU Terrorist Content Regulation.[100]

Another impetus supporting the development of an EU legal framework for the use of automatic content filtering mechanisms is the CJEU case law. In the *Glawischnig-Piesczek v. Facebook* judgment, cited earlier, the Court not only accepted the implementation of the pre-filtering of content (the so-called ***upload filters***) by service providers, but also allowed proactive analysis of all publications to identify ***similar*** content to that previously deemed unlawful. It is worth bearing in mind that, in this respect, the CJEU de facto issued a response partly going beyond the request for a preliminary ruling. Indeed, the request focused on the permissibility of extending a court order to an obligation to remove content with "an equivalent meaning." The problem concerning the definition of this concept drew the Advocate General's attention.[101] However, the Court did not fully take into account the Advocate General's arguments and, in its judgment, opted for a very broad interpretation according to which "the illegality of the content of information does not in itself stem from the use of certain terms combined in a certain way, but from the fact that the message conveyed by that content is held to be illegal."[102] Such an interpretation effectively rules out the possibility for a service provider to use only simple techniques to eliminate the repetition of unlawful publications. The standard set by the CJEU requires full content analysis to be implemented, and given the vague notion of nearly identical content it will in fact be up to the service provider itself to decide on the content moderation rules to be applied.

The problem with the *Glawischnig-Piesczek* judgment does not relate to the CJEU's adoption of a debatable interpretation of a general monitoring

98 Conseil constitutionnel 18 June 2020 (2020-801) FR:CC:2020:2020.801.DC <https://cli.re/pZr2Jw> accessed on 6 September 2023.

99 Emmanuel Dreyer, 'Présentation de La Proposition de Loi Avia' (2020) 63 *Légipresse* 13.

100 For more on the proportionality of expedited content removal, see: Marcin Rojszczak, 'Gone in 60 Minutes: Distribution of Terrorist Content and Free Speech in the European Union' (2023) *Democracy and Security* 1.

101 Opinion of AG Szpunar of 4 June 2019 *Eva Glawischnig-Piesczek* (C-18/18) EU:C:2019:458 at [74].

102 *Glawischnig-Piesczek v. Facebook* (C-18/18) EU:C:2019:821 at [40].

obligation – based on the assumption that a service provider's search of all publications for speech similar to that challenged does not breach the prohibition on general monitoring – but to its acceptance of the use of extensive and highly intrusive preventive content moderation measures.

The validity of the interpretation set out in *Glawischnig-Piesczek* was confirmed in a recent judgment in which the CJEU examined Poland's complaint concerning measures introduced in Directive 2019/790 on copyright and related rights in the Digital Single Market (the CDSM Directive).[103] The Directive is a *lex specialis* in relation to the general liability framework for service providers introduced in the e-Commerce Directive (now the DSA),[104] in particular requiring service providers to "make their best efforts in accordance with high industry standards of professional diligence to avoid the availability on their services of unauthorised works and other subject matter, as identified by the relevant rightholders."[105] Hence, this mechanism requires service providers to respond proactively to copyright infringements, and therefore to eliminate identical and similar works – taking into account all works registered with rights management organisations. Clearly, in a world of global digital services, a system to pre-analyse and filter the tens of millions of pieces of content that are published every day cannot be set up manually and requires the implementation of sophisticated algorithmic systems.[106]

The CDSM Directive thus establishes more far-reaching content filtering obligations than those traditionally associated with the *notice and takedown* model known from the DSA. The discussion concerning the proportionality of the solution adopted in the Directive – and consequently its compliance with EU law – lasted for several years and eventually led to a complaint to the CJEU in which the Polish government demanded that the preventive content filtering mechanisms established in the Directive be declared invalid.[107]

However, the Court found that the concerns the Polish government and human rights organisations raised were not justified.[108] Although it considered in detail the risks related to the protection of freedom of expression and the

103 Directive (EU) 2019/790 of the European Parliament and of the Council of 17 April 2019 on copyright and related rights in the Digital Single Market and amending Directives 96/9/EC and 2001/29/EC, OJ 2019 L130/92.

104 For more on the relations between both acts, see: João Pedro Quintais and Sebastian Felix Schwemer, 'The Interplay between the Digital Services Act and Sector Regulation: How Special Is Copyright?' (2022) 13 *European Journal of Risk Regulation* 191.

105 Recital 66 of the CDSM Directive.

106 Felipe Romero Moreno, '"Upload Filters" and Human Rights: Implementing Article 17 of the Directive on Copyright in the Digital Single Market' (2020) 34 *International Review of Law, Computers & Technology* 153.

107 See the arguments presented by Poland, summarised in: Bernd Justin Jütte, 'Poland's Challenge to Article 17 CDSM Directive Fails before the CJEU, but Member States Must Implement Fundamental Rights Safeguards' (2022) 17 *Journal of Intellectual Property Law & Practice* 693.

108 *Poland v. Parliament and Council* (C-401/19) EU:C:2022:297.

right to information, it held that the introduction of an obligation for service providers to monitor content did not go beyond what was acceptable in a democratic state.[109] In doing so, however, it did not address in detail the failure to establish effective legal safeguards – i.e. the requirement for a judicial review within a certain period of time, on pain of the decision to block content becoming invalid. The Court's interpretation means acceptance of a state of affairs in which access to a publication can, in reality, be blocked for many months (or years), resulting in the permanent elimination of its impact on the ongoing public debate.

While the area of application of the CDSM Directive is the protection of private interests, similar measures have been adopted for years in the area of public security. NetzDG, which imposes obligations on service providers to block content due to its illegal nature (penalised by criminal law), is a model also in this respect. However, a question arises in this case as to exactly whose interests exactly the service providers are protecting. If it is considered that they are carrying out activities commissioned to them by public authorities (performing public tasks, e.g. preventing access to terrorist content), this should lead to the conclusion that also the assessment of the permissibility of this interference should take into account the standard for the use of surveillance by public authorities.

This conclusion becomes more relevant when it is the task of a private entity (a service provider) not only to analyse and block user publications, but also to report the violations it has identified to law enforcement authorities. Such mechanisms were introduced, for example, in Regulation 2021/1232, establishing a specific measure to combat the dissemination of paedophilia (the so-called CSAM Regulation).[110] According to the Regulation, if a service provider implements this measure, it is obliged to report any violations identified to the competent law enforcement authorities. While the CSAM Regulation concerns a specific area of application of content filtering mechanisms, a similar mechanism – but concerning all cases "involving a threat to the life or safety of a person or persons" – is explicitly provided for in the DSA. Moreover, while the CSAM Regulation requires human confirmation of the correctness of an algorithmic assessment before a suspected crime is reported, no identical requirement has been introduced in the DSA. Not only does the DSA not require manual analysis of the data before they are submitted to law enforcement, but it even extends the reporting obligation to "any information giving rise to a suspicion that a criminal offence . . . has taken place, is taking

109 Willemijn Kornelius, 'Prior Filtering Obligations after Case C-401/19: Balancing the Content Moderation Triangle' (2023) 14 *JIPITEC* 123.

110 Regulation (EU) 2021/1232 of the European Parliament and of the Council of 14 July 2021 on a temporary derogation from certain provisions of Directive 2002/58/EC as regards the use of technologies by providers of number-independent interpersonal communications services for the processing of personal and other data for the purpose of combating online child sexual abuse, OJ 2021 L274/41.

place or is *likely to take place* [emphasis added]."[111] The mechanism adopted thus includes the mandatory reporting of hate speech, e.g. incitement to violence, to law enforcement authorities as well.

Against this background, it is worth revisiting the NetzDG Act. One of the main elements of its amendment that came into force in 2022 was the introduction of specific obligations to report infringements to the competent public authorities. In particular, content infringing the designated criminal provisions should be compulsorily reported to the Federal Criminal Police Office (BKA).[112] According to BKA's analysis, compliance with this obligation will lead to the submission of around 250,000 reports each year, leading to the initiation of around 150,000 new criminal proceedings.[113]

The new legislation was challenged by technology companies (including Google and Meta) on the grounds that it was not in compliance with not only German constitutional provisions, but also with EU law and the ECHR. In its ruling, the Cologne Administrative Court found certain provisions of NetzDG to be incompatible with EU law. In particular, this concerned the infringement of the regulations of the e-Commerce Directive to the extent that NetzDG obliged entities not based in Germany to apply German law. However, the Court did not find that the obligations to analyse content and report the infringements detected to law enforcement authorities constituted an impermissible interference with fundamental rights. In this regard, it noted that the legislation under review "does not impose an obligation to actively search for facts or circumstances that could possibly indicate illegal information" – from which it concluded that there was no breach of the prohibition of a general monitoring obligation.[114]

Of particular interest, however, is the Court's consideration of the compatibility with EU law of the obligations to report publications to law enforcement authorities. In this regard, it recalled that the possibility of establishing such a mechanism stemmed directly from Article 15(2) of the e-Commerce Directive.[115] At the same time, it pointed out that Member States may oblige service providers to submit information on "alleged illegal activities" to law enforcement authorities. However, the norm cited by the Court should be read in conjunction with Article 15(1) of the same Directive, i.e. the prohibition of establishing a general monitoring obligation. Therefore it seems that the reasoning put forward by the Cologne Court does not cover cases where the law mandates the reporting of the infringements detected using active

111 Art. 18(1) of the DSA.

112 See Sec. 3a of NetzDG.

113 Oliver Noyan, 'Big Tech Opposes Germany's Enhanced Hate Speech Law' *Euroactiv* <https://cli.re/bpeKrN> accessed 6 September 2023.

114 *Verwaltungsgericht Köln* 1 March 2022 (6 L1354/21) DE:VGK:2022:0301.6L1354.21.00 at [108].

115 This is now Art. 18(1) of the DSA, but this provision is not really equivalent to the earlier Art. 15(2) of the e-Privacy Directive.

content filtering mechanisms. Unfortunately, the Court did not address in detail the assessment of the compatibility of the German regulation with the Charter, with the result that some of the arguments regarding the applicability of NetzDG have remained de facto unresolved.

An interesting aspect of the application of NetzDG also relevant in the context of the broader discussion on the surveillance effect of content filtering regulations is the procedure applied in relation to notifications submitted to BKA. The legislature established specific safeguards, including, *inter alia*, an information obligation vis-à-vis the author of blocked content, which the service provider has to fulfil within 4 weeks of reporting the content to law enforcement authorities.[116] As NetzDG requires service providers to report infringements electronically, and given the large estimated number of notifications (approximately 250,000), it is to be expected that the information transmitted to BKA alone will form a large (and detailed)[117] database. It is clear that these data should be used to prosecute the perpetrators of the crimes reported. However, NetzDG does not explicitly lay down an obligation to delete the information submitted, in particular if no criminal proceedings have been initiated on its basis. The Federal Administrative Court in Cologne confirmed that the submission of such a wide range of data met the necessity condition. In the Court's view, this is due to the lack of availability of a less intrusive measure. This assessment seems debatable, especially because such a measure could, for example, be the implementation of a two-stage content reporting process covering, first, the links to contested publications alone, and only in a second step, after preliminary verification by law enforcement authorities, provide more detailed information making the author identifiable. The adoption of such a procedure was, in fact, discussed during the legislative process, and the Court also referred to the legitimacy of its implementation.[118] However, it considered that it would be too time-consuming and, as a result, create the risk that the necessary information would not be secured in time. Thus, it considered that the measure provided for by the law was *necessary* because it was *effective*.[119] This is a flawed argumentation, however, similar to that used to support other overly extensive forms of surveillance. Effectiveness does not predetermine the need for a particular measure, especially when other tools are available that achieve the same objective and are less intrusive.

Transferring the lessons from the NetzDG case to the EU level, one can conclude that the reporting of all potential violations of law to law enforcement authorities using algorithmic means, combined with the failure to establish rules on the minimisation of the data submitted and oversight over

116 However, BKA can order the service provider to withhold sending such a notice.
117 Including, in addition to the contested content, e.g. the username and the user's IP address.
118 *Verwaltungsgericht Köln* (n 114) at [154].
119 Ibid. at [152].

their use, seems a ready recipe for the creation of a system of mass surveillance without public authorities having to take any active steps to intercept user data.[120]

Ensuring the security of online services – including countering crimes, in particular those targeting children's safety or glorifying violence or extremism – is nowadays one of the most important tasks of public authorities in the sphere of ensuring order in cyberspace. At the same time, however, as with other forms of surveillance the mass analysis of data in search of violations of the law involves a high risk of constructing a regime that will impose excessive restrictions on individual freedom and privacy. Therefore it may be helpful in discussing automatic content control measures to relate them to the standards developed in the field of electronic surveillance. This would provide an opportunity to verify whether, for example, a vague order to search for content of a similar nature meets the standard of the foreseeability of the law. Or whether establishing rules which impose an obligation to automatically make available to law enforcement authorities detailed information on contested content, including data beyond those necessary for the prosecution of the perpetrator, meets the standard of strict necessity.

Any technique for the mass surveillance of online user activity by public authorities should be subject to similar restrictions and controls. Only then will the resulting regulatory model actually be effective and efficient in countering the risks of abuse of power and erosion of democratic principles.

6.6 The fading public/private surveillance divide

Historically, the use of intrusive electronic surveillance measures has been the domain of public authorities. It is only in recent years, as a result of mainly technological but also social changes, that measures applied by private entities have been increasingly debated as well. The distinction between privacy surveillance and public surveillance reflects, first and foremost, the different purposes of their use: the former is intended to protect private interests, e.g. to ensure security in the workplace or protect business secrets, while the latter serves the purposes of general security.

Moreover, the two forms of surveillance are also evaluated differently by the public, which is no doubt also influenced by historical and personal experiences and the perception of the risks associated with the use of each type of surveillance.[121]

120 It is a separate issue whether measures such as those adopted in NetzDG can at all be considered effective in the fight against the distribution of illegal content on the Internet. Rachel Griffin, 'New School Speech Regulation as a Regulatory Strategy against Hate Speech on Social Media: The Case of Germany's NetzDG' (2022) 46 *Telecommunications Policy* 102411.

121 Nili Steinfeld, 'Track Me, Track Me Not: Support and Consent to State and Private Sector Surveillance' (2017) 34 *Telematics and Informatics* 1663.

In reality, however, the division between private and public surveillance is increasingly of historical interest only. The technical capabilities at the disposal of big tech can be considered to far exceed public authorities' data collection and processing capabilities in most countries – including European ones. The global data market has also significantly affected the ability of public authorities of the country from which the data acquired originated to control private entities. In addition, as a result of the dynamic development of technologies with a high surveillance potential, even relatively small companies can nowadays quickly achieve the capacity to carry out mass surveillance of hundreds of millions of users online.

The disappearance of the boundary between public and private surveillance is also the result of the progressive privatisation of public tasks, which is leading to the gradual takeover by private entities of duties traditionally associated with public bodies. Commercial companies have been developing and implementing technologies used in the area of electronic surveillance for years. Currently, there are many surveillance tools manufacturers in the market who are ready to supply their products to any recipient – including countries under international sanctions, such as Syria or Libya.[122]

However, whereas external subcontractors were suppliers of products and systems a few decades ago, today they are de facto providers of surveillance services. As a result, a new type of public-private partnership is emerging – one which, to paraphrase the terms describing cloud services – can be called surveillance as a service. Viewed in this light, public authorities benefit from a service provided by a private entity. Examples of such services are Pegasus or ClearView, discussed earlier.

In the case of the Pegasus system, the system provider (the NSO Group) provides the entire platform to manage the surveillance process – from distributing spyware to specific smartphones through to overseeing the data collection process and to the subsequent data processing. Significantly, the private entity also controls the technical infrastructure necessary for the surveillance activities. This leads to obvious questions about the existence of adequate safeguards to prevent unauthorised persons (e.g. NSO Group employees) from accessing the data.[123]

According to the manufacturer's assurances, it is the user of the system (a public authority) who decides on the scope and manner of using the tool.[124]

122 Claire Helen Lauterbach, 'No-Go Zones: Ethical Geographies of the Surveillance Industry' (2017) 15 *Surveillance & Society* 557.

123 For a detailed analysis on the Pegasus spyware case, see Marcin Rojszczak, 'EU Criminal Law and Electronic Surveillance: The Pegasus System and Legal Challenges It Poses' (2021) 29 *European Journal of Crime, Criminal Law and Criminal Justice* 290.

124 'Response from NSO Group to the Pegasus Project' *The Washington Post* (18 July 2021) <https://cli.re/NJmoey> accessed 6 September 2023. See also the statement of the NSO Group presented in the *WhatsApp Inc. v. NSO Group Ltd.* case (US District Court for the Northern District of California, case 3:19-cv-07123-JSC) 7 <https://cli.re/ZeEeyb>.

At the same time, however, the information disclosed shows that the manufacturer has the capacity to verify how its system is used – in particular, whether it is used for unlawful activities.[125] This circumstance alone is unusual: a foreign private entity (linked to Israeli intelligence) assesses whether the use of the technology supplied by it by a third country's public authorities is lawful. While it is difficult to assess the credibility of the NSO Group's assurances as to the legal safeguards established, the lack of transparency regarding the technology used raises questions. Indeed, the authority using the NSO Group's platform is only ostensibly in control of the surveillance process. Without knowing (or having any control over) how the data is intercepted, transmitted, and processed, it is unaware of not only who else has access to them but even whether the data have not been tampered with and whether they constitute all the material obtained.

These ambiguities are of particular importance when surveillance is used in the field of fighting crime, as they can lead to the evidence presented being challenged in court. This is why the FBI, although it purchased access to the system, chose not to use it as part of its investigations.[126] Bureau representatives argued that their interest in Pegasus was purely due to its desire to learn more about the product's technical capabilities.[127] Interestingly, however, even after President Biden banned the use of commercial spyware tools by US public bodies,[128] it turned out that Pegasus had been used by an FBI subcontractor to gather information on suspects in Mexico.[129]

The above example illustrates another problem concerning the disappearing division between public and private surveillance. Nowadays, when talking about the surveillance activities of ***public authorities***, it is necessary to establish not only whether these activities are not carried out entirely in commercial systems, but also whether they are not carried out by private subcontractors. Although Edward Snowden is commonly referred to as an NSA analyst, he was in fact an employee of Booz Allen Hamilton, the NSA's subcontractor. Called "the world's most profitable spy organisation,"[130] Booz Allen employs more

125 For example, the NSO Group has repeatedly stated that Pegasus "was not associated in any way with the heinous murder of Jamal Khashoggi."

126 Ellen Nakashima, 'FBI Acknowledges It Tested NSO Group's Spyware' *The Washington Post* (2 February 2022) <https://cli.re/Bvv9e9> accessed 6 September 2023.

127 This version is contradicted by internal FBI materials made public in 2022: Mark Mazzetti and Ronen Bergman, 'Internal Documents Show How Close the F.B.I. Came to Deploying Spyware' *The New York Times* (12 November 2022) <https://cli.re/yPAJ94> accessed 6 September 2023.

128 Executive Order of 27 March 2023 on Prohibition on Use by the United States Government of Commercial Spyware that Poses Risks to National Security.

129 Mark Mazzetti, Ronen Bergman and Adam Goldman, 'Who Paid for a Mysterious Spy Tool? The F.B.I., an F.B.I. Inquiry Found' *The New York Times* (31 July 2023) <https://cli.re/A5X9k5> accessed 6 September 2023.

130 Matthew Rosenberg, 'At Booz Allen, a Vast U.S. Spy Operation, Run for Private Profit' *The New York Times* (6 October 2016) <https://cli.re/yPnDKp>.

than 25,000 staff, nearly 10,000 of whom hold the highest security clearances granted by the federal government. A significant proportion of the staff work for the US Intelligence Community on a permanent basis. As a result, it is employees of Booz Allen Hamilton and similar companies who design, implement, and oversee the operation of indiscriminate electronic surveillance programmes. It thus appears that "NSA analysts" are, in many cases, private subcontractors who – like Snowden or Martin, who was also charged with unauthorised removal and retention of highly classified information[131] – actually supervise the processes of both the collection and subsequent use of data.

The increasing outsourcing of public surveillance tasks is leading to the transfer to private parties of responsibility not only for specific activities. but also for the organisation of the entire process. An example is the regulatory trend discussed in the previous section, concerning the use of automated content filtering mechanisms by digital service providers. It is based on the creation of a legal framework transferring responsibility for a specific area of surveillance use to private actors, leaving them a large degree of freedom in the choice of the means used to achieve this objective.

Previously, however, the ***privatisation*** of electronic surveillance defined in this way did not include the performance of tasks related to eavesdropping on electronic communications. Even where legislation imposed obligations on businesses in this area, these related to making infrastructure available or allowing the installation of certain types of equipment by SIAs. An example is the regulations of the French Internal Security Code imposing obligations on service providers to cooperate with secret services in maintaining the surveillance equipment provided.[132] The telecoms operator does not manage or supervise the operation of these devices, and its role is limited to enabling their installation by authorised public authorities.

One of the first signs of a shift in this paradigm was the adoption of EU Regulation 2021/1232, establishing a specific measure to combat the dissemination of paedophilic material (the CSAM Regulation).[133] The Regulation created a legal framework for the application by providers of certain electronic communication services[134] of measures to analyse users' communications – covering not only metadata but also the content of correspondence. At the same time, however, the act did not impose an obligation to implement such measures but relied on a voluntary decision by a service provider to do so. In other words, if a service provider decided to put the communications of its users under surveillance to identify paedophilic content, it was legally obliged

131 Ellen Nakashima, John Woodrow Cox and Matt Zapotosky, 'NSA Contractor Charged with Stealing Top Secret Data' *The Washington Post* (5 October 2016) <https://cli.re/bpkWNK> accessed 6 September 2023.

132 See Art. L851-3 of the Internal Security Code.

133 Regulation (EU) 2021/1232 (n 110).

134 Its scope includes number-independent communications services, also referred to as OTT – see section 2.1.

to organise this process taking into account the safeguards indicated in the legislation, and also to compulsorily report the cases of abuse identified to law enforcement authorities. Of course, the adoption of this Regulation led to heated discussions on the limits of interference with individual rights, including in the context of the permissibility of using surveillance in a preventive manner.[135] Against this background, it suffices to recall that according to the CJEU's position a generalised analysis of the entirety of communications violates the essence of the right to privacy and is, therefore, per se incompatible with EU law.[136]

Additional ambiguities regarding the CSAM Regulation concern the voluntary nature of the surveillance. If the fight against the sexual exploitation of children requires such measures – which are, therefore, *necessary* – it is difficult to justify why their implementation should depend on a private entity's decision. Accepting this state of affairs would create the impression that it is the service provider who examines the need for the use of surveillance and that, de facto, its implementation does not serve public purposes but the protection of private interests.

Doubts about the CSAM Regulation will be partially resolved once a new piece of legislation – the draft regulation presented in 2021 setting the framework for the use of surveillance in the area of combating sexual abuse of children – comes into force.[137] The draft regulation eliminates the voluntary use of surveillance, imposing instead a legal requirement for its implementation on providers of certain electronic communications services.[138] Once adopted, this act will introduce into EU law a hitherto unknown general surveillance measure that covers all communications, including their content. Surveillance will be used by private actors according to the requirements and under the supervision of public authorities. However, unlike the provisions of the French Internal Security Code discussed earlier, it will still be up to a service provider to decide on how the data will be processed and, therefore, on the algorithms used to identify unlawful content. It is worth noting that also in this respect the draft regulation proposes an important novelty related to the establishment of the EU Centre on Child Sexual Abuse. One of the Centre's tasks will

135 In fact, similar discussions have also been held outside the European Union concerning analogous regulations adopted by other legislatures – see e.g. Joseph Zabel, 'Public Surveillance through Private Eyes: The Case of the Earn It Act and the Fourth Amendment' (2020) 2020 *University of Illinois Law Review Online* 167.

136 *Maximillian Schrems v. Data Protection Commissioner* (C-362/14) EU:C:2015:650 at [94]. See also Christian Thönnes, 'Automated Predictive Threat Detection after Ligue Des Droits Humains' (2023) *Verfassungsblog: On Matters Constitutional* <https://intr2dok.vifa-recht.de/receive/mir_mods_00015520> accessed 19 September 2023.

137 Proposal for a Regulation laying down rules to prevent and combat child sexual abuse, COM/2022/209 final.

138 However, these are still OTT services, so the new law is not intended to apply to classic telecoms operators.

be to develop and make available free of charge a reference model (system) for the analysis and detection of unlawful material.[139] Although service providers will not be obliged to use this system, its availability will certainly have a positive impact on the standardisation of solutions used by telecommunications service providers.

Leaving aside the assessment of the legality of the proposed provisions – in particular, their compliance with the criteria of necessity and proportionality (discussed earlier)[140] – what merits attention is the almost complete transfer of responsibility for the ongoing use of surveillance from public authorities to private entities. It will be the service provider (e.g. Meta or Google) that will be not only entitled but also legally obliged to analyse all user communications and report violations to public authorities. Given the indiscriminate way in which the data is processed, this will, in fact, be the first legally sanctioned use of untargeted surveillance measures by private parties – yet for the purposes of carrying out a public task. At this stage of the legislative work, it is impossible to predict the final form of the new regulation, but the need for its adoption is linked to the expiration of the current CSAM Regulation in 2024. It should be expected that the discussion of the new regulation will also provide an opportunity to assess the appropriateness of the direction taken by the EU legislature in privatising electronic surveillance tasks.

6.7 The transatlantic cooperation in the shadow of surveillance

The discussion on the future of the European Union model of electronic surveillance regulation focuses, for obvious reasons, on the specifics of the measures implemented in individual Member States. Despite the differences arising from statutory law, its practical application, and national case law, the surveillance regimes in place in particular countries are subject to similar restrictions, built on respect for the same rights and values and international human rights systems.

However, electronic surveillance, especially that based on indiscriminate surveillance measures, is most often not strictly national in nature. Hence, a holistic discussion of this issue requires an adequate consideration of its cross-border aspects. For European countries, cooperation with the United States is particularly important in this regard. This is due to the mutual economic importance of the European Union and the United States, as well as to their close intelligence ties and the multitude of programmes implemented jointly by the services of individual European countries and their US counterparts.

139 Art. 50(1) of the draft CSAM Regulation.

140 Anna Pingen, 'New Controversies around Proposal to Combat Child Sexual Abuse Online' *eucrim* (2 September 2022) <https://cli.re/53n4KA> accessed 6 September 2023.

At the same time, the US model for the regulation of electronic surveillance is structured in a fundamentally different way to the European one. This is increasingly leading to controversy, not only in the sphere of economic cooperation but also in the area of cooperation in criminal matters or, more broadly, cooperation related to the performance of public security tasks. The mismatch between the European and US frameworks for the regulation and supervision of electronic surveillance is particularly hotly debated with regard to covert programmes carried out in the field of national security. Suffice it to say that the CJEU has concluded that the US legal model does not provide an adequate level of protection compared with that provided under EU law.[141] These conclusions have led the CJEU to find that the electronic surveillance rules established in the US violate the essence of the right to privacy and personal data protection for Europeans whose data has been transferred to the United States.[142] To this extent, they can, therefore, be considered fundamentally incompatible with EU law.[143]

Understanding the differences between the American and European legislation and discussion of the possibility of overcoming them are among the issues that may significantly influence the future shape of the European electronic surveillance model. This also requires referring the concepts of ***adequacy*** (CJEU) and ***comparability*** (ECtHR) present in the case law of the European courts to the realities of the US legal model. Only then can a comprehensive assessment be made of the extent to which agreement on common legal safeguards and standards is possible. And if it is not, how a common transatlantic agreement on the permissible limits of the use of electronic surveillance can be built in a way that protects the EU-US partnership, which is crucial for ensuring not only regional but also global security.

The US Constitution does not explicitly define privacy-related guarantees. The right to privacy has been articulated by the US Supreme Court through precedent-setting rulings against the backdrop of the application of the Fourth Amendment, which forbids unreasonable searches and seizures.[144] An essential Fourth Amendment criterion for assessing the legality of surveillance by public authorities against US residents is the so-called ***probable cause*** test. This condition, in principle, limits the implementation of measures that interfere with fundamental rights to cases where public authorities have obtained (lawfully) reliable information linking a specific person to criminal activity.[145]

141 See the *Schrems* and *Schrems II* cases, discussed in section 5.4.

142 In terms of privacy, this conclusion flows directly from the *Schrems* case (see *Maximillian Schrems v. Data Protection Commissioner* (n 136)), while with regard to the protection of personal data, it is related to the failure to establish an independent supervisory authority, a requirement which directly stems from Art. 8(3) of the Charter.

143 Maria Lorena Flórez Rojas, 'Legal Implications after *Schrems* Case: Are We Trading Fundamental Rights?' (2016) 25 *Information & Communications Technology Law* 292.

144 See earlier in section 2.4.

145 Andrew Manuel Crespo, 'Probable Cause Pluralism' (2019) 129 *Yale Law Journal* 1276.

The manner of assessing *probable cause* and the criteria for recognising the fulfilment of the *probable cause* condition are extensively discussed in the case law of American courts. The fulfilment of this condition is verified in light of the circumstances of each particular case,[146] but without the need to demonstrate respect for the principles of necessity or proportionality as they are understood in Europe.

In the case of the United States, the constitutional standard of protection of fundamental rights can be supplemented by international legal norms only to a limited extent, despite the fact that the United States has acceded to and ratified the International Covenant on Civil and Political Rights. However, as a result of the reservations made during the ratification procedure, this treaty has no direct effect in US domestic law. In consequence, individuals are unable to invoke its guarantees in disputes before American courts. As a result, the practical relevance of the provisions of the Covenant from the perspective of the individual is low, and it does not have the effect of strengthening guarantees or extending rights and obligations beyond the applicable constitutional standards.[147]

The Fourth Amendment model of privacy protection is also characterised by limitations on the circle of right holders and duty bearers. The Fourth Amendment's personal scope covers only citizens and residents of the United States (so-called US persons),[148] has only vertical effect,[149] and has little effect on public authorities' actions outside the United States.[150] As a result, the Fourth Amendment guarantees must be fully applied by public authorities only within the territory of the United States and only in relation to persons permanently residing there.

It should be noted that a consequence of the lack of explicit inclusion of the right to privacy in constitutional provisions (as this right is defined in the European Union) is also the lack of guarantees related to the protection of personal data. In the European model, personal data protection is a right derived directly from the right to privacy (in the ECHR) or defined as a separate subjective right (e.g. in the Charter). The way in which the right to privacy is defined – through a non-exhaustive list of protected interests – allows

146 Andrew Taslitz, 'What is Probable Cause, and Why Should We Care? The Costs, Benefits, and Meaning of Individualized Suspicion' (2010) 73 *Law and Contemporary Problems* 145.

147 Catherine Redgwell, 'US Reservations to Human Rights Treaties: All for One and None for All?' in Michael Byers and Georg Nolte (eds), *United States Hegemony and the Foundations of International Law* (Cambridge University Press 2003) <www.cambridge.org/core/product/identifier/CBO9780511494154A027/type/book_part> accessed 19 October 2020.

148 *United States v. Verdugo-Urquidez*, 494 U.S. 259 (1990). See also Mary Lynn Nicholas, 'United States v. Verdugo-Urquidez: Restricting the Borders of the Fourth Amendment' 14 Fordham International Law Journal 267.

149 Eric Johnson, 'Lost in the Cloud: Cloud Storage, Privacy, and Suggestions for Protecting Users' Data Note' (2017) 69 *Stanford Law Review* 867, 878.

150 Elizabeth A Corradino, 'The Fourth Amendment Overseas: Is Extraterritorial Protection of Foreign Nationals Going Too Far?' (1989) 57 *Fordham Law Review* 617, 618–619.

its subject matter scope to be extended in a way that reflects social changes and technological progress. Therefore in the European model the extension of the scope of protection does not require a change in the substantive law.[151] The US Constitution is devoid of this flexibility. An analysis of the US Supreme Court case law leads to the conclusion that the substantive content of the right to privacy under the Fourth Amendment is significantly narrower than that under the European standards. In particular, it does not cover guarantees concerning the protection of personal data at all.[152]

The different constitutional norms in the European Union and the United States also result in the introduction of different statutory provisions and the shaping of different obligations on the part of public authorities to protect privacy. In the European Union, legislation serves to supplement and clarify constitutional guarantees (derived from primary law). The European data protection model, which is currently based on the GDPR (complemented in the field of law enforcement by the LED), provides for the introduction of identical public law obligations for all entities processing information, regardless of whether they belong to the private or public sectors. As the right to privacy is a fundamental right, its protection derives from public law regulation.

In the United States, legislation establishing privacy safeguards is implemented on a sectoral and fragmented basis. In the US legislation, the closest equivalent to the European General Data Protection Regulation is the Privacy Act of 1974,[153] which only regulates data collection and processing activities by federal authorities. The provisions of the Privacy Act also contain a number of exemptions, *inter alia* in terms of obliged entities as well as the purpose of processing. For instance, processing by law enforcement authorities carried out in connection with ongoing investigations is exempted from the provisions of the Act.[154] The lack of constitutional guarantees related to privacy protection means that the state is not obliged to enact appropriate legislation to regulate horizontal relationships.

In the US legal system, the executive's powers to impose measures interfering with fundamental rights are also more extensive than the analogous regulations in place in European countries. The US Constitution grants the executive branch broad prerogatives in the area of public security.[155] Their exercise may not in every case be limited by acts of Congress. In addition, in a number of laws Congress has delegated to the executive the

151 An example is the ECtHR's recognition that Art. 8(1) is a sufficient basis for extending protection to the content of electronic communications. See e.g. *Copland v. the United Kingdom* (62617/00) 3 April 2007 ECtHR at [44].

152 To the extent that this right is defined under European law – see section 3.4.

153 Pub Law No. 93-579, 88 Stat 1896.

154 See 5 U.S.C. §552a(a)(8)(B)(iii).

155 William C Banks and ME Bowman, 'Executive Authority for National Security Surveillance' (2001) 50 *American University Law Review* 1.

authority to enact regulations influencing national security.[156] The combination of vague constitutional standards, fragmented statutory provisions, and extensive federal government powers has resulted in a legal system in which, in many cases, national security objectives prevail over personal rights and liberties.

A practical example of the distribution of powers in US legislation is Executive Order (EO) 13768, issued by President Donald Trump in January 2017, which required the federal government not to apply the rights under the Privacy Act of 1974 to foreign nationals.[157] Notwithstanding the other controversies surrounding the Order, the introduction of measures limiting statutory rights in a non-statutory act is noteworthy.

The dispersed powers in the area of national security also result in the US legal model having several equivalent legal bases for the implementation of electronic surveillance programmes. Among the most important are the federal Foreign Intelligence Surveillance Act (FISA)[158] and EO 12333.[159] Both allow the conduct of indiscriminate electronic surveillance programmes and establish various legal safeguards in this regard, including those related to the process of authorising surveillance, the purpose of such surveillance, and judicial review of the actions taken. Importantly, however, both legal regimes are used for the implementation of surveillance by the same secret services. As a result, while various intrusive programmes conducted by the US NSA are discussed in the public domain, when assessing their legality it is important to bear in mind that some are conducted under the FISA and some under EO 12333.[160]

The main purpose of the enactment of the FISA was to set out rules for the conduct of intelligence activities against foreign nationals in a way that would prevent the same means and techniques from being used to monitor US citizens' activities. The FISA bill was submitted and passed as a direct consequence of the legally questionable activities of US secret services related

156 However, it would be a mistake to point to only one reason why the executive's powers prevail over the other authorities in the US political system. *See* William P Marshall, 'Eleven Reasons Why Presidential Power Inevitably Expands and Why It Matters Symposium: The Role of the President in the Twenty-First Century' (2008) 88 *Boston University Law Review* 505.

157 See Art. 14 of Executive Order 13768: Enhancing Public Safety in the Interior of the United States, 82 FR 8799 (25 January 2017); repealed.

158 Foreign Intelligence Surveillance Act of 1978; Pub Law No. 95-511, 50 U.S.C. §1801.

159 Executive Order 12333: United States Intelligence Activities, 46 FR 59941 (4 December 1981).

160 However, some surveillance activities are implemented on a legal basis other than the FISA and E.O 12333. An example is the STELLAR WIND programme, implemented based on direct Presidential Authorisations. For more details, see section 5.1. See also 'Report on the President's Surveillance Program' (Inspectors General of the DoD, DoJ, CIA, NSA and DNI 2009) <https://cli.re/VJnJ3P> accessed 6 September 2023.

to, *inter alia*, the surveillance of the opposition and political competitors (e.g. concerning Martin Luther King or the Watergate scandal).[161]

The Act introduced two main mechanisms for the implementation of surveillance activities. The first, stemming from Article 102 of the FISA,[162] can only be used in the case of electronic communications carried out between actors of foreign influence subject to the condition that there is "no substantial likelihood" that communications of US persons will be obtained as a result of the surveillance activity.

Alternatively, the FISA provides for the possibility of carrying out electronic surveillance activities in any case on the basis of a court order issued by the US Foreign Intelligence Surveillance Court (FISC), established by the Act for this purpose. Created under Section 103 of the FISA, this judicial body originally consisted of 7 (later 11) judges, one for each of the federal judicial circuits, selected by the Chief Justice of the US Supreme Court. Together with the appellate court (the US Foreign Intelligence Surveillance Court of Review, FISCR), both bodies have exclusive jurisdiction with respect to approving applications under the FISA, which means, in particular, that their decisions cannot be appealed before other federal courts and the legality of these decisions cannot be challenged using any other legal procedure. An exception to this is the possibility of filing a petition for a writ of certiorari with the US Supreme Court to challenge a judgment rendered by the FISCR.[163] However, in practice this is a right available only to the government party as only representatives of public authorities participate in the proceedings before FISC/FISCR.[164] Moreover, under the statute the activity of the courts is, by definition, secret, which includes hearings, applications filed, and orders issued. In addition, the entities to which the orders are addressed (e.g. telecommunications operators) are obliged by law to keep secret all activities related to the execution of the orders, as well as the very fact that they have been issued.[165]

The original wording of the FISA has been amended several times. Particularly significant changes were introduced by the so-called Patriot Act of 2001, passed in response to the 9/11 attacks.[166] It was under this reform that Section 501 of the FISA was amended,[167] which resulted in an expansion of

161 Stephen Dycus and others, *National Security Law* (Sixth edition, Wolters Kluwer 2016) 507.
162 50 U.S.C. §1802.
163 See 28 U.S.C. §2106.
164 See 50 U.S.C. §1881a(h)(6)(B).
165 See 50 U.S.C. §1861(d).
166 It should be noted that the Patriot Act had been criticised even before the first revelations about the extensive surveillance programmes implemented based on it appeared. See Peter G Madrinan, 'Devil in the Details: Constitutional Problems Inherent in the Internet Surveillance Provisions of the USA Patriot Act of 2001 Note' (2002) 64 *University of Pittsburgh Law Review* 783.
167 This amendment was introduced in Sec. 215 of the Patriot Act of 2001. Hence, the measures applied under it have over the years been referred to as 'Sec. 215 surveillance' – see e.g. Casey

the NSA's power to conduct indiscriminate surveillance programmes involving the collection of metadata from electronic communications. An example of the application of the regime under the amended rules is the FISC order of 25 April 2013, disclosed in the public domain, which requested Verizon, one of the major US telecommunications operators,[168] to provide metadata on all domestic and international calls made by all users of the operator.[169] The order indicated that the data to be transmitted were to include, among other things, the calling station and called station numbers, the IMSI and IMEI identifiers, and the duration of the call. It should be noted that the scope of the data to be transmitted was in no way related to the need to obtain this information in connection with ongoing criminal proceedings – data on all calls of each subscriber were requested. In essence, therefore, this was a measure similar to a general retention obligation applied in EU law at the time, with the difference that, in the case of the US model, even the measure's application itself remained secret. Moreover, the FISC, when issuing the order, did not verify the justification for the transfer of the requested data but only carried out an assessment of the compatibility of the request with the legal basis – in this case, Section 501 of the FISA.

Another amendment introduced by the Patriot Act – concerning Section 702 of the FISA – became the basis for the implementation of mass surveillance programmes that also included access to the substantive content of communications (e.g. voice calls, emails, or content exchanged via instant messaging). While both provisions of the FISA directly affected the privacy of the users of electronic communications services, at the same time they formally constituted the basis for implementing different surveillance programmes.

Due to the numerous controversies that arose in the wake of Snowden's revelations about the scale of surveillance activities, the FISA has been subject to successive amendments, which did not always lead to increased oversight over the area of state surveillance activities. Examples include the Freedom Act of 2015 and the FISA Amendments Reauthorization Act of 2017, which in some areas expanded the scope of communications that could be subject to surveillance measures. The earlier legislation had not allowed for the lawful collection of the so-called about data, i.e. communications exchanged by third

McGowan, 'The Relevance of Relevance: Section 215 of the USA Patriot Act and the NSA Metadata Collection Program' (2014) 82 *Fordham Law Review* 2399.

168 It should also be emphasised that Verizon – in addition to the international connections operated by MCI Networks – also manages a significant part of the Internet backbone network within the United States (the so-called *tier 1*). See Chapter 1 for detailed information on how bulk capturing of data from a Tier 1 network can, in fact, lead to the establishment of a global surveillance regime.

169 Similar orders directed at all telecommunications operators have been issued since 2006. HL Pohlman, *U.S. National Security Law: An International Perspective* (Rowman & Littlefield 2019) 258.

parties, the content of which could indicate a (usually distant) reference to the object of surveillance.[170]

Apart from the procedures arising from the FISA, a separate basis for the implementation of surveillance programmes by US services is EO 12333. This Order is of particular importance in the case of programmes implemented outside the territory of the United States, as in such cases the restrictions arising from the FISA do not apply. This instrument has been amended three times since its issuance in 1981,[171] with each successive amendment leading to a relaxation of the requirements and an expansion of the powers of the Intelligence Community.

The Executive Order sets out the conditions for conducting electronic surveillance activities, including in relation to US persons (i.e. US citizens and residents). In doing so, it establishes less restrictive requirements than those arising from both the Fourth Amendment and the procedures provided for in the FISA. The Order identifies a catalogue of nine conditions allowing for applying surveillance programmes, which taken together provide a very broad framework for the lawful collection of data, including on US citizens.[172] Moreover, even when none of the conditions are met, the Order allows for incidental data collection "that may indicate involvement in activities that may violate Federal, state, local, or foreign laws." As the Order does not draw any boundaries or limitations related to "incidental data collection" based on this provision, it is possible to collect any dataset, however large, that is related (even remotely) to information of legitimate interest to the services.[173]

Unlike the FISA, activities conducted under Executive Order 12333 do not require court approval, nor are they subject to periodic judicial review. The Order does not impose any restrictions on the scope of information obtained; in particular, it does not provide additional conditions to be met by mass surveillance programmes involving bulk and unlimited data collection. According to information declassified in 2014, the NSA conducts most of its electronic reconnaissance activities exclusively under Executive Order 12333.[174]

The provisions of both the FISA and EO 12333 were taken into consideration in the CJEU's analysis, which led to the precedent-setting *Schrems* judgment, in which the Court found that the US legal model did not provide

170 The use of *about collection* led to the bulk collection of data of individuals outside the search criteria used – see Barton Gellman, Julie Tate and Ashkan Soltani, 'In NSA-Intercepted Data, Those Not Targeted Far Outnumber the Foreigners Who Are' *The Washington Post* (5 July 2014) <https://cli.re/dp2keR> accessed 6 September 2023.

171 The amendments were made pursuant to E.O. 13284 of 23 January 2003, E.O. 13355 of 27 August 2004 and E.O. 13470 of 30 July 2008.

172 See Sec. 2.3 of E.O. 12333.

173 Mark M Jaycox, 'No Oversight, No Limits, No Worries: A Primer on Presidential Spying and Executive Order 12,333' (2021) 12 *Harvard National Security Journal* 58.

174 'Legal Fact Sheet: Executive Order 12333' (National Security Agency 2013) <https://cli.re/BvkE42> accessed 6 September 2023.

adequate safeguards under EU law.[175] In turn, in the *Schrems II* judgment, concerning the new legal framework for transfers of personal data to the United States adopted in the wake of *Schrems*, the Court reiterated its earlier conclusions, this time pointing to the failure to establish any means of judicial review in the case of schemes based on EO 12333.[176]

This led to the development of another – the third in a decade – transatlantic programme for exchanging economic data between the European Union and the United States.[177] This time, however, the US government's declarations were backed up by the adoption of a new executive order, namely Executive Order 14086.[178] Its purpose was to establish new legal safeguards, in particular a judicial review mechanism concerning violations related to the exercise of surveillance powers under EO 12333.[179]

In principle, the act equates the conditions for the use of information on foreign nationals with the pre-existing rules for the use of information on US persons.[180] In this respect, the Order thus establishes a kind of ***adequacy*** of protection against unauthorised interference – understood, however, not as the introduction of safeguards equivalent to those in force in Europe, but safeguards adequate in relation to those enjoyed by US citizens.

The Order also establishes a multi-stage complaint process and sets up a specialised judicial body – the Data Protection Review Court – with the power to investigate cases of potential abuse in the application of surveillance measures.[181] In this way, the US side sought to address one of the fundamental problems hindering the free flow of data between the European Union and the United States: the lack of judicial redress.

While the issuance of EO 14086 certainly represents an important step in the transatlantic dialogue on the forms and scope of extensive electronic surveillance measures, the Order does not appear to address all the key issues effectively.

First, EO 14086 is an act of the executive branch, applicable to EO 12333 – and therefore to surveillance activities conducted under it. It has no effect whatsoever on surveillance programmes conducted under other US laws, in

175 *Maximillian Schrems v. Data Protection Commissioner* (n 136) at [81–82].

176 *Schrems II* (C-311/18) EU:C:2020:559 at [192].

177 Commission Implementing Decision EU 2023/1795 of 10 July 2023 pursuant to Regulation (EU) 2016/679 of the European Parliament and of the Council on the adequate level of protection of personal data under the EU-US Data Privacy Framework, C(2023) 4745 final.

178 Executive Order 14086: Enhancing Safeguards for United States Signals Intelligence Activities, 87 FR 62283 (7 October 2022).

179 'The United States and the European Union Begin Implementation of the European Union-U.S. Data Privacy Framework' (2023) 117 *American Journal of International Law* 346.

180 See Sec. 2(c)(iii)(A)(1)(a) of E.O. 14086.

181 The organisation and functioning of the authority are defined in Attorney General Order No. 5517-2022: See Data Protection Review Court, 87 FR 62303 (14 October 2022).

particular the FISA.[182] This leads to the conclusion that an EU resident should first know which (covert) surveillance programme they have been subjected to (and thus under which programme their personal data have been intercepted) to be able to use the appropriate legal procedure. At the same time, the "no confirming–no denying" model in place means that US authorities (including the Data Protection Review Court) cannot indicate whether the reason for not granting a complaint is that it is not justified, or perhaps that the applicant used the wrong legal procedure. This will be the case, for example, if the data of the person concerned are indeed used unlawfully by US authorities, but the basis for their actions is a programme under the FISA rather than EO 12333.

The measures provided for in Order do not even apply to all programmes authorised under EO 12333. Indeed, they apply only to untargeted surveillance measures meeting the definition indicated in EO 14086, which excludes activities involving the use of selectors – "for example, . . . specific identifiers or selection terms."[183] As indicated earlier, the mere definition of the term "selector" is problematic. Under a strict approach, any untargeted surveillance programme uses selectors. However, it is possible to adopt an interpretation according to which filters used at the initial stage – as not related to the substantive analysis of content – are not selectors. The definition set out in the Order seems to have the effect of deliberately excluding from the scope of application of the mechanisms provided for therein any programme which uses any selectors, also "due to *technical* [emphasis added] or operational considerations."[184] In this view, none of the known bulk surveillance programmes run by the NSA would qualify as a bulk collection under EO 14086.

Moreover, although the Order establishes new safeguards for the processing and further use of the information, it does not actually create additional restrictions on the interception process itself. In particular, it does not require that the conditions of proportionality or necessity be met in order for the actions taken by the US services to be legal. Moreover, equating the rights of EU citizens with those of US persons under EO 12333 only superficially fulfils the European partners' expectations of a more complete protection of the personal data transferred. Indeed, the failure of successive cases brought by non-governmental organisations against US secret services proves that judicial control of the electronic surveillance in the area of national security is largely illusory in the United States, and certainly significantly deviates from the standards in place in Europe.[185] In this sense, for federal law to provide adequate protection under EU law standards, EU citizens would have to receive more extensive legal protection in the United States than that enjoyed by US citizens – a demand that is obviously impossible to meet in a democratic state.

182 See Sec. 2(e) of E.O. 14086.

183 See Sec. 2(c)(ii)(D) of E.O. 14086.

184 Sec. 4(b) of E.O 14086.

185 For a detailed comparison between the European and American legal models in this aspect, see section 4.2.

There is no doubt that the adoption of EO 14086 was intended as a response to the European partners' concerns about the impact of the extensive US surveillance programmes on the possibility of building a common data market. However, leaving aside the assessment of whether the regulation adopted comprehensively achieves this objective, it is necessary to take a broader view of the issue at hand.

The differences between the European and US models for the application of surveillance measures are profound, and despite a common legal tradition founded on respect for the democratic principles and the rule of law, an attempt to overcome them by establishing a common standard of legal safeguards based on the application of the same legal concepts in the same way is simply not feasible. Just as the European Union was built on respect for the differing constitutional traditions of the Member States, it would seem that trust and relationships with third countries should be built in a similar way. Therefore while the CJEU has correctly assessed the risks associated with the transfer of data to the United States, the position it has adopted should at the same time encourage the construction of an intergovernmental treaty on the legal regulation of electronic surveillance. It is a mistake for the parties to limit themselves to the implementation of yet another half measure (such as EO 14086), which obviously fails to resolve the problem for which it was devised and only provokes further court cases.

Therefore, because neither the European Union (and its Member States) nor the United States will adapt their legal model to each other's expectations, the only possible – and sustainable – solution seems to be to resort to instruments of international law. In this respect, it is worth recalling the initiative developed under the auspices of the Special Rapporteur on the right to privacy discussed earlier,[186] which, however, did not gain the approval of either the United States and EU Member States. Revisiting this proposal – perhaps formulated differently and based on a broader view of the right to data protection – may create the future conditions for creating a secure and transnational space for the development of modern digital services.[187] In such a view, the general criteria for using electronic surveillance would be just one of the areas that the new treaty could regulate.

6.8 Summary

In July 2023 – partly against the backdrop of the discussions about a new law on special measures for the 2024 Olympics – the French government presented draft legal amendments allowing secret services to use spyware to

186 See section 5.5.

187 Another proposal is the so-called intelligence codex – see: Eliza Watt, 'The Right to Privacy and the Future of Mass Surveillance' (2017) 21 *The International Journal of Human Rights* 773.

remotely activate the microphones and cameras on the phones of individuals suspected of terrorism and other serious crimes.[188] In principle, the new regulations are expected to lead to the legalisation of a function that has been available in such software for years. All known spyware packages marketed for the so-called lawful interception can not only intercept communications (phone calls or text messages), but also access any information stored on the device (e.g. a photo library) or accessible from the device (e.g. data stored in cloud services). Therefore it should not come as a surprise that tools of this type also allow for the recording of video and audio – and thus the continuous monitoring of the environment in which the device is running.

The case of the French legislation is interesting for several reasons. First, it illustrates the differences in approaches to using the available technology by different European countries. While there is an ongoing debate in France about whether and how to control the technology that turns a user's smartphone into an eavesdropping device, the same solutions have been used for years in many other European countries,[189] in some of them without any specific statutory regulation. An example is Poland, where the current legislation does not introduce a specific legal basis for implementing this type of intrusive surveillance measures, and security services use general provisions on eavesdropping on electronic communications.

Second, surveillance using spyware can be carried out anywhere in the world, thus overcoming the territorial restrictions associated with the classical forms of eavesdropping (the need for access to telecommunications links, precluding easy eavesdropping on individuals in third countries). Therefore the French, Polish, or other European services have the technology to eavesdrop on any person with a mobile phone, no matter where they are.[190]

Third, although this type of software (such as Pegasus) is essentially used for targeted surveillance, this is mainly due to its licensing and distribution restrictions. If, instead of external software (which must be supplied and installed on the phone), the surveillance functionality were to be mandatorily built into a device's operating system by its manufacturer and made available to secret services, targeted surveillance would, de facto, become indiscriminate surveillance.

The above example – one of many – proves that in the era of dynamic technological changes, sticking to decades-old concepts on the ways or forms

188 Camille Ducrocq, 'Caméras et Micros Activables à Distance Par La Justice: Pourquoi Cette Mesure Fait Polémique' *La Parisien* (8 June 2023) <https://cli.re/97oZ5K> accessed 6 September 2023.

189 Quentin Liger and Mirja Gutheil, 'The Use of Pegasus and Equivalent Surveillance Spyware' (PEGA Committee of the European Parliament 2023) <https://cli.re/o4ZRbp> accessed 6 September 2023.

190 In fact, Roman Giertych, an opposition politician who was reportedly under surveillance by the Polish authorities, was in Italy at the time.

of using electronic surveillance actually limits the usefulness and protections of the standards developed in this field. Moreover, it creates a regulatory grey area, facilitating the implementation of new surveillance measures without adequate legal safeguards. New terms are being coined in an attempt to hide behind the marketing message, i.e. hide the actual potential of the novel technologies. In this way, "bulk surveillance" is becoming "automated content moderation."

As indicated earlier, surveillance is increasingly ceasing to be a tool used to gain knowledge about individuals. and instead is ever more turning into a means of influencing them.[191] To achieve this ultimate goal of many modern forms of surveillance, it is not necessary to resort to socially objectionable techniques designed for the mass interception of communications. As it turns out, the same effect can be achieved by imposing new obligations on electronic service providers or consumer electronics manufacturers. The same solutions as those used on a mass scale to determine purchasing preferences are already being deployed today to predictively identify threats for law enforcement purposes.

It is too early to say whether the new generation of surveillance measures will require a completely new regulatory approach. For the time being, however, it is apparent that disregarding the already existing standards for the use of electronic surveillance in legislative analysis leads to the establishment of measures that raise serious concerns, not only with regard to compliance with the principles of necessity or proportionality, but also with regard to respect for the essence of particular fundamental rights.

References

Alpaydin E, *Machine Learning: The New AI* (MIT Press 2016).

Angwin J and others, 'Machine Bias' *ProPublica* (23 May 2016) <https://cli.re/mp8mRz> accessed 6 September 2023.

'Annual Report of the Investigatory Powers Commissioner 2021' (Investigatory Powers Commissioner 2021).

Bajak F, 'Germany Seizes Server Hosting Pilfered US Police Files' (9 July 2020) <https://cli.re/7EVbvX> accessed 6 September 2023.

Bamford B, 'The United Kingdom's "War Against Terrorism"' (2004) 16 *Terrorism and Political Violence* 737.

Banks WC and Bowman ME, 'Executive Authority for National Security Surveillance' (2001) 50 *American University Law Review* 1.

Bauman Z and others, 'After Snowden: Rethinking the Impact of Surveillance' (2014) 8 *International Political Sociology* 121.

Baumgärtner M and Knobbe M, 'Sonderermittler Spricht von Klarem Vertragsbruch Der NSA' *Der Spiegel* (30 October 2015) <https://cli.re/97VNQR> accessed 6 September 2023.

191 Zygmunt Bauman and others, 'After Snowden: Rethinking the Impact of Surveillance' (2014) 8 *International Political Sociology* 121.

Biermann K, 'BND Stores 220 Million Telephone Data – Every Day' *Die Zeit* (2 February 2015) <https://cli.re/XA7j4Y> accessed 6 September 2023.

Brouwer E, 'Ligue Des Droits Humains and the Validity of the PNR Directive: Balancing Individual Rights and State Powers in Times of New Technologies' (2023) 60 *Common Market Law Review* 839.

Corea F, 'Introduction to Artificial Intelligence' in Francesco Corea (ed), *An Introduction to Data*, vol 50 (Springer International Publishing 2019) <http://link.springer.com/10.1007/978-3-030-04468-8_3> accessed 18 September 2023.

Corradino EA, 'The Fourth Amendment Overseas: Is Extraterritorial Protection of Foreign Nationals Going Too Far?' (1989) 57 *Fordham Law Review* 617.

Crespo AM, 'Probable Cause Pluralism' (2019) 129 *Yale Law Journal* 1276.

De Hert P and Papakonstantinou V, 'Framing Big Data in the Council of Europe and the EU Data Protection Law Systems: Adding "Should" to "Must" via Soft Law to Address More than Only Individual Harms' (2021) 40 *Computer Law & Security Review* 105496.

Donelle L and others, 'Use of Digital Technologies for Public Health Surveillance during the COVID-19 Pandemic: A Scoping Review' (2023) 9 *Digital Health* <https://doi.org10.1177/20552076231173>.

Dreyer E, 'Présentation de La Proposition de Loi Avia' (2020) 63 *Légipresse* 13.

Ducrocq C, 'Caméras et Micros Activables à Distance Par La Justice: Pourquoi Cette Mesure Fait Polémique' *La Parisien* (8 June 2023) <https://cli.re/97oZ5K> accessed 6 September 2023.

Dycus S and others, *National Security Law* (Sixth edition, Wolters Kluwer 2016).

Eberle EJ, 'Observations on the Development of Human Dignity and Personality in German Constitutional Law: An Overview' (2012) 33 *Liverpool Law Review* 201.

Echikson W and Knodt O, 'Germany's NetzDG: A Key Test for Combatting Online Hate' (Centre for European Policy Studies 2018) 2018/09 <https://cli.re/Bvv1Zx> accessed 6 September 2023.

Ertel W, 'Machine Learning and Data Mining' in Wolfgang Ertel (ed), *Introduction to Artificial Intelligence* (Springer 2011) <https://link.springer.com/10.1007/978-0-85729-299-5_8> accessed 18 September 2023.

Fazelpour S and Danks D, 'Algorithmic Bias: Senses, Sources, Solutions' (2021) 16 *Philosophy Compass* e12760.

Flores AW, Bechtel K and Lowenkamp CT, 'False Positives, False Negatives, and False Analyses: A Rejoinder to Machine Bias: There's Software Used across the Country to Predict Future Criminals. And It's Biased against Blacks' (2016) 80 *Federal Probation* 38.

Flórez Rojas ML, 'Legal Implications after *Schrems* Case: Are We Trading Fundamental Rights?' (2016) 25 *Information & Communications Technology Law* 292.

Gellman B, Tate J and Soltani A, 'In NSA-Intercepted Data, Those Not Targeted Far Outnumber the Foreigners Who Are' *The Washington Post* (5 July 2014) <https://cli.re/dp2keR> accessed 6 September 2023.

Glover P, *Protecting National Security: A History of British Communications Investigation Regulation* (Routledge 2022).

Griffin R, 'New School Speech Regulation as a Regulatory Strategy against Hate Speech on Social Media: The Case of Germany's NetzDG' (2022) 46 *Telecommunications Policy* 102411.

Gruszczak A, 'Intelligence Fusion for the European Union's Common Security and Defence Policy' (2022) 19 *Politeja* <https://journals.akademicka.pl/politeja/article/view/4784> accessed 19 September 2023.

Gryz J and Rojszczak M, 'Black Box Algorithms and the Rights of Individuals: No Easy Solution to the "Explainability" Problem' (2021) 10 *Internet Policy Review* <https://policyreview.info/articles/analysis/black-box-algorithms-and-rights-individuals-no-easy-solution-explainability> accessed 28 November 2021.

Haddad GM, 'Confronting the Biased Algorithm: The Danger of Admitting Facial Recognition Technology Results in the Courtroom Notes' (2020) 23 *Vanderbilt Journal of Entertainment & Technology Law* 891.

Hafetz J, 'Homeland Security's Fusion Centers Show the Dangers of Mission Creep' *The Hill* (19 March 2019) <https://cli.re/PAM5eE> accessed 6 September 2023.

Heldt A, 'Reading between the Lines and the Numbers: An Analysis of the First NetzDG Reports' (2019) 8 *Internet Policy Review* <https://policyreview.info/node/1398> accessed 7 June 2022.

Iliadis A and Acker A, 'The Seer and the Seen: Surveying Palantir's Surveillance Platform' (2022) 38 *The Information Society* 334.

Jaycox MM, 'No Oversight, No Limits, No Worries: A Primer on Presidential Spying and Executive Order 12,333' (2021) 12 *Harvard National Security Journal* 58.

Johnson E, 'Lost in the Cloud: Cloud Storage, Privacy, and Suggestions for Protecting Users' Data Note' (2017) 69 *Stanford Law Review* 867.

Jütte BJ, 'Poland's Challenge to Article 17 CDSM Directive Fails before the CJEU, but Member States Must Implement Fundamental Rights Safeguards' (2022) 17 *Journal of Intellectual Property Law & Practice* 693.

Kaminski ME, 'The Right to Explanation, Explained' (2019) 34 *Berkeley Technology Law Journal* 189.

Kappler K, 'Consequences of the German Constitutional Court's Ruling on Germany's Foreign Intelligence Service: The Importance of Human Rights in the Cooperation of Intelligence Services' (2022) 23 *German Law Journal* 173.

Keshet Y, 'Fear of Panoptic Surveillance: Using Digital Technology to Control the COVID-19 Epidemic' (2020) 9 *Israel Journal of Health Policy Research* 67.

Kornelius W, 'Prior Filtering Obligations after Case C-401/19: Balancing the Content Moderation Triangle' (2023) 14 *JIPITEC* 123.

Lauterbach CH, 'No-Go Zones: Ethical Geographies of the Surveillance Industry' (2017) 15 *Surveillance & Society* 557.

'Legal Fact Sheet: Executive Order 12333' (National Security Agency 2013) <https://cli.re/BvkE42> accessed 6 September 2023.

Leloup D, 'Palantir, l'embarrassant Poisson-Pilote Du Big Data' *Le Monde* (9 October 2018) <https://cli.re/KDYevQ> accessed 6 September 2023.

'Les Mesures de Vidéosurveillance Algorithmique Introduites Par La Loi JO 2024 Sont Contraires Au Droit International' *Le Monde* (6 March 2023) <https://cli.re/4Rodb3> accessed 6 September 2023.

Liger Q and Gutheil M, 'The Use of Pegasus and Equivalent Surveillance Spyware' (PEGA Committee of the European Parliament 2023) <https://cli.re/o4ZRbp> accessed 6 September 2023.

Madrinan PG, 'Devil in the Details: Constitutional Problems Inherent in the Internet Surveillance Provisions of the USA Patriot Act of 2001 Note' (2002) 64 *University of Pittsburgh Law Review* 783.

Marshall WP, 'Eleven Reasons Why Presidential Power Inevitably Expands and Why It Matters Symposium: The Role of the President in the Twenty-First Century' (2008) 88 *Boston University Law Review* 505.

Mayson SG, 'Bias in, Bias Out' (2018) 128 *Yale Law Journal* 2218.

Mazzetti M and Bergman R, 'Internal Documents Show How Close the F.B.I. Came to Deploying Spyware' *The New York Times* (12 November 2022) <https://cli.re/yPAJ94> accessed 6 September 2023.

Mazzetti M, Bergman R and Goldman A, 'Who Paid for a Mysterious Spy Tool? The F.B.I., an F.B.I. Inquiry Found' *The New York Times* (31 July 2023) <https://cli.re/A5X9k5> accessed 6 September 2023.

McGowan C, 'The Relevance of Relevance: Section 215 of the USA Patriot Act and the NSA Metadata Collection Program' (2014) 82 *Fordham Law Review* 2399.

Mchangama J and Alkiviadou N, 'The Digital Berlin Wall: How Germany (Accidentally) Created a Prototype for Global Online Censorship – Act Two' (Justitia 2020).
Mitib A, Amin L and Corderoy J, 'Ex-MI6 Chief Put US Firm on Path to £27m Border Software Contract' *The Times* (5 September 2023) <https://cli.re/ax22xQ> accessed 6 September 2023.
Nakashima E, Cox JW and Zapotosky M, 'NSA Contractor Charged with Stealing Top Secret Data' *The Washington Post* (5 October 2016) <https://cli.re/bpkWNK> accessed 6 September 2023.
Nakashima E, 'FBI Acknowledges It Tested NSO Group's Spyware' *The Washington Post* (2 February 2022) <https://cli.re/Bvv9e9> accessed 6 September 2023.
Nicholas ML, 'United States v. Verdugo-Urquidez: Restricting the Borders of the Fourth Amendment' (1990) 14 *Fordham International Law Journal* 267.
Nolan T, 'Fusion Centers' in David Gray and Stephen E Henderson (eds), *The Cambridge Handbook of Surveillance Law* (Cambridge University Press 2017) <www.cambridge.org/core/product/identifier/9781316481127%23CN-bp-6/type/book_part> accessed 24 September 2023.
Noyan O, 'Big Tech Opposes Germany's Enhanced Hate Speech Law' *Euroactiv* <https://cli.re/bpeKrN> accessed 6 September 2023.
Papis-Almansa M, 'The Polish Clearing House System: A "Stir"ring Example of the Use of New Technologies in Ensuring VAT Compliance in Poland and Selected Legal Challenges' (2019) 28 *EC Tax Review* 43.
Pingen A, 'New Controversies around Proposal to Combat Child Sexual Abuse Online' *eucrim* (2 September 2022) <https://cli.re/53n4KA> accessed 6 September 2023.
Pohlman HL, *U.S. National Security Law: An International Perspective* (Rowman & Littlefield 2019).
'Privacy and Security: A Modern and Transparent Legal Framework' (Intelligence and Security Committee of Parliament 2015) HC 1075.
Quintais JP and Schwemer SF, 'The Interplay between the Digital Services Act and Sector Regulation: How Special Is Copyright?' (2022) 13 *European Journal of Risk Regulation* 191.
Redgwell C, 'US Reservations to Human Rights Treaties: All for One and None for All?' in Michael Byers and Georg Nolte (eds), *United States Hegemony and the Foundations of International Law* (Cambridge University Press 2003) <www.cambridge.org/core/product/identifier/CBO9780511494154A027/type/book_part> accessed 19 October 2020.
'Report on the President's Surveillance Program' (Inspectors General of the DoD, DoJ, CIA, NSA and DNI 2009) <https://cli.re/VJnJ3P> accessed 6 September 2023.
'Response from NSO Group to the Pegasus Project' *The Washington Post* (18 July 2021) <https://cli.re/NJmoey> accessed 6 September 2023.
Rich ML, 'Machine Learning, Automated Suspicion Algorithms, and the Fourth Amendment' (2015) 164 *University of Pennsylvania Law Review* 871.
Rojszczak M, 'Compliance of Automatic Tax Fraud Detection Systems with the Right to Privacy Standards Based on the Polish Experience of the STIR System' (2021a) 49 *Intertax* 39.
–, 'EU Criminal Law and Electronic Surveillance: The Pegasus System and Legal Challenges It Poses' (2021b) 29 *European Journal of Crime, Criminal Law and Criminal Justice* 290.
–, 'Extraterritorial Bulk Surveillance after the German BND Act Judgment' (2021c) 17 *European Constitutional Law Review* 53.
–, 'Gone in 60 Minutes: Distribution of Terrorist Content and Free Speech in the European Union' (2023) *Democracy and Security* 1.

Romero Moreno F, '"Upload Filters" and Human Rights: Implementing Article 17 of the Directive on Copyright in the Digital Single Market' (2020) 34 *International Review of Law, Computers & Technology* 153.

Rosemain M, 'A French Alternative to Palantir Would Take Two Years to Make, Thales CEO Says' *Reuters* (23 October 2020) <https://cli.re/372ezq> accessed 6 September 2023.

Rosenberg M, 'At Booz Allen, a Vast U.S. Spy Operation, Run for Private Profit' *The New York Times* (6 October 2016) <https://cli.re/yPnDKp>.

Rudin C, 'Stop Explaining Black Box Machine Learning Models for High Stakes Decisions and Use Interpretable Models Instead' (2019) 1 *Nature Machine Intelligence* 206.

Selbst AD and Powles J, 'Meaningful Information and the Right to Explanation' (2017) 7 *International Data Privacy Law* 233.

Singer N and Chen BX, 'In a Post-Roe World, the Future of Digital Privacy Looks Even Grimmer' *The New York Times* (13 July 2022) <https://cli.re/VJxBq8> accessed 6 September 2023.

Sprenger J and Brodowski D, '"Predictive Policing", "Predictive Justice", and the Use of "Artificial Intelligence" in the Administration of Criminal Justice in Germany' (2023) *e-Revue Internationale de Droit Pénal* 5.

Steinfeld N, 'Track Me, Track Me Not: Support and Consent to State and Private Sector Surveillance' (2017) 34 *Telematics and Informatics* 1663.

Taslitz A, 'What Is Probable Cause, and Why Should We Care? The Costs, Benefits, and Meaning of Individualized Suspicion' (2010) 73 *Law and Contemporary Problems* 145.

Thönnes C, 'Automated Predictive Threat Detection after Ligue Des Droits Humains' (2023) *Verfassungsblog: On Matters Constitutional* <https://intr2dok.vifa-recht.de/receive/mir_mods_00015520> accessed 19 September 2023.

Tosza S, 'Internet Service Providers as Law Enforcers and Adjudicators. A Public Role of Private Actors' (2021) 43 *Computer Law & Security Review* 105614.

'The United States and the European Union Begin Implementation of the European Union-U.S. Data Privacy Framework' (2023) 117 *American Journal of International Law* 346.

van der Veer R, Bos W and van der Heide L, 'Fusion Centres in Six European Countries: Emergence, Roles and Challenges' (International Centre for Counter-Terrorism 2019) <https://cli.re/838YPz> accessed 6 September 2023.

Watt E, 'The Right to Privacy and the Future of Mass Surveillance' (2017) 21 *The International Journal of Human Rights* 773.

Zabel J, 'Public Surveillance through Private Eyes: The Case of the Earn It Act and the Fourth Amendment' (2020) 2020 *University of Illinois Law Review Online* 167.

Index

Note: Numbers in **bold** indicate a table. Numbers in *italics* indicate a figure on the corresponding page.

Index of surveillance programmes: